THE LIFE AND TIMES OF THE EQUITABLE

Henry Baldwin Hyde
Founder
1834-1899
Painting by Leon J. Bonnat, 1881-1882

Collection of The Equitable

THE LIFE AND TIMES OF THE EQUITABLE

BY JOHN ROUSMANIERE

THE EQUITABLE COMPANIES INCORPORATED

NEW YORK

ISBN 0-9648761-2-4

Printed in the United States of America

Printed by The Stinehour Press

Typeset in Caslon 540
Paper, Mohawk Superfine Softwhite Smooth and
Eloquence White Silk

Design: DLJ Graphics Communications

TABLE OF CONTENTS

ILLUSTRATIONS
*Black and white illustrations are interspersed throughout the text,
while color illustrations are grouped in sections.*

COLOR SECTIONS
Henry Baldwin Hyde (frontispiece)

The Equitable's public image in the nineteenth century (between pages 18 and 19)

The Protection Group (between pages 78 and 79)

Equitable Buildings, 1870-1961 (between pages 140 and 141)

Paintings in The Equitable Collection (between pages 200 and 201):
    The Atlantic Cable Projectors, *by Daniel Huntington*
    America Today, *by Thomas Hart Benton*
    Grover Cleveland, *by William McGregor Paxton*

The Equitable's Chief Executive Officers, 1859-1995 (between pages 264 and 265)

FOREWORD

"The Equitable's strengths and weaknesses have been dramatic stories," Davidson Sommers, a former Chairman of the Board, told me as he looked back on the long history of The Equitable Life Assurance Society of the United States. Although drama is not often considered a feature of the life insurance business, if I have accomplished anything in this book, it is to show that — at least at The Equitable — a large life insurance company, much because of its size and significance, may experience plenty of excitement.

The Equitable enjoys one of the longest and most intriguing histories of any major American financial institution. Part of our story — the "times" of our title — is how this company has acted with or reacted against the social and economic trends and tensions around it. The other part of the story is the "life" that has been breathed into the company by its people. Founded in 1859 by a dominating figure in the formative era of American capitalism, Henry Baldwin Hyde, The Equitable survived growing pains to become, with the help of the tontine, an extraordinarily successful type of annuity policy, the world's largest life insurance company, with representatives in almost every foreign country where money was exchanged.

Priorities and strategies have been in almost constant flux. In the early years, well before the appearance of Social Security and corporate pension plans, Equitable offered some of the very few products that provided financial security for Americans. The company has long been one of the most important sources of capital for building the country's cities, farms, homes, industries, and transportation systems. It has twice been owned by stockholders, but for decades it was a mutual company controlled by its policyholders. It has been a leader in the integration of minorities and women into the work force. Today its main product once again is an annuity, and, because of the global partnership it recently formed with a French insurer, AXA, it has returned to the international arena. A recurring theme in this history, in fact, is the one of renewal of old structures and ideas.

Based on extensive archival research and dozens of interviews, this is the story of the meshing of (and, sometimes, conflicts among) the broad, challenging financial and social environment and Equitable's personalities, ambitions, theories, inventions, risks, and public concerns. Any organization in which the three most important jobs are as diverse as retail selling, investing hundreds of millions of dollars, and calculating the rigid laws of probability is, I think, inherently interesting. This is all the more the case when billions of dollars and the hopes and aspirations of millions of people are at stake.

One theme running through these pages is the development of insurance products and sales systems in response to changing consumer, regulatory, and internal needs. Another is shifting investment policy in response to changing markets (a major chapter in the history of life insurance is the history of interest rates). A third is the colorful story of the ways in which The Equitable has presented itself to the world through advertising and promotion.

As Davidson Sommers put it, Equitable's history is one of dramatic stories of all flavors. The Equitable has seen good times and also difficult times — what institution of fourteen decades has not? The slings and arrows of the surrounding American economy have bruised and pricked the Society's skin, and The Equitable itself has made mistakes. We will fairly and thoroughly describe those occasions and the reasons that lay behind them.

This book was commissioned by The Equitable, but the company's hand on my shoulder has been extremely light. Richard H. Jenrette, Equitable's Chairman and Chief Executive Officer, has an interest in the company's history that is ardent, knowledgeable, and objective. Like other readers who work or have worked at the company, he has noticed and corrected factual errors, yet the writing, organization, and interpretations in these pages are mine.

At The Equitable, I have enjoyed and benefitted from the encouragement and support of Eleanor Hamill, Nancy Green, and Maribel Saleem. In the Equitable Archives, Jonathan Coss and, earlier, Arline Schneider gave me access to valuable source materials. Jon's role as a research guide in this long project has been invaluable, and his essay on Equitable's century-long sponsorship of company baseball teams has shed light on a little-known but important aspect of its past.

Dozens of friends and acquaintances in and outside Equitable, too numerous to list here, provided insight and information; those who submitted to formal interviews are listed in the Sources section at the end of this book. I thank Jean Strouse, the biographer of J. Pierpont Morgan, for sharing her valuable research on the period of his ownership of Equitable. I was introduced to The Equitable by another Morgan biographer, Ron Chernow. My parents, James A. and Jessie P. Rousmaniere, reviewed drafts with care, and Leah Ruth Robinson Rousmaniere loyally listened to more than she ever thought she would hear about life insurance.

In order to minimize distraction for the reader, the endnotes have been made as concise and as infrequent as possible. They serve solely to provide brief citations of sources for quotes and data, and are limited to one note to a paragraph. Full citations of published sources may be found in the bibliography. Abbreviated citations of the two major sources of documents are as follows: EqAr refers to the Equitable Archives in the company's New York Home Office headquarters; and HBS refers to the Equitable Life Assurance Society Collection in the Baker Library at the Harvard University Graduate School of Business Administration in Boston, Massachusetts. For permission to quote from documents, I thank those two archives and the Oral History Office at Columbia University.

John Rousmaniere
Stamford, Connecticut
August 1995

THE LIFE AND TIMES OF THE EQUITABLE

"A half-way course never produces any good results." Henry Baldwin Hyde overlooks his confident signature around the time he founded The Equitable in 1859.

CHAPTER I

THE YOUNG MAN
FROM CATSKILL

T he mainspring of Henry Baldwin Hyde's existence, he once said, was "call it *pressure*," and when he gave an instruction, he ordered, *"jam it through."* On a Saturday evening in March 1859, twenty-five year-old Henry Hyde called upon his employer, Frederick Winston, the head of America's largest life insurance company, at his Manhattan home to make a business proposition. Addressing Winston as an equal, Hyde announced that he was quitting the Mutual Life Insurance Company of New York to form his own insurance enterprise. And he asked — in fact, he demanded — that Winston provide referrals, cooperation, and general good will. He himself, Hyde promised, would be pleased to return the favor. Winston did not consider Hyde an equal or regard his offer as a favor. He fired Hyde on the spot and ordered him to clear out his desk by Monday morning.[1]

Undiscouraged, Hyde said good-bye, went to Mutual Life's office building, rented space above his former employer's, and out the window he hung a thirty-foot banner proclaiming the arrival of The Equitable Life Assurance Society of the United States. Thirty years later, Equitable was the largest insurance company in the world.

Henry Hyde has been justifiably praised by historians as "the most daring and inventive insurance man of his time" and "the greatest organizer in the history of life insurance marketing." Yet the hinge of his and Equitable's success was not so much his business boldness and managerial adroitness but, rather, his innate sympathy for the predicament of

Americans. In a time of almost no protection for families against an economy that another historian has called "reckless, booming anarchy," Americans needed help and Henry Hyde understood their need. It would be too much to claim that he and life insurance were made for each other, but his boyhood experiences surely prepared him for this particular line of work. So to understand the rise of Equitable and life insurance, we must begin with the family and surroundings of young Henry Baldwin Hyde in the boom-to-bust riverfront hamlet of Catskill, New York, at the time of Andrew Jackson.[2]

The Hydes came from rugged, pietistic, and determined stock. His first ancestor in America emigrated in 1633 from England to the Massachusetts Bay Colony with the radical Protestant Nonconformist Thomas Hooker, and then moved to western Connecticut. Around 1800, Wilkes Hyde (grandfather of the founder of The Equitable) moved farther west, across the Hudson River, to Catskill, about 115 miles north of New York City. There he opened a store, and his magnetic personality and keen business sense — characteristics that would be passed on to his grandson — made him prominent and prosperous. A measure of his success was a half-admiring, half-teasing story about his parsimony: while taking a friend on a tour of his garden, he picked a cherry, cut it in half, and offered one portion to his guest. Wilkes's son Henry Hazen Hyde inherited his father's scrupulousness and amplified it with vigorous religious faith. He worked in the family's general store, taught Sunday school at the local

Equitable's original office at 98 Broadway.

Presbyterian church, and married a clergyman's daughter, Lucy Beach.

Henry Hazen Hyde's second son, the founder of The Equitable, Henry Baldwin Hyde, was born on February 15, 1834. As an adult he seldom spoke of his childhood, and then only of lonely wandering down to Catskill's busy wharf to watch the great Hudson River steamboats come and go. We know that he was gifted intellectually, that he could read complicated words before he turned five; that his father was ambitious, his mother tubercular, his sister retarded; and that when he stood on that wharf he sometimes

Henry Hazen Hyde.

had fantasies of boarding a paddlewheeler and escaping downriver to the great city of New York.

We also know that all around him lay a fever of speculation and failure. An early Dutch settlement, Catskill lies on the west bank of the Hudson and near the northern tip of the mountain chain whose name comes from its native wildcats and rushing streams, or *kills*. In the tales of Washington Irving and the paintings of Thomas Cole, the leader of the Hudson River school of landscape painters, this is the dreamy territory of the Headless Horseman and Rip Van Winkle, of towering castles and isolated Dutch villages, of cascading waterfalls and deep glens rumored to harbor buried treasure and bearing such names as Storm King, Hell Hole, Devil's Lake, and Devil's Kitchen. While romance surrounded Catskill (and surrounds it to this day), it had a long history as a thriving commercial center. Its woodworking factories built furniture; its mills ground local wheat into flour; and its tanneries, set among forests of tannin-rich hemlocks, turned cattle hides shipped from Argentina into leather. The traffic of wagons, river sloops, and steamboats was constant and heavy.

Although Catskill was thriving at the time of Hyde's birth in 1834, the hemlocks were thinning out and the wheat growers and flour millers were picking up and following the recently finished Erie Canal into western New York. Catskill's financial lifeline became tourism and what Cole called "the wild magnificence of the Catskill mountains." In 1832, an enterprising young local, Charles L. Beach, invested a nest egg made from selling life insurance in a new stagecoach company that carried visitors up the steep, twisting roads to his hotel, the Catskill Mountain House, which became one of America's premier resorts. The appeal of the Catskills was not only their picturesque setting but also their clean air. As

The rise and fall of Catskill taught Hyde his first lessons about the need for financial protection.

outbreaks of cholera, yellow fever, and "the fevers" swept through the cities, doctors advised their patients to flee to the mountains. This sanctuary was available only to the financially comfortable. The round trip on Beach's stage cost the equivalent of a workingman's daily pay, so the people whom young Henry Hyde watched disembark at the wharf were monied as well as prudent.[3]

With the arrival of these vacationers and the fading of its traditional industries in the mid-1830's, Wilkes Hyde and the other merchants of Catskill saw an opportunity. Fifty local families pooled $746,000 (the equivalent of more than $10 million today) to develop property to sell to the visitors for summer homes. They bought old farms and empty lots, laid out new roads and boundaries, and distributed thousands of sales brochures. A speculative mood swept across the county on the crest of a wave of cheap money set off by English bankers. But the wave collapsed during the winter of 1837 after the bankers, suddenly doubtful about the American economy, cut off credit. The resulting panic set off a vicious, nationwide, three-year depression. Catskill was devastated. A local historian observed mournfully that the promoters' hopeful maps showed "streets and lots [that] were as plentiful as are brambles on the same location at this day." Drained of its industry, its energy, and its capital, Catskill became little more than a byway to the Mountain House. By 1840, the kindest observation that one visitor could offer about the town was, "It is a thrifty little village in which the most prosperous vocations are those of inn-keeper and stage proprietor."[4]

This civic collapse paralleled that of the Hyde family. Henry Hazen Hyde lost his father when old Wilkes Hyde was thrown from a buggy and killed, his wife when Lucy Beach Hyde died, and his oldest boy when James (nicknamed "Caleb") was sent off to Yale to study to be a missionary but died of typhoid fever. The second son, Henry Baldwin, had to be sent to live with Connecticut relatives for a time. And so Henry Hazen Hyde began to seek an escape from the ruins.

A route out was provided by the local schoolteacher and Catskill's Don Quixote, John C. Johnston, a friend of the Hydes. When he was not teaching or supplementing his meager income with odd jobs in a wheelchair factory, Johnston reveled in his role as commander of the local brigade of the state militia, a duty that permitted him to claim the title of brigadier general.

John C. Johnston.

Though the outfit's activities consisted mostly of marching in Independence Day parades, they were Johnston's glory. "He was a tall, active man, with long gray hair and a commanding personality," someone wrote of him, adding, "He was a good talker." A portrait shows a handsome, intense man of military bearing, with a sharp jaw jutting out of a high collar, deep-set heavy-lidded eyes, and two enormous hoop earrings.[5]

This was not the sort of fellow who would be satisfied to end his days in a dying village. Sometime in the 1840's, when he was about sixty, Johnston came upon a brochure recruiting insurance agents. Published by the Mutual Life Insurance Company and titled *A Treatise on Life Insurance*, it described life insurance as ideal both for families beaten about by the erratic economy and for aspiring entrepreneurs looking for a product to sell. Johnston's ambitions

Sheppard Homans.

stirred. In 1849 or 1850, he departed Catskill for New York and soon opened a Mutual Life agency in Manhattan. Before leaving, he spoke of his ambitions with his friend Henry Hazen Hyde, the religious storekeeper.

Johnston found Hyde a job as an insurance agent in northeastern Pennsylvania. Hyde packed up his mother, his retarded daughter, and sixteen-year-old Henry Baldwin, and was on his way. An insurance historian wrote of the farewell of the Hydes and Johnston, "The departure of that trio from the village of Catskill marks an epoch in the history of American life insurance."[6]

Johnston quickly built Mutual Life's most successful agency to the point where it was selling almost one-fifth of the company's new policies. Meanwhile he amassed enough proxies from policyholders (who, since the company had a mutual structure, controlled it) to force out the old president and install a new one more to their liking, Frederick S. Winston. With his man in place, Johnston retired, collected $30,000 against future commissions on the renewals of policies he had sold, and moved to Wisconsin to raise cattle. He promised he would never go back to insurance but, vigorous as ever in his seventies, became bored by ranching and founded the institution that would develop into the Northwestern Mutual Life Insurance Company.

Henry Hazen Hyde also found his calling in life insurance and made a quick success. Exerting a magnetic personality and peppering his sales talks

Frederick S. Winston.

with Biblical references, he became Mutual Life's top agent. The company soon sent him on the road to recruit and train agents. "A genuine apostle of life insurance," Hyde was characterized by an agent whom he recruited in Indiana; "the first man that we ever heard talk life insurance on the high key that is now so familiar among the best workers, and he actually talked until he not only brought tears into our eyes, but into his also, and all with the utmost sincerity." Hyde's energy and industry were extraordinary. He described his daily routine:

I come to my office in State Street at eight o'clock; I work with all my might; at two o'clock I dine; I work until half-past six o'clock; I go home tired in body and mind; I rest, and doze, and retire to bed at half-past nine; arise at five; at half-past five I mount a spirited horse with a good friend, and we dash off ten miles, returning in one and a half hours.

Mutual Life called him back to its New York headquarters (known as the Home Office in the insurance business), but the assignment failed. In not the last clash between the contrary cultures of insurance sales and management, Hyde took offense when the New York businessmen belittled his evangelical convictions and fervent style. He settled in Boston and ran a big agency first for Mutual Life and later for his son's new enterprise, Equitable. At his death in 1873, he was hailed as "without doubt the most successful life insurance canvasser in the world."[7]

As for Henry Baldwin Hyde, his entry into life insurance was slightly delayed. When the family settled in Pennsylvania in 1850 he was sixteen. There was no work for him there, so he went to New York City and found a job as a clerk in a dry goods store. "He entered heartily into the business," remembered an acquaintance. When John Johnston tracked him down, all the boy could talk about were the fine opportunities for young men in the city's stores and banks. His old teacher demurred. Hyde remembered him saying:

Mr. Hyde, the banking houses and the mercantile houses that you have been speaking of will all pass away. You may enter them and rise to such position as will suit you and only live to see all your future hopes darkened by unforeseen circumstances which you yourself would be unable to prevent.

The path, Johnston told his former student, lay in life insurance. Young Hyde followed his mentor's advice and, in 1853, went to work at Mutual Life's Home Office as a clerk. Within a few years he was cashier, working regularly and closely with President Winston. He accepted premium payments from policyholders, issued commissions and advances to agents, and generally watched over the company's daily commerce.[8]

Caught up in the daily activities of the most successful and innovative American insurance company, and in regular contact with his wide-traveling father in the field, Hyde was on the cutting edge of the business. Mutual Life's actuary, Sheppard Homans, a Harvard-educated mathematician, was collecting data for the first American mortality tables. Until then, policyholders' longevity was predicted and premiums were set using mortality tables based on old European demographic studies, including one from seventeenth-century Russia. In 1858, Homans issued his first report on what he called the American Experience Table (the table was still in use, though much modified, sixty years later). In the spring of 1859, Homans, Hyde, Massachusetts insurance

Elizur Wright.

New York's business district in the mid-nineteenth century: hundreds of low wooden office buildings housing many small, unstable businesses.

superintendent Elizur Wright, and other insurance actuaries, agents, and managers gathered at New York's Astor House for the first convention of the American insurance industry. They exchanged ideas on all the newly arising technical issues in the business and formed the industry's first organization, the Life Convention, and its first think tank, the Bureau of Life Insurance and Annuities. That same year, reflecting the diversity of new companies and technical solutions to insurance-related problems, as well as the expanding popularity of life insurance, the New York State legislature created one of the first insurance regulatory agencies and began tentatively to tell insurers how to do their business in a way that was both healthy for them and fair to their customers.

This rise of a distinctly American insurance technology stimulated Hyde's ambitions. Working in the cashier's office of a vital, growing company, he studied what was right and what was wrong about the way the insurance business was managed. He concluded that Mutual Life and other companies were not progressing as they should. He had three complaints. First, companies were accepting promissory notes from policyholders instead of insisting on cash payments. Hyde was sure that this practice not only prevented companies from building the capital base they needed but induced them to take needless risks. Anybody who bought insurance by potentially leaving survivors burdened with debt was not a good prospect. Second, Hyde thought insurers were overly cautious in their marketing strategy by limiting their product line to policies with a face value of only $5,000 or less (approximately $75,000 today). The insurers claimed they were trimming their risks, but it seemed to Hyde that they were ignoring an extensive market.

And third, Hyde was convinced that insurance companies were not selling their products as hard as they could and should.

The fundamental management principle of a big life insurance company was that for the enterprise to work, the law of averages must be allowed to minimize the company's exposure to concentrated risks. Spreading risks required that a large, varied population of policyholders be gathered. Where the traditionalists and Hyde disagreed was over strategy for accomplishing that goal. Older companies attracted policyholders by allowing them to pay with promissory notes, not cash. They also capped the face values of policies at small amounts on the assumption that anybody wealthy enough to buy big policies for cash was too elderly to be a good risk. Likewise, experienced insurance men believed that aggressive sales drives would be too costly and would pull in too many bad risks.

But it seemed to Henry Baldwin Hyde that a market for large policies with cash premiums was growing among the generation of young and middle-aged urban merchants, bankers, and lawyers who were thriving in the mid-century economic boom that came on the heels of the depression of the 1830's. The mid-nineteenth century was the era of the clipper ships, the California gold rush, and the annexation of Texas; of the first great railroad expansion, the invention of the telegraph and the reaper; and of the greatest wave of immigration and urbanization in the country's prior history.

Hyde was familiar with the concerns of this mercantile generation because he knew many of its representatives through his chief social activity, which was attending church. At the Fifth Avenue Presbyterian Church, at 19th Street and Fifth Avenue, he met the men and women who showed him this other, new market and who later went on to provide the vital financial backing for his enterprise. His friends

Equitable's birthplace, the Fifth Avenue Presbyterian Church.

included the church's most important parishioners, the family of the rector, James Waddell Alexander. A son of a founder of Princeton Theological Seminary, the chief Presbyterian divinity school, Alexander was an exponent of the influential theology of New Light Calvinism, which de-emphasized the harsh fatalism of traditional Calvinism and stressed the powers of reason and the need to confront the problems of the world. A popular, talented preacher with deep, liberal social convictions, Alexander challenged the well-to-do businessmen in his congregation to address the grinding poverty on the streets outside their comfort-

The Rev. James W. Alexander.

United States Insurance Advertiser.

THE EQUITABLE LIFE ASSURANCE SOCIETY OF THE UNITED STATES.

(PURELY MUTUAL.)

Office, 98 Broadway, New York.

This Company is now fully organized, having complied with the laws of this State and lodged the required Securities with the Comptroller.

This Society is now prepared to receive applications for Life Assurance, and will underwrite policies upon the most favorable terms.

This is the only Stock Company in America that divides its ENTIRE PROFITS, PRO RATA, among its Policy Holders (legal interest, 7 per cent. only, paid on its Stock), thereby giving the assured all the advantages of the Purely Mutual system, with the pledge of a Perpetual Capital Stock, and the added security that its Board of Directors have a permanent moneyed interest in conducting its affairs with Prudence and Strict Economy.

Its rates are based upon the most approved English Tables of Mortality, verified by American experience to the present time.

By the Charter, Dividends to the Assured are to be declared every five years, and may be applied to the reduction of premium, or will be credited upon the policy, thereby increasing the amount insured.

Parties desiring to insure will be furnished with the Society's publications, rates, etc., (gratis), upon application, or if desired, will be waited upon at whatever place they may designate, by one of its officers.

DIRECTORS.

Hon. Wm. C. Alexander,	John Slade,	Thomas A. Cummins,
William Walker	Hon. Henry J. Gardner,	Francis B. Cooley,
Henry Young,	Henry H. Hyde,	H. D. Newcomb,
Irad Hawley,	E. Spencer Miller,	Moses A. Hoppock,
James Low,	Sol. R. Spaulding,	Geo. D. Morgan,
James M. Beebe,	Hon. Dudley S. Gregory,	H. V. Butler,
Henry A. Hurlbut,	Hon. Steph. H. Phillips,	Ezra C. Reed,
Thomas A. Biddle,	John Auchincloss,	Dwight Townsend,
Benj. E. Bates,	Henry S. Terbell,	Henry M. Alexander,
John T. Moore,	Henry G. Marquand,	William T. Blodgett,
Thomas U. Smith,	James M. Halsted,	Benjamin F. Manierre,
Wm. Whitewright, Jr.,	Thomas S. Young,	E. J. Hawley,
Wm. G. Lambert,	Bennington F. Randolph,	Alanson Trask,
Wilmot Williams,	Wayman Crow,	Edward W. Lambert, M.D.,
Peter McMartin	Geo. Talbot Olyphant,	Daniel D. Lord,
George H. Stuart,	Alexander Young,	Robert Bliss,
Jas. Lenox Kennedy,	Sam. Frothingham, Jr.,	Henry Day,
	Henry B. Hyde.	

HON. WILLIAM C. ALEXANDER, *President.*
HENRY B. HYDE, *Vice-President.*

EDWARD P. WILLIAMS, *Secretary.*
GEO. W. PHILLIPS, *Actuary.*
    E. W. LAMBERT, M.D., *Physician.*   W'LD PARKER, M.D., *Consulting Physician*
    HENRY DAY, *Attorney.*   DANIEL LORD, *Counsel.*

Bankers—METROPOLITAN BANK.

The Society's first advertisement. Its best endorsements were the prestige of its stockholders and the reputation of mutuals.

able homes and offices. Henry Hyde joined the church, was active in a young men's committee, and became friendly with the rector's family. Observed one of the rector's sons, William Alexander, "Mr. Hyde had the impression that talent of various kinds was discoverable among members of the Alexander clan." The rector's brothers William and Henry were to become Equitable's first President and second attorney, respectively. James W. Alexander, another of the rector's sons, was Hyde's closest friend when he was starting out; they lived in the same boarding-house, and Alexander was an usher at Hyde's marriage to Annie Fitch in 1864. Thirty-five years later, he would succeed Hyde as President. His brother William, who observed Hyde's reliance on his family, was Equitable's Secretary for fifty-seven years, from 1880 to 1937. As late as 1951, there would be an Alexander on Equitable's Board of Directors. The rector himself expressed interest in the enterprise before he died in 1859. The fact that his widow was supported by an annuity from a church insurance fund reinforced the value of insurance in the minds of his family as Henry Hyde approached them for help in assembling his new enterprise.[9]

Confident that he had a pool of potential backers and colleagues, Hyde, helped by his father and a few friends, began to develop his insights into a business plan. On March 12, 1859, he went to Frederick Winston to announce that he was founding a new insur-ance company offering large policies. Hyde probably was aware that Winston himself was about to form a new company for large poli-cies, Washington Life Insurance Company. If so, it would have been typical for Hyde to make a preemptive strike to keep a competi-tor off guard. In any case, Winston, who was once described as "a man of commanding energy, of despotic and choleric temper," furi-

The first President, William C. Alexander.

ously threw Hyde out of both his house and his employment.[10]

Hyde moved quickly. He rented a room in the back of the second floor of Mutual Life's Home Office at 98 Broadway. He bought a box of good cigars, commissioned a long banner dis-playing the name of his new enterprise, and borrowed some cheap desks and chairs. Offering a life insurance policy as security, he purchased office supplies and account books on credit. He talked his neighbors on the second floor into loaning him a couple of clerks, whom he seated at the desks and told to look busy. The neighbors also allowed him to hang his banner out the front windows directly over the Mutual Life sign. Then he opened his doors, placed the box of cigars on the mantel as a sign of welcome, and waited for customers to arrive.

He also recruited financial backers. A New York law, passed in 1852, addressed the failure of many undercapitalized mutual insurers by obligating new insurance companies to deposit $100,000 in state bonds as a reserve against potential losses. The interest would go to the company, but the principal would remain with the state government. Since Hyde did not have $100,000, he had to raise it from backers, and the only term they would accept was to have an equity interest in the new enterprise. So he issued 1,000 shares with a par value of $100 and offered an annual yield of 7 percent. He and his father between them owned a minority interest of seventy shares. Half the remainder was bought by congregants at the Fifth Avenue Presbyterian Church with the understanding that the Alexanders would be represented on the board of directors and in management.

In this way, Equitable — unlike Mutual Life, New York Life, Northwestern Life, and most of the other life insurers formed in this period — was founded not as a mutual company owned by its policyholders but, rather, as a stock company owned by its investors. Yet through force of personality and practicality, Henry Baldwin Hyde succeeded in turning this titular stock company into a functioning mutual. In a stock company, all profits go to the proprietors. In a mutual, the policyholders participate in the investment performance of the assets, recouping profits as dividends. The most successful insurance companies at that time were mutuals, due to a bleak history of proprietors' absconding with assets before death benefits were paid out. Hyde insisted that stockholders' dividends be limited to 7 percent so that there be sufficient money to allow policyholders to participate substantially. However, his backers resisted the idea, demanding that they receive a 10 percent return on their investment. Hyde, who understood from his experience at Mutual Life just how strong was the appeal of mutuality, threatened to quit. His fighting words were remembered this way:

Gentlemen, I have made up my mind that this company shall be a purely mutual company, and if this provision limiting the dividends for all time on the stock to legal interest isn't put into the charter, I will take my hat and walk out of this room and have nothing further to do with the enterprise.

His ultimatum won the battle with the loss of only one backer. Hyde was able to exploit the company's hybrid corporate structure in promotional materials suggesting that since Equitable enjoyed the best features of both sides, it had a special claim on the public's trust. Equitable's first sales brochures described the new company as "Organized upon principles purely mutual, and managed by gentlemen whose names must command public confidence."[11]

Hyde at first assumed he would be President, but his chief backer, William Lambert, warned him that he was too young and unseasoned to win the full confidence of his investors, whom, of course, he had already challenged. After the first candidate refused, they settled on a brother of the Fifth Avenue Church's rector. This was William C. Alexander, a Virginia-born lawyer who had unsuccessfully run for governor of New Jersey. Considerably older than Hyde and better-known in the business community, Alexander had the authority to control the huge and potentially disruptive fifty-two member board of directors, which was dominated by the investors. Among the powerful men on the board was the attorney Daniel D. Lord, whose authority was so respected that he was known as the Lord Almighty. While Hyde

Daniel D. Lord.

was disappointed not to be the titular head, he understood the problem and realized that he had no option but to cooperate; a public association with the Lord Almighty and his friends was one of the best advertisements a new enterprise could have. Hyde also was confident that though Alexander's name was at the top of the letterhead, he himself held the reins. The other William Alexander, the long-time Secretary, once wrote of his uncle: "Mr. Hyde always treated him with great deference, but there was no conflict of opinion. His confidence in Mr. Hyde was complete, and he always cooperated in carrying out Mr. Hyde's most daring plans." When the first President died in 1875, Hyde assumed the title and kept on doing what he had been doing for sixteen years, which was to dominate The Equitable.[12]

Getting the Society established on a mutual basis was an accomplishment, but keeping it in business during its growth years was no less trying. Perhaps Hyde's most daring feat in Equitable's first decade occurred in 1867 and reflected his Catskill days.

Just as the company was struggling to a secure footing, a wave of Asian cholera swept the country. The Society's actuary warned Hyde that if he insisted on paying the dividend promised policyholders that year, they would be ruined by the death claims that were sure to pour in. Hyde disagreed. No doubt recalling his boyhood at a time when wealthy people escaped cholera by fleeing to the Catskill Mountain House, he decided that anybody who had sufficient caution and money to purchase a life insurance policy was, by definition, careful enough to take the right precautions in an epidemic. He was correct. Mortality among Equitable policyholders during the cholera attack was even lower than usual. Rarely again would anybody ever challenge his authority. He once characterized his personality in an aphorism of his own: "A half-way course never produces any good results."[13]

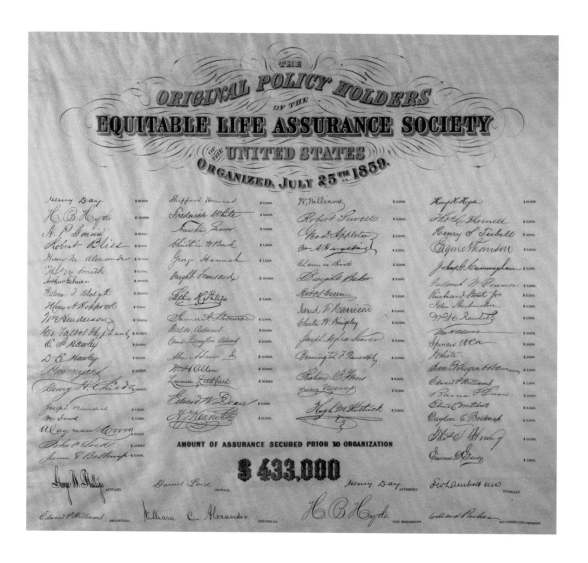

As this poster indicates, a life insurance company was known in part by the reputations of the people who purchased its policies. Although Hyde was Vice-President, his huge signature indicates his true authority.

CHAPTER II

THE BIRTH OF
AN ENTERPRISE

"Choose any American at random and he should be a man of burning desires, enterprising, adventurous, and, above all, an innovator," Alexis de Tocqueville wrote in *Democracy in America*. He could have been referring to Henry Baldwin Hyde, that master of both innovation and boldness. Observed the best historian of insurance, J. Owen Stalson, "Hyde's genius for *thinking* his way through marketing problems produced the beginnings of merchandising in life insurance." And as he developed the sophisticated idea of an aggressive, functionally mutual company, he expressed his bold ambitions in the language of the trenches. Where his father's vocabulary was of the church, his was of the army: every decision was either a "retreat" or an "advance," and life itself was a war on shifting battlefields. "I am as confident of our united ability to whip everything out of sight in our business in the future as I am that I live," he bragged as he set out on a sales tour of the South in 1870. His reports from the tour overflowed with cheerful blusters. From Charleston, where business had been slow: "You will see a change or my name is not HYDE." From Mobile, *"We must do double the business of any company in 1871 — How would that be for high!"*[1]

Oddly, this fierce competitiveness does not radiate from the best-known image of Hyde, a statue made after his death in 1899 by John Quincy Adams Ward that has stood in the lobby of various Equitable Home Office buildings in New York. Ward captured a more reflective Hyde caught in midstride and midthought. "The attitude of contemplation is not characteristic," complained William Alexander about the statue. "Mr. Hyde did a great deal of thinking, but he held his head high, with a forward gaze, and his whole air was one of activity and not one of repose and reflection." Alexander remembered Hyde this way:

Mr. Hyde was a very handsome man with a tall and striking figure. His eyes were fine and piercing, and he had a well formed, sensitive mouth.... Most people were awed by Mr. Hyde's manner and presence, and when he glared at anyone with whom he was talking, great trepidation was usually manifested.[2]

And for good reason, for his decisiveness could be Napoleonic. After moving from his first offices to a larger suite, Hyde found that he still required more space and solved the problem expeditiously by renting an adjacent room and personally kicking a hole in the wall so he would not have to wait for city building permits. Late one night, while addressing envelopes for a direct-mail campaign, he discovered that he had run out of postage stamps. He sent a clerk to wake up the postmaster, who, impressed by Hyde's nerve, roused an assistant to produce the stamps. Alexander speculated:

I have often thought that he would have made a great military leader, such as Stonewall Jackson, for he never began a drive without studying every phase of the situation in advance. He considered every difficulty, he provided for every possible emergency.... [T]he moment he started every pound of pressure that could be brought to bear was concentrated on the object in view; and then his confidence was absolute, and his activity and daring unlimited.[3]

To appreciate Hyde's innovations, we should understand a little of the situation of life insurance at the time he founded Equitable.

Although property insurance dates back to 3000 b.c., when Babylonian traders cooperated to form pools of cash reserves against future losses, life insurance did not appear until around 400 b.c. Groups of Greeks and Romans formed fraternal organizations — some based on common social background, others on shared business interest — that cov-

This statue of Hyde, made after his death in 1899, has stood in a number of Equitable Buildings.

ered members' burial costs either by establishing reserves through dues or by making assessments at the time of a member's death. This simple fraternal benefit society (or "burial" society) was the typical life insurance company until the seventeenth century, and it survives in the form of the friendly and provident society. The burial society was not much more than a neighborhood savings bank. A few members, all known to each other and sharing styles of life, made fixed deposits into an account that was cautiously invested, and withdrawals were made to meet the contracted expenses. Shortfalls were covered by assessments. There was no purpose other than to meet the needs of the group, whose commonality assured that natural longevity, likelihood of accidents, exposure to plagues, and other risks could be predicted relatively easily by extrapolating from the experiences of a few. Fraternal benefit societies of well-traveled seamen charged higher dues than societies of other workers less prone to risk, like bankers. Yet even a city's population of bankers might be wiped out by a financial panic or a local plague. The ideal was to hedge one group's very specific set of risks against another's, yet the tools for doing that were not yet available.

Actuarial science and, with it, life insurance began to take their modern shape in the seventeenth century with the compilation of the first mortality tables from government population data and the development of probability theory. The first insurance actuaries (the word is derived from a Latin term meaning keeper of accounts) produced theories and mathematical formulas for calculating the expected average longevities of men and women of different ages, occupations, and residences. The key term was *average*. Said the important nineteenth-century American actuary Elizur Wright, "While nothing is more uncertain than the duration of a single life,

Hyde reveals the wear and tear of strenuous work: (counterclockwise from below left) at ages thirty, fifty, and fifty-five.

nothing is more certain than the average duration of a thousand lives." With reliable
mortality tables and actuarial tools, actuaries
could reliably estimate insurance risks for
much larger and more diverse groups than the
membership of a fraternal benefit society.
From these estimates, and by relying on
assumptions about the future behavior of
interest rates (which determined the earnings
of the policyholder payments that were
invested by the company), insurers could predict the correct size and schedule of premium
payments. There were two goals: policyholders
must receive their guaranteed death benefits
and, often, dividends; and the insurers themselves must make enough of a surplus to
provide a healthy foundation of capital that
would cushion them during depressions and
other hard times. Besides setting premiums at
levels that were both competitive and remunerative to the company, the trick lay in
finding a sufficiently extensive population of
varied policyholders — people of different
ages and occupations, residing in different
locations — to spread the risks, permit the law
of averages to apply, and cut the company's
exposure. A modern-day actuary, Harry D.
Garber, a former Equitable Vice-Chairman of
the Board, has described the approach this
way: "Actuaries tend to go down the middle,
play the averages, travel down the central path.
The fundamental principle of insurance is that
you not concentrate the risk — in an age
group, in an industry, in an asset, in a product." Overconcentration of risks was to be
avoided at all costs. A company must insure
both the seaman and the downtown banker (as
well as the rural farmer and the village shop-
keeper) and charge them premiums
commensurate with their particular risks
according to occupation, age, and residence.[4]

The difficult, expensive part was selling
enough policies to all those thousand (and
many more) lives. Marketing burial coverage

to members of a fraternal benefit society was
one thing; they all knew and influenced each
other. But selling coverage on a wide scale
was an expensive task, yet one that had to be
done so risks were not overly concentrated.
The costs (and the potential rewards) were
such that the first English and American life
insurers, unlike the fraternal benefit societies,
were not owned by their members but were
financed by venture capitalists. A small number of investors earned all the profits after the
payment of contracted death benefits and
dividends. Beyond that, the policyholders did
not share (or as insurers put it, participate in)
the profits of the company. Most of these
companies were subsidiaries of banks, property insurers, or religious denominations
offering financial assistance to clergymen and
their families. The first nonfraternal, commercial American company to specialize in
life insurance was The Pennsylvania
Company for Insurance on Lives and
Granting Annuities, founded in 1809. It sold a
wide range of policies but, like all life insurers, trimmed its risks by banning certain
activities. For example, it refused to pay benefits on deaths due to duels, suicide, or "the
hands of justice," or ones occurring in places
of high mortality, such as ships at sea, remote
parts of Canada, and the deep South, with its
fever-ridden swamps.[5]

The early problem of life insurance was
that the need for it was stronger than the institutions that provided it. The biggest risk for
policyholders often was the insurance company itself. Before the 1840's, the life
insurance business did not have a particularly
good reputation for stability or even integrity.
All too often, companies were undercapitalized or their promoters and stockholders fled
with premiums — one historian has described
the early English companies as "like gnats on
a summer evening, and disappearing as suddenly." Of the twenty-three life insurers

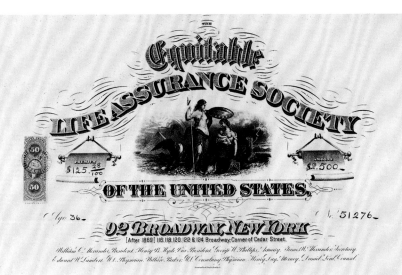

An Equitable life insurance policy of 1870.

TRUTH
IN A NUTSHELL.

By Rev. Henry Ward Beecher.

&

READ THIS CAREFULLY, AND HAND IT TO YOUR WIFE.

In this pamphlet, published in 1862, Henry Ward Beecher wrote that Americans had a "moral duty" to purchase a life insurance policy.

A widely reproduced Equitable advertisement from about 1900.

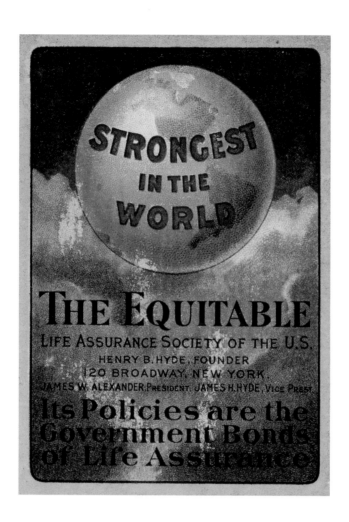

The cover of an Equitable calendar of the turn of the century.

founded in America between 1812 and 1842, only five survived. But this dreary history of fraud and incompetence did not snuff out the human need for insurance, which offered the only form of financial protection available to most families. Throughout most of the nineteenth century — a time, unlike ours, of big families, life expectancies rarely exceeding sixty years, sweeping plagues, weak government supervision, and frequent accidents — protection for the widowed and the orphaned did not exist outside life insurance and the disaster relief provided by the occasional industrial company. Not until labor unions, worker's compensation, Social Security, and corporate pension plans developed in the early to mid-twentieth century would other forms of protection be widely available. Life insurance, therefore, filled a large social need. For this reason justifications of it often were couched in a language and enthusiasm redolent of declarations of religious faith. "I remember the emotion which the possession of that policy awakened in my heart," recalled the politician and editor Thurlow Weed about his first purchase of a life policy. "I have paid in premiums and interest more than four times the amount of the policy, but there is no pecuniary claim that I meet more cheerfully."[6]

The problem was how to meet that deep demand with strong, viable, trustworthy institutions. The most lasting solution was the mutual structure, in which there were no shares and the company was controlled by its policyholders, who were given all the profits after a prudent capital foundation was built up. Whether the policyholders legally owned a mutual was and remains a subject of long debate; the usual explanation was that nobody owned it but that the policyholders, through their votes, controlled it. The key was policyholder participation in earnings, which meant that no investors were around to run off with premium payments. *Mutual*, therefore, came to be a synonym for *safe*.

The best-known and most successful insurance company in Britain, if not the world, was a mutual, The Society for Equitable Assurances on Lives and Survivorships, founded in London in 1762. The two key terms in the title were "Equitable" and "Assurance"; they meant that the company promised prompt, fair payment of dividends and death benefits. (Until the early twentieth century, *assurance* was a common synonym for *insurance*.) The rule was caution, not high sales volume. The company rationed the number of policies it sold through lawyers and merchants, who received small commissions for recruiting high-quality applicants from among their normal customers. More aggressive solicitation was expected to be expensive and an invitation to risk-prone customers.

The English Equitable's reputation was so widely respected that Henry Hyde would appropriate its name, with only a couple of small changes, when he formed his company in 1859. After that, the two companies were known as the "old Equitable" and the "new Equitable." Yet as respected as the mutual concept was, it had an inherent problem: capital raising was limited solely to selling policies. Some mutuals were formed in America, mostly for groups (such as clergymen) and in forms not distinguishable from fraternal benefit societies; many of these companies did not survive, and life insurance generally was sold by banks and property insurance companies.

Ironically, the triumph of the mutual system in the United States was brought about by a pair of catastrophes in the 1830's. The first was the great fire of December 23, 1835, which destroyed almost the entire business district between the East River and Broadway in lower New York City. More than 640 structures valued at $20 million went down, and took with them the burgeoning industry of

EDITORIAL FROM THE

NEW YORK EVANGELIST,

OF THURSDAY, SEPTEMBER 21, 1876.

[EDITOR—THE REV. HENRY M. FIELD, D. D.]

Lessons for Hard Times—Mistaken Economies—Life Insurance.

A typical church tract recommendation of life insurance.

stock, all-lines insurance companies. Of twenty-six companies, twenty-three were done in by their obligations to policyholders who owned property destroyed by the fire. Two years later came the panic of 1837, which shattered the hopes of Catskill, if not the entire country, and dried up pools of venture capital for the next decade. "Poor New York!" cried former Mayor Philip Hone in 1840. "A garden sowed with sand and running fast into desolation.... Business at a standstill." More than any other event in the first half of the nineteenth century, the depression drove home to Americans the value of life insurance. Insurance dividends and accumulated cash values were the only protection that many families had. Some states endorsed this first widespread financial umbrella by passing statutes favoring insurance. The first general law to deal exclusively with life insurance was the so-called Married Women's Act, passed by the New York State legislature in 1840, which protected the insurance benefits of the poor and middle-class widows of deceased bankrupts from attachment by creditors (to exclude

wealthy people, the statute did not apply if premium payments exceeded $300). To encourage private saving through insurance, many states passed laws exempting insurance dividends and other benefits from income and inheritance taxes. This benefit, which gives life insurance and annuity products a unique feature among savings and investment instruments, is one of the strongest appeals of life insurance, and it remained hotly contested until well into the twentieth century.[7]

After the fire and depression, it was almost impossible to find investors to start new insurance companies. American promoters instead borrowed the mutual scheme of organization of the English Equitable. They did not, however, appropriate its cautious, selective marketing. The American mutuals' approach, which Henry Hyde would develop, was to encourage agents to sell aggressively by offering high sales commissions and then to put the applications submitted by agents through a screening process, known as "underwriting," that included medical and credit evaluations. Under this system that combined mutuality, a strong sales effort, and careful underwriting, there came in the 1840's the first great expansion of American life insurance. New companies, all mutuals, included Mutual Life (now MONY) and Nautilus Insurance (later New York Life) in New York, Mutual Benefit in New Jersey, New England Mutual in Massachusetts, and Penn Mutual and Connecticut Mutual in other states.

To raise capital and sell enough policies for the law of averages to apply, sales would have to be substantial and rapid — and that required organization and capital. The pioneer in the field, before Hyde, was Morris Robinson, who headed Mutual Life between 1842 and his death in 1847. He introduced the American style of insurance marketing as he assembled the first serious life insurance sales force. Robinson was guided by an insight that is now familiar but that he is credited as first verbalizing: life insurance does not sell itself. People, he observed, came up with any number of reasons why they did not require insurance. Some were sure that they would not die (or, if they did, that they would have been sufficiently successful to leave their families pots of money). Others distrusted insurance companies in principle, having heard that some had failed. Still others thought the entire concept of life insurance a violation of religious principles. Whatever the cause, people did not take readily to the idea of purchasing financial protection for their families and, therefore, had to be talked into it. Robinson's insight has come down to us as "Life insurance is not bought, rather it has to be *sold*."

Robinson, therefore, struggled to make insurance more appealing. He simplified contracts by leveling the premiums so that policyholders paid the same amount throughout the life of the policy. A level-premium policy (which came to be called "ordinary" insurance) made ownership more convenient. It also indirectly provided capital for the company: in the early years of the policy, when the policyholder was young and had a low risk, the premium was higher than what was demanded by the mortality expectations, and the excess of premium over reserves could be invested. But Robinson's chief effort was to see that insurance was marketed competently by well-motivated, well-compensated, commissioned sales agents.

The agents had to be trained to address the main obstacle to insurance sales in the mid-nineteenth century — religious conviction. Many faithful Christians were sure that the purchase of

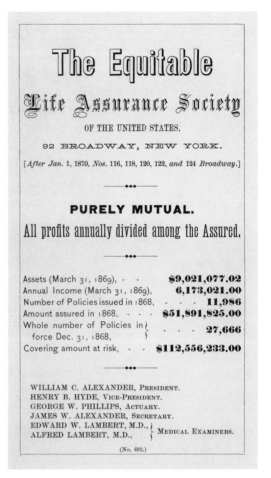

Advertising often was a simple financial statement.

Morris Robinson.

an insurance contract challenged their dependence on God, invited Providential punishment, and made humans into mere articles of commerce. One Episcopal bishop went so far as to ban his people from buying life insurance altogether. It was easy to poke holes in these arguments by pointing out, for instance, that most church steeples had lightning rods. Yet many Americans were sure that life insurance was mere gambling. People in trouble should seek shelter where they always had, in family and church. These convictions probably were a defense of the old, rural, stable way of life against the confusions of the time — the terrible depression, the massive immigration from Ireland and Germany, the rapid urbanization, and the growth of transportation in the first railroad boom. The United States of Abraham Lincoln in 1859, when Henry Hyde founded Equitable, was a far less settled, far more diverse country than the country of Andrew Jackson in 1830.

The fundamentalist religious critique of life insurance, therefore, was sharp. The mutuals had an ingenious reply: life insurance itself fulfilled a social service, missionary purpose. This was not a trick of clever salesmanship. The 1850's in America were swept by deep, fervent concern about the rights of citizens and the moral health of the nation. This was the time of the abolitionist, temperance, and suffrage movements, and of intense religious revivals (in, among other places, the Fifth Avenue Presbyterian Church). Then, the design and sale of life insurance policies was widely considered to be a beneficent, socially redeeming, and pious enterprise because a life policy brought a financial security otherwise unavailable to average Americans. That the famous Alexander family of New Light Calvinism, Princeton Seminary, and the Fifth Avenue Church endorsed life insurance — even to the extent of backing a new life company — was testimony that the idea was moral.

Today, when an insurance policy is widely thought of as little more than an investment alternative with some tax and other financial advantages, many might think it curious that a simple, dry life policy once carried weighty ethical significance and was even widely regarded as an agent of social and religious reform. Yet the early success of The Equitable and other life companies was grounded on the conviction that life insurance was a social benefit. As we will see, the religious and reform appeal of a big financial company that cared deeply about the welfare of its individual clients was integral to the identity of mutual life insurance companies.

In the nineteenth century, the most articulate spokesman for the social reform ideology,

which Equitable and other companies echoed in their advertising, was the most influential actuary and insurance regulator of the time, Elizur Wright. He saw no dissonance between his profession and his beliefs as a social reformer and fervent abolitionist. Wright was sure that the dry certainties of actuarial intelligence, properly represented by capable agents, would bring about cultural transformation as surely as would the demise of slavery. Insurance, he said, was not just a gamble; rather it was "gambling made useful." His biographer has called this idea "mathematically determined altruism." Many insurance people went even further. Agents did not just sell insurance policies; rather, they "preached the gospel of protection." After the death in 1873 of Henry Hazen Hyde, the father of Equitable's founder, a writer for an insurance magazine memorialized him in sermonic language:

> [L]ike St. Paul, [Hyde] suffered no hardship, no fatigue, no infirmity, to prevent him preaching the truth in season and out of season to all men. He reasoned with husbands and fathers with a force and address they found it impossible to escape; but although he insured them almost in spite of themselves, thousands of these men lived and died thanking him for their conversion.

The language of conversion reached back to the recruiting brochure, written by Morris Robinson, that had attracted Henry Hazen Hyde and John Johnston to leave Catskill a quarter of a century earlier. In A Treatise on Life Insurance, the sale of a life policy was characterized as an act of divine will acting through human reason to reduce worry and concern and, thereby, to lengthen human life. One insurance company went so far as to claim in an advertisement that a life policy was a proof of the doctrine of the immortal soul, since through the agency of a policy, the deceased reaches back from beyond the grave to protect his family.[8]

Until the 1880's, the main advertisers in the hundreds of religious magazines were life insurers, and the church attendance of insurers' officers, investors, and board members was frequently mentioned in advertisements. Morris Robinson, Henry Hyde, and other pioneers often recruited clergymen and schoolteachers to be part-time agents; not only were they credible, respected believers in God, family, and community, but they already were well-trained, professional persuaders. In recruiting agents, the companies also exploited the era's faith in entrepreneurial activity, which was called "the theology of success" and preached from the pulpits and taught in the schools and the pages of the famous McGuffey readers that were the precursors of such modern self-improvement manuals as *The Power of Positive Thinking* and *The One-Minute Manager.* In 1836, one clergyman produced an inspirational manual titled *The Book of Wealth: In Which it is Proved from the Bible that it is the Duty of Every Man to Become Rich.* All this was a wonderful appeal for prospective agents.

The idea that insuring a life is an ethical calling is one of the elements of the ideology of mutual insurance that we call "insurance fundamentalism": life insurance is no more and no less than a rigid, scientific, low-risk system for guaranteeing essential financial protection for the good of the average American. Insurance fundamentalism was the glue of an industry that has frequently gone off in very different directions, often to be pulled back by the sharp, clear ideal that life insurance is more than just a financial instrument.

Riding the crest of the wave of the mutuals and Morris Robinson's intelligent merging of insurance with current needs and issues, American life insurance companies almost tripled in number from eighteen to forty-eight between 1840 and 1850, and the value of

insurance in force grew twenty-fold, from less than $5 million to $96 million. In an increasingly migratory, urbanizing, and market-driven culture, the ever growing number of people far from the traditional support systems of family and church were attracted by the idea of financial protection against the unstable economy. The largest group of clients for the new life insurance companies was the urban middle class, and the occupation that provided the most policyholders was that of merchant. Yet there remained problems. Many of the mutuals were frightfully undercapitalized. Nautilus had less than $60,000 to work with, and when John Johnston launched his new enterprise in Wisconsin in the 1850's he had to borrow money in order to pay his first death claim. To protect policyholders from the collapse of weak mutuals, New York State required new companies to put up $100,000 as a bond against their survival — a law that effectively required promoters to find shareholders, even if they, like Henry Hyde, had their companies function as mutuals.

Such was the setting as Equitable struggled through its first months. The new enterprise's success was anything but instantaneous. Hyde knew the business, had good advisors (including his father and Sheppard Homans, Mutual Life's actuary), was backed by wealthy people who trusted him, and was on the forefront of the new actuarial technology. He was also lucky in his timing, for with the start of the Civil War in 1861, the relative advantage of Mutual Life and other older companies shrank as they lost their well-developed business in the South. (Like many men in the North, Hyde avoided military service by hiring a substitute for his army call-up.) But with all these strengths he faced many hurdles. Since he would not offer the convenience of accepting IOU's, his sales efforts had to be more intense and, therefore, more expensive than those at

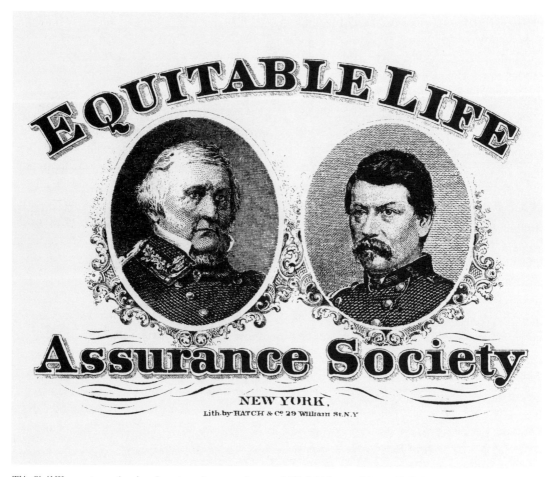

This Civil War-era promotional card carries endorsements by generals Winfield Scott and George McClellan. Agents customized it by writing their names and addresses across the bottom.

other companies. He soon found that the people interested in relatively large policies were not as numerous or eager as he had hoped (he did not sell a policy with a face value larger than $10,000 until 1862), and that they and most other prospects had already been thoroughly canvassed by Mutual Life and other established companies. Frederick Winston started a whispering campaign against Equitable. And the cold-call sales trips that he took through New York's office buildings, accompanied by the Society's doctor, Dr. Edward W. Lambert, at first were extremely discouraging. Lambert, who owed his job to the fact that his father was Hyde's main backer, looked back on these tough early days with the mingled romanticism and humor of a combat veteran:

Mr. Hyde and I were very young men, and our reception by the majority was chilly and often discourteous. We were never actually kicked out, but discretion on our part probably saved us. One man whose office was in John Street was persuaded to submit to an examination, but he was found to be ineligible on account of organic heart-trouble. He became so angry at what he considered the impudence of the whole transaction that we had to retreat very hastily.

As gloomy as their prospects were, Lambert related, Hyde gamely kept the enterprise alive: "The energy, persistence, and hopefulness of Mr. Hyde during the months from February to

July were so great that he held together the eminent men whom he had interested in this new project." Yet Hyde was far more discouraged than he let on. Years later he said, "I knew when The Equitable had been going about eighteen months, it seemed as if the heavens were brass over my head and as though it were utterly impossible to make anything out of the little company."[9]

As he peddled policies, Hyde recruited salesmen by appealing to entrepreneurial ambitions: "I want hustling agents to get business." The two most energetic agents were himself and his father, who between them, in New York and Boston, were responsible for more than half the 800 policies sold in 1859. The son's commissions totaled $5,200 and took care of most of the company's first-year overhead. When he was not selling, he often traveled around the country to recruit and train an agency force. And when he was doing neither, he was firing off spirited advisories to agents:

> Make use of all your friends and associates. Get lists from your doctor of insurable people, and, if necessary make it an inducement to him to smooth the way. Make your clergyman help you insure his flock, join literary societies and clubs — in order that you may insure the members.

Yet it was nowhere that easy. To attract capable agents, Hyde boosted sales commissions from the usual 10 percent to 50 percent of the first year's premium while providing the chief agents in the field, called general agents, with monopolies over huge territories. Soon Equitable was offering the highest commissions in the business — as much as 100 percent of first-year premiums, plus 10 to 20 percent on annual policy renewals for as long as twenty years, plus bonuses and prizes. He was one of the first to offer agents written contracts, rather than vague oral agreements, and

to cover specified expenses in exchange for an exclusive call on the agent's time.[10]

It was an expensive program, but it accomplished Hyde's goal, which was to attract many agents to approach many more prospects. At the end of 1860, Equitable had 229 agents, more than all but three of the older New York companies. Five years later, the Society had the largest sales force in the industry with 525 agents, almost twice the size of Mutual Life's. Fearing that the cost of these tactics could drag the new company down, the board of directors encouraged Hyde to control expenses and build a strong capital base by paying him and President Alexander annual bonuses equal to a percentage of the year's surplus.

"Great is the power of system, order, and discipline," Hyde once said. He was in the first wave of American managers who exerted what the business historian Alfred D. Chandler has called "the visible hand" — the conscious use of the tools of functional administration. Hyde closely watched all expenses; every charge had to be approved by at least two officers. He tolerated no slack. When an officer who had been in on the planning at the beginning, Robert Bliss, became delinquent on his mortgage to Equitable, Hyde demanded that he sell his house. But as meticulous as it seemed, Hyde's operation was not management in the modern sense of the word, with oversight committees and delegated decision-making, but rather a feudal system that freed him to assert his seignorial dominance throughout the company. According to his theory of administration, the genius of Henry Hyde should be freed to roam unimpeded throughout the company. He explained it when he commanded his successor, James W. Alexander: "Your work, to be of value to The Equitable, must be personal. You cannot depute your work to others, expecting them to do it as well as you can."[11]

Hyde defined himself not by his feelings but by his achievements, foremost of which were The Equitable's success and his control over it. "His nervous system apparently interpenetrated the whole Equitable system," noted an observer. It could have been said of every relationship in his life. To the point of physical breakdown, he seized and exercised large, detailed duties everywhere. From his wife he commandeered every detail of his household. From his father he appropriated most family duties, including caring for his retarded sister, Lucy. Annie Hyde spent her time drawing and engraving, often with their son James. Henry Hazen Hyde was less accommodating. He complained of being abandoned emotionally by his overworked, distracted son. Henry Baldwin did not take the charge seriously until too late, after the old man's death. Even then he could only speak of his grounding in his work: "It takes away the pleasure I had in transacting the business of life insurance," he wrote an acquaintance, "because I have no one to sympathize with me in it as my father did, and perhaps no one living can have the gratification over my success that he had."[12]

The collection of Hyde's letters in the Baker Library at the Harvard Graduate School of Business Administration is filled with commands and admonitions — relevant and petty — about costs, appointments, products, and authority. On one day alone, August 3, 1896, he fired off a barrage of commands to employees: to the manager of his farm in Bay Shore, Long Island, ordering him to take the plow in out of the rain; to the farm's housekeeper ordering her to save string and instructing her how to wind the grandfather clock; to the manager of the Equitable Building to locate a bootblack stand in a particular corridor; to employees of a railroad in which he had an investment to place signs precisely where he specified; to a vice-presi-

dent to purchase three umbrellas. Officers returning from vacations were accustomed to finding on their desks memorandums demanding tighter management and stricter accounting. Vice-presidents ill at home were told to expect him to visit with a stenographer and a briefcase full of papers. It was an astonishing performance. "Henry B. Hyde is an orchestra — tenor, alto, soprano, and bass all in one!" marveled a columnist for an insurance newspaper.[13]

If there was a problem, it was that he lacked proportion. "To insure success," Alexander recalled, "he often put on a hundred pounds of pressure where ten pounds would have been sufficient, thus wasting superfluous energy." Without apology or explanation, he drove his people as hard as he drove himself. His chief actuary, George Phillips, was in such a perpetual state of anxiety that the only way he could work off his tensions was to spend his nights roller-skating through the Society's halls. At least Phillips had an outlet. Hyde's usual response to the sustained pressure that he created as he supervised the many technical and marketing aspects of his business can be summarized in three words: total physical collapse. He did take some pleasure in constructing new buildings, but otherwise he drove himself into breakdown. Some thought him a hypochondriac, although (according to his applications for insurance) he did suffer from rheumatism and dyspepsia. His chief health problem was the debilitation that comes from addictive overwork and the ruthless drive to control and excel. Sometimes when he was in this state he would order his staff to his sickbed to report to him between his bouts of vomiting, but usually he simply disappeared for several weeks or months, abandoning his family and heading off on a long vacation — once, a trip around the world — accompanied only by an Equitable employee.[14]

"Life assurance was to him more than a business," Alexander said of Hyde; "it was a faith, a cult. Dominated by it himself, he speedily imbued others with its imprint." Of his commitment to Equitable, Hyde would only speak of "this one thing I do."[15]

☞ By a **NEW METHOD OF LIFE ASSURANCE**, more favorable results than any hitherto experienced may be enjoyed by persons possessed of constitutional longevity, who keep their policies in force until the middle or latter part of their lives.   These results are obtained by a novel application of the Tontine principle to the distribution of dividends, and by allowing the assured to sell his policy to the Company only after stated periods.

THE NEW

TONTINE SAVINGS FUND POLICY

IS BASED ON THE ABOVE CONDITIONS, AND PRESENTS THE FOLLOWING DISTINGUISHING FEATURES, WHICH ARE ILLUSTRATED BY A *CALCULATION OF PROBABLE RESULTS* ON A POLICY OF TEN THOUSAND DOLLARS, AT **ORDINARY LIFE RATES**, AGE 37, ANNUAL PREMIUM, $281.70.

FIRST—SALE OF POLICY TO THE COMPANY.

At the end of 10 years ....104 per cent. of premiums returned.
"   " 15 " 151   "   "   "   "
"   " 20 " 201   "   "   '   "

SECOND PAID-UP POLICY.

At the end of 10 years... $7,000
"   " 15 "   14,000
"   ' 20 "   22,000

THIRD—AN ANNUITY

AT THE END OF 15 YEARS THE PROFITS WILL *EXTINGUISH THE ANNUAL PREMIUM*, AND, WITH THE SUBSEQUENT ANNUAL DIVIDENDS, WILL PURCHASE A YEARLY INCOME OF $173 30
OR, AT THE END OF 20 YEARS, OF 647 40

THESE ESTIMATES ARE DERIVED FROM A CAREFUL DIGEST OF PAST EXPERIENCE, *AND ARE ENDORSED BY*

SHEPPARD HOMANS, Consulting Actuary.

☞ PERSONS INTENDING TO ASSURE THEIR LIVES WILL FIND IT TO THEIR ADVANTAGE TO EXAMINE THIS NEW PLAN WITH CARE.   DOCUMENTS, GIVING FULL PARTICULARS OF THE RULES OF THE COMPANY WITH REGARD TO THE ISSUE OF THE ABOVE SAVINGS FUND POLICY, EXTENDED TABLES OF RATES, AND OTHER INTERESTING MATTER, MAY BE OBTAINED BY APPLICATION TO THE

EQUITABLE LIFE ASSURANCE SOCIETY,

120 Broadway, New York,

OR ANY OF ITS REPRESENTATIVES THROUGHOUT THE UNITED STATES AND CANADA.

FOR further information desired, address either the officers of the Company or any one of its agents.

THE EQUITABLE LIFE ASSURANCE SOCIETY OF THE UNITED STATES,

No. 120 BROADWAY, NEW YORK.

Equitable's success was built by the tontine, an annuity originally designed by a seventeenth-century Italian doctor, Lorenzo Tonti, that it introduced in 1868.

CHAPTER III

RACING AT HOME
AND ABROAD

E quitable's new business was doubling in 1862 when pietistic Henry Hazen Hyde wrote his son, "It is truly wonderful that your company has so far outstripped its fellows. The power and ability has been conferred by Him who gave us being. Let Him have all the praise." But faith in divine sanction did not prevent him from giving his son some business advice: he must resist the temptation to make public comparisons between Equitable and the other companies, "especially with the Mutual as to outstripping them or anything of the sort." Henry Baldwin Hyde, who never knew a fight he did not like, ignored his father and added this boast to the Society's advertisements: "The Success of this Society has not been equalled by that of any Company ever organized, either in Europe or America."[1]

This was the warm-up to a decades-long fight between Equitable, Mutual Life, and, later, New York Life, described by the turn-of-the-century historian Burton J. Hendrick:

The one striking fact in the life insurance situation for the last fifty years has been the rivalry and hatred existing between these companies. Even now a Mutual official bristles whenever The Equitable is mentioned; and to a loyal Equitable man the Mutual's name is still anathema.

That fierce rivalry shaped the way the big companies did business, and in the end it came close to wounding them fatally. As the three companies battled each other to become the world's largest insurer, they came to be called "the racers."[2]

The skirmishing between Hyde and Frederick Winston of Mutual Life commenced the day Hyde hung his sign in its insulting position, but the war did not start for real until 1867, when Winston announced that he would declare policyholder dividends annually instead of every few years, which was the general practice. Until then, no company had been confident enough of its finances to pay dividends more frequently than every two years. Because Mutual Life was far more secure financially than the younger company, it seemed impossible that Equitable could match Winston's new policy for more than a year or two. Hyde hopefully announced that he, too, would pay annual dividends, and then went to work to figure how to meet his promise. He decided that the solution lay in inventing a successful new product.

He did not have to look far. In his hands, the tontine (also called the semi-tontine) became the very heart of Equitable's growth. Instead of guaranteeing benefits for survivors, like an insurance policy, the tontine provided for the policyholders themselves in their old age through the payment of dividends deferred over agreed upon periods of time. The longer the policyholder lived, the bigger the payout. The appeal for the sponsoring company was that it could invest the premiums as it wished during the period of the deferment, with no obligation to produce dividends. Because money built up before dividends were paid, tontines sometimes were called accumulation policies or deferred dividend policies.

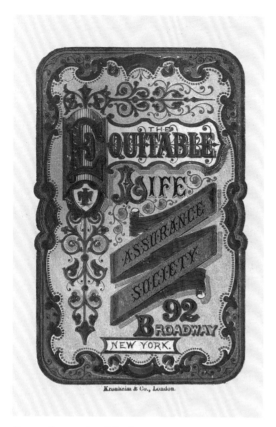

Some early promotional circulars were ornate.

Over the next four decades, the tontine became the most popular product in the life insurance business and the foundation for Equitable's rise. Although Hyde was the first American insurance executive to fully exploit the tontine, he did not invent it. The tontine, like many of his products, was an adaptation of an old policy. The idea was introduced in 1653 by an Italian doctor and banker, Lorenzo Tonti, as a fund-raising scheme for the French government, which was fighting several expensive wars. In all, the French floated more than thirty-five tontines in a little over a century. The immense popularity of tontines was shaped by the need for financial protection and also by two human passions — optimism about one's longevity and a delight in gambling. A set number of subscribers paid the same sum of money into a pool, which was then invested. The principal and some of the earnings remained with the sponsor, while most of the earnings were paid out to living subscribers as dividends, either annually or on some other schedule determined by the sponsor or policyholders. The length of the contract and schedule of premiums and dividend payments varied from one tontine to another. For example, participants younger than twenty-five might start out with a 7 percent annual dividend while those over seventy earned 14 percent. As subscribers died off, the shares increased in size until the last living subscriber enjoyed the entire payout. Meanwhile, the sponsor accumulated a sizable fund of its own.

The tontine idea was contagious. English and American promoters used tontines to finance the construction of buildings. Many towns had "tontine societies," just as we have our lotteries. The first U.S. secretary of the treasury, Alexander Hamilton, attempted to institute a national tontine to help raise money to liquidate the national debt built up by the American Revolution, but protests against the idea of betting on human longevity scotched the plan.

Henry Hyde did not inch his way into the tontine business. Rather, he made a frontal assault by essentially converting Equitable from an ordinary life company to a tontine company. His enthusiasm can be explained in part by his all-or-nothing personality, in part by the sometimes desperate struggle for survival against Mutual Life. But it also was rooted in legitimate business concerns about the cost of introducing new products — concerns that have not declined in importance since Hyde's day. The time-consuming actuarial work needed to design and price an insurance contract is expensive, as is the effort to educate agents about the product and to encourage them to sell it by offering favorable commissions. Advertising is costly; so are sales materials and the Home Office's normal support of the agents. Inevitably there is a lag of several years between the product's launch and its first profits, since the first year's premium rarely covers the cost of selling a policy. Therefore, marketing pressure must be exerted for several years in order to build the renewals that finally make a policy profitable to the company. With such high start-up expenses built in to the design, marketing, and sales system, economies of scale must be effected through selling in high volume. It was a constant challenge. In 1993, an Equitable actuary and officer, Harry Garber, summarized the problem and its solution, "They need to make a lot of sales; that's the only way you can make this system work." This would be the pattern for Equitable's introduction of most of its new insurance contracts throughout its history.[3]

On the last day of 1868, Henry Baldwin Hyde announced that Equitable would sell not one but four types of tontine policies, with maturities ranging from five to fifteen years before deferred dividends would be paid. The policyholder would receive a guaranteed death benefit and dividends based on whatever interest rate prevailed. Projections were made according to compound interest based loosely on current rates. The plans were designed by Equitable's chief actuary, George Phillips, and Hyde's old friend Sheppard Homans, who still was at Mutual Life but somehow found a way to assist his employer's bitter competitor. The policies were aimed at people in upper income brackets described (somewhat awkwardly) in promotional material as "many persons who from vigorous health, comfortable position in life, great family vitality, or from a hopefulness of disposition, which often secures the end it anticipates, are very confident of living long." In other words, they were people needing financial security for their old age and death benefits for their survivors, and desiring the

freedom to make their own choices about the timing of the dividend payments, depending on their needs and their understanding of economic trends.[4]

Besides a projection of yields well above bank interest rates, tontines had the additional advantage of giving consumers an unusual degree of choice in maturities, which affected the size of dividends. Unlike most other insurers, who offered few options other than the size and duration of the policy, Hyde provided enough alternatives to leave the policyholder with a sense of active control over the policy. Homans stressed this feature in his endorsement: "[T]he assurants will, when assuring, choose the class which they instinctively feel will be most profitable to them...." This early example of what we now call consumerism was a brilliant marketing touch. A later Equitable Chief Executive Officer who closely studied Hyde's career, Richard H. Jenrette, noted just how original the tontine was:

> *He realized that the risk of living too long is just as insurable and valuable as the risk of dying prematurely. He got life insurance into the savings business, and he was the father of modern insurance marketing. He got the industry out of the minor leagues.*[5]

At first, tontines did not sell well. They were somewhat more complicated than traditional insurance policies, and their commission schedule was lower. Hyde tinkered with the contracts and, to induce agents to sell them, lowered first-year commissions on traditional life policies to 35 percent and raised those for tontine policies to 50 percent. (At times of intense competition among the racers, commissions went as high as 100 percent of first-year premiums.) Hyde also changed the names of the policies from the formal Tontine Dividend Policy to the more suggestive

THE NECESSITY OF REFORM

IN

LIFE INSURANCE.

There has existed in this country for more than thirty years a British system of life-insurance, which includes some important benefits, with several grievous defects. One of the latter is, that it locks up many millions of dollars in the vaults of corporations which had better be in the hands of the people, to whom it really belongs; and another is, that the management of the business is extravagantly costly.

As a sample of this costliness, I give below the commissions paid to agents for procuring business and collecting premiums for the last twelve years in a single company:—

COMMISSIONS.

1866,	$686,622 94	1873,	$835,400 22
1867,	913,162 94	1874,	800,559 96
1868,	1,055,830 06	1875,	762,365 09
1869,	1,063,846 85	1876,	733,128 34
1870,	725,066 72	1877,	1,172,853 68
1871,	594,476 53		
1872,	667,463 55		$10,010,776 88

An attack on Equitable and its agency system.

Tontine Savings Fund Assurance. Between 1868 and 1872, Equitable's market share of new insurance business rose by almost half from under 8 percent to 11 percent. In 1873, the product became extremely popular, which was fortunate because a devastating four-year depression began that year and the Society's capital base was badly depleted.

The insurance industry at first was ambivalent about the introduction of tontines. While some companies raced to follow Hyde, others harshly attacked the tontine as an immoral lottery on human life expectancy, and a few critics went so far as to predict that policyholders would murder others in order to increase their dividends. To Elizur Wright, by then Massachusetts Insurance Commissioner, and other insurance fundamentalists, tontine policies violated the rigid, inalterable mathematical principle of life insurance in which

they had placed so much faith. The law of averages meant nothing if one policyholder's benefits depended on another's death. "Life insurance cannibalism" was Wright's caustic evaluation of how agents were urging policyholders to switch from ordinary life insurance to tontines: "It is as if a temperance society should endeavor to promote its cause by establishing a liquor saloon under its lecture room, or a church should support its minister by a lottery." Besides Wright, the chief opponent of the tontine was the head of Connecticut Mutual Life, Jacob L. Greene. "Its principle is gambling, and gamblers must expect to fall into the hands of sharpers, and sharpers are the only ones who make money by gambling," Greene proclaimed in one of his many anti-tontine publications. "The simple, plain facts can lead to no other conclusion. The lamb who ventures among Tontine wolves must expect to be devoured."[6]

The violence of his language reflected Greene's desperation. Whatever its philosophical merits, the tontine debate was no contest financially, for tontines were sensationally popular among the public as well as lucrative for insurance companies, and for very good reason: in a tontine, everybody would not only get something but also could hope to get everything. As Jacob Greene discovered to his increasing frustration, the tontine was an extremely stiff competitor to ordinary life insurance. He watched his company drop from the second largest U.S. insurance company in 1865 to the eleventh largest in 1900, far behind insurers selling tontines. Equitable, meanwhile, had risen from seventh largest to third largest, just behind Mutual and New York Life and far ahead of the pack. For a while, in the 1880's, the Society had been the largest.

Tontine sales built The Equitable Life Assurance Society. According to the account-

TONTINE:

What It Is;

How It Works.

PUBLISHED BY H. FRANKLIN FORD, 71 BROADWAY,
NEW YORK.

A LIBEL EXPOSED.

WHAT IT CONSISTS OF.

An anonymous pamphlet entitled, "TONTINE, WHAT IT IS, HOW IT WORKS," has just appeared and is being circulated diligently and gratuitously. Its objects are: (1) to show that the Tontine Savings Fund plan of insurance introduced by the Equitable Life Assurance Society of the United States, is a delusion and a snare, and the attempt is to prove this by giving information purporting to have been gathered from letters written by persons who have allowed Tontine policies to lapse and who are dissatisfied; and, (2) to make invidious comparisons between the Equitable and certain competing companies to the advantage of the latter.

This attack is *deliberately false* and *intentionally misleading*, and furnishes too good an opportunity to expose the dishonesty of the class of attacks to which it belongs, and to emphasize the merits of the system attacked, to be passed without notice.

WHERE IT ORIGINATED AND WHY IT HAS APPEARED.

The Equitable Society has done, and continues to do, a larger business than any other company in the world;

Hence the envy of its rivals.

The Tontine Savings Fund method of insurance is the most popular form of policy extant;

Hence the rivals of the Equitable have circulated in the past, and continue to circulate, attacks upon it. The pamphlet entitled, "TONTINE, WHAT IT IS, HOW IT WORKS," is of this character and from such a source.

NEW YORK, November 1, 1881.

Entered according to Act of Congress in the year 1881, by the Equitable Life Assurance Society of the United States, in the office of the Librarian of Congress, at Washington.

FEBRUARY, 1872.

A LIBEL

SQUARELY MET.

BEING A

STATEMENT FROM THE OFFICERS

OF THE

Equitable Life Assurance Society

OF THE UNITED STATES

TO THEIR AGENTS.

FEBRUARY 12th, 1872.

NEW YORK:
LEES & SKEEN, Printers, 208 & 210 Fulton Street.
1872.

ing rules of the time, insurance companies were not required to establish reserves against tontine accounts until the policies matured, so insurers were free to invest all the money at the going interest rates of 6 to 8 percent for as long as twenty years. Surpluses ballooned. Another advantage of tontines was the high lapse and forfeiture rate due to non-payment or tardy payment of premiums. For many years until anti-forfeiture laws required them to refund part of the premiums previously paid, insurance companies were permitted to keep the funds of lapsed policies. Lapses accounted for a vast amount of money. A study of an Equitable twenty-year tontine sold in 1871 revealed that of the money accumulated in the fund before dividends began to be paid out in 1891, 30 percent consisted of money left by lapses and forfeitures and investment yields on those funds; 12 percent

Another attack, this time on tontines (above left), stimulated Equitable to return fire (above).

consisted of money deposited by deceased policyholders; and 58 percent was money accumulated by living policyholders who had not forfeited their tontine policies. Any money not paid out as dividends was retained by the company.[7]

The tontine, in short, was extremely good to Equitable and all other insurers that sold it. By 1905, the total face amount of all tontine policies in force was more than $6 billion — just under two-thirds the value of all life insurance in force and the equivalent of 7½ percent of the total national wealth of the United States. Between 1869 and 1899, Equitable's insurance in force increased almost eight-fold, from $134 million to over $1 billion, its annual dividend payments almost tripled from $1.2 million to $3.5 million, and the company's assets expanded almost thirty-fold from $10.5 million to $280 million.

Most suggestive of the success of tontines is the story of Equitable's surplus, or capital derived from profits. An excellent indicator of financial health is the proportion of assets comprised by the surplus. In 1865, just as the Society was climbing to its feet, surplus was 19 percent of assets, but Mutual Life's wearing attacks dropped the proportion to 4½ percent in 1868 and then 3 percent for two years, as Hyde spent large sums to launch the tontines. In 1871, surplus, fed by compound interest on tontine premiums and the high lapse rate, began to build. Between 1876 and 1899, it averaged 18¼ percent and frequently was as high as 22 percent of assets. In other words, one dollar out of five of the company's assets was surplus, or profits. At Hyde's death in 1899, the surplus, at $57 million, was almost triple its level just ten years earlier. This huge capital base, the vast majority of which was derived from the tontine business, made The Equitable one of the largest and most powerful financial institutions of the nineteenth century.

Equitable, 1859-1899 *(in millions)*

YEAR	INSURANCE IN FORCE	PREMIUM INCOME	ASSETS	SURPLUS
1859	1.1	0.02	0.12	0.96
1869	134.2	5.8	10.5	0.4
1879	162.4	6.4	37.0	4.7
1889	631.0	25.4	105.4	20.8
1899	1,054.4	42.4	279.4	57.3

As Equitable and, eventually, Mutual Life and New York Life exploited the tontine, the war between the racers intensified. One of Winston's favorite tactics to attempt to undermine his younger, less secure rival was to cut Mutual Life's premiums drastically. He did this three times between 1865 and 1879. The smaller Equitable could not respond in kind, but Hyde fought back with marketing plans offering consumer benefits to policyholders, such as prompt payment of death benefits. A ruthless, cunning competitor, Hyde also could be subtle: he once acquired lists of Mutual Life policyholders, found a few discontents, and helped them bring lawsuits against the company. But usually he made open, well-publicized assaults against Mutual Life with the weapons of more appealing products, aggressive sales campaigns, and new marketing schemes. These sieges demanded long stretches of intense work. William Alexander remembered a battle with Mutual Life in 1872 with special affection: "It was a real war. Mr. Hyde, and all the officers, clerks, and agents worked night and day until the fight was over. And nothing ever benefitted Equitable more than this conflict." Overwhelmed, Winston sent his chief assistant, Richard McCurdy, to Hyde to surrender and work out a face-saving compromise by trimming its rate reduction by half. The combat was intensely personal. Winston once waited until Hyde was out of the country on a long vacation before cutting premiums, and for many years after that, Hyde refused to leave New York City whenever he sensed that Winston would mass his troops on Equitable's border. In 1885, when Hyde, on vacation in Florida, learned that Winston had died, he rushed back to New York to be prepared for a surprise offensive by his successor, McCurdy.[8]

These bitter wars were not a good advertisement for the life insurance industry. "The bane of the business... has been its jealousies," complained a New York State insurance superintendent. "[A]ttacks and counterattacks, charges and counter charges have been made, till very many of the great insuring public have lost confidence in, and become suspicious of, the system." Occasionally the public (or sheer exhaustion) prevailed upon the combatants to call a truce. Winston and Hyde once went so far as to agree to exchange contract forms and sell each other's policies, but the companies' general agents complained, and a rare armistice in the long war was broken by another battle.[9]

As Equitable developed its tontine business, it was also expanding abroad in a wave that made life insurance the first large international financial industry. So long as big insurance companies were ambitious to grow — and they rarely felt otherwise — they were obligated to spread their risks, which meant moving into new geographical regions. Yet Hyde had his doubts about going into foreign countries: "Time expended in cultivating the American field will produce ten-fold more than any money expended in Great Britain or any part of Europe," he insisted in 1870. That observation was supported by the record until then. The first known Equitable policy sold outside North America was on the life of a missionary outbound to Siam in 1860. In the next three years, policies were sold on the lives of three Americans living in China, Chile, and Argentina. The foreign business

Alexander Munkittrick, The Equitable's first European agent.

slowly picked up after Hyde, in 1868, permitted his actuaries to establish standard premiums for tropical and semitropical areas (allowing for the estimated additional risks, they increased the normal premiums by one-half and one-fourth, respectively).[10]

At around that time, Sheppard Homans and other American insurance men were returning from Europe with reports that foreign companies could not come near matching modern American marketing techniques. For once, Hyde did not see this as a challenge; he preferred to concentrate his forces in America. But after the Germania Insurance Company (later renamed Guardian Life) developed a lively foreign business in the late 1860's, Hyde reluctantly appointed his first European agent. He was Alexander Munkittrick, the former head of a small American insurer. His opening appeal was to a British group of Presbyterian clergy. During his first year in Britain, he sold some 11,000 policies, almost four times more than any British company. Munkittrick then established agencies in France and Germany.

Hyde, who was fanatical about retaining personal control over his operations, almost certainly would not have given in to his advisors and expanded abroad had it not been for the implementation in 1866 of the first transatlantic cable, which allowed him to communicate with his foreign agents almost as quickly as he could with his general agents scattered around the United States. (The cable's promoter, Cyrus W. Field, was an Equitable director; a painting of Field and other officers of the Atlantic Cable Co. now hangs in Equitable's board room.) To keep cable messages secret from prying competitors, Equitable developed its own fifty-five-page codebook. All coded words began with the letter "r": annual premium was *ringachat;* blood pressure, *richly;* age nine, *rialto;* a fifteen-year term policy, *rijkskroon;* Mexican currency, *righteous.* Reflecting the reality of the domination of the insurance business by the three racers, the code book listed only three insurance companies — Mutual Life, New York Life, and Equitable itself, whose code name was *rimantiene.*[11]

While Hyde never abandoned his doubts about expansion overseas, it became a large and critical part of the business in the late nineteenth century. Competitive pride played a part — Mutual Life and New York Life also expanded abroad — but the major cause for expansion was the flattening of American sales during the depression of the 1870's. The Equitable simply could not be allowed to stop growing. Between 1860 and 1893, the Society placed agencies in ninety-one countries, with at least one on each continent. By 1893, almost one-fourth of premium income was derived from foreign sales. The company flourished abroad for the same reason it flourished at home. As J. Owen Stalson described it, the Society's "bold, persistent, unremitting, person-to-person solicitation" was not matched by domestic companies. But these successes

were costly: expenses ran two to five times those of domestic business; transferring funds across borders was complicated; remote agents were hard to supervise. To Hyde's disgust, many agents who were not connected to him by cable went native and lost touch with the Home Office altogether until he dispatched officers to chase them down and close up their agencies. But the main problem with the foreign business was dealing with governments. After the first wave of American insurance invaders, governments began to protect their domestic insurers either by banning the American companies' most profitable product, the tontine, or by requiring them to establish extremely large reserve deposits in local banks. Americans responded with bribes, which only added to the cost. In Russia, the chief Equitable agent happened, not coincidentally, to be a government insurance regulator. In Mexico, Equitable's advisory board was chaired by the nation's president.[12]

Some countries were opened more slowly than others. After a decade of fumbling in France by local agents, Hyde in 1881 finally sent an American to Paris. He was the Reverend Stephen H. Tyng, Jr., a New York Episcopal priest. Tyng had won Hyde's attention by writing a spirited defense of the life insurance industry in a popular magazine. Whether or not Tyng's payoff was the offer of the Paris post, within a few weeks he resigned his pulpit and was on a ship to France. He opened Equitable's offices in a building that the Society purchased on l'Avenue de l'Opéra and, to attract American prospects, installed English-language reading rooms and information services. But Hyde was not favorably impressed by Tyng's entrepreneurship and replaced him after only a year. His successor, James A. Taber, did better under Hyde's meticulous, sometimes disruptive supervision. In 1883, Hyde went to Paris and instructed Taber

Some of Equitable's foreign buildings: (clockwise from top left): Berlin, Melbourne, Paris, Madrid, Vienna, and Yokohama.

The same techniques were used abroad that worked at home, including aggressive marketing by agents with supplies of brochures.

to hang on the building a huge Equitable sign like the one he had put up outside his first office in 1859. Characteristically, he did not trust Taber with the design; on returning to New York he ordered a sample made and sent over. Like a child on Christmas Eve, he anxiously awaited Taber's reaction: "I am watching every steamer for a letter from you, with regard to affairs in Paris," he wrote. "I am sure you will be delighted with the sample sign sent." Whether or not the sign had any effect, Equitable's sales in 1887 totaled $138 million in face amount, two and one-half times the sum of all the policies sold that year by the eighteen largest French companies.[13]

The entrepreneurship that Hyde encouraged had something of a frontier quality. In late 1885 or early 1886, Sidney S. Schmey, a German-born Equitable agent attached to the agency in Prussia, traveled to St. Petersburg, Russia, with some German-language policies. Schmey did not care that he knew no Russian, that the government had not granted him a license to sell insurance, nor that Henry B. Hyde was completely unaware that he had departed Germany. He settled in St. Petersburg and sold policies to many members of the large cosmopolitan community of Russia's capital. In 1889, he won the legal right to do the business that he had been conducting for three years, subject to government approval of The Equitable's insurance contracts. He had Russian-language contracts printed up, bought a large house, hired a French cook, and entertained lavishly. His invitation list of likely prospects included (according to a colleague) "artists, diplomats, painters, Russian Senators, [and] famous Italian singers." As one of only two agents of American insurers in Russia, he prospered.[14]

The Russian government decided to ban Equitable's tontine policies because, it claimed, they gave the Society an unfair advantage over domestic companies. The government was dissuaded briefly by a flamboyant man of vague nationality who referred to himself by the title General but was known in St. Petersburg's small insurance community as the tontine ambassador. It was rumored that he was helped by the American ambassador. All the same, the government banned tontines in 1894 by requiring that dividends be paid annually. Schmey, undiscouraged, continued to live it up at Equitable's expense. Henry Hyde sent over his Vice-

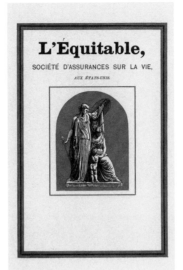

All brochures had the same themes: the benefits of life insurance protection, and the security offered by The Equitable.

President for Foreign Agencies, George T. Wilson, to fire him. Schmey returned to Germany and was succeeded by Dr. P. J. Popoff, a Russian-born American citizen who made the agency profitable with the help of a new policy that looked like an ordinary annuity but functioned like a tontine. New Russian business doubled until Popoff, shattered by the death of his daughter, resigned in 1904. He was succeeded by his assistant, Herman Ivanovich Schoofs, a multilingual Russian who had worked in the government insurance department. During the revolution of 1905, Schoofs shut down the office and stopped sell-

ing new policies, although he was kept busy handling existing policyholders. After the Russian Revolution, the Bolshevik government outlawed all contracts between Russian citizens and foreign companies, and Equitable finally ended its Russian business by moving Schoofs to Paris, where he spent the remainder of his days dealing with lawsuits filed by émigré policyholders. By then the financial problems that Hyde had long since anticipated — plus some crises that he never would have dreamed of — had led Equitable to close down its entire foreign empire after half a century of colorful adventures abroad.

Hyde built big buildings in part to advertise The Equitable's strength, relevance, and security.
The Home Office at 120 Broadway had the first elevators ever installed in an office building.

CHAPTER IV

FAITH, TRUST, AND SIZE

The Equitable had no hope of success if public trust in its services, agents, and reliability were lacking. To inspire that trust, and also to instill in Equitable's people the sense of purpose that drove him, Henry Hyde created one of the pioneering consumer and public relations programs. He used advertising and other forms of publicity in a wide variety of media, from agents' brochures to newspapers to architecture.

The double challenge was how a large life insurance company should think of itself so its employees had the requisite sense of mission, and then present itself and that mission to the world. The company could not deny that it was a business; after all, people were trusting it with their money. Yet the business purpose must somehow be expressed in a way that made it seem, if not a philanthropy, at least an institution devoted to the public service that its product, life insurance protection, was said to provide. In other words, profits and good works must go hand in hand. That, of course, was one of the doctrines of mutual status, but since Equitable was not a true mutual, it had to go a step further to assert its social concerns. Hyde therefore presented The Equitable as a blend of a large, successful business and a social service, missionary enterprise working for the good of humanity. The idea often used to summarize this blended identity was *security*, whether it was expressed in words or in such seemingly contradictory images as a balance sheet listing Equitable's surplus, or a sentimental painting of a mother embracing a child. What the two illustrations had in common was the theme of secure protection against danger. This was not callous manipulation; Hyde, his agents, and his employees believed in their calling to preach and administer "the gospel of protection."

The security idea was apt for its time and for many years to come. In Equitable's 101st year, in 1960, the company's advertising agency would characterize its public image as "big, caring, gentle, corporate, tender as a mother, historic, a friendly giant."[1]

Hyde propagated these two themes energetically, consistently, and often ingeniously. The most visible usually was public service, which was represented in Equitable's mutual system of operations as well in the Latin motto that Hyde placed on the corporate seal and that is translated "Of benefit alike to rich and poor" *(Aeque pauperibus prodest locupletibus aeque)*. Hyde expressed this benevolence by identifying Equitable with religion and the protection of those in need, symbolized by the helpless widow and the orphan. To represent the doctrine of social service visually, Hyde conceived and displayed striking symbols, foremost among which was the "Protection Group" image that served as the Society's logo beginning in 1860. Its most prominent figure, the Goddess of Protection, has been Equitable's icon for 135 years, with only a brief hiatus during the 1980's. As for the second theme, Equitable's strength and reliability as a financial institution were repeatedly represented in a variety of ways. One was the company's motto, "Not for a day, but for all

Ingeniously titled brochures kept appearing to counter attacks on Equitable and life insurance itself.

time" (in French, *Pas pour un jour mais pour toujours*). This motto is a clever borrowing of Ben Jonson's description of Shakespeare as "Not of an age, but for all time." Another, more dramatic display of financial strength was Hyde's international program of constructing monumental buildings that carried Equitable's name.

The founding idea of Equitable's public image was that mutual, participating life insurance offered benevolent social services that complemented the churches' spiritual services. Hyde and his advertising directors assiduously pursued the theme of mutuality by explaining that although the Society was a stock company, it worked on the mutual scheme. Because this explanation was complicated and subject to attacks by competitors that were pure mutuals, Hyde chose to promote his benevolent intentions in a different manner by aligning Equitable with the church. The church paper, or tract, would be the main outlet for Equitable's advertising until the 1880's.

In a time of religious revival that was tied into some of the great social causes of the day, including civil rights for minorities and

women, this appeal reached a wide audience. Thanks to heavy government postage subsidies for newsprint, all papers thrived in the mid and late nineteenth century. While fewer than 200 papers were published in the country in 1800, by the time Hyde founded Equitable there were more than 3,000 papers, which were responsible for more than half of U.S. mail deliveries. Among them were hundreds of religious weeklies, monthlies, and broadsides fighting the lively theological, denominational, and social-reform disputes that swept the country between the 1840's (when the crucial issue was slavery) and the 1890's (when it was poverty). In New York alone in 1850 there were fifty-two religious journals, many of them published and edited by popular preachers. A clergyman of the time estimated that three-fourths of all reading by Americans was "purely religious." Equitable advertised widely in church newspapers and, taking advantage of their quid pro quo offers of free editorial space, filled their columns with endorsements by friendly clergymen. One of Hyde's consultants, a Baptist preacher from Newark, the Reverend Henry Clay Fish, wrote some of Equitable's first promotional pamphlets endorsing life insurance in general and Equitable in particular — with titles like *Words to Wives* and *Why Not?* — as well as the first training handbooks for agents, *Agents' Companion* and *The Agents' Manual*.[2]

To attract word-of-mouth advertising in the churches, Hyde provided clergymen with policies and assistance with sermons and articles, conducted them on guided tours of the Home Office, and introduced them to directors and officers. Anticipating questions about the Society's financial reliability, he even opened its books to them. After one visit, a prominent Presbyterian clergyman and editor of a denominational magazine, the Reverend S. Irenaeus Prime, wrote that Hyde, the Alexanders, and the directors were "chiefly religious and benevolent men" who "know that intelligence and virtue tend to prolong life, and that the most safe and profitable life insurance will be among enlightened religious communities." Prime urged pastors to recommend insurance and "its rich advantages" to their congregations. Addressing Equitable's board he concluded, "I believe your Society is one of the most purely benevolent institutions in our land." A million dollars could not buy that kind of publicity.[3]

The publicity coup of Equitable's early years was an endorsement by the country's most famous preacher, the Reverend Dr. Henry Ward Beecher, of Plymouth Church, Brooklyn. In 1862, Hyde gave Beecher a policy and helped him write a complimentary article in his tract. Purchase of a life policy in the troubled times of economic disruption and the Civil War was "a moral duty," Beecher explained. "Once the question was: Can a Christian man rightfully seek such assurance? That day has passed. Now the question is: Can a Christian man justify himself in neglecting such a duty?" Hyde liked such questions. He invited Beecher to write more of them for *Our Mutual Friend*, Equitable's magazine, but first

TRAPS

BAITED WITH ORPHAN;

OR,

What is the Matter with Life Insurance?

BY

ELIZUR WRIGHT,

EX INSURANCE COMMISSIONER.

BOSTON:

JAMES R. OSGOOD AND COMPANY,

(Late Ticknor & Fields, and Fields, Osgood, & Co.)

1878.

Elizur Wright was the conscience of life insurance.

he reprinted most of the original piece in a widely distributed pocket-sized pamphlet titled *Truth in a Nutshell*, on whose back page ran a picture of the massive new Equitable Building at 120 Broadway over a commanding caption: "Read this Carefully, and Hand it to Your Wife."[4]

The heyday of the religious press ended in the 1870's with the rise of large-circulation, general-interest newspapers and of a secular "niche" press in many fields, including insurance. Each major insurance company supported its own pet industry paper with heavy advertising and used it as an outlet for favorable publicity. Elizur Wright, the conscience of insurance fundamentalism, complained that the relationships were so cozy that no insurance periodical would dare run "any searching criticism of life insurance companies." When he and other watchdogs and reformers published critiques of tontines and misleading sales tactics, they appeared in pamphlets with provocative titles like *Traps Baited with Orphan; or, What is the Matter with Life Insurance?* Still, company control of a trade periodical could not always be taken for granted. In 1872, Mutual Life's main defender, the *Insurance Times*, suddenly switched over to Equitable and began pounding out harsh attacks on its old supporter. Frederick Winston successfully sued the editor, Stephen English, for defamation. English was thrown into jail; Winston bailed him out after he promised to transfer his allegiance back to Mutual Life.[5]

Less controversial and more practical for agents were promotional handouts, the most enduring of which was the corporate calendar, invented in 1869 by George Coburn, a printer in Hartford. "If a calendar does nothing more than to make an initial call possible and add one prospect, it has paid for itself," an Equitable advertising director, Arthur H. Reddall, wrote in his textbook on insurance publicity. Other promotional handouts, all carrying Equitable's logo and the name of an agency, included posters, pencils, and blotters. One popular blotter showed a worried man, his head surrounded by tiny devils, with a caption promising that the insurance agency "will blot 'em out." With the arrival of motion pictures in the early twentieth century, many of these slogans were reformatted onto transparencies that were projected onto the screen before the feature film was shown.[6]

As secularized as the marketing of life insurance became, religious imagery remained lively. Two articles in a 1902 issue of the Society's agents' magazine, *The Equitable News*, were "Sermons for Agents," which cited Bible verses apt for sales presentations, and "How Theological Students Can Support Themselves," which encouraged managers to recruit clergymen as agents:

[T]he pastor, while exhorting a member of his flock to make provision for his welfare in the world to come, can charge him to look out for his welfare in old age, and for the welfare of his family in the event of his death.... Many of the best life assurance agents have been men trained for the ministry.

The last statement was true. Then and later, many ministers supplemented their income by selling life insurance. And today, some agents describe their job as "preaching the gospel of protection."[7]

Equitable's advertisements often referred to the economically helpless, whom the Society promised to protect. The typical expression of this theme was the "widows and orphans" motif, which Hyde and his advertising advisors illustrated in hundreds of pictures of distressed children and infants, some in utter despair and others on the verge of being rescued by Equitable agents. This social service theme was replayed in many ways in the advertisements and promotional brochures produced by William Alexander, the Secretary for many years. It was capsulated in an advertisement whose caption was, "Some wives do not recognize the value of insurance. All widows do." As sentimental as it was, this portrayal expressed a very real concern in the nineteenth and early twentieth centuries, when there was no Social Security, the poorhouse was a reality, and few remunerative jobs were available to women.

The idea of the helpless widow and orphan took visual symbolic form in Hyde's choice of one of the very first corporate symbols in history. This is the statue group known as the Protection Group (sometimes the Protector), with its image of a protective female warrior holding her shield over a young mother and child. The first version of the Protection Group appeared in Equitable's seal,

The Protection Group (shown here in its plaster model) was unveiled on the Equitable Building during a visit by a Russian duke in 1871.

designed by the American Bank Note Company, that was embossed on Equitable policies beginning in March 1860. Originally, the female figure carried a stave. In 1868, Hyde commissioned a statue on the "protection" theme from John Quincy Adams Ward, a well-known American sculptor who specialized in impressive public statues. Ward simplified the image but made one dramatic alteration: instead of a stave, the guardian now held a spear. The change clearly identified her not as a vague maternal figure but as Pallas Athena, the all-triumphant Greek goddess of both war and generosity. This addition mirrored Henry Hyde's own aggressiveness and sharpened Equitable's image.

Carved in Italy over a period of two and one-half years, Ward's statue weighed ten tons and stood eleven feet tall. In 1871, it was installed in the pediment of the Equitable

Building at 120 Broadway and, a few months later, was unveiled to honor a visit by the Russian Grand Duke Alexei. For the event, Equitable commissioned a twelve-stanza heroic ode, whose last lines read:

> *Thy shield "Assurance," providence thy*
> *spear*
> *Invulnerable Queen! Thou reignest here.*

Many art critics refused to take the Protection Group seriously because it was located on an office building on commercial Broadway. However, one reviewer commended Equitable for introducing true art to an area unfamiliar with it; the Group, he wrote, was "the most dignified and successful, if not the only dignified and successful, sculptural monument of our chief thoroughfare." Hyde thought so highly of the Group that he asked Ward to produce bronze copies to install on The

Equitable's buildings under construction in Boston, Madrid, and Berlin. Sadly, the original Protection Group sculpture had a short life. The marble soon became so pitted and corroded that it was taken down and put into storage, where it disintegrated altogether except for two heads, which Hyde saved in his personal museum of Equitable memorabilia. Although Ward's plaster model was still available, another statue was not made. The model was destroyed when the Equitable Home Office burned down in 1912. A plaster replica was displayed as part of the Society's exhibit at the 1939 New York World's Fair. As for the heads, they disappeared after Hyde's death in 1899, resurfaced in Florida many years later, and were purchased at auction by Equitable. In 1995, they were displayed on the forty-ninth floor of the Home Office building.[8]

Besides the religious connection and the "widows and orphans" idea, Equitable's extensive promotion effort concentrated on the theme of trustworthiness and strength. It was an important message at a time when many insurers offered only a few inflexible products, delayed paying death benefits for months, and regularly contested policyholders' claims. Here Hyde made some innovations in the area that we now call consumerism. The tontine was one; it offered unprecedented flexibility for policyholders. Equitable also was one of the first American insurers to offer policies to women, the first to give policyholders the benefit of the doubt in disputes over contractual terms, and the first to make policies incontestable.

Incontestability was a substantial innovation. Insurers commonly challenged claims for death benefits that did not seem to conform strictly to the letter of the law. Hyde was convinced that a policy of challenging claims would hurt the company's reputation, so in 1879 he guaranteed that benefits would be paid on the day the Home Office received a copy of the death certificate so long as there were no obvious questions about a death claim and the policy had been in force for at least three years. (He later reduced the period of contestability to one year.) The introduction of incontestability was a brilliant stroke that ended years of public brawls among insurance companies over who was most favorable to policyholders' interests. Similarly, Hyde made it a policy to avoid the litigiousness that seemed epidemic among insurance companies. "The company has a great horror of litigation, its special pride being that it keeps itself out of the Courts," said an Equitable officer. Equitable went to court against policyholders only two-thirds as often as New York Life and Mutual Life in the late nineteenth century. When the Society did have a dispute with a policyholder, it usually settled quickly before the story reached the newspapers.[9]

The government's interest in regulating life insurance grew with the industry. While state and federal courts were generally favorable to business, they were extremely hard on life insurers in cases involving policyholders. In one decision after another, judges and juries ruled for policyholders and tighter state regulation. This hoisting of insurers on the petard of their own public relations campaigns had dramatic consequences. Between 1890 and 1908, of the 2,000 insurance regulations reviewed by courts, only 1 percent were ruled unconstitutional. Equitable felt the brunt of this trend in the 1890's, when Hyde, concerned about rising overhead, briefly refused to settle many suits. But he quickly reversed himself in the face of a barrage of negative publicity to the effect that heartless Equitable was exploiting helpless policyholders through the legal system.

The regulation of insurance was wholly a state matter thanks to an 1869 Supreme Court

Depicted in poignant advertisements, the widows and orphans theme reflected a legitimate worry in a time when there was no Social Security.

decision, in *Paul* v. *Virginia*, that life insurance did not fall under federal jurisdiction because it was not interstate commerce. Ironically, many insurance officers at the time would have welcomed federal regulation so there would be consistent rules from coast to coast, rather than a patchwork of conflicting state laws. Yet Hyde preferred the status quo of state regulation. He knew that a big company like Equitable enjoyed much more influence over a state legislature than it would over Congress. He was correct. Reformers and competitors for dollars (including banks) constantly challenged the theory of life insurance exceptionalism and its outgrowths, including the tax exemptions and deferrals on death benefits and dividends. It did not hurt that the New York State Insurance Department was a haven for favoritism. Every few years, a reform governor would sweep out the hacks or

try to untangle the byzantine regulations, without much long-term effect. Hyde recruited politically sophisticated and well-connected directors who served as paid lobbyists in Albany. One, Cornelius N. Bliss, was the longtime treasurer of the Republican Party, which dominated national and state politics after the Civil War and to which Equitable made sizable donations. Another was Chauncey M. Depew, a one-man New York powerhouse with legendary persuasive powers (he was known as the best after-dinner speaker in America). Depew headed the New York State Republican Party, was a United States Senator, and served as president of the New York Central Railroad, which dominated state life. (The alley for delivery trucks on the east side of Grand Central Terminal is named after him.) Equitable paid Depew a $20,000 annual retainer, and when a new town called

Depew was built around a New York Central station near Buffalo, the Society chipped in there, too.

These and other lobbyists influenced legislators and insurance regulators by providing entertainment, campaign funds, and other services. Largely because the well-organized, well-financed insurance lobby successfully defended life insurance as the last barrier against poverty, bills intended to raise taxes of insurance companies above nominal levels, and to end the traditional exclusions from levies on dividends, surrender values, and death benefits, were regularly beaten back in state legislatures. Still, the tax exemption was hardly a sure thing; it was not in the original draft of the 1913 Federal Revenue Act, the first federal income tax passed after the adoption of the Sixteenth Amendment, and was inserted only late in the congressional debate.

As successful as lobbyists were at representing most insurance industry concerns, they could not keep the pot from boiling. As the number of policyholders grew, legislators paid attention to consumer protection, and investigations of sales practices were frequent. An investigation usually turned up something that shocked people who had believed completely (and naively) that the companies were as purely beneficent as their advertising claimed, or that every agent was selfless. Sometimes real violations of trust were unveiled, but often the public did not know what to think. "[M]en and firms lauded as statesmen and giants in one year," observed an historian, "were castigated as crooks and frauds in the next, with no factual charge except the press of events and bankruptcy laying open their affairs and books to public scrutiny and hindsight." The hearings came in waves. In one three-month period in 1877, Henry Hyde testified at three of them. "I can't transact any business. I spend all my time being investigated," he complained.[10]

As usual, he had a strategy. When a government investigation seemed likely, Hyde sometimes arranged for an informal one by a panel of friendly or neutral actuaries, policyholders, or regulators. This group, he knew, would pay at least one compliment that he could publicize to distract people from the more hostile evaluations. (As shrewd as Hyde was, he did not stoop to the level of one competitor who in order to hide a critical report, copyrighted it and withheld all permission to quote from it.) Another way to counter the poor publicity surrounding investigations was to publicize endorsements of Equitable and its products from prominent figures. Besides famous clergymen, they included businessmen, King Kalakana of Hawaii (who in 1883 bought a policy from the Society's San Francisco agency), and various celebrities. Hyde's fiercely independent critic Elizur Wright, in financial need in his old age,

Surplus as the arch of "the bridge of prosperity."

allowed Hyde to use his name in an endorsement in exchange for a $2,000 annual retainer as a consulting actuary.

In promoting Equitable's reliability, Hyde always emphasized that it functioned as a mutual by distributing much of its earnings to policyholders. Sometimes he went so far as to claim it was "purely mutual" (as the Society's first advertisement boasted); this of course was not the case, since Equitable was owned not by its policyholders but by Hyde and a few other stockholders. As Hyde's opponents pointed out the inaccuracy of this claim, he replaced it in the 1870's with another: Equitable was reliable because it was too big to fail. The new slogan was "Strongest in the World." This promise came true in 1886, when the Society had the largest capital base (counted as surplus) with $16.3 million and close to the largest assets, with $75.5 million. In emphasizing capital as a sign of integrity and reliability, Hyde skirted the touchy subject of profitability, a measure that seemed to many critics to be inappropriate in an institution run on the principles of mutuality. While his early advertisements mentioned the word *profit*, and it sometimes was used internally as an indicator of success and efficiency, that word disappeared from Equitable's public language in the 1870's as true mutual insurers pressed their attack on the Society's stock ownership. Profit would not return to public use until the 1980's, though its idea was partially hinted at by surplus, which also suggested strength.

The "Strongest in the World" message was conveyed in several ways. In advertisements, it was illustrated in imaginative artwork involving thermometers, bar graphs, and other measures. One much-reproduced ad, created by Secretary William Alexander, showed people marching across a bridge, labeled "surplus," high above a raging torrent identified as "ruin"

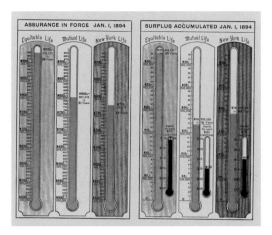

Strength was portrayed in different ways, even on an envelope.

and "despair." The bridge's keystone was labeled "management." (Alexander claimed this intricate image first came to him in a dream.) But no promotion made the point about the Society's financial strength half as well as its immense, elegant buildings in America and a dozen foreign countries. Hyde was a pioneer in the idea of making an office building a promotional tool as well as a workplace, and Equitable was the first American business to build its own corporate headquarters and put its name on it. In all, Hyde built fifteen Equitable Buildings around the world in forty years at a total cost of $38 million (the equivalent of about $600 million today). The program, which he called "building buildings for glory," came easily to a man whose appetite for the biggest of everything was voracious. For example, when ordering wildlife remains to decorate a room in the Equitable Building in New York, he insisted, "I would very much like

The Home Office in the early 1870's.

to secure the largest elk's head and the largest deer's head in the world."[11]

The initial justification of the building program was as an investment. Since 1849, insurance companies based in New York were prohibited from owning real estate other than their own office buildings and properties taken in mortgage foreclosures. The way around this restriction was to build a large office building, take some space in it, and rent out the remainder to tenants of good name whose reputation would enhance that of the building's owner. Hyde's first development of this plan was in 1868, when he asked his board for $1 million to construct a seven-story office building on the site of a hotel across from Trinity Church in lower Manhattan. Equitable would take two upper floors, and the remaining space would be leased out. The directors were appalled. Equitable had assets of only $5 million, had an

uncertain new product in the tontine, and was beleaguered by Mutual Life. Besides, every other office building in the world was only four or five stories high. The proposal that the owner should be on upper floors, or that anybody would take space far above the valuable ground-floor offices, at the height of Trinity's tall steeple, seemed ludicrous.

Hyde placated the board by taking personal responsibility for renting out the upper floors and working closely with the architect, George B. Post, to make the Equitable Building as attractive and functional as it could be. He talked the Delmonico family, proprietors of the city's most popular restaurant, into setting up a branch with a special entrance from the building. And to make the upper offices attractive and accessible, he and Post installed two well-furnished, nicely paneled versions of a new gadget, called the "safety hoister," that Elisha G. Otis had recently placed in a Manhattan hotel. Equitable's elevators, the first ever installed in an office building, became tourist attractions and convinced prospective tenants to escape the dirt and dark of a street-level office. A bank leased the ground floor, Equitable took the second and third stories, and several law and insurance firms rented the space under the mansard roof. Equitable installed a Lawyers Club and an Insurance Club, where tenants could gather for conversation, lunch, and reading in well-appointed libraries. The Insurance Club soon merged with the Lawyers Club, which came to have its own elevator, a 35,000-book library, and a membership of 1,820, including many Equitable employees whom Hyde commanded to join up.

The Equitable Building opened in 1870, but it was never completed to Hyde's satisfaction. He had it under an almost continuous expansion that cost another $3 million and earned the building such nicknames as "Hyde's folly" and "marble quarry." The unending con-

THE COMPLETED BUILDING OF THE EQUITABLE LIFE ASSURANCE SOCIETY, NEW YORK CITY.—Drawn by Hughson Hawley.—[See Page 559.]

These illustrations of the enlarged Home Office appeared in Harper's Weekly, *America's most popular magazine.*

struction so annoyed the Delmonicos that they moved out, and Hyde replaced them with a restaurant owned by Equitable called Café Savarin, whose produce and milk were supplied by his working 200-acre farm on Long Island. (The arrangement apparently was motivated not by greed but by his obsession with controlling every aspect of every project in which he was involved.) The Equitable Building gradually expanded to fill a large block and dominate the Wall Street area. The structure was so tall, said a contemporary, that it was "as if it were standing upon a hill in the middle of the city." It acquired one of the city's first electric-light systems and a spectacular, marble-rich aura that the *New York Times* called "an indescribable impression of splendor." Its reputation, in the words of the *New York Tribune*, was as "the hub around which the business affairs and the noonday life of the city

revolved" — which, as Hyde knew very well, only added to its appeal to prospective tenants. To further guarantee that Equitable would not be forgotten, Hyde placed the Protection Group frieze over the entrance and installed the local weather bureau on the top floor and gave it a flagpole from which to fly pennants reporting the day's forecast. The building was featured in Equitable's advertising, especially when the Society's assets and surplus were listed, and Hyde produced an array of souvenir photographs and prints to remind people of its (and its sponsor's) size and permanence.[12]

The Equitable Building and its iconography set the standard for insurance architecture. When William Dean Howells, in his 1890 novel, *A Hazard of New Fortunes*, wanted to set a scene in which the subject was life insurance, he placed his characters in an edifice like Equitable's Home Office, and described them

"An indescribable impression of splendor," was how one reporter characterized the building.

walking down "the marble halls and stairs of the great building" and standing "on the outside steps of the vast edifice beetling like a granite crag above them, with the stone groups of an allegory of life insurance foreshortened in the bas-relief overhead" — a clear reference to the Protection Group.[13]

As Equitable expanded abroad, it carried this monumental style to its regional offices. Besides good advertising and a source of income from rentals, this building program stimulated a warm welcome for Equitable by local business leaders and politicians. After Hyde announced he would put up two new office buildings in Australia, a national newspaper there editorialized glowingly: "The shrewd business men who manage the affairs of The Equitable Life Assurance Society have shown that they have unbounded faith, not only in the future of Melbourne, but also of Sydney."[14]

This chain of grand structures and high hopes served as a vivid image of the Society's global strength and scope. Advertisements circulated in various languages displayed them lined up in ranks, like troops, under banner headlines that announced, once again, that Equitable was "Strongest in the World." But such claims (and the costs behind them) were not admired by insurance fundamentalists. Already critical of tontines, they leaped upon the accumulating luxury of 120 Broadway and the construction of many other large Equitable Buildings in America and abroad as indications of the downfall of the idea of cautious, responsible mutuality and protection. Hyde did not take these criticisms seriously. He wrote one of his vice-presidents:

If we do not have attacks of one kind, we have them of another. One day it is the building; another day it is the way the President parts his hair; and another day

it is with regard to the general rascality of the concern. There must be in business and in politics, as on the surface of the earth, active volcanoes to relieve the situation, like a bilious attack, and we can never expect to be free from them. Perhaps if it takes the shape of attacks on the buildings, it is about as good as any other attack.[15]

Still, Hyde was more sensitive about the buildings than about most other corners of his empire. Besides promoting Equitable and bringing in rental income, they satisfied his own needs. "With him, building was almost an obsession," an Equitable historian, R. Carlyle Buley, has written. But Buley had it backward, for while some people have had edifice complexes, Henry Hyde had edifice therapies. Building was his only release. When his extraordinary nervous energy hit a dead end, he turned for renewal to the creation or redesign of tangible objects — the Equitable Building, a new office abroad, his town house, his farm, a college apartment or stable for his son, James, or the Jekyll Island Club, an exclusive businessmen's retreat on a barrier island off the coast of Georgia whose members included J. Pierpont Morgan.[16]

His extraordinary construction program was one of the few public outlets for Hyde's ego. He himself was a part of Equitable's publicity, for on every advertisement and brochure, his name was printed under Equitable's and an image of the Protection Group. Otherwise, he made it a rule to keep his face and private life out of the newspapers. He violated the rule for only one reason, he said: "I have not been modest or backward, however, in upholding the banner of The Equitable under all circumstances, and have endeavored to secure all the honors that properly belong to the cause I represent."[17]

For many years the Equitable Family coalesced around the Society's baseball teams.
Here is an Equitable squad around the turn of the century.

CHAPTER V

"THE EQUITABLE FAMILY"

Crossing Manhattan's rivers on ferryboats, and making their way along the financial district's narrow streets by foot or on horse-drawn trams, came the Home Office's army of workers — actuaries, stenographers, mathematicians, clerks, auditors, doctors, agents, messengers — and their chief, Henry Baldwin Hyde. Each morning, Monday through Saturday, they filed through the front door, signed the attendance book, and moved on to their places. Once the doors were opened for business, there followed policyholders to collect their dividends or pay their premiums, all transactions in cash.

The offices could have been found in a Dickens novel. Though there was a telephone system as early as 1880 (it was managed by a decisive, clear-voiced stenographer named Emma Jackson), in every other way operations were slow and unaided by technology. Policies were recorded by hand in large ledgers and bound in huge reference books called policy ticklers. Despite the widespread use of typewriters in the 1880's, at Equitable all envelopes were addressed using steel-tipped or even quill pens, which also were used to write many letters. Before the turn of the century, there were no calculating machines. The actuary's and mathematical departments were populated by geniuses like Joel G. Van Cise, the chief actuary, who had been hired after demonstrating that he could add four columns of figures in his head simultaneously. As for gaining income from the Society's huge portfolio of bonds worth hundreds of millions of dollars, every quarter a team of men was sent down to the huge basement vault to clip coupons to send to the issuers as demands for interest payments. Coupon cutting, said one man who briefly did this work, Arthur H. Reddall, was "a dreaded chore." Each man had memorized a different sequence of numbers in the elaborate combination for opening the locks, and they took turns turning the dials. Once inside the vault, they set to work:

After fussing with endless stacks of bonds, each stack containing packages of fifty $1,000 bonds, twenty packages equalizing a million dollars, we would finally swing closed the big doors, set the time locks, then reach down in our jeans and try to find 15 or 20 cents for a luncheon sandwich.[1]

The rest of the Home Office army labored over less exotic tasks through the day and, if called upon, into the night at the then high overtime wage of fifty cents an hour. Some sent out bills, others mailed copies of *The Equitable Record*, the agents' magazine, filled with advice on improving sales. Advancement through the ranks was slow but certain, for Equitable never fired anyone except for the most blatant cause. After arriving at the age of sixteen or eighteen, some staff members treaded water in their jobs for years on end, while the most talented and luckiest recruits — watched carefully by Hyde from his office on the mezzanine above the main work area — gradually rose through the system until by their retirement, forty or fifty years later, they had reached the high status of officer. To elevate workers' spirits during these long careers of performing routine work, and to keep the entire company unified around a common mission, the Society sponsored luncheon and evening educational programs, social gatherings, company baseball teams, and employee clubs. The lead cheerleader for the entire company, Home Office and far-flung sales force alike, was William Alexander. Though his job was Secretary, or chief in-house attorney, his duties spread everywhere in the areas of advertising and public relations. He enthusiastically spread such inspirational slogans as "the Equitable spirit" and "the Equitable family" in hundreds of advertisements, books, pamphlets, and company magazines (one of which he titled *The Equitable Spirit*). He did this for more than half a century after coming to the Society as a young man, and when he retired in 1937, he was the last of the Alexanders who worked at Equitable.[2]

Baseball was the most popular recreational activity. Like other companies, The Equitable sponsored amateur (and, later, semi-professional) baseball teams of talented athletes who happened to be (or often were recruited to be) company employees. Baseball was serious business in most industries between the 1860's and the 1950's. As the president of the National Cash Register Company explained his sponsorship of a company ball team, "There is no charity in anything we do. Isn't it just good business?" A company team — especially a winning team — encouraged company loyalty and camaraderie, and exercise was believed to foster good character and cooperation that benefitted employee and employer alike. And games between companies in the same industry could be relied on to sharpen competition at all levels. By the 1880's, there were industrial baseball leagues across the country. In New York, Detroit, Chicago, Hartford, and Springfield, Massachusetts, there were enough insurance companies to put

together insurance leagues. Later, there were leagues of teams representing financial companies and services, including banks and the New York Stock Exchange.[3]

Equitable's first known baseball game was played in August 1866 against Mutual Life, which won by the amazing score of 40–21. Six weeks later, Equitable beat the Metropolitan Fire Insurance Company, 42–18 (it was a time when batters had the advantage over pitchers). Over the next ninety years, Equitable sent out teams to play in many New York industrial leagues, some limited to insurance companies, others to financial institutions, and a few open to all comers. The team also played in charity games for such good causes as raising money for the victims of an epidemic or a natural disaster like the Johnstown flood. But the main business was competition with other insurers. After Equitable beat Mutual Life in 1886 before 1,000 spectators at the Polo Grounds, then in Central Park, the team received this message from Henry Hyde: "Hooray! Let the eagle scream congratulations to the Club on its victory; do it some more!" That was a good year for baseball at the Society, which formed an intramural league, the Equitable Base Ball Association. One team was called the Semi-Tontine Nine; another the Incontestable Growlers.[4]

Beginning in the 1920's, industrial league baseball reached a new level of competitive-

Industrial league baseball in the 1880's was serious business.

Many sports were important to company morale. This is the finish of the 100-yard dash at the 1915 Field Day for employees.

ness as companies recruited and sometimes compensated players mainly to play industrial ball. A survey of benefits offered to employees by industries in North Carolina in the 1930's yielded the startling information that while forty companies offered group insurance plans and twenty-eight provided scholarships for education, fully 127 of them supported base-ball teams. During World War II, an Equitable team traveled across America to play teams of servicemen, and for several years Equitable represented New York in a national amateur baseball championship in Ohio. After the war, the star was briefly Edward ("Whitey") Ford, the son of a Home Office telephone operator. In 1946, when he was sixteen, Ford came to work as a messenger and became a pitcher on the company team. In his first game, he pitched a shutout against IBM. That year the team won the New York Industrial League, and Ford was signed by a scout for the New York Yankees, where he had a Hall of Fame career. Other athletes who worked at, and sometimes played for, Equitable included Ernie Banks of the Chicago Cubs and Ed ("Rinty") Monahan of the old Philadelphia Athletics. When Equitable offered Monahan a job that paid him better than baseball (it was the time long before free agency), he came to work at the Home Office in 1956. By then industrial league baseball was on its last legs after almost a century.

In organizing his sales force, Hyde borrowed the structure of the general agency from Mutual Life. The general agency was a large operation with exclusive rights to a sizable terri-tory, often an entire state. It was owned and run by the general agent, who took overrides on the local agents' commissions and also sold insur-ance. The general agent passed on a portion of the agency's total commissions to the Home Office, which provided the products to sell and distributed commissions through Equitable's salaried on-site representative, the cashier. The general agent had broad freedom to run the ter-ritory much as he pleased, so long as the agency and he (general agents were male until the twentieth century) sold Equitable policies exclusively and aggressively. All Equitable agencies worked this way except those in New York and other large cities. There agencies were responsible for so-called metropolitan districts owned by Equitable, and were run by salaried agents called agency managers. Working directly below the general agent (or agency manager) was the district manager (sometimes called unit manager). His job was to recruit, train, and supervise several agents; he, too, was compensated through commissions on his own sales and overrides on his subordinates' com-missions. The agents themselves worked either full-time or part-time. Some agents were repre-sented in rural areas by a subagent. From the top of the pyramid to the bottom in a general agency, from general agent to subagent, everybody had an individual contract with Equitable, worked solely on commission (although some expenses were covered), and sold Equitable policies exclusively.

The three-tier structure provided close supervision (Equitable was well ahead of other companies in programs for training agents), but was more expensive than the two-tier agency forces of most other companies, which lacked the district manager level. This high cost often prevented Equitable from offering premiums as low as those of other insurers. Hyde, to gain a competitive advantage, was forever striving to develop new versions of old policies or entirely new types of products. "I have a great and abiding faith in Mr. Hyde's ability to get up a new policy that will be a seller," one of his sales managers, Gage E. Tarbell, confidently told a colleague during a time when Equitable was falling behind the other "racers" in sales. Hyde often justified that faith. And so, out of necessity, Equitable developed a reputation as one of the most innovative insurance companies.[5]

Besides high cost, another problem with the Equitable system was that it gave an unusual amount of autonomy to the general agents. Some officers feared they might recognize their power, band together, and attempt to influence or even displace a weak President. But Hyde was confident that he could discipline the agency force to his purposes through perpetual vigilance and constant travel by himself, his traveling agents, and his regional and Home Office sales managers. The field force was his army, he explained:

Thus the whole territory may be brought under steady control. The Local Agent is supported by the Special or District Agent, while all are sustained and assisted by the Traveling Agents, under the orders of their general-in-chief, the General Agent himself.[6]

Hyde's own role in the field was like the one he assigned himself in the Home Office: commander-in-chief above the generals, creator and enforcer of discipline and standards. In recruiting agents, Hyde always preferred newcomers to the insurance business. While he might steal an agent from a competitor in the heat of one of the regular battles, he distrusted anybody trained outside Equitable and regarded candidates for transfer from other insurance companies as enemy turncoats. "Men brought up in The Equitable have, as a rule, more fidelity and more zeal in the company's service than those coming from other companies," he explained. Life insurance, after all, was not just a job but a faith.[7]

Hyde's leadership of the sales force was intensely personal. He wanted his agents to know that he considered them the most important people in the company. To demonstrate the depth of his solicitude, he often visited them in the field and hosted them in the Home Office. He once explained why he kept a board member waiting while he talked with an agent: "I can get a good Director any time, but a good agent is another matter." Henry Hyde's epitaph, said an Equitable officer, should have been, "Here lies the friend of life insurance agents." He used that concern to lash them to improve sales volume. The Society committed about 8 percent of its surplus to cash advances, which agents paid back on extremely liberal terms. (The Home Office's Agency Department once gave an agent a $1,000 advance to stop him from taking a vacation trip during a sales campaign.) Hyde also set up competitions for various prizes, including cash bonuses, silver pitchers, and what he enjoyed calling "a massive and valuable gold watch and chain." On one occasion he engineered a competition for a watch between an agent in Vermont and the man's son in New Hampshire (the father won).[8]

J. W. Alexander V.P.

I agree (between November 15th and December 15th) to double the business of my best month this year.

General Agent.

Nov.   75.

Fall Campaign, 1875.

New York, September 6th, 1875.

To the General Agents of the Society.

GENTLEMEN:

As the Summer season draws to a close and the invigorating atmosphere of Autumn admonishes us of the approach of another busy term, we address you again on the subject of the Society's work during the rest of the year 1875. In the hot months we have not pressed our agents to intense effort, for during the dog days business energy is relaxed, and there are fewer opportunities for brilliant achievements. The time has now come, however, when we should all of us—at the head office, at the branch offices, and at every remote outpost of the Company—be nerving ourselves for determined and continued PRESSURE.

It is not necessary for us to tell you that this year has been unprecedented as a dull one in business circles. From every quarter of the country and from every branch of industry has come up the same cry. The business of life insurance has not been an exception. We hear from other leading companies that they are running behind their record for 1874. Under circumstances like these, what is the obvious duty of the officers and agents of the Equitable? Is it to succumb to the lassitude which seems to enervate so many enterprises, or is it to show the true spirit of a laudable ambition and to rise superior to all obstacles? We know too well the pluck and nerve of the agents of the Equitable Life to have any doubt about what their unanimous response will be.

We have a better organization than we had last year; we have a Company in better condition than it ever was before; we have a better variety of canvassing matter; and we have the actual results of our Tontine system, after an experience of seven years—a lever in the hands of a good agent which ought to give him double the advantage he had before. Under these circumstances, we confidently appeal to our general agents to co-operate with us, by increased industry, ingenuity, and liberality, and to roll up such a heavy business between this time and the 15th of January next as will weigh the scales far down in favor of 1875 as against the previous year.

The inquiry may arise in some minds, how are we to accomplish such results? We might point with satisfaction and pride to some of our general agents who have achieved better results during this year than the last in spite of increased difficulties, and advise the others to emulate their example of skill attention and indomitable enthusiasm ; but, believing that each of you has the desire to do his utmost and will second the efforts of the officers, we will, even at the risk of repetition of what has been heretofore said, urge upon you a few things, which we know, from long experience and trial, to be of great importance in the business.

First: We urge you to co-operate with us in our system of allotments. Some of you may, too hastily, imagine that this system is not calculated to produce business. If so, you are mistaken. Experience, that unerring teacher, has proved its efficiency. Even among yourselves, there can scarcely be one at all fit for his position who has not some pride about meeting the deserved commendation of those at the head of the Company. If this be true, how much more so is it the case with every subaltern? Our system of allotments is based on the supposition that every man has some pride in achieving success and derives keen satisfaction from the recognition of it, with

The Home Office used a variety of ways to urge agents to increase production.

Every angle was exploited. Leading agents were urged to send their photographs to the Home Office to be displayed in places of honor. To hang on agency walls, out from 120 Broadway went cardboard "motto cards" displaying one of Hyde's fervent inspirational messages in large boldface type. The energy of his expression usually compensated for the vague grammar, as we see in this motto card from 1871:

> It may be that you do not THINK enough — that you are not thoroughly awake. Some men go all through life half asleep. Others, until some tremendous event awakens them and they develop their latent energies; and then the world admires and respects WHAT IS CALLED THEIR GENIUS. Let us give a name to this awakening and developing power. Call it PRESSURE. PRESSURE makes those of us who are successful what we are.

And pressure was the rule at Equitable. Besides three or four large sales campaigns a year honoring an Equitable officer or a national holiday, agents were constantly instructed to become better producers. In 1875 the Home Office sent out a flyer to all the general agents. Handwritten on ruled paper to resemble a personal memorandum, the text was a short promise: "I agree (between November 15th and December 15th) to double the business of my best month this year." Each general agent was obligated to sign and return it to the Home Office, and then proceed to double his business.[9]

Encouragement poured out of the Home Office onto agents' heads to build loyalty, trust, and teamwork. Hyde knew that agents marched to a different drummer than his clerks. Theirs was not the steady, scheduled, daily routine but the jagged leap and fall that is the salesman's lot — long bouts of discouragement as one prospect after another rejected advances, broken by an occasional wave of euphoria on closing a big case, or sale. To keep agents motivated, Hyde and his general agents devised new challenges and sales goals, each

MOTTOES FOR 1888.

(Extracts from Circular to Agents, of Feb. 1, 1871.)

"LET THE PROBLEM BE TO PRODUCE A GIVEN RESULT IN YOUR AGENCY. Consider all the present means of accomplishing it; go out of the old ruts; think it over deeply; invent new ways; choose the best plan; develop it distinctly; weigh every point; WHEN APPROVED, CHANGE YOUR ANXIOUS THOUGHT TO DETERMINED ACTION, and press through all discouragement; and, if your energy increase in the same ratio that obstacles thicken around you, you will, as a rule, ACCOMPLISH YOUR PURPOSE."

"It may be that you do not THINK enough—that you are not thoroughly awake. Some men go all through life half asleep. Others, until some tremendous event awakens them and they develop their latent energies; and then the world admires and respects WHAT IS CALLED THEIR GENIUS. Let us give a name to this awakening and developing power. Call it PRESSURE. PRESSURE makes those of us who are successful what we are. We all yield to it and obey it; and we would that your love for the Equitable, your recollections of the glorious victories won under its banner, and your responsibility as co-workers in its service and supporters of its reputation in the future, should so PRESS upon you that every latent power of body and mind should be aroused and perfectly developed in the discharge of the trust

The President requests that General Agents will forward the Motto Cards promptly to all local agencies.

WM. ALEXANDER,
Secretary.

Motto cards were sent out as inspiration.

Secretary William Alexander wrote many of the promotions.

incrementally higher than the last, to guide them through the tough campaigns of their apprenticeships and later careers. The Home Office laid out its challenges in the rotund, rousing motivational language characteristic of many other types of campaigners — military, political, and athletic. James W. Alexander, the friend of Hyde's youth and his head of sales, told agents in 1886:

The interests and aims of all who are connected with a great mutual association like The Equitable are identical. The success of the Society is the success of the Agent, and if the Agent fails to do his part, the Society suffers to that extent.

In 1894, the Woods General Agency in Pittsburgh mailed out 3,000 copies of an energetic announcement of a new campaign in honor of Alexander's successor as sales head, Gage E. Tarbell:

[E]very agent throughout the United States would eagerly embrace any opportunity to express to Mr. Tarbell by a

concerted action their appreciation of the phenomenal services rendered by him to the agents of the Society during the past year.... This can only be done by concentrated, continuous, and systematic application to business during every hour of every day of September.

Although the letter was signed by Edward A. Woods, the dynamic Equitable general agent in Pittsburgh, and eight other general agents, a note on a copy in the Equitable Archives reveals that the author of this appeal was none other than Tarbell himself.[10]

Even fireworks become routine if they are shot off every night. Hyde learned that the best way to encourage his troops was to periodically declare war on another insurer, most often Mutual Life, and send out a battle cry for solidarity. "There never has been in the Society's history a time more auspicious, nor reasons more urgent, for entering upon the uncompleted work of a year with indomitable zeal and prompt determination," James Alexander told the agents at the start of a campaign in 1893. The moment was auspicious:

1st. Because the unexampled advantages offered to the public by The Equitable have made it pre-eminently popular at the present moment... 2nd. It is necessary to check the audacious methods adopted by a certain rival institution to outstrip other companies in business, if only for a single year, and no matter whether by fair means or foul.[11]

It was exciting stuff, but Hyde knew that insurance wars were too expensive and exhausting to be fought every day. So he and the Home Office people whom he assigned to sales and agency management were constantly visiting the general agencies during months-long trips on the road. Until the 1890's, Hyde stayed in regular circulation, residing for a few days at a general agency, speaking at morale-boosting dinners, and then piling into a train to carry him overnight to the next agency. "[T]he important thing is to stay long enough in every place to get your men and get them to work," he said of his tours. "If things are not ripe in one place, you can of course pass to another, and return, but I regard this steady, energetic, intelligent work on the spot as what is most valuable." He reported that he spent so many weeks on the road that he felt more at home in Pullman cars than in a hotel. Once Equitable became secure financially, it purchased its own railroad car to provide Hyde and his sales managers with a degree of homey comfort on the rails. Using this car, Gage Tarbell spent more than one-third of his working time on the road, often on cross-country tours of agencies.[12]

The enthusiasm and challenge that Tarbell, Hyde, and others imparted on the road were recalled by Wyman Ellis, who in 1894 was appointed general agent for Montana by the manager of Equitable's Southern Region,

Edward A. Woods of Pittsburgh, the most powerful general agent.

Harry H. Knowles. Ellis reminisced about how Knowles inspired him:

I was taught that The Equitable was the "strongest in the world"; that it was the first company to write Tontine insurance; the first to make policies incontestable in three years; the first to reduce the period of contestability to two years, and later to a period of one year; that it was the first company to make death claims payable on the day proofs were received.

Ellis was pleased and proud. "Imagine what all this meant to me at the time?" he asked rhetorically years later as he remembered Knowles's lecture.[13]

The general agents passed this message down the line as they supervised their own agents. One agent, Jerome J. Wilson, recalled his terror at the prospect of trying to sell his first large policy: "Up to that time I was writing only 'ones' [face values of $1,000] and 'twos' and very rarely a 'five.' But on that date I struck a prospect for a $20,000 policy, and I got cold

Dr. George Woods founded the Pittsburgh agency in 1880.

feet." Nervous, Wilson asked his general agent, Archibald C. Haines, who had recently written a $100,000 policy, to accompany him and close the deal. Haines refused. Wilson recalled, "He put his arm around me and said: 'J.J., if I go with you, it means I will write it and not you. You are just as able to write it as I am.' And I went and wrote it — $20,000 Endowment with a $1,000 premium." The most successful agents got over this hump quickly and could write their own ticket. For example, there were the three Dinkelspiel brothers. One, known in the insurance industry as the good Dinkelspiel, was much admired for his honesty, but his brothers William, an Equitable agent, and Sam, an agent for New York Life, were infamous for their ability to earn high commissions by playing off companies against each other and for their attempts to "twist," or switch, a client away from one company's policy to a policy they were selling. Despite their notoriety, when the two "bad" brothers lost $50,000 at the track, New York Life and Equitable leaped to the rescue and covered their losses.[14]

In the field, the authority was the general agent. The most important and influential general agency in Hyde's day, and for many years after, was the one in Pittsburgh. Though known officially as the Western Pennsylvania Agency, it was always called the Woods Agency in honor of the family that dominated it. By 1900, the Woods Agency was the largest agency in Equitable and perhaps the world, responsible for 5 percent of all Equitable's sales as it annually placed $9 million in new policies and took in $1.5 million in premiums (the equivalent of about $144 million and $24 million respectively, today).

Equitable policies were sold in Pittsburgh as early as 1862 by itinerant agents. Hyde, during his long trips around the country to visit established agencies, always made a point of dropping in on areas where Equitable was not represented, just to look around. In 1880, he stopped at Pittsburgh, which was becoming the steel capital of the world. Hyde sensed possibilities. Always alert to the direct and indirect sales value of personal influence exerted by well-known individuals — what we call networking — Hyde looked around for a prominent local citizen to set up a general agency. His eye fell on George Woods. For twenty-one years Woods had been chancellor of Western University (now the University of Pittsburgh), but in 1879 he was forced to resign during a dispute with his cautious board of trustees over his plans to enlarge the university. Known as Doctor Woods because he had been granted an honorary doctor of laws degree, George Woods was widely respected in Pittsburgh. Accepting Hyde's offer, he rented a tiny office in the only Pittsburgh office building with an elevator and staffed it with his fifteen-year-old son, Edward, whom (apparently forgetting his previous commitment to education) he took out of school. George Woods then went on the road to preach the gospel of protection.

Edward Woods (flanked here by his brothers, Charles and Lawrence) became an industry leader in marketing and education.

Edward grew into the business. When not processing applications to send back to the Home Office for approval, he sold insurance. William Alexander congratulated Dr. Woods on his boy's progress, confiding, "I have found your son in all respects fulfilling the opinion expressed of him." Henry Hyde offered Edward a new general agency in Ohio, but Edward declined. When his father retired in 1890, there was a debate back at the Home Office as to whether twenty-five year-old Edward was too young to approach Andrew Carnegie, Henry Clay Frick, and Pittsburgh's other steel tycoons. Edward won and soon joined the ranks of the city's leading citizens. He rapidly expanded the territory from seven counties until by 1910 it included sixty-one counties in three states, stretching east over the Alleghenies to Lancaster, west through the spur of West Virginia almost to Columbus, Ohio, and north to Lake Erie. To cover this 55,000-square-mile territory, Woods had as many as 500 agents who, seemingly, called at every farm and village. One enterprising rural agent forwarded four applications from people he had visited during a grueling sales trip that he described as "a drive of 113 miles through mud a foot deep."[15]

Edward Woods, wrote J. Owen Stalson in his history of life insurance marketing, "probably originated or stimulated the development of more ideas for selling life insurance and training agents than any other man in the history of the business." Woods was among the first to target ethnic groups and recruit agents who would have

Bertha Straus.

credibility with them. In 1893, he appointed his secretary, Bertha Straus, as an agent not to develop a sales program for women, but as part of an effort to assemble a team of Jewish agents to sell to members of Pittsburgh's growing Jewish community. Woods also hired the first full-time agency publicity officer; he put him to work preparing ads and press releases for local newspapers, instructional manuals for agents, and sales pamphlets for their customers. The Woods Agency had a publication for every occasion. One of the most popular brochures could be characterized as a kind of gossip sheet: it listed the agency's prominent clients, individuals and businesses alike, with names organized by the face value of the policies in descending order. Sure that a happy benefi-ciary of an Equitable policy was his best advertisement, he set up systems for rapid pay-ment of death benefits. ("He gives twice who gives quickly" was one of his slogans.) Working in the Leads Department in the agency's research office were people whose job was to study the obituary pages in all the local news-papers and check the names of the deceased against the agency's records. If a policyholder died, an agent promptly visited the doctor and funeral director to have them sign a death cer-tificate, and the family received the death benefit before they even started to think about filing a claim.[16]

The Woods Agency's vast territory.

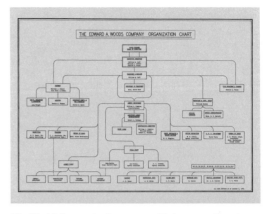

Woods's tightly organized agency provided a range of services.

Like many agents, Woods saw himself as part missionary, part teacher, and he pursued every aspect of those roles with Hyde-like resoluteness and authority. Portraits of him made at the turn of the century show a lean, thick-mustachioed man in a vest and big bow tie staring fiercely out at a world in need of his services and purposefulness. When Woods preached the gospel of protection, he was likely to quote liberally from the hundreds of inspira-tional phrases that he faithfully recorded in his pocket-sized looseleaf notebook. Now in the Equitable Archives, this well-worn notebook is a mine of bromides, anecdotes, and eco-nomic figures. On one page is Woods's formula for success: "Work, Enthusiasm, Experience, Knowledge = WEEK." Elsewhere are listed such obscure data as the costs of a typical funeral and rates for inheritance taxes. A sec-tion titled "Making Salesmen," which he called upon when recruiting and motivating agents, was filled with such diverse tips as "We trade with people we like," "75 percent of people have impressions from sight: color; motion," "Keep idea continually rapping," "Have him hear, see, and handle," and "As in physics: an idea once started will continue unless stopped."[17]

Woods's agency was a family operation in fact as well as in model. One brother was Edward Woods's chief assistant, another was his legal counsel, and a nephew was an agent. For his non-related staff and agents, Ed Woods served as father figure steering them always onto the straight and narrow path toward higher sales. "There was a very great amount of tradition in the Edward A. Woods Agency. There was *noblesse oblige*," recalled Robert I. Peters, who started out in the Cashier's Department in 1921. Woods's paternalistic arm pushed his agents and other employees in directions he believed were constructive and productive. He covered the costs of the staff's social club, paid 10 percent interest on deposits made by the agency's thrift club, and sponsored picnics and evenings at the theater. To honor the agency's golden anniversary in 1930, Woods had Equitable create its first group pension plan for his agency. For years he led agency groups on tours to summer resorts and educational sites; in 1899, President McKinley received him and his staff at the White House. Back home, the Woods agency took over a local amusement park for an annual summer office party that Woods, focused as always on serious purpose, called an "education conference" and also turned into a promotional event: when the staff orchestra played, the concert was broadcast over a local radio station. On the first Friday of every November, the agency held a veterans' dinner in the ballroom of the William Penn Hotel, where Woods handed out a commemorative lapel pin to each agent celebrating a significant anniversary with the agency. Each pin had a stone — an emerald in a twenty-year pin, a diamond in a fifty-year pin. And under the agents' plates were bonus checks, the amount increasing with longevity in the agency. The next day, Woods gathered his agents for a day-long seminar in insurance salesmanship and technology.[18]

To further nourish agents' loyalty and ambition, Woods took some unusual steps. In 1911, when the agency had more than $100 million of insurance in force, he incorporated it and presented his long-term agents with stock because, he told them, he wanted "to hold your personal undivided connection and interest in the Agency." The Pittsburgh Veteran Legion was for agents who had served at least five years. The Century Club, founded in the mid-nineties, was for agents who sold policies whose face amount totaled at least $100,000 (the idea spread throughout the industry and, with inflation, the limit was increased to $1 million). The Equitable Luncheon Club, founded by Woods in 1891, grew from eleven local agents into the Society-wide Equitable Agents Association; in 1930, it had several hundred members from the Woods Agency alone. During Equitable's crisis in 1905, he helped organize and was the first president of the potent general agents' association that came to be called the Old Guard. Later, as we will see, Woods played crucial roles in developing Equitable's pension business and the American College of Life Underwriters and its Chartered Life Underwriter certification program.[19]

For more than twenty years, Hyde headed the sales operation, but several years after he became Chief Executive Officer in title as well as function in 1875, he turned the job over to his old friend James W. Alexander, who in 1893 was succeeded by Gage Tarbell. Hyde continued to alternately cajole and hector the agents, as well as look closely over Tarbell's shoulder. "[Y]ou have to keep at them all the while and make them earn their living," he once commanded Tarbell. "There is no use trying to reconstruct a dead-and-alive man and make a good man of him."[20]

Tarbell was up to the job. In him Equitable had its first sales officer who had come up through the field force. Born in 1856 in Smithville Flats, a small farm town in central New York, Tarbell studied law in a local attorney's office by day while keeping the

Gage E. Tarbell, described as "born to make things come to pass," was chosen by Hyde to head agency operations.

books of a grocer by night. He practiced law and soon felt sufficiently successful to purchase a life insurance policy. That simple transaction apparently transformed Gage Tarbell's life. The story, as related by an Equitable man who knew him well, Frank L. Jones, says much about Tarbell and the importance of life insurance to many nineteenth-century Americans:

> When he was a young man and without funds he was induced to buy a life insurance policy in The Equitable. He occupied a small room in a village in upper New York State. When the policy came by mail he took it to his room and, as he related, he walked up and down the room reading aloud the provisions of the policy. When he had completed reading it, he looked up and saw his countenance reflected in a small mirror in the room. He stated that he uttered in a loud voice, "Tarbell, you are different! What's the matter with you? I know Tarbell, you are now a capitalist!"[21]

It was the sort of epiphany that turns new believers toward the priesthood — and insurance policyholders into insurance agents. In 1878, Tarbell wrote to Henry Baldwin Hyde to ask if he could bring similar enlightenment to others as an Equitable agent. An agent soon came over from Binghamton to inquire about the young lawyer, and he was put under contract as a subagent for the Binghamton agency, which in turn was under contract to a general agency in Syracuse. Tarbell sold his first two policies to local grocers (who may well have been his former employers) and quickly built a fine sales record. He was appointed general agent for some areas of New York and then, in 1888, was transferred to Milwaukee to take over a weak general agency that covered Wisconsin and northern Michigan. He revived the agency and in 1891 was appointed Equitable's resident secretary in Chicago, putting him in charge of all upper midwestern general agents as he continued to make his own sales. In 1892 alone Tarbell sold $2 million worth of insurance. Early in 1893, as a major war between the three racers was building, Hyde and Chauncey Depew appeared unannounced in Tarbell's office and asked him how soon he could go to work supervising the sales force. The next day he was on his way to the Home Office in one of the New York Central's private railroad cars.

Tarbell's sales tactics often were questioned. He was so well known for rebating premiums or making other special deals with prospects that he was known as the king of the rebaters in Chicago. But in force of personality, egoism, and vitality, he was in Henry Hyde's league. He was once described this way: "Of inexhaustible physical and mental energy, built on a large plan, and born to make things come to pass. His circulars to agents reflect the glow of his fiery nature." When Gage Tarbell went about his business, observed James Alexander, he did it "hammer and tongs." Like Hyde, he was a Dutch uncle, blending encouragement and command. "We must have the results" was a recurring phrase in his warlike letters to agents. A general agent in Louisville and Cincinnati, Henry J. Powell, remembered:

After signing my contract Gage E. Tarbell patted me on the back and said, "Now, my boy, it is up to you." He had fulfilled his part — he had given me the contract — it was up to me to make good in good times and in bad. Mr. Tarbell's action indelibly impressed upon me that he was putting the job squarely up to me. This gave me confidence. I had to win — not only for myself but for him.

The tolerance disappeared several years later when Tarbell suspected that Powell was allowing too many risky sales. "You should go over your list and dismiss every man that has not your confidence." Tarbell demanded. "I do not care to talk long about it, and I do not want you to spend too much time in thinking about it, but I do want you to see that nothing of this kind or nature is permitted to occur again in Kentucky."[22]

Tarbell's problem was that there was no room for two strong personalities at The Equitable. He was too much like Hyde to be allowed to share center stage. Hyde, who was never good at giving up authority, allowed himself to be whipsawed into undercutting Tarbell by general agents whom Tarbell had disciplined. When some agents complained that Tarbell was too demanding, Hyde took their side and fired off a severe seventeen-page, handwritten memorandum in which he accused Tarbell, "You have at times a most disagreeable, overbearing, imperious manner which makes people dislike you." When Tarbell argued back, Hyde pulled rank: "You came from Chicago about three years ago. I organized the Equitable about the time you were born...." Late in 1896 Tarbell filed another futile appeal for authority: "I think we can write Fifty Millions more business in 1897 than in 1896 — if you will allow me to use my ordinary judgment." But Hyde, though his health was failing, was characteristically unable to release the reins of his great empire. His judgment remained The Equitable's policy.[23]

One of the most famous of Equitable's nineteenth-century posters, the "lighthouse picture" appeared just before
Henry Hyde's death in 1899. This was a new expression of the old security theme.

CHAPTER VI

NEW AND OLD IDEAS

Equitable had risen in four decades to become one of the world's largest financial institutions, alongside the Bank of England, Mutual Life, and New York Life. But in 1905, six years after its founder's death, it would be in near ruin after a fight for its control between Hyde's two delegated successors — his son, James, and his old friend, James W. Alexander. One of the most dramatic events in American business history, the fight for Equitable was also one of the most consequential, for it directly led to the first pervasive, rigorous regulatory system in American finance, New York State's Armstrong laws of 1906. This legislation shaped the life insurance business for the next ninety years, and continues to do so today.

The events of and reasons for the fight for Equitable have long been hidden by a myth that the Society's problems were caused solely by the extravagances of young James Hazen Hyde. But the truth is very different and much more fascinating. It involves national economic disruptions, political machinations reaching to the White House, the ambitions of financiers, and an internal leadership crisis created largely by Henry Hyde's dynastic dreams. To be sure, there were waste and scandal, some of it traceable to James Hyde. But they were far less significant than the rapidly changing environmental factors that he and James Alexander were forced to wrestle with, the most important being the country's perilous economic situation. This chapter concerns those factors and how Equitable dealt with them, and the next chapter will tell the story of the war for Equitable.

By the mid-1890's, the seed of Henry Baldwin Hyde's vision had come to full blossom. Thanks to his marketing skills, the tontine, the sound and stable returns on the government bonds in which Equitable invested, and the extraordinary demand for life insurance and annuities, Equitable had grown from a dream to an international giant with almost $250 million in assets and $60 million in surplus (equivalent today to almost $4 billion and $1 billion). That success was a triumph, but it had its shadow side: it distracted people, even Hyde, from the old disciplines. Equitable was walking a tightrope. Sales costs were so high that they had to be subsidized by investments, and should any harm come to Equitable's investment income — a collapse of interest rates, for example, or the end of the tontines whose deferred dividends made up such a large portion of the portfolio — the rope would sway wildly. That something eventually would intrude upon the seemingly charmed life of The Equitable seemed clear to some people who knew the company well. Elizur Wright, the aging consulting actuary and prophet of insurance fundamentalism, predicted, "Some day there will be a terrible crash in The Equitable. Its disruption is only a matter of a few years."[1]

Hyde had little patience with the disciplines of investing, whether for his own account or that of his company. No doubt he was frustrated that he was unable to control market interest rates and other external forces the way he could alter, say, insurance sales

No. 1.—MUTUAL LIFE.

Comparison between the Equitable and the Mutual Life, based on Annual Statements and Insurance Department Reports.

Printed for the information of Agents.

For the sake of uniformity, in giving Assets and Surplus, 20 per cent. is deducted from Due and Deferred Premiums, to reduce them to their net value.

DECEMBER 31st, 1898.

	EQUITABLE.	MUTUAL LIFE.
Commenced Business,	*1859*	*1843*
Years older than Equitable,		*16*
Assurance in Force,	$987,157,134.00	$970,496,975.00
New Business in 1898,	168,043,739.00	134,118,295.00
Assurance in Force in New York,	196,654,201.00	171,767,919.00
New Business in 1898 in New York,	35,541,354.00	18,264,029.00
Gross Assets,	258,233,839.74	277,629,976.06
Total Liabilities,	201,058,809.27	233,058,640.68
Gross Surplus,	57,175,030.47	44,571,335.38
Dividends to Policyholders	3,059,744.86	2,255,244.85
Ratio of Assets to Liabilities,	128.44%	119.12%
Ratio of Surplus to Liabilities	28.44%	19.12%

These ratios illustrate the respective financial strength of the two companies, and show that the Equitable could afford to dispense with over $18,700,000 of its Surplus and still maintain a financial strength equal to that of the Mutual.

	EQUITABLE.	MUTUAL LIFE.
Increase in Premium Income	$808,147.94 —	$374,453.48 DECREASE
Increase in Total Income	1,677,017.25	844,021.20
Percentage of Expenses to Mean Amount in Force,	0.90%	1.10%
Percentage of Death Claims Paid to Mean Amount in Force,	1.34%	1.39%
Percentage of Death Claims Paid, and Expenses to Mean Amount in Force,	2.24%	2.49%
Percentage of Surplus Earned to Mean Reserve,	5.16%	5.06%

An Equitable ad attacking Mutual Life.

simply by adjusting sales commissions by a few percentage points. He became rich thanks to his high salary and bonuses voted by the board of directors, and he invested his surplus in real estate, in trust, mining, and electric companies, and in eight commercial sailing schooners (one of which was named for him). But most of his excess cash almost automatically went to buy Equitable stock. He succeeded in the early 'nineties in acquiring a majority interest of 502 of the 1,000 shares.

But as for managing the Society's investments, he called it "a serious and crushing responsibility" and delegated the job to an investment company affiliated with Equitable, Mercantile Trust Co., run by Louis Fitzgerald,

a well-connected financier whom J. Pierpont Morgan often called upon to manage transactions. Yet Fitzgerald could not handle all the investment problems. Hyde complained, "Every time there is a panic or disturbance on Wall Street, I have to attend to the Trust Company as well as The Equitable, and all this gives me a good deal of anxiety." Henry Hyde took his pleasure in knocking his head against other people, not numbers.[2]

He was unprepared when market interest rates plummeted during the 1890's. Since the 1870's Equitable's yield on investments, most of which were long-term bonds, had averaged about 6 percent, but in the depression-ridden 'nineties, the Society, like all investors, had trouble getting 4 percent and, toward the end of the decade, far less. "[O]f late years it has been almost impossible to find profitable remuneration for idle funds," complained a financial newspaper in 1898, when New York banks were getting less than 1½ percent on loans to businesses and individuals. Declining yields sliced income and drove up the purchase prices of the bonds that made up the largest portion of the Society's investment portfolio. The cause of the low yields lay in the conflicting interests of domestic debtors and European creditors. Debt-ridden farmers in the 1880's and early 'nineties pressed for an inflation-stimulating shift from the gold standard to the silver standard. On the other side were European investors and their American representatives, who were important backers of U.S. railroads and industry and saw inflation as an attack on the value of their assets, almost all of which were in bonds. The passage of the Sherman Silver Purchase Act of 1890 triggered massive withdrawals by foreign investors from the country's gold reserves, a panic in 1893, and a subsequent depression that lasted through the remainder of the decade. In terms of misery and financial disruption, the depression was on a par with that of the 1930's. The Cleveland and McKinley administrations, opposed by populists and backed by insurance companies, banks, and other financial institutions, vigorously opposed silver and inflation. Under their deflationary monetary policy, there was a long period of declining interest rates until just after the turn of the century, when newly discovered stockpiles of gold in Alaska and South Africa sent rates climbing.[3]

All of this struck at Equitable's investment income, which, with premiums, was one of the two legs holding up the Society. Ninety years later, there would be a third leg — large fee income earned from managing assets for other parties — that would absorb some of the shocks of a volatile economy, but in the 1890's Equitable's only cash flow was derived from investments and premiums. Those two legs became shaky in the deflation and depression of the decade. Investment income dropped precipitously. Meanwhile flat insurance sales meant that premium income was eaten up by "loading," or sales costs. Under Hyde's growth-oriented marketing system, Equitable's loading usually was higher than that of other companies. The problem, and its competitive fallout, was summarized by the Society's actuary, Joel G. Van Cise, in one brutally succinct sentence: "[F]or many years up to 1905 our expenses made up about all our loading on premiums, while the Northwestern [Mutual Life] was saving a considerable part of their loading." Other insurers began to offer higher dividends than the Society could afford to pay, and that cut further into Equitable's sales. At the turn of the century, Equitable's assets and surplus — which had long made it "Strongest in the World" — grew in smaller increments. In 1903, for the first time in thirty-four years, the surplus actually decreased.[4]

This decline in investment income reached into the pockets of policyholders. When twenty-year tontines were sold in 1871,

Actuary Joel G. Van Cise was the watchman over the surplus.

the Society projected a return of 10½ percent on their maturity in 1891. The actual rate turned out to be 6½ percent — healthy enough at a time when bank yields averaged less than 4½ percent, yet still below the original projection. Policyholders, led to expect more, were furious. James Alexander complained about "the general cry of disappointment among the policyholders." Even Equitable's agency head, Gage Tarbell, demanded an explanation from Alexander as to why his own twenty-year tontine policy (taken out, Tarbell noted, when he was "a struggling country boy") was at maturity worth less than half what the sales agent had projected.[5]

All this was hard news for Hyde, Alexander, and Tarbell. Their experience had been that since investment income was predictably healthy, the solution to any problem was to create another new insurance product or launch another vigorous sales campaign. The notion that they were prisoners of financial conditions apparently beyond their control was hard to

The aged Henry Hyde, exhausted but still battling.

accept. Hyde decided to start a cost-cutting program and shift from a strategy of expansion to one of consolidation. "We have all got to get out of the old-fashioned ideas to accomplish anything now at the end of the nineteenth century," he nagged his associates.[6]

His first step was to trim the dramatic but expensive international empire. He had invaded foreign territories as a defensive maneuver when competitors attempted to circle his flanks. He had a convenient excuse for withdrawing his outposts when governments banned tontines; an attack on tontines — specifically, deferred dividends — was an attack on Equitable's financial health. Van Cise warned Hyde in 1897, "I do not believe, under the present conditions of the business, that we can make any money in any country where we are not allowed to issue policies with the payment of profits deferred for periods of fifteen and twenty years." Equitable began to retreat from foreign territories well before Mutual Life, New York Life, and other

competitors. Hyde ordered Alexander to close up foreign agencies:

> The time has come when we have got to adopt an entirely new method of doing business…. The South American business may be profitable but it is disagreeable, as you have to violate every great principle of life insurance to do business there at all; it is a perfect game of chance. We are now seeing that we shall be driven out of the whole of Europe with the exception of England, Spain, France, Belgium, and Holland…. I am very glad we are out of Austria and Hungary. It was a roaring farce that we stayed so long and spent the money we have for the business received…. France will drive us out eventually.[7]

Due to "instructions of Henry B. Hyde" (according to the records), in the early 'nineties Equitable shut its agencies in Bulgaria, Romania, Serbia, Switzerland, Dutch Guinea, French Guinea, the Friendly Islands, six nations in Central America, nine Caribbean islands, India, the Philippines, and the Straits Settlements of Singapore, Malacca, and Pinang. When the government of Prussia, for twenty years a prime market for American insurance, demanded that foreign insurers deposit half their premium income in Prussian government bonds, Equitable closed up shop there, too, in 1894. The retreat from Prussia, said Hyde, was merely a "small matter." In October 1895, two months after Brazil's legislature approved a national insurance company, Equitable abandoned its Rio de Janeiro office — its most profitable foreign agency. By 1904, the number of foreign agencies had been halved to forty-one, and the volume of the Society's new foreign business was half its peak of a decade earlier.[8]

In some countries, the withdrawal was hastened by the new century's revolutions and national movements. The Russian business was all but ended during the 1905 revolution, which was triggered by the country's defeat in the Russo-Japanese War. In Japan, whose war effort had been partially financed by Equitable, national pride eventually led to the Society's voluntary retreat there, too. Equitable had been selling insurance profitably in Japan since 1866 and had become the largest insurer. When domestic insurance companies demanded protective legislation, in 1912, the Diet approved punitive reserve requirements on foreign companies. Facing additional costs of more than $1 million, Equitable gave its manager, John T. Hamilton, only two days' notice to close up. Hamilton, distraught, complained to the head of foreign agencies, George T. Wilson: "The worst of the whole thing is the disbanding of the field force, as I feel considerable sympathy with my men." He went off on a farewell tour of the agencies to tell them the bad news and thank them for their service. A few years later, when the French agencies were terminated during World War I, the once earth-girding Equitable empire consisted of sales representatives in only Canada, Great Britain, and the Netherlands. When the Society withdrew from those three countries in 1921 it was a purely American company for the first time in seven decades.[9]

As Hyde began this mammoth cutback of the foreign business in the early 1890's, he was faced with an ambitious new chief rival. New York Life had recently survived a painful scandal that led to the expulsion of its old administration. Its new president was John A. McCall, Equitable's former Controller and a former New York State insurance superintendent. McCall's chief assistant was a dynamic thirty-year-old second-generation insurance agent, George H. Perkins, Jr., who had run successful agencies in western states before going to New York Life's home office in 1892. Perkins' hero was Henry Hyde, and he followed Hyde's

Equitable's man in Japan, John T. Hamilton.

lead in introducing a program of radical innovation. New York Life was the first big insurer to drop many premium surcharges for people living in swampy southern regions, the first to offer policy loans to distressed customers to pay premiums during the depression, and the first to replace the general agencies with less costly, company-owned branch offices run by salaried managers. New York Life's sales costs soon decreased by one-fifth even though it expanded its foreign operations while Equitable was cutting them back.

George H. Perkins, Jr.

Perkins' initiatives set off a new war between the racers. Although the companies in 1895 agreed to ban rebates on premiums and other costly sales features, most of them ignored the truce (Equitable doubled the amount of bonuses it paid agents). Hyde was less quick to meet New York Life head to head on policy loans. He had built Equitable on the idea of selling contracts for cash on the barrel-head and still thought loans risky and costly. His actuary, Joel Van Cise, backed him, but eventually the general agents convinced him that, to remain competitive, Equitable had to offer the feature. In 1899, insurance regulators dropped the restriction that policy loans could be used only to pay premiums, and many policyholders began to borrow heavily against their policies in order to invest in the rising stock market. Between 1900 and 1910, the value of policies with loan features almost tripled industry-wide.

Perkins, like Hyde, thrived on competition. He convinced the government of Prussia to grant a monopoly to New York Life. Hearing the good news, his home office sent him a cable referring to the recent ambitions of Czar Alexander of Russia to conquer Prussia: "Please Alexander, do not weep because there are no more Prussias to enter." Perkins wittily replied with a slap at the other Alexanders, at Equitable: "I'm not the Alexander who weeps. Try 120 Broadway." To Hyde's frustration, New York Life kept gaining. From a distant third-place position in 1890 it rose to become the world's largest insurance company in 1899, as measured by assets. Perkins' success was rewarded two years later when, though still at New York Life, he was presented by J. P. Morgan with a partnership in his powerful bank.[10]

Once the rebel in American life insurance, Henry Baldwin Hyde had become its senior statesman; he even permitted himself to be talked into giving a speech at Mutual Life's golden anniversary celebration in 1892. He began to talk vaguely of retirement. Though only in his sixties, he was worn down by exhaustion and multiple infirmities, and his attention wandered sentimentally to the past. In his town house he assembled a museum of Equitable artifacts, including the sign he had brazenly hung on the Mutual Life building in 1859, the skimpy set of furniture that he rounded up for his first office, and the remains of John Quincy Adams Ward's great Protection Group. He sentimentally wrote Ward, "I have two heads of the dear old group which commemorates a period of my life when I was attaining success after success; the building of the Equitable Building, etc., etc."[11]

But Hyde's fires still flared up. Returning from a long European vacation in 1896 and finding things not to his liking, he unleashed rounds of complaints at James Alexander and Gage Tarbell, whom he briefly relieved of duty as head of the field force. He commanded one of his officers:

> *Don't deal with Perkins unless absolutely necessary. The less he knows about our business the better…. The way to treat them is to shut down on them absolutely. They brag about their July business. Let them say that they have got a walkover, and we are not in it! The less they think we are doing, the better.*

What Equitable needed to pick itself up, Hyde decided, was another good war. Getting wind of a scheme by Mutual Life's president, Richard McCurdy, to slice premiums, Hyde excitedly commanded his assistants to prepare for counterattack. When McCurdy called off his blitz, Hyde seemed as disappointed as an eager young soldier who just missed his first firefight. "It is really too bad I am not going to have an old-fashioned fight with McCurdy," he complained. "It would be a splendid thing for our business, and I would wipe him from the face of the earth. I have done it two or three times before, and I could do it again." The excitement broke his fragile health completely, and the Board of Directors appointed an executive committee to manage the company. Early in 1899 Hyde dictated a fierce letter to Tarbell insisting that he clean up an agency mess in Chicago. "It is worth a good deal of time and money," he thundered.[12]

That was his last explosion. Hyde became too feeble even to sign his name. He died on May 2, 1899. The Home Office was draped from its roof to the street with black crepe, and he was buried out of the Fifth Avenue Presbyterian Church.

He was eulogized everywhere and in every way, but his best memorial was the financial record of what he, Equitable, and American life insurance had accomplished. By 1890, more life insurance was in force in the United States than in the entire British Empire. Between 1860 and 1900 — very close to Hyde's tenure at The Equitable — life insurance industry assets increased twenty-fold, annual life insurance premiums *eighty*-fold. In 1860, income from life insurance premiums constituted just one-fifth of 1 percent of national income. Forty years later, it was almost 3 percent (and this at a time when national wealth was quadruple what it had been in 1860). Moreover, fifty cents of every dollar of family savings in 1900 was in a life insurance or annuity policy.

The giants of the business were the three "racers." The only financial institution in the world larger than Equitable, Mutual Life, or New York Life was Great Britain's national bank, the Bank of England. In 1899, they almost simultaneously reached a level of insurance in force of $1 billion (Equitable reached that mark in only forty years, the others in more than fifty years). Their combined assets — $1.2 billion — were equal to almost one-half the deposits in all the country's savings banks, and their total annual premium income was equal to more than three-fourths of the gross income of all 4,900 nationally chartered banks. Among them, the racers controlled

NOTED MEN AT MR. HYDE'S FUNERAL.

Friends of President of the Equitable Life Assurance Society Gather in Great Numbers at Impressive Ceremonies in Fifth Avenue Presbyterian Church.

Hyde's funeral was front-page news.

almost two-thirds of American life insurance. Equitable's surplus alone was equivalent to one-fourth of all U.S. customs duties.[13]

Hyde had carefully laid out a plan of succession. At his death, his twenty-three year-old surviving son, James Hazen Hyde, inherited his father's majority interest in the Society under a trust whose trustees included James Alexander. It would expire when Hyde turned thirty in 1906 and assumed full personal control. Until then, Equitable was to be run by Alexander, who had been instructed by Henry Hyde to tutor the young man in the ways of business and insurance.

A valued friend of Henry Hyde's since they had first met in his father's church, James W. Alexander — Equitable's third President — was a lawyer who for many years had titular responsibility for the agency force. Hyde named him his immediate successor in 1888. This early laying on of hands drove away some talented officers, including John A. McCall, who left Equitable to run New York Life. Late in 1897, Henry Hyde wrote a five-page instructional letter to Alexander in which he laid out his theory of business. "My rule in everything that is

James Hazen Hyde once said, "I got too much power when I was young."

to be done has governed all my labors for The Equitable," he opened. This rule was "to use my best skill regardless of time, engagements, and everything else." He told Alexander that he hoped it would be his rule, too.[14]

Unfortunately, Hyde did not also give Alexander the two things he required most. One was unambiguous authority over Equitable. The other was his own decisive, scrappy temperament. James Alexander was full of amiable good intentions — "a man of delicate sensibilities," was how one friend described him. "The handsomest and the most polished gentleman I ever came in contact with," said a journalist acquaintance. Alexander was determined to recast Hyde's feisty entrepreneurial operation into establishment solidity. "[W]ise guidance," he said, "has become of more importance than intrepid work and constructive skill." It was time, he said, to end the unseemly battling that Hyde enjoyed so thoroughly:

> [T]he institution of life assurance is one of such dignity and usefulness; it deals with such sacred interests; it is so vast, so serious, so important, that in the opinion of some, among whom this writer desires to be included, it is worthy of the best endeavors of the best people in the community to keep it decent, pure, and dignified.[15]

Fine as those sentiments were, the times called less for dignity than for decisiveness. As Henry Hyde had appreciated, the insurance business and the economy were going through wrenching changes that required Equitable to hunker down and make some painful decisions about overhead. But when an actuary reported that sales costs, or loading, had run almost half a million dollars over budget, Alexander could only scribble a limpid notation on the memorandum: "Here is the very essence of our problem. We must study, study, and strive. We are spending more than the 'loading' provided for that purpose." He carried his helplessness even on vacations abroad. From Italy he complained to James Hyde:

> Take out the banks, and the miscellaneous real estate, [and] the buildings, and we are earning a fine interest rate on our assets. Indeed it must be very large, for our average has been fair with all that handicap, but the handicap is growing and our prestige as a Company in surplus and dividends will depend on a large degree in the interest account. The other companies are both doing better than we are.

And what steps did he recommend? Alexander equivocated yet again: "Here," he told Hyde, "is a fine field for study and for action." And there the letter ended.[16]

James W. Alexander was described as "a man of delicate sensibilities."

While Alexander reflected, Second Vice-President Gage Tarbell acted. In 1899, to induce agents to look toward the long term and profitability, he reduced first-year commissions and increased renewals, capped advances to agents, and eliminated rebates and bonuses. Before long the actuaries were pleased to report that loading had dropped substantially, that lapses were down, and that profits were up. Yet the commitment to profits did not stick in a company that for so long had measured its success largely by sales volume. As Tarbell was slicing first-year commissions, Equitable's exhibit at the 1900 Paris world's fair featured a display in flashing colored lights that showed growth, assets, and surplus. That same year, Tarbell engaged George Perkins in an old-fashioned, costly war for agents. Perkins struck first by attempting to lure Equitable agents discouraged by the commission reductions to New York Life, but Tarbell won first blood by bringing over Perkins' chief agent in New York City and 167 of his 170 agents, using as bait the promise of a $250,000 advance. Perkins fought back in Buffalo, where he stole most of Equitable's agents. At that, the battle ended, but so did the experiment with cost-cutting. Under pressure from general agents, the reforms were rescinded in 1902 and overhead rose back to its previous level. Meanwhile, James Hyde was going around Alexander to boost executives' salaries by an average of 51 percent. Hyde's own pay was increased from $25,000 in 1899 to $100,000, the same as Alexander's salary.

Responding to higher costs and lower income everywhere, George Perkins made a surprising proposal: the big insurance companies should consolidate. "The old idea that we were raised under, that competition is the life of trade, is exploded," he said. Insurers had sometimes cooperated — for example, to set premiums and ban rebates — but never to the degree that Perkins proposed. The big companies, he urged, should have a joint litigation committee and stand in solidarity when any one of them was threatened by legislation. He saved his most audacious scheme for a meeting in Paris with Alexander and Richard McCurdy of Mutual Life in 1901. He proposed that just as J. P. Morgan, with Perkins' help, had recently brought together fifteen companies to form the United States Steel Corporation, the three of them should merge their companies into one. Alexander was less impressed by the idea itself than by its audacity. He cryptically summarized the conversation in a letter to James Hyde:

> *Become the arbitrator of life assurance in the world. Be so large as to be able to cope with foreign governments. Cut down expenses to the quick. Make everything purely mutual, and be the exponent of real and justifiable socialism. Buy out your and everybody's stock for some millions. Buy out all the general agents'*
> *commissions as New York Life has done. Form an executive control — triumvirate or otherwise — from present officers — have the whole under immediate management of one competent man.*

Alexander added, with disapproval, "Perkins would consent to be this man." He characterized the plan as a "little two-penny scheme," nothing more than a gambit by Perkins to enhance his own power. Gentlemen, he told Hyde, really must behave better. Alexander drew no other lesson from the proposal and thoroughly disregarded Perkins' implicit point, which was that insurance companies had best transform themselves voluntarily before their environment and history forced change on them.[17]

Perkins did not repeat his offer, but the idea of consolidation was catching. At least twice between 1901 and 1904, Mutual Life offered to buy out James Hyde, reportedly for $10 million. Equitable continued to go its own costly way.

Since the effort to cut costs in a time of intense competition appeared to be a losing battle, the best solution to Equitable's problems appeared to lie in improving investment income. One insurance historian, Burton J. Hendrick, summarized life insurance simply: "This great institution rests upon two solid bases: the law of human mortality and that of compound interest." With the value of compound interest eroded by the depression and deflation of the 1890's, Equitable, led by James Hyde, began to look in new directions to improve its investment performance. This search led it into the developing field of corporate finance. Many dozens of industries and railroads, and their investment banks, were eager for financing from the Society, which controlled one of the world's largest pools of investable assets.[18]

EQUITABLE

THE EQUITABLE LIFE ASSURANCE SOCIETY OF THE UNITED STATES

A lithograph poster of the Protection Group.

*The Protection Group in a stained glass window made in 1879 by
Nicolas Lorin of Chartres, France.*

The heads of the goddess and the widow, now in the Home Office,
are all that remain of the Protection Group.

*Customized for an agent, this poster from the early 1860's shows the business cards of
Equitable's fifty-two directors.*

A recent graduate of Harvard, where he had majored in French, James Hyde had no experience or interest in technical life insurance despite James Alexander's attempts to tutor him. But Hyde was fascinated by investments. With plenty of his own inherited money to invest, he formed a syndicate, called James Hazen Hyde & Associates and including Alexander and Tarbell, that began putting funds into many of the financings in which Equitable participated. (This was legal at a time when the concept of conflict of interest was in its infancy and was decades from being laid down in statutes.) Hyde, assigning himself the job that today would be called chief investment officer, pressed Alexander and the board of directors to switch the Equitable's investment concentration from government to corporate securities.

Hyde was not alone in favoring new investments in corporate securities either by buying equities or loaning industries and railroads money through bond purchases. Tarbell went so far as to propose that the three big insurance companies combine to purchase the Pennsylvania Railroad (the idea was not taken seriously). The favored security was corporate bonds. Common stock investments were not banned by most state insurance regulators, but there were good reasons for insurance companies not to become deeply involved with them. Besides the stock market's risk in a time of almost no securities regulation, there was the problem of matching assets whose values varied from day to day against the known, long-term liabilities of insurance policies. This was a fairly easy task with bonds, which promised fixed interest rates.

The new policy was a break with the past. Historically, Equitable had placed almost all its portfolio in government bonds. The few corporate securities that it owned in the nineteenth century were a relative handful of railroad bonds. (The chief financiers of nine-

teenth-century railroads and industries were British and German banks, not American financial institutions.) After hundreds of railroads and industries failed during the depression of the 1890's, a wave of consolidations and reorganizations was put into motion by J. P. Morgan, Edward H. Harriman, and other American bankers and investors. This was the first great movement of mergers and acquisitions in American history. Morgan would look back on the turn of the century and marvel that "for months at that time nearly every day, somebody was negotiating for some line or buying, or trying to buy, a railroad." This merger movement required financing. With many foreign investors having withdrawn to lick their wounds during the silver movement and the depression, the vacuum was largely filled by domestic life insurance companies. Between 1898 and 1905, Equitable entered finance in a substantial way, purchasing more than $200 million in corporate bonds. The proportion of corporate securities in its investment portfolio increased exponentially from a tiny fraction to one-third. Sometimes Equitable purchased the securities directly, but usually it worked with an investment bank, like J. P. Morgan & Co. and (most frequently) Kuhn, Loeb & Co., that underwrote an issue of securities in exchange for a fee.[19]

So it was that Equitable and the other racers at the turn of the century moved from the financial sidelines to become the largest backers of American corporations. "[L]ife insurance companies emerged as the most important non-bank intermediary for the mobilization and interregional transfer of capital," writes an economic historian, Stuart Bruchey. A perspective on the change was offered by George Perkins, the son of an insurance agent: "When I was a boy, insurance companies had to buy [securities] at second, third, or fourth hand," he told a legislative committee. "We have generally moved up closer and closer, and the ultimate situation will be that these life companies will get to the point where they will, between them, come more directly to the financial situation."[20]

By law, insurance companies were mildly constrained in their use of their assets. For example, New York insurance law prevented insurers from buying real estate other than office buildings, restricted direct investments in securities, and capped advances to agents. One way to get around these controls was to channel funds through an investment bank; but the best route was through a trust company, a type of bank that had unusually broad powers to manage other people's money. Beginning in the 1870's, Equitable purchased majority or minority interests in eleven trust companies in New York, New Jersey, and Missouri. These investment affiliates were expensive to manage and paid Equitable less than competitive interest rates, but the services they offered seemed worthwhile to turn-of-the-century insurance executives and to the investment banks, railroads, and industries that needed insurance investments and loans. As a financial figure familiar with the system, Thomas W. Lawson, observed, "The trust company is the irrigating canal of Wall Street, the insurance company the reservoir."[21]

The most important trust company for the insurance companies was the National Bank of Commerce, into which several other trust companies were merged between 1900 and 1904. The affairs of The Equitable were tied up with the affairs of this bank. Advantaged by a charter that relieved stockholders of some liabilities usually imposed on owners of shares of other banks, the Bank of Commerce, through a series of mergers with banks and trust companies, had become the largest bank in New York State by 1904. Further mergers soon would make it the nation's second largest bank and the second largest holder of other banks' balances. It had long been known as

J. P. Morgan's bank because of the financier's dominance of its affairs. While Morgan may have held sway over the bank, he did not own it. One of its principals was Thomas Fortune Ryan, a speculator who would come to play a crucial role in The Equitable. Other stockholders included Equitable and Mutual Life. The Bank of Commerce was sometimes called the insurance bank because of these investors and also because the racers relied on it for their daily operations. Besides having trust powers that allowed it to manage large sums of money, the bank was extremely well organized and could process checks and other paperwork more efficiently and faster than other banks. Each day it handled as much as half the money flowing in and out of New York City's financial institutions, including the three racers. To pick up on Lawson's metaphor, the Bank of Commerce was the system's spigot. The hand on that spigot controlled vast pools of funds as well as the administration of America's (if not the world's) three largest financial institutions.

The Bank of Commerce was the most important of several trust companies affiliated with Equitable. Another was Fidelity Trust, based in Newark, New Jersey, an arm of the fast-rising Prudential Insurance Company of America, which briefly considered merging with Equitable. The story is interesting.

Prudential's background was very different from Equitable's. From its beginning, it had specialized in door-to-door selling of low-premium term insurance called industrial insurance to manual laborers who paid small weekly premiums. Prudential had copied Equitable by creating a vivid, striking logo to suggest its own reliability — a sketch of the rock of Gibraltar. In 1902, Prudential was the fourth largest insurance company in America when its founder and president, U.S. Senator John F. Dryden, facing a suit by dissident stockholders, came up with a plan to merge the insurer with Fidelity Trust. The plan was sunk by the courts, but in the meantime the Massachusetts insurance commissioner threatened to ban Prudential from his state unless it released some of its control of Fidelity. Equitable obliged Dryden by buying 2,500 shares of Fidelity stock. There soon arose talk about a merger between these two big and very different insurance companies. The merger did not come about, but it stimulated Mutual Life, New York Life, and other traditional insurers to look seriously into combining with such industrial insurers as Metropolitan Life or creating their own industrial insurance subsidiaries. Had the fight for the Equitable and the other events of 1905 not stimulated tight regulation of insurance companies and stopped the expansion of the racers, the kind of massive consolidation envisioned by George Perkins undoubtedly would have occurred among industrial and traditional insurance companies.

To return to investments, all this meant that Equitable, out of the necessity to earn a better return on its assets, in just a few years became a participant in an increasingly huge, complex system of corporate finance that was gradually making America independent of foreign capital. The question was whether Equitable would control its own destiny or be ruled by the clients it was serving.

The stability of this system was crucial to all participants, and its intricacy could be seen in the membership of Equitable's own board of directors, which included some of the period's most powerful financiers, railroad executives, and industrialists, many of whom were Equitable's clients or prospective clients. Among them were Jacob Schiff of Kuhn, Loeb & Co., Equitable's usual investment banker; Schiff's associate, Edward H. Harriman, head of the Union Pacific Railroad; August Belmont, American representative of the Rothschild

interests and promoter of New York's first subway; James J. Hill, the "empire builder" who ran the Great Northern and Northern Pacific railroads; Chauncey Depew, president of the New York Central Railroad; and Henry Clay Frick, one of the most important officers in the steel empire of Andrew Carnegie.

Most of these men were exceptionally able, but few had time to learn about the unique legal, accounting, actuarial, and marketing aspects of life insurance. They felt little need to do so, for they had respected and trusted Henry Hyde to get the job done. Sometimes James Alexander was unable even to gather a quorum for board meetings. Although he complained mildly, he enjoyed having a free hand to run the Society as he pleased. "It is something of a feather in our cap to have prominent men on our list of directors," Alexander once said of a director whom he characterized as "an inoffensive man in our Board and makes no trouble." The director's qualifications were that he had friends in the foreign service, a large bank account, and little interest in the details of the Society's affairs.[22]

Part of a director's job was to steer Equitable to worthwhile investments. It was not illegal or considered unethical if those investments involved the director. Schiff was most valuable because, as senior partner at Kuhn, Loeb, he provided a number of helpful services and introductions. Always in need of institutional investors to take a big block of securities to launch an offering, Kuhn, Loeb gave discounts if the Society took sizable shares. Once the securities found a market (as they usually did, thanks to Kuhn, Loeb's excellent reputation), Equitable might sell them at a profit.

Most of these securities were railroad bonds with attractive yields of 4 percent or more. The interest rates were relatively high because the bonds' maturities were extremely long. Officers and investment advisors at

Jacob Schiff.   *Chauncey Depew.*

Equitable and other insurance companies were convinced that the deflation would last for decades and that railroads would always be healthy. Therefore they bought thirty-, fifty-, and even hundred-year bonds with rates of 4 percent or higher. The size of this bet on the future of American railroads is remarkable: in 1906, four dollars out of ten in Equitable's portfolio were invested in securities with maturities after 1940 (amazingly, one–third of those securities had maturities between 1990 and 2010). Though this attempt to lock in favorable rates for generations to come may have seemed shrewd at the time, the gamble did not pay off. Not only did short-term interest rates soon recover, but within a generation many of the railroads in which Equitable invested failed.[23]

Equitable also invested in securities offered by an increasing number of foreign countries, including Sweden, Mexico, Japan, and Great Britain. The first big international financing occurred in March 1900 when J. P. Morgan & Co. managed a $150 million American loan to the British government to help pay for the Boer War in South Africa. Equitable, New York Life, and Mutual Life each took $5 million of these bonds. Perhaps the most dramatic financings occurred in 1904 and 1905, when the Society and James Hyde's investment syndicate, working through Kuhn, Loeb, between them bought $10 million worth of bonds as loans to the Japanese government

to help it win the Russo-Japanese War. Schiff took an intensely personal interest in this financing because, as a Jew, he was offended by Russia's anti-Semitic policies. The issues totaled more than $200 million and involved bond sales to more than 20,000 individuals and institutions. When Schiff visited Japan in 1906, he was given a hero's welcome and an audience with the emperor, an extremely rare privilege for a foreign commoner.

With the counsel and advice of Schiff and other directors, James Hazen Hyde took the lead role in managing Equitable's investments. His efforts often were profitable for Equitable, but the style with which he made them and lived his life almost fatally damaged the Society. As an old man, Hyde explained his six unfortunate years as his father's heir apparent very simply: "I got too much power when I was young."[24]

James Hyde was the founder's only surviving son. His older brother, Henry Baldwin Hyde, Jr., had died in 1880 at age eight, the second of Hyde's offspring to pass away in childhood, leaving James and his sister, Mary. Hyde had the deceased boy's likeness inserted into a stained glass window in the Equitable Building and transferred his intense sentiments and high hopes to James. He gave him vast amounts of money, educated him at Harvard, and sent him on long trips to Europe. His checkbooks were balanced by Equitable accountants, his horses were shipped by Equitable maintenance people, and the details of his life were overseen by his father's private secretaries. When he chose rooms at Harvard, his father had them reconstructed to his taste and then, at year's end, paid to have them restored to their original form. His father dominated the boy to the point of giving him the same nickname, Caleb, that his own domineering father had given his brother. And he made it clear what he expected of him. Said

James Hyde makes his record coach ride.

James, "I had always been brought up to consider my legitimate life work to succeed my father in The Equitable." Expectations of carrying on in the family business were not limited to James. In 1885 Henry Hyde appointed Mary's husband, Sidney Dillon Ripley, as Equitable's Cashier.[25]

James rebelled against his father's dogmatic, heavy hand. Asserting his individuality, he adapted a persona radically different from that of the decisive American entrepreneur: the Parisian *boulevardier*. Hyde studiously developed a style that was accepted in chic circles in Paris but that in New York was bizarre: hiding his delicate features behind a goatee and sunglasses, dressing in silks and satins, favoring exotic flowers, and carrying himself like a prince around the two cities in elaborate livery. He was well known in fashionable society as the first American to wear yellow gloves with a blue suit and the man who helped set a speed record for a round-trip coach run

between New York and Philadelphia (it took nineteen hours and thirty-five minutes and wore out seventy-eight horses). After Henry's death, James transformed his father's beloved, simple working farm on Long Island into a hub of elaborate parties for the young, fashionable inheritors of the great fortunes created in the Gilded Age. When in New York, he made his journey to the Equitable Building, as a newspaper reporter put it, by heading "jauntily downtown in his private hansom cab, a bunch of violets nodding at the side of the horse's head." It was rumored that he once said, "I have wealth, beauty, and intellect; what more could I wish?" Even if Hyde did not actually mouth that conceit, the fact that it was attributed to him suggested his reputation for a lack of consequence. His appearance only added to this image. "Altogether, Mr. Hyde was about as handsome and graceful a figure as one could find," observed a reporter, "quick, polished, suave — the highly bred, much-travelled university graduate — manly in stature and in bearing, but with a curiously boyish air, notwithstanding."[26]

There was no question that James Hyde had brains enough to master the technology of life insurance, but, clearly, his youthful heart felt confined by the unspectacular, bureaucratic, long-term existence that life insurance had assumed in the 'nineties. Why his father, who was so observant in so many other ways, convinced himself that James would happily accommodate himself to Equitable can be seen as yet another piece of evidence both of Henry Baldwin Hyde's confident sense of control over his environment and of the limits of that control. Here the founder was far less powerful than he believed, for his son was equally willful in getting his way and would turn out to be equally domineering.

Having so energetically declared his independence during his father's lifetime, James Hyde equally assiduously identified with him after his death. Following the funeral, he commissioned John Quincy Adams Ward, who had produced the Protection Group, to make a full-size statue of Henry Hyde; and over the next three years he had Ward produce eighty-one bronze statuettes based on it. He presented them to friends, Equitable officers, and agents. (Some of these statuettes are still passed down by Equitable officers.) James Hyde's loyalty seems to have been motivated by a concern that his standing in the company depended on his identification with the founder, for his attitude toward Henry Hyde's designated heir as the company's President, James W. Alexander, was characterized by ambivalence and, sometimes, contempt. When Alexander assigned him the job of supervising the Home Office building — a position that would provide him with an intimate perspective on the Society's inner workings — James Hyde on his own authority packed up and moved to Paris, where he insisted on living for six months of each year. When Alexander appointed him head of Equitable's unprofitable Paris agency, Hyde lobbied against the French government's plan to impose harsh reserve requirements on foreign insurers, which would have forced Equitable's withdrawal from the country (which Henry Hyde had long favored, anyway). In 1902, with Equitable funds, Hyde gave a dinner in New York for the retiring French ambassador to the United States, Jules Cambon. He also announced his wish to build a new French headquarters building in Paris. The pressure worked. The French government softened its reserve requirements, and Equitable constructed the building. (Sold after the Society withdrew from France in 1916, the building returned to the fold in 1992 when it was purchased by AXA, a French insurance company that took a major stake in Equitable.)

Such successes went to Hyde's youthful head. His father had enjoyed friendships with wealthy businessmen but had been careful to keep their attention in perspective. Not so his son, who naively believed that because they asked him to join the boards of forty-six banks, railroads, and industries, he was their equal. It probably did not cross his mind that these directorships came his way because he owned the controlling interest in one of the very largest financial institutions in the world.

Relations between James Alexander and James Hyde worsened. While on vacation in Italy in 1903, Alexander came across some gossipy clippings from New York newspapers that led him to fire off a cautionary letter: if Hyde insisted on "getting thick with all the young Rockefellers, Goulds, and other billionaires," he should at least avoid having his name publicly mentioned with theirs. A proud, dignified man from a family that had much to do with Equitable's success, Alexander must have suffered deeply as he observed the founder's callow heir tripping through life.[27]

James Hyde's eyes show that he had inherited his father's intensity.

Yet Alexander ceded much investment responsibility to Hyde. It was difficult to tell whom Hyde's decisions were meant to benefit, since he was investing for Equitable, himself, his syndicate, and two of the Society's affiliated trust companies. Sometimes the syndicate used the Society's funds as if they were its own (for instance, paying $1.25 million for bonds of the Oregon Short Line Railroad, of which Hyde was a director, then five days later selling them to Equitable at a profit of $25,044). While such behavior seemed to violate the premise of insurance fundamentalism — and of Equitable's own advertising — that a life insurer's duty was to handle its policyholders' funds with caution, inside the Home Office it was generally winked at. There had long been a consensus that the Hydes should be permitted to use some of the company's money as their own because, although they owned a

majority interest in one of the world's largest and most profitable companies, New York law limited the value of their stock to the original $100 par value and 7-percent yield — or only $3,514 a year. Meanwhile, entrepreneurs in other, less regulated businesses were reaping vast rewards from the capital gains of much smaller enterprises. The only way the Hydes could benefit substantially would be to sell out, and nobody wanted that because there was no guarantee that the buyer would treat Equitable's policyholders fairly. Therefore the board paid the Hydes very well, allowed them to earn other salaries from the affiliated trust companies, gave them healthy bonuses, and tolerated a small amount of intermingling of funds to support their investments.

But James Hyde took gross advantage of these freedoms. In 1902, he and his syndicate invested in one of the affiliated trust companies, Equitable Trust, and took over its board of directors. Over the next three years, they raised the value of the stock several times by recapitalizing at increasing levels with Equitable funds, until in 1905 they sold their Equitable Trust stock to the Society at a 430 percent profit. The outside accountants who later audited Equitable's investment records would report that "the many transactions... have been wrapped in much mystery."[28]

Alexander (who benefitted from some of these transactions) continued to look on helplessly when the Society's interests were involved. Hyde's investment operations were so impulsive and busy that the Society sometimes was strapped for cash. "What does The Equitable get?" Alexander asked rhetorically after learning that Equitable might have to postpone an investment because cash was committed to a trust company. "[O]ur names are being used and are carrying weight," he similarly complained in 1903 about Fidelity Trust. "Things look lovely there but we ought to *know;* they have more money than ever to

This confident cover of a company magazine appeared early in the new century, not long before the fight for The Equitable between James Hyde and James Alexander.

put out, and all hands there are living like nabobs...." He concluded with another of his sighs, "Prevention is better than cure."[29]

The sudden shift into corporate finance was so dramatic that people inside Equitable began to wonder if the social service ideals of insurance fundamentalism had become irrelevant. "Let us hoist the black flag and stop sailing as a missionary ship," pro-

posed an officer. But as important as finding rewarding investments had become in the straitened economy of the turn of the century, social service and mutuality were so ingrained in the Society's culture and public image that Alexander and his officers could not conceive of publicly presenting Equitable as a capitalistic, profit-driven institution. The risk of loss of public trust simply was too great. They continued to repeat the traditional formulas about sacred trust and widows and orphans, ignoring, at least in their public statements, the new involvement with a whole new set of clients and businesses in the dawn of American corporate finance. These formulas had long served to protect the insurance companies from the general American distrust of big financial institutions that had made such entities as Pierpont Morgan's bank and United States Steel so distrusted. The insurance companies also were screened from the attacks on bigness by their claim that insurance was not only philanthropic but thoroughly scientific. Should the public begin to doubt the law of averages, their trust in life insurance might instantly fade. Gage Tarbell understood the risk as he looked back on a time, in the 1880's, when "the opinion prevailed with the public that the computation of premiums and reserves was really based upon scientific principles." Tarbell warned Alexander in 1900, "The change in this respect of late has caused people to say that there was nothing in the scientific principle theory, that it was like any other merchandising, selling goods for what you could get, etc."[30]

But try as Alexander and the others might, the traditional public trust in the promises and integrity of life insurance — a trust built in large part by Henry Hyde in his ingenious, enormous advertising campaigns and his attempts to make Equitable responsive to policyholders' needs — was beginning to waver at the turn of the century. The first wave of tough questions swept in from social and moral reformers in the Progressive movement in the Midwest, like Robert M. La Follette of Wisconsin, who were taking over statehouses in the midwestern states. In the summer of 1904 his insurance commissioner attacked deferred dividend policies. When he came to New York to examine Equitable, Alexander refused to cooperate. Alexander was sure that the entire insurance industry — large and small company alike — when faced with what James Hyde called "the Western Barbarian Host" would stand shoulder to shoulder with Equitable and the other giant companies to defend against increased regulation. Alexander exhorted Tarbell, "Anyhow we could make the welkin ring throughout the country, and rouse the insurance interests to a modification of the insurance laws of all the States. The powers of the superintendents should be curtailed." One superintendent seemed to be on The Equitable's side. The New York State Insurance Department, which directly or indirectly regulated more than 95 percent of the country's life business, was heavily influenced by Equitable and the other big companies. The three racers supported a lobbyist, Andrew Hamilton, who spent $1.3 million in ten years, and whose tools of persuasion included maintaining a hospitality house for legislators and insurance commissioners known as "the house of mirth."[31]

The question was whether President Theodore Roosevelt, who was presenting himself as a reformer, would support the Progressives' demand for more (and federal) regulation. Two of Roosevelt's strongest New York supporters, Chauncey Depew and Cornelius Bliss, sat on Equitable's board, and the Society made sizable contributions to the Republican Party. With all the changes in a business that was so large and so involved with the public interest, could The Equitable survive in the form that Henry Hyde had created?

The headline underestimated the roles of James Alexander and James Hyde in the 1905 crisis, but accurately portrayed its notoriety, which swept up Wall Street and all the Society's agents.

CHAPTER VII

THE FIGHT FOR THE EQUITABLE

I n 1904, the fifth anniversary of Henry Baldwin Hyde's death, skepticism about life insurance for the first time became an issue in a presidential campaign. Theodore Roosevelt, campaigning as a reformer, included life insurance companies in his list of "malefactors of wealth" that deserved tight federal regulation. James Alexander, blind to the shift in public perception, denied that anything had changed. In a speech during the campaign, he attacked "the popular delusion that [life insurance] is a monster money-making scheme." Invoking the traditional language of insurance fundamentalism and Hyde's advertising, he called the business "a purely altruistic and beneficent agency."[1]

But back in his office, Alexander admitted that one thing had changed: The Equitable was not earning money the way it used to. In a tone of desperation he complained to James Hyde in March 1904 about poor investment yields: "the very great handicap we have in low interest on our real estate holdings; low interest on the value of our bank and trust company stocks; low interest on our thirty-odd millions of deposits; etc." At only 4 percent, the Society's net investment return was the worst among forty-seven big American insurers. (Relatively low returns, however, were typical among the very largest companies, which had the most extensive portfolios of investments — some remunerative, others not — as well as biggest territories, sales forces, and office staffs. Mutual Life ranked forty-third on the list, New York Life thirty-ninth.) If the new relationship with Wall Street had not wrought

a financial miracle, Alexander was aware that it also had taken away some of his autonomy. He had been given a seat on the board of directors of a trust company, the Western National Bank, with assurances that he would be fully consulted on all its important affairs. Learning, after the fact, that the bank had been sold to the Morgan interests, he muttered, "They are a slick crowd!"[2]

Outside Equitable's walls the worry was that, as the only big stock company, it would be the target of a takeover attempt. A Massachusetts insurance commissioner predicted that some "bold manipulator" would eventually buy it in order to exploit its vast assets. There was no question about its vulnerability. The majority interest lay in the hands of a young, somewhat erratic man who had demonstrated no interest in life insurance, James Hazen Hyde. Most of the remaining shares were owned by the elderly men who, as adventurous young merchants in the 1850's, had backed the young man's father. Their heirs, reasonably, were hoping for a better return than a mere $7 per annum per share. Another indication of an impending split was that Alexander and Hyde, like partners in a mismatched marriage, regularly disagreed about such basic matters as officers' appointments and salaries, and elections to the board of directors. While Hyde was jealously staking out his position as Equitable's imminent head, influential persons (including an important director whom he counted as a friend, Edward H. Harriman) were working behind his back to remove him from the scene.[3]

The Equitable's size and relationships brought J. P. Morgan into its sphere of interest.

National and state politics were involved in these intrigues. Between bouts of bashing big business, Theodore Roosevelt was personally soliciting campaign donations from wealthy businessmen to bolster the 1904 Republican campaign. One of the people he approached was Harriman, whose railroad interests Roosevelt had only recently attacked in the successful Northern Securities antitrust suit. At Roosevelt's personal request, Harriman donated $50,000 to the New York State Republican Party, which was putting up a weak gubernatorial candidate that year, and arranged with friends for another $150,000. The Republicans carried New York, Roosevelt won the election, and Harriman began insisting that his donation had given him special influence in Albany and Washington. On December 10, Harriman wrote the White House to ask the president to appoint a new ambassador to France. His nominee was James Hazen Hyde.

Ned Harriman was a brilliant, often ruthless railroad promoter and investor who worked closely with Jacob Schiff of Kuhn, Loeb & Co. The father of Averell Harriman, the statesman and New York governor, he had started out in the 1870's with a program of acquiring small railroads, sometimes in unfriendly raids. By 1901 he owned the Union Pacific Railroad, had a solid minority stake in the Southern Pacific, and (in a hostile takeover attempt that brought about Wall Street's worst crash in history before 1929) was going after the Northern Pacific, which was controlled by J. Pierpont Morgan. If his raid on the Northern Pacific had succeeded, most of the major railroads west of Chicago would have been in his empire; as it was, he dominated the roads of the far West and Southwest.

Despite his grand ambitions and accomplishments, Harriman seemed very ordinary. Arthur H. Reddall, an Equitable employee who saw him often in the Equitable Building, where Harriman had his offices, described him as "a quite really unimpressive figure" who "wore his derby closely pulled down to his eyes" and usually went about unrecognized. Inside that modest shell lived a calculating mind and a bold, commanding spirit. "[T]he worst little devil in his class, and always at the top of it," was how he was remembered by a schoolmate. The years did not change Harriman. "[N]o one worked *with* him," one of Harriman's close associates said. "He was always the sole director, and sometimes imperious and arbitrary." As a takeover artist, one of his favorite tactics was to buy a small part of a company that he coveted, visit it frequently, and eventually overwhelm its officers.[4]

Theodore Roosevelt.

Having reorganized the Union Pacific into the most important railroad in the West, and beginning to assemble a railroad in Russia, Harriman set his sights on building an international railroad empire. Already allied with Kuhn, Loeb and several small trust companies, he went hunting for large assets to finance the scheme — which meant an insurance company and a national bank. By taking over Equitable, he would gain considerable say in the affairs of the National Bank of Commerce.

The fox was let into the chicken coop in 1901, when Hyde, without consulting Alexander, invited Harriman to join The Equitable's Board of Directors. Hyde was so eager for the time, in 1906, when he no longer would be burdened by the advice of his father's old friend that he decided to ignore him anyway in some decisions, including the choice of his chief financial advisor. He told Harriman that when he would take over in five years, he would require "independent men" to advise him. Harriman bought some stock, came to the Society for financing for his raid on the Northern Pacific and for the reorganization of the Union Pacific, and encouraged and flattered Hyde. But he also attempted to get him out of the way by performing what appeared to be the favor of nominating him ambassador to France. Harriman justified his support of the young man to Roosevelt with a few words about his business experience and affection for Paris and, more pointedly, about Harriman's own donation to the Republican Party; the appointment, he told Roosevelt, would be a wonderful personal favor to himself. Supporting Harriman's proposal were another prominent Equitable director, the coal and steel executive Henry Clay Frick, and outgoing New York governor Benjamin G. Odell.[5]

Bringing in Odell was a big mistake, for his reputation was cloudy at best. The previous March, after then Governor Odell had lost

Edward H. Harriman worked to gain control of Equitable.

more than $100,000 in an investment syndicate sponsored by an Equitable affiliate, Mercantile Trust, he had backed a legislative bill that would have rescinded the trust company's New York charter. The bill did not pass, so Odell sued Equitable, which settled with him for $75,000. Understandably wary of attaching his name to Odell's, Roosevelt turned Harriman down.

Harriman's attempt to have Hyde removed from the scene was just one indication late in 1904 that a play for Equitable and its vast assets was forthcoming. One potential raider was thought to be Thomas W. Lawson, a stock speculator and critic of Wall Street (his book *Frenzied Finance* was a best-seller), another was Mutual Life, and a third was Harriman himself. Alexander, with the other trustees for Hyde's stock, opposed selling out. But worried about what would happen after Hyde took control, Alexander decided that the way to remove Equitable from play was to convert it from a stock company dominated by a single, impressionable shareholder to a purely mutual company controlled by its tens of thousands of policyholders. Mutuality meant stability and permanence.

In November 1904, to look into the legal issue and propose a plan for mutualization, Alexander retained a group of lawyers (among them was a meticulous former law professor, Charles Evans Hughes). He did not notify James Hyde of this initiative.

It was January 1905, and Gage Tarbell was optimistic. "Yes, this should be a marvelous year," he wrote a friend on January 16. "Everything is ripe for it. All that is necessary is men, method, and push. While the two former are generally considered sufficient, they must be supplemented by the latter."[6]

The reality was far less rosy and simple. On January 25, James Alexander — who had finally found an issue on which he did not equivocate — visited James Hyde at home and insisted that Equitable be mutualized according to the plan devised by his legal advisors. The Society's charter had always provided for votes by holders of policies with face values of $5,000 or more, but this provision had never been enforced. Now, Alexander told Hyde, it was time to fulfill that obligation and include holders of smaller policies as well. Hyde should be prepared to sell his stock. Alexander warned that he would take his proposal to the Board of Directors at its next meeting, on February 8. Hyde resisted the proposal. Back in the office, Alexander enlisted Tarbell's support, and in letters marked "confidential" or "personal" they urged directors to attend. "I *very much* desire to have you present," Tarbell emphasized to several directors. "Matters of great moment will probably come up," Alexander ominously promised others. Each requested the directors to visit them for personal briefings at the Home Office. As the letters went out, Alexander and Tarbell circu-

lated among their colleagues a petition demanding mutualization. Carefully avoiding a personal attack on Hyde, the petition expressed worry about "the future management of the affairs of the Society, the conservation of its business, and the due administration and protection of the trust funds in its charge" and insisted on control by "the real parties in interest" in The Equitable — its 50,000 policyholders. Thirty-five officers, including some of Hyde's closest associates, signed the petition. As the day of the meeting neared, Alexander and Hyde engaged in frequent shouting matches.[7]

A temporary truce was called on the evening of January 31, 1905, when Hyde hosted and Alexander joined the 600 guests at a debutante party given by Hyde for his niece, Annah C. Ripley. It was held at Sherry's, a stylish New York restaurant, and the theme was Versailles during the heyday of Louis XV. The restaurant was exotically decorated with thickets of rose bushes and other furnishings by Whitney Warren, the architect of the New York Yacht Club and coarchitect of Grand Central Terminal. The guests, who included the city's political and financial leaders (Equitable officers among them), appeared in appropriate costumes, and there were performances of French texts and music by actors, singers, and the Metropolitan Opera's orchestra and ballet corps. The event was up to James Hyde's usual standard: exotic, carefully planned, and altogether splendid.

Such a party was not rare in New York at that time, but the gossip columnists promptly got to work misrepresenting it: the guests danced the cancan on the tables, Champagne flowed like water, Hyde was having a love affair with the middle-aged French actress who was the star of the show, Gabrielle Réjane. And the party not only was wildly expensive ($200,000 was one figure bandied about) but was paid for by the policyholders of The

Equitable Life Assurance Society of the United States. So went the rumors. The truth was very different. The cost was close to $20,000, which Hyde covered personally, and the party, while opulent, was reported by its guests to have been in good taste. Hyde later claimed that the reason for the hostile newspaper coverage was that he had declined to invite Mrs. Joseph Pulitzer, the wife of the publisher of the scandal-mongering *New York World*. Pulitzer, Hyde was sure, took his revenge by misrepresenting the event as an orgy conducted at Equitable's expense. While there may be something to this interpretation, the party might well have gone relatively unnoticed had it been held in a private home or been hosted by someone who was not a flamboyant, publicity-seeking heir and officer of a life insurance company that advertised that its main concern lay with the welfare of orphans and widows.

Alexander quickly seized upon the sensational press coverage as a justification for mutualization; it was his duty, he announced to Equitable's staff and board members, to unseat such a wastrel. Alexander was fudging the chronology, of course, for he had decided at least two months before the party to mutualize Equitable. But focusing on Hyde's extravagance and notoriety was an effective tactic, considering the importance of public trust and morality to the business of life insurance. The newspapers took Alexander's side. "Large responsibility ill becomes a social butterfly," said one New York paper, and a magazine unfavorably compared "the Strenuous Life as exemplified by Mr. Roosevelt" with "the Equitable Life as exploited by Mr. Hyde." Finley Peter Dunne, who in the persona of the barkeep "Mr. Dooley" was the Doonesbury of his time, soon laced into Hyde as an incompetent layabout, writing in his usual Irish brogue:

Afther dispatchin' a messenger boy f'r a bunch iv orchids an' dhrawin' on th' threasury f'r a pound of caramels, he sint f'r th' head bookkeeper. "Me man," says Caleb, "what is th' meanin iv this here wurrud Tontine I see used so often?" The bookkeeper explained. "Ye surprise me," says Caleb. "I thought 'twas something f'r th' hair," he says.

With his opponent the butt of such jokes, Alexander did not have to overexert himself to blame Hyde for stimulating a conflict that, in fact, Alexander himself had already stirred up. And so the debutante party came mistakenly to be identified, then and for decades afterward, as the single cause of Equitable's subsequent problems and the bitter fight for its control.[8]

Hyde's resolve only stiffened. Within a week after the party, Alexander circulated a second petition, which went beyond a defense of mutualization to attack Hyde personally. It was signed by all but one of the thirty-five officers who had put their names on the previous one. (The exception was William H. McIntyre, Henry Hyde's longtime secretary and one of the trustees for the stock.) The second petition changed the tenor of the debate. Tarbell, who had supported Alexander, backed away and disclaimed any responsibility for the attack. After that he positioned himself between the two sides in hopes that his close relationship with the general agents would help him. But, just in case he was forced by the winning side to leave, Tarbell negotiated a settlement for the renewal commissions due him from his days as an agent and unloaded his 250 shares in the Equitable Trust Company (at a 30 percent profit).

At the board meeting on February 8, Alexander handed the directors the two petitions and presented his proposal for a change in the charter allowing mutualization.

There was little sympathy for the proposal, which seemed to some directors to be an illegal seizure of stockholders' property. After an angry exchange between Alexander and Hyde, the board appointed a committee of twelve directors to look into the controversy. Among its members were Alexander, Hyde, Wilson, Tarbell, Harriman, and Jacob Schiff. Although the newspapers referred to the Committee of Twelve as "a committee on conciliation," its first job was to establish the facts for the outside directors, few of whom knew much about the controversy or Equitable itself. While some directors favored one side or the other, many suspended judgment.

Within a week the dispute was public knowledge, and the real and imagined foibles of the two opponents were publicized for all to read in Pulitzer's *World* and other papers. Too late to call a truce, should the two antagonists even desire one, the situation was rapidly cascading into a tragedy of Shakespearean proportions. Given the complex network of obligations and egos that had linked the Hydes and the Alexanders for half a century, it was surprising that tensions between Equitable's two talented founding families had not erupted sooner after the death of the domineering genius who had kept the house in order. James Alexander had every right to be proud that the Alexanders had been the first to identify and nurture the brilliance of the boy from Catskill. James Hyde, for his part, was a rebel thrust by his demanding father's dynastic hopes into a position he had not wanted and that he was aware he was not qualified to fill. (Tellingly, the specialty he chose, investments, was an area in which his father had taken little interest.) Alexander had every right to feel humiliated by Hyde's immature slights and disobedience, and it was understandable that Hyde was ill-pleased to be subverted to the older man's authority.

Still, these long-bubbling frustrations might have been contained had not Henry Hyde, in a rare moment of irrationality, succumbed to dynastic aspirations and left Equitable with a caretaker President in a highly ambiguous position at just the time that the Society required forthright leadership to steer it through tough times. Alexander perhaps was not capable of providing that leadership in even the most favorable conditions, but his situation at the turn of the century would have been untenable for most chief executives. He had to attempt to assert himself while standing in the long shadow of the recently deceased, powerful founder, all the while aware both that the founder's heir soon would assume control and that painful, unpopular changes were needed — changes that even Henry Hyde had not been able to implement.

Given those pressures, it was understandable though unfortunate that the tone of the debate over mutualization descended into personal invective. Alexander told the Committee of Twelve:

> *A personal proprietary regime has thus been established, based upon stock control — a control utterly out of place in a mutual company and fundamentally at variance with the theory and practice of mutual insurance which is conducted by the policyholders through their chosen agents and for their exclusive benefit.*

As for facts, Alexander focused on Hyde's unauthorized activities and expenses, including securities purchased with Equitable's money, his high salaries from Equitable and three trust companies, steep travel and living costs, the famous debutante party, and the dinner for the French ambassador in 1902, which Alexander characterized as a purely private function even though Hyde clearly had used it to lobby the French to liberalize their insurance laws. As for his own lapses, Alexander said nothing of his $100,000 salary and investments in Hyde's syndicates. He did, however, admit to one mistake: purely out of affection for the memory of Henry Baldwin Hyde, he had hired the young man to work at Equitable. For his pains he had been shoved aside rudely. Still, he told the directors, he had charity in his heart for the boy. "[H]is youth and inexperience entitle him to a measure of indulgence," Alexander said, but the time had come to face up to Hyde's weaknesses and save him from further public humiliation by expelling him from control of the Society.[9]

Alexander went too far by half. Not only had some of Hyde's activities long been winked at by the board out of concern for what they regarded as proper compensation for his and his father's controlling interest, but the directors were far too experienced and practical-minded to swallow Alexander's innocence whole. Everybody knew that Hyde had come by his stock and position because of his father, not through the charity of the Alexanders. Many were aware of Alexander's activity in Hyde's investment syndicate, and the others learned of it when Hyde produced checks and buy and sell orders signed by him. Alexander was not as pure as he seemed. Hyde's best defense would have been to ignore Alexander's provocative attacks, calmly point out who had been President of Equitable since his father's death, and then promise to tame his youthful spirits. He briefly followed this line in March when he reimbursed the Society a little more than $63,000 for what he claimed were his profits from the syndicate and another $13,089.41 for the cost of the dinner for Ambassador Cambon, although he continued to insist (reasonably) that it was a business event in the interests of the Society.

Yet restraint and apology came no more easily to James Hyde than they had to his father. His public pronouncements and letters to his critics could be so tactless that his secretary regularly toned them down. His chief legal advisor, Elihu Root, went so far as to pro-

Lawyer Elihu Root was one of The Equitable's saviors in 1905.

hibit him from making public statements without his permission. But Hyde could also be effective. Who, he asked, had been President for the past five years? Referring ominously to "serious and radical questions affecting the management of the Society," Hyde placed the blame for Equitable's troubles on Alexander, a poor administrator, he said, and Tarbell, whom he accused of being overly concerned with enhancing volume (a policy that Hyde characterized as "rush, rush, rush"). When Hyde was not disparaging his erstwhile colleagues, he muttered about "the enemies of the Equitable Society" at Mutual and New York Life who, he said, were punishing him for Equitable's friendly relations with Prudential. When he was really furious, Hyde tried to assert a kind of royal prerogative: Alexander owed his job to Henry Hyde and to him, and it was time he recognized that fact and either marched to his command or quit.[10]

Alexander effectively turned Hyde's claim of prerogatives on its head by alleging that

Hyde's "open, aggressive, and misguided emphasis and outward assertion given to the fact of his stock control" only reinforced the importance of promptly mutualizing Equitable. The point struck to the core of the weakness of Hyde's position, and Hyde knew it. When asked what he would do when he took over Equitable in 1906, Hyde made only one commitment, and it showed just how deeply he had been wounded by Alexander's probes: he promised to place his stock in trust for another five years.[11]

As the directors learned more about these two men and Equitable, they became increasingly independent and impatient. Chauncey Depew observed that when bad boys throw mud it invariably sticks to their own hands. August Belmont wondered out loud why, if one-man rule was the "tremendous evil" that Alexander portrayed, Equitable had long thrived under it when Henry Hyde was alive. The question, Belmont insisted, was not corporate structure but simply who was the right man to run Equitable. As the nasty battle wore on, he and the other directors came gradually and reluctantly to the conclusion that neither combatant was qualified for the job.[12]

All this time, Gage Tarbell was looking after his own interests. On February 12 he met with Hyde at the Union League Club. In a memorandum afterward, Hyde wrote that Tarbell, "while polite, was very firm and threatening." Hyde reported that Tarbell had at first intimated that he would lead an agents' revolt against him, and then offered him $1 million to resign. But by the end of the meeting, Hyde claimed, Tarbell confessed that he wished he had never left Chicago.[13]

And then there was Ned Harriman, always circling and playing the political hand. In one meeting he proposed a simple solution to the problem: divide up the surplus among the policyholders, and quickly go out of business.

It was a silly idea and he knew it, for he had his own eye on that surplus, if not the larger pool of assets. After the February board meeting, he regularly met with Hyde, former governor Odell, and Hyde's loyal secretary, McIntyre, to assure them that, thanks to his political influence, the insurance superintendent and the legislature were bound to reject mutualization and Alexander was sure to lose. "Now, more than ever, Albany is yours," he told Hyde one day. "We are in control," he said on another. There was no question who "we" were, as Harriman assumed a domineering personality that heretofore he had shielded from his young protégé. Hyde, shocked, reported that Harriman had shouted at Alexander, "God damn you! I'll chuck you where you belong, I've got you where I want you, and I have the power to do it."[14]

Word of Harriman's ambitions leaked out, and the press speculated that Equitable was another battleground for Harriman and his old enemy, J. Pierpont Morgan. A headline in the *New York American* ran: *"Equitable Fight Really Is One for Control by Great Money Borrowers of Wall Street."* To cover all its bases, the *American* in the same issue speculated that Hyde's problems stemmed from his sartorial elegance, so different from the bowler-topped sturdiness of the bankers. "Hyde's chief mistakes," wrote one reporter, "were that he wore a pot hat and cultivated the manners of a Frenchman."[15]

It was all very emotional, colorful, and unseemly. Many people involved with the participants removed themselves as quickly as they could. The newspaperman Adolph S. Ochs had taken out almost $1.5 million in personal and business loans from Henry Hyde and The Equitable in order to buy the *New York Times* in 1896 and build the Times Building in midtown Manhattan. Now he scrambled to pay off his personal debts before Pulitzer spread them across the front pages of the *World*. Meanwhile, an attorney who did

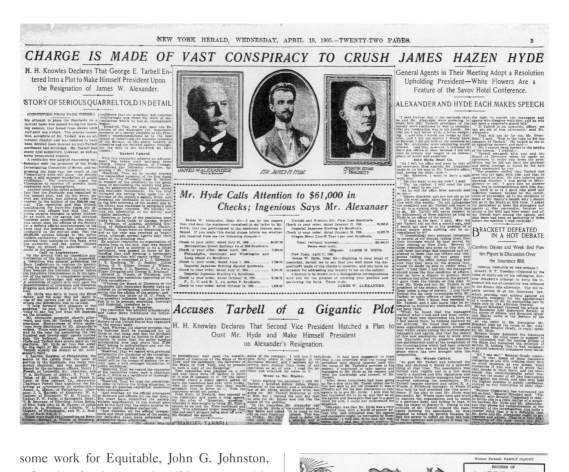

CHARGE IS MADE OF VAST CONSPIRACY TO CRUSH JAMES HAZEN HYDE

H. H. Knowles Declares That George E. Tarbell Entered Into a Plot to Make Himself President Upon the Resignation of James W. Alexander.

General Agents in Their Meeting Adopt a Resolution Upholding President—White Flowers Are a Feature of the Savoy Hotel Conference.

STORY OF SERIOUS QUARREL TOLD IN DETAIL

ALEXANDER AND HYDE EACH MAKES SPEECH

Mr. Hyde Calls Attention to $61,000 in Checks; Ingenious Says Mr. Alexanaer

Accuses Tarbell of a Gigantic Plot

H. H. Knowles Declares That Second Vice President Hatched a Plan to Oust Mr. Hyde and Make Himself President on Alexander's Resignation.

BRACKETT DEFEATED IN A HOT DEBATE

some work for Equitable, John G. Johnston, refused a fee because he did not want his name publicly associated with what he called "such a damnable scandal about everything connected with The Equitable."[16]

Faced with so many conflicting, heated ambitions, the Equitable Board of Directors conditionally decided to remove the Society to the safety of status as a mutual. They gave authority to rewrite the charter to a panel of six lawyers chosen from the elite of the New York and Philadelphia bars. The chairman was Elihu Root, characterized by Theodore Roosevelt as being as "sane and cool-headed as he is high-minded." Root had just stepped down as secretary of war and was resuming his legal career. At the time he was retained by Equitable, he was preparing to go before the Supreme Court to argue Morgan's side in a huge, complicated suit brought by Harriman

The vituperation seemed endless. Some thought Hyde might have done better if his appearance had been more American.

over title to the stock of the Northern Securities Company after it was broken up by Roosevelt. (Harriman had also tried to retain Root, but Morgan reached him first.) As Root learned more about the Society's predicament and the effects of the bad press, he became so disturbed by what he called "a very difficult and disastrous situation" at Equitable that he asked the Supreme Court to postpone the scheduled argument so he could concentrate on Equitable's problems (the Court approved the request).[17]

A majority of the lawyers decided that mutualization presented a congeries of demanding legal and business problems. One was the risk that a hostile takeover could be engineered by somebody who gained control of proxies. Another concerned property rights; already, an Equitable stockholder, Franklin B. Lord (son of "the Lord Almighty"), had filed suit claiming mutualization was an illegal seizure of property. But Root recognized that Equitable's problem was far broader than the legal issue of corporate structure: public trust was at stake. Without it, the Society never would have thrived in the past and was doomed in the present. Taking the pulse of his friends and clients in the financial world, he concluded that the well-publicized, bruising dispute was stimulating a crisis in confidence that might well lead to a run in which policyholders cashed in their policies. The contrast between, on one hand, the values of social service that Equitable had long stood for and, on the other, the behavior of its officers during the winter and spring of 1905, was stimulating a credibility gap. At issue was not Equitable's business strength. Rather, the issue was moral: nobody wanted to be a member of Equitable's family when the parents were acting so irresponsibly.

Root and the other lawyers understood the crucial importance of public trust to the country's growing financial independence and self-sufficiency and to the institutions that were its warp and woof. Because the fabric of interlocking private and public interests was so tightly woven, a run on Equitable could easily stimulate the collapse of other institutions (including, very likely, the enormous National Bank of Commerce) and then — worse yet — a hysteria that might spread throughout the entire American economy. Root was not alone in having these fears. On returning from a meeting with Root and the other lawyers on the panel, Hyde's attorney, W. C. Gulliver, hurriedly sent his client a memorandum in which he spoke of fears of a "great panic" and "personal and financial disaster."[18]

The panel recommended a stopgap compromise that they hoped would cool tempers: mutualization would be put on hold, but policyholders would be given a majority of the Board of Directors. Equitable's board agreed. After first approving the recommendation, Hyde backed out and dismissed Gulliver. When Hyde bragged that he had defeated Alexander, Jacob Schiff warned him that the board's rejection of mutualization was not a vote of confidence in him and that he should adopt a more modest mien. It was advice that Hyde ignored. The board now disbanded the Committee of Twelve and, on April 6, appointed a new internal investigative committee of five outside directors, chaired by Henry Clay Frick and including Harriman, whose patronage of James Hyde was ending.

Even before the Frick Committee got to work, Equitable's agents had joined the fray. The general agents and agents were becoming jumpy as business declined in the wake of the wild reports coming out of 120 Broadway. The first agents to assert themselves were the managers of the New York City agencies, who convened as the Board of Managers of Equitable's New York Metropolitan District. The board had been formed in the 1880's by Henry Hyde to keep agents' unrest under control. It met on April 3, 1905, to seek a way to express the managers' concerns about the Society's obvious disarray and the collapse of sales caused by it — or what the secretary described in the minutes as "the various pending efforts to disturb the business and injure the reputation of The Equitable." The situation was so precarious that the board even discussed going on strike against Equitable in order to get the officers to focus on the agents' problems. While they decided not to strike, the board did form a national "protective organization" of all general agents and agency managers and sent a delegation to Alexander, Hyde, and Tarbell to demand that their personal quarrels be ended, or at least kept out of the newspapers. But the brawl continued, and the Board of Managers decided to address it at an upcoming agents' convention in New York.[19]

Companywide agents' conventions were a relatively new phenomenon. In 1899, the Society's fortieth anniversary, all the agents and general agents had gathered for the first time in Equitable's history. Subsequent meetings went so well that Tarbell scheduled four regional meetings to boost a national sales campaign in 1905. The main convention was already scheduled for New York on April 18–20. The crisis was a strong magnet, and 243 general agents and agency managers — just about everyone in Equitable's system — met in New York at the Waldorf-Astoria Hotel. They invited Hyde, Alexander, and Tarbell to speak. Everybody knew how crucial the field force's backing would be, and if anybody had an advantage it was Tarbell, the agency head, who had been taking advantage of his close relationship with the general agents, managers, and agents. To revive sagging sales, he had hastily scheduled a March sales campaign that he called Tarbell Month, including a day called Loyalty Day. Just how much loyalty Tarbell felt for Equitable

was an open question, but of the three men embroiled in the controversy he was the one whom the general agents knew best.

The first speaker was Alexander, who was greeted by a standing ovation. In the traditional language, he assured the managers that they were his personal friends and "the heart and soul of the Society itself" and that every Equitable job — even those of President and Vice-President — was expendable except that of agent. Hyde came next. His advisors had worked with him on a speech that they hoped would communicate deep concern for the agents' personal interests. James Hazen Hyde, however, was not a man of the people. In his first sentence he patronized the general agents as "insurance workers," and he went on to reiterate that he was his father's son, referring to Henry Hyde no less than nine times in less than ten minutes. He built on the family theme by declaiming about "this brother of mine, The Equitable" and confiding, "I drank in a great love for its principles and its traditions when a babe at my mother's breast." The agents sat through this quietly until Hyde spied Tarbell and made a critical comment about him. When some agents hissed, Hyde lost control. He yelled at one agent, "You may hiss, you owe $50,000 to Mr. Tarbell! Only two animals hiss, a goose and a snake." Tarbell advanced on him threateningly until Alexander pushed them apart, shouting, "Gentlemen, I beg of you!" After that disastrous appearance, all Tarbell had to do was say a few complimentary words about the agency force, accept loud applause, and sit down.[20]

The general agents and agency managers then gave the "protective organization" a formal structure and name, the Association of Managers and General Agents, and elected their most powerful colleague, Edward A. Woods, as president. (Over the years, the association would come to be called the Old

Guard.) They unanimously passed motions endorsing Alexander, Tarbell, and mutualization. The next day the officers went to Hyde's home and asked him to resign. Hyde defied them, and the agents and managers scattered to renew the war in their agencies. Although the convention bolstered the field force's confidence in the Society and stimulated a sales boost, its heat demonstrated how far the battle for Equitable had disintegrated in less than three months from a boardroom debate over corporate governance to a bitter personal battle that polarized the entire company. One unanticipated effect of the convention was that it dampened the Board of Directors' support for mutualization; the general agents and managers had organized themselves so well that the directors feared they could control enough policyholders' proxies to take over a mutualized Equitable.

Still more heat followed. On May 3, Alexander resigned as a trustee for James Hyde's Equitable stock. The other trustees rejected his resignation and brought suit to depose him. Henry Hyde's dynastic dream now swarmed with snakes.

This sad story had a happy ending because of three men: Elihu Root, Henry Clay Frick, and Thomas Fortune Ryan. While Root was focusing his energies on preventing runs on or hostile takeovers of Equitable and the National Bank of Commerce, Frick and his committee were hard at work studying Equitable. A fiercely factual, unsentimental businessman, Frick had made his name and his fortune in the rough-and-tumble of the coal and steel industry in Pittsburgh. As Andrew Carnegie's right-hand man, he gained notoriety — admirable in the eyes of some businessmen, damnable in those of most other Americans — for his ruthlessness in putting down labor unrest at the Homestead steel mill in 1892. Surviving an attempt on his life by an anarchist, Frick had left the Carnegie interests and become a major figure in the nation's moneyed establishment, so much so that in the middle of Equitable's brawl Theodore Roosevelt secretly urged him to purchase the *Washington Post*.

The Frick Committee could have made the easy decision: back the owner, Hyde; dismiss the troublemaker, Alexander; and slap the wrist of the gadfly, Tarbell. Instead, they made the courageous one: to behave independently and forcefully, less like a detached grand jury than a prosecutor. To the three men the committee presented long lists of pointed questions. While the trio answered them more or less honestly, they prepared and passed around memorandums revealing each other's secret compensation agreements and management deficiencies. The committee's patience was short. "The Society needed a president who would do something besides circularizing," one member, Melville E. Ingalls, complained. Schiff himself, though long a close friend and intimate investment advisor of the Hydes, shared the pox-on-all-their-houses conviction. In one meeting he announced in a flood of metaphors that "Alexander and Hyde had each other by the throat, and that in the meantime the Society was being destroyed…. [W]hile the doctors are disagreeing the patient is dying." With Equitable obviously floundering, there was nothing to do, Schiff told the others, except to sweep out all three high officers.[21]

The committee agreed in its scathing report, which it issued on May 31, 1905. Equitable, the committee stated succinctly, had lost its way. What the Society and its policyholders needed was "systematic but uninteresting plodding," not the search for investment coups that had been the recent pattern. Equitable had forgotten its purpose when it became a tool of finance: "In other words, it should be a life insurance company." In its obsession with becoming the largest company

Thomas Fortune Ryan ended the crisis.

and "the rush for business," the Society had allowed agents to become too important. And "moral obliqueness" had become the rule in investments; officers too often were motivated by greed. For these misdeeds the Frick Committee blamed Hyde and Tarbell in part but primarily President Alexander, who, as chief executive and Hyde's trustee, should have disciplined the young man and steered him in the right direction. The committee presented its report to the Board of Directors on June 2. Tarbell mildly protested the criticisms of the sales system that he had inherited from Henry Hyde, Alexander denied almost everything, and Hyde launched into an intemperate monologue in which he accused Harriman of betraying him in order to take over the company. Hyde's and Alexander's supporters, for once finding something to agree on, succeeded in tabling the report.[22]

Most members of the Frick Committee resigned from the board, and the remaining directors resolved that Hyde sell his stock to a buyer of their choice. They discussed naming a chairman of the board to supersede Alexander, but Schiff proposed turning Equitable over to a small committee comprising men of national prominence who would hire a new chairman to reorganize the company. Among the names mentioned were those of former President Grover Cleveland and former secretary of war and ambassador to Britain Robert Todd Lincoln, Abraham Lincoln's son. When Alexander and Hyde refused to cooperate, Schiff resigned — but not before chastising them for blocking necessary change.

The management question could not be addressed until the ownership problem was dealt with. A buyout syndicate was formed by William Rockefeller and George J. Gould, an Equitable director and railroad developer who had already offered Hyde $5 million for his shares. Hyde turned down their offer and proposed putting the stock in trust or selling it to Equitable, but there were legal barriers to both ideas. Then Harriman stepped forward. Whether he made a bid is not known, but clearly he presented himself to Equitable's board as their only hope. Others were not so sure, such were the size of the stake and the instability of the situation. As The Equitable was being shaken to its roots, a large block of stock in the National Bank of Commerce went up for sale in Europe. The possibility of a foreign stockholder taking control of the bank and shredding the fabric of finance in which the bank and Equitable were so crucial so horrified one banker, George F. Baker of the First National Bank, that in June 1905 he seriously considered merging with the Bank of Commerce rather than be vulnerable to a hostile takeover attempt.

Harriman was regarded in some quarters as equally disruptive. The possibility that Equitable (and the Bank of Commerce) might fall into his hands stimulated the appearance of a new player. He was Thomas Fortune Ryan, a financier with interests in various trust companies, among them "the insurance bank," the Bank of Commerce. Sometime between the board meeting on June 2 and June 8, Ryan offered Hyde $2.5 million for his stock with the understanding that it would be placed under the control of independent trustees and that Ryan would continue to earn the usual dividends totaling only $3,514.

Why Ryan would make this apparent sacrifice was a mystery, for his reputation was for robber baron–style ruthlessness, not philanthropy. "If Ryan lives long enough," his partner William C. Whitney once joked, "he'll have all the money in the world." He had made a fortune from investments in the American Tobacco Company, the Royal Typewriter Company, and Manhattan's tram and trolley lines. By 1905, Ryan was living in a Fifth Avenue mansion of such ornateness that people called it the American Louvre. Through his attorney, Elihu Root, he had followed Equitable's struggles from the time they became public. Ryan's concern, like his lawyer's, was that because of the Society's size, its internal conflicts would, if not tamed, spill over into Wall Street and upset the entire financial community. A run on Equitable would lead to runs on banks and the federal treasury. The analysis was not inaccurate, and the concern was not unreasonable. The interlocking system of financial reservoirs, sluices, canals, and spigots was large and extensive. "There was hardly such a person as a prominent New York financier who could have been called disinterested in The Equitable's troubles," observed Root's biographer. But of all those men, Thomas Fortune Ryan was probably best qualified to deal with the problem of bringing order to the potentially out-of-control situation brought about by the fight for The Equitable. Not only did Ryan have a large stake in the National Bank of Commerce and

its related trust companies, but he knew something about the life insurance business. He was a member of the syndicate that late in 1904 had taken over the failing, mismanaged Washington Life Insurance Company (which Frederick Winston of Mutual Life had founded in 1860), refinanced it, replaced all but one of its officers, slashed overhead, and reoriented its investment policies. He had been criticized for self-interest; many of Washington Life's new investments were in companies he controlled and were made through a brokerage run by his sons. As questionable as these proceedings seem to us today, at the time they were not illegal, and they had helped return Washington Life to solid footing.[23]

Yet at the time there was widespread incredulity that Ryan, who was known as an avaricious raider, had agreed to buy Hyde's Equitable interest in a way that yielded him a pittance and no access to Equitable's assets. His explanation that he was serving the public interest was greeted by widespread skepticism.

But few people at the time realized that, in this case, it was worth more to Ryan and his

Ryan was suspected as a raider but put his stock in trust.

The fight badly bruised the image of The Equitable, all but destroying half a century's worth of public trust.

business partners to be protective, not avaricious. In securing Equitable, he was buying an insurance policy for his and their investments in the Bank of Commerce, if not the entire system. There was a subtle side to Ryan, whom Whitney called "the most adroit, suave, and noiseless man" he had ever known. The fact of the matter was that while Equitable's fate deeply concerned the tight network of bankers and investors who were building and profiting from America's new, independent, stable capitalism, it also concerned the public interest. What most of the interested parties shared was a desire for stability. Not for another nine years, when the Federal Reserve system went into operation in 1914, would there be a national central bank to provide that permanence. Therefore, it was up to the bankers themselves. In an article titled "Why I Bought The Equitable," published in 1913, Ryan described the stakes in language very similar to that used by Root

during the crisis: "No more serious quarrel has disturbed business for a generation than that which rose out of conditions that became known as existing in The Equitable early in 1905." In other words, as valuable as Equitable's assets might be to him if he could draw on them, they were even more valuable if they were kept out of the hands of people who threatened to upset the new corporate finance system — like Harriman. On Ryan's side as the system's policemen were J. Pierpont Morgan and a few other substantial bankers. Morgan had large financial interests in Metropolitan Life, and his partner, George Perkins, remained an officer of New York Life. Morgan encouraged Ryan to purchase control of Equitable, and there is hearsay evidence, at least, that Morgan provided funds to help him accomplish it.[24]

If Ryan was motivated to buy Equitable for mixed reasons of public and private interest, why did James Hyde sell it?

First, he clearly had to sell to somebody, for he had lost the support of Equitable's directors and the trustees for his stock. While there were higher bids than Ryan's, what Ryan offered that the other bidders did not was the trust arrangement, which effectively removed Equitable as a target for speculators and regained for it the confidence of its policyholders and agents. By thereby "saving" Equitable, Hyde may well have felt justified that he had retained for himself the distinguished place in history to which his father had consigned him and from which his former friends, Alexander and Harriman, had attempted to oust him. Now Hyde, still a young man, could go on with his chosen life in good conscience.

On June 9, 1905, Hyde and Ryan, accompanied by their attorneys, Elihu Root and Samuel Untermeyer, signed an agreement under which Ryan purchased the stock and immediately placed it in trust. Legal questions as to whether Hyde had the right to sell the stock were covered by a blizzard of paperwork and a codicil to his will. Ryan immediately appointed the trustees: Grover Cleveland, industrialist George Westinghouse, and Judge Morgan J. O'Brien, presiding justice of the Appellate Division of the New York State Supreme Court. With their approval, he appointed secretary of the navy Paul Morton as Equitable's new Chief Executive Officer. When Ned Harriman learned of the sale, he rushed to Ryan and, threatening retribution by the state legislature, demanded half the stock, a say in the appointment of the new management, and positions on the board of trustees. Ryan flatly turned him down. Harriman threatened, "I will use any effort I can to defeat an unworthy object," and continued to apply pressure. Morton wrote his wife:

We are likely to have a great row before we get through because Harriman is so mad

— he got terribly left in the shuffle and is horribly broken up about it. He shook the tree for months and months and Ryan walked off with the plums and now Harriman is hostile….

And so the fight for Equitable ended with some feelings bruised but the Society still intact.[25]

A few weeks later, President Roosevelt appointed Elihu Root secretary of state. Root later was elected senator from New York and received the Nobel Prize for Peace — not for his crucial role in saving Equitable, but for his service as President of the Carnegie Endowment for International Peace. Henry Clay Frick for the remainder of his life looked back with frustration on his attempt to reform Equitable. Gage Tarbell was kept on because he was trusted by the general agents. James Alexander, however, was let go and suffered a nervous breakdown; before he died in 1915, he compensated Equitable for some profits on investments financed by the Society. James Hazen Hyde also paid back Equitable for some expenses and investment profits.

In November 1905, James Hyde sold the Long Island farm and his stables and fled to Paris, where he had always felt more at home than in his father's long shadow. There he lived for thirty-five years without returning to New York. He became a leader of the American community, worked on projects involving Franco-American cultural relations, and was elected an honorary life fellow of the Royal Society of Arts and a member of the Institute of France. After the German occupation forced his return to New York, Hyde remained active in cultural relations. He died in New York in 1959 on the exact date of Equitable's centennial. James Hyde was married three times (twice to countesses) and had a son, Henry Baldwin Hyde. The other lineal descendants of The Equitable's founder were the children of his daughter, Mary Ripley. (A grandnephew, S. Dillon Ripley III, headed the Smithsonian Institution in the 1970's and 'eighties.)

According to James Hyde, he and Alexander crossed paths only once again. In Egypt, on camelback, they came upon each other near the base of the Pyramids. Hyde reported that neither man acknowledged the other as they rode into the desert in opposite directions.

Appointed by Ryan and the trustees, Paul Morton, a former railroad man and Equitable's fourth President, restored the company's finances and reputation in his brief, often controversial tenure.

CHAPTER VIII

THE MORTON RECOVERY

A fter the Society resiliently snapped
back from one or another of its crises,
William Alexander, its longtime Secretary,
would breathe a sigh of relief and say, "God
watched over The Equitable." Yet credit for the
Society's quick recovery from the year of troubles of 1905, and the problems that led to it,
must go to Thomas Fortune Ryan and the
men he recruited, Paul Morton and Grover
Cleveland. Through Morton's determination,
Cleveland's integrity, and the self-discipline of
Ryan (and the subsequent majority shareholder, J. P. Morgan), The Equitable and public
trust in it were gradually, if painfully, restored.[1]

Morton was born on the Nebraska frontier
to an accomplished family. His father was secretary of agriculture under President Cleveland;
his brother Joy ran the Morton Salt Company
(Joy Morton and his son Sterling were Equitable
directors). Paul began his career at sixteen as a
clerk in a freight office of a railroad in which his
father had an interest, and twenty years later he
was vice-president of the sprawling Atchison,
Topeka & Santa Fe Railroad. In 1904, Theodore
Roosevelt appointed him secretary of the navy.
Surviving a scandal involving charges that, at the
Atchison, he had approved rebates to shippers,
Morton served effectively for a year. In May
1905, Thomas Fortune Ryan hired him to manage the subway system that Ryan and August
Belmont were building in New York. Morton
accepted the job, left on a short European
vacation, and returned to New York to
discover that Ryan had bought the controlling
interest in Equitable and named him
Chairman of the Board. As Morton left govern-

ment, Roosevelt praised him in a public letter:
"[Y]ou have undertaken perhaps the greatest and most important work now open to
any businessman."[2]

Equitable people quickly saw Morton as a
refreshing change from the equivocating James
Alexander and impulsive James Hyde. Massive,
robust, forthright, and decisive, he was the man
to deal with a crisis. "Paul Morton, Human
Dynamo" was the title of a contemporary magazine profile. His philosophy of life, he said,
was, "So live your life each day that you can at
any time look any damn man in the eyes and
tell him to go to hell." During his first week at
120 Broadway, he told his daughter, "[T]he situation is interesting and I like it. I am always
happiest when things are doing and if the
bricks begin to fly we will have lots of fun." As
the enormity of his challenge became clear a
few days later, he wrote her:

> It is a big position — one of the biggest in
> the world and naturally we all feel quite
> good about it. Brings me in New York and
> places me at once among the financial
> leaders of the City — The Equitable has
> over $420 million of securities and invests
> over $20 million of income — It ought to
> be a life work and I think I have made no
> mistake in taking it.[3]

Morton identified Equitable's chief problem as regaining the trust of policyholders and
agents, who were leaving the Society in droves.
In his first week he wrote the agents to declare
that the leadership crisis was past, and he
proved it in a string of decisive actions. He dis-

Grover Cleveland at the time he was an Equitable trustee.

avowed $1 million in liabilities carried on Equitable's books but incurred by James Hyde's investment syndicate. He sliced overhead by $600,000 by, among other things, cutting executive compensation by 20 percent and ending a $25,000 annuity to Henry Hyde's widow. He demanded letters of resignation from all officers, pocketing those of the top salespeople, Gage Tarbell and George T. Wilson, and accepting those of Hyde, Alexander, and Controller Thomas D. Jordan. (Jordan promptly disappeared on a permanent vacation in Europe, far from the reach of American prosecutors who wanted him to explain some questionable accounting in the company's books.) And Morton filled most of the seats on the Board of Directors that had been held by officers with policyholders (soon, twenty-eight of the fifty-two directors were policyholders). To indicate that management would be subservient to the board, he changed his own title from Chairman to President. And he commissioned a thorough study of the Society by teams of outside accountants from two auditors, Haskins & Sells and Price, Waterhouse.

All of this was accomplished in consultation with Grover Cleveland, who chaired the panel of trustees for Ryan's stock. The only President of the United States to serve two nonconsecutive terms (in 1885–89 and 1893–97), Cleveland was regarded much as Harry Truman is regarded today, as a man of rock-hard principle and independence. For good reason, the best biography, by Allan Nevins, is subtitled *A Study in Courage*. Since his second departure from the White House, Cleveland had been living quietly in Princeton, New Jersey, scratching out a living as a writer and public speaker and turning down most business offers because they involved apparent conflicts of interest or struck him as undignified. (Pensions for Presidents were still far in the future.) He had met Ryan through William C. Whitney, who was secretary of the navy in his first administration and, later, Ryan's business partner. When Ryan approached Cleveland, through a friend, to serve as a trustee for his Equitable stock, Cleveland at first hesitated because Ryan had donated money to his campaigns. When Ryan promised he would stay clear, Cleveland took the job with the understanding that he would not be compensated. This relationship between the robber baron and the moralist generated widespread incredulity, but Ryan kept his word. "I can say to you that from that day to this Thomas F. Ryan has not offered a suggestion nor has he approached the trustees directly or indirectly," Cleveland told a reporter in 1908. "If he had not done what he did in Equitable, nobody can tell what would have happened." Cleveland eventually accepted a nominal $1,000 a month as president of the Association of Life Insurance Presidents, the trade association for the big insurance companies, and agreed to accept small compensation as an arbitrator of disputes between insurers.[4]

Cleveland preached insurance fundamentalism. Equitable's mission, he declared repeatedly, was solely to sell life insurance protection. As he put it, Equitable must strengthen the "powerful cable binding life insurance to the immovable rock of popular confidence," relearn "our old, simple American standards of honesty," and flush speculation out of its system. He was helping to bring that about by attaching his name and reputation to the Society, but Cleveland did not stop there. In selecting new members of Equitable's board, he and the other trustees — George Westinghouse and Judge Morgan J. O'Brien — agreed not even to consider insurance agents, financiers, stock brokers, and investment bankers. (Explaining the last group, Cleveland said, "I feel that underwriting just at the present time is, or ought to be, a little out of fashion among the directors of The Equitable Assurance Society.")[5]

At the end of 1905, the outside auditors reported to Morton that though Equitable was sound financially, Alexander and the Society's other officers had overvalued real estate and securities holdings, allowed sales costs to get out of hand, misled the Frick Committee about their compensation agreements by $900,000, and allowed the Society's operations to decline. Morton wrote down the surplus by 15 percent and set about modernizing the infrastructure by ordering the installation of new office machinery. In his first speech at an agents' meeting, Morton promised that "six months of tempest and storm" were over and that he intended to make the new administration "honest, conservative, and courageous." Equitable would no longer try to be the largest insurer, he announced; henceforth it would be the best and safest.[6]

Other investigations by outsiders were already under way. One was run by Louis D. Brandeis, a Boston lawyer (and future Supreme Court justice) who had introduced savings bank life insurance in Massachusetts; representing a group of Equitable policyhold-ers, he attacked high agent commissions. Another was held by New York State Insurance Superintendent Francis Hendricks. Edward Harriman dispatched Chauncey Depew and former governor Odell to control Hendricks, but the situation was far too advanced to be muffled. Hendricks blamed the Hydes, father and son, for all Equitable's problems. The search for scapegoats continued when the New York attorney general, pressured by policyholder groups, sued forty-nine members of the old Equitable board for diverting assets from policyholders. Though the suit eventually was dropped, it kept the issue of widespread culpability for Equitable's troubles in the public spotlight.

But no investigation of Equitable was as important as the Armstrong Committee's. On July 20, 1905, Governor Frank Higgins, after months of chiding by Joseph Pulitzer's *World*, called for an official investigation of all fourteen life insurance companies headquartered in New York. The state legislature formed an investigative committee of three senators and five assemblymen chaired by State Senator William W. Armstrong. Many insurance executives welcomed an investigation by the same body that had winked at many of their misdeeds; they (and Senator Armstrong himself) expected a quick and relatively bloodless persecution of a few scapegoats that would little change the insurance business. But what they got was something very different, and that because of the man whom Armstrong hired as chief counsel.

Armstrong made what he believed was a safe selection: a corporate lawyer who had worked for Equitable on its mutualization plan, forty-three year-old Charles Evans Hughes. Armstrong could not have misread his man more thoroughly. Known as Charles the Baptist in part for his denominational affiliation but chiefly for his rigorous ethics and self-discipline, Hughes was hardly the man for a merely

Triggered by the Equitable crisis, the Armstrong Committee hearings, run by Charles Evans Hughes, ventured into delicate areas.

sensational but unsubstantial cover-up. After submitting the mutualization plan to Alexander, Hughes had spent several months as counsel to a state committee investigating the public utilities industry. In July he and his wife were on vacation in Germany when he received a telegram from Armstrong asking him to run the insurance investigation. When his wife complained about the interruption, Hughes told her, "My dear, you don't know what this investigation would mean. It would be the most tremendous job in the United States."[7]

Hughes made it clear from the beginning that he endorsed the idea of life insurance; he owned policies and would later buy some more from Equitable. But what he set out to do was return the business to the principles of insurance fundamentalism. Asking most of the questions during fifty-seven days of testimony, Hughes studiously ignored the sentimental widows-and-orphans defenses of insurance practices presented by many wit-

nesses and politely but firmly probed for detailed factual information. "[H]is was an intellectual moralism; he believed in God but believed equally that God was on the side of the facts," another lawyer, Robert T. Swaine, said of Hughes, who, Swaine continued, handled the investigation "as unemotionally as a teacher finding a mild enthusiasm in leading a child to concede the irrefutable verities of mathematics." The inquiry ventured into some extremely sensitive areas. When Richard McCurdy of Mutual Life learned that the Armstrong investigation would be serious, he spoke anxiously about what he called "the dreadful controversies and the frightful disclosures that are occurring very near to us." The committee discovered, among other misdeeds, that after McCurdy's son died, Mutual Life had issued him a backdated life policy. "We had a lot of money coming in that we did not know what to do with," was McCurdy's weak explanation for the pattern of self-dealing by himself and his officers. And when Hughes began to ask about the cozy alliance between the insurance companies and legislators — a relationship that led all the way to Theodore Roosevelt's White House — the leaders of the state Republican Party tried to lure him off the trail by offering him its nomination for Mayor of New York in the upcoming 1905 election. Their persuasion was so lengthy and intense that Mrs. Hughes was convinced Hughes would not hold out against it. But he did, and the political connections were exposed.[8]

Though McCurdy's embarrassments were worse than anything Equitable could produce, the Society had the committee's and the public's full attention if only because its scandals were the first to be widely known. All its main figures testified except for James Alexander, who was emotionally shattered, and Jordan, who was beyond the reach of a subpoena. Edward Harriman, James Hyde, Jacob Schiff, Henry Clay Frick, Gage Tarbell, and Thomas Fortune Ryan all testified, some more forthrightly than others. Taken as a whole, the seven volumes of transcripts and exhibits of the Armstrong Committee's hearings provide one of the best portraits of the workings of insurance companies and Wall Street at the turn of the century.

In the committee's final report, which he wrote and which was released in February 1906, Hughes laid out meticulous recommendations for legislation that, he thought, would prevent life insurance companies from again being distracted by large sales volume, high finance, and greed. The root problem, he believed, was the tontine — not so much the annuity-type policy itself but its deferred dividends. Before they were distributed to policyholders, these dividends grew into large amounts that tempted insurance executives into actions that could not be countenanced. The tontine made life insurance companies

too wealthy and too subject to the pressures of speculators. Life insurers, Hughes wrote,

were not incorporated to make money by speculation, by purchase for resale, or by the development of industry. They were chartered to furnish life insurance, and the true measure of their power and their duty in the handling of their funds is to invest them with due conservatism, to the end that they may be able to discharge their obligations. If in this manner they should make less money they would also be less likely to court disaster....[9]

Within two months after Hughes filed his report, the New York legislature passed eight bills based closely on his wording and intended to protect companies and their policyholders from financial distress. Known as the Armstrong laws, these new insurance statutes had two themes: first, life insurers should be in no business except life insurance; second, the business henceforth would be held by a short regulatory leash, and anything not specifically permitted by the laws or approved by the New York State Insurance Department was illegal.

Hughes (center) would not be distracted from the facts.

The laws themselves transformed the business in both the investment area, which Hughes believed lay at the core of The Equitable's troubles, and the insurance sales area. In order to end the practice of insurers' owning trust companies and other institutions not engaged in life insurance, the statutes prohibited ownership of any common stock. To stop accumulations of large amounts of money that might tempt insurers to engage in speculative investments, the laws capped the surplus at 10 percent of assets, banned deferred dividends, and tightened accounting standards that defined surplus. To discourage overemphasis on sales volume, the Armstrong laws banned rebates to policyholders, advances to agents, and many subsidies to agencies. New sales volume was severely restricted; Equitable and all other insurers with more than $1 billion of insurance in force were prohibited from new business totaling more than $150 million a year — only a third Equitable's new business in 1904.

To add weight to these disciplines, the laws isolated companies from the influence of stockholders. Mutualization was mandated, and the Board of Directors was made accountable as fiduciaries for policyholders' money; for example, they had to approve every investment and most salaries. In addition, almost every aspect of the business required insurance department approval — agents' commissions, officers' salaries, surrender values, the language of contracts (the product was to be called insurance, not assurance, though Equitable was not forced to change its name). The department would hold a regular, detailed audit of every insurer's business at the company's expense. Other states passed similar laws, some adding more stringent restrictions. After Wisconsin limited the salaries of executives of insurers doing business there to $25,000, and Texas imposed high taxes and reserve requirements, Equitable withdrew from those states altogether, not to return for many years.

In a phrase, the Armstrong laws took the life insurance industry to boot camp. "Some of the recommendations came as a rude shock to the men who have been brought up in the insurance business as heretofore conducted," Equitable's lawyer, Paul Cravath, told Hughes. But while a few recommendations appeared "rather drastic," Cravath assured Hughes of Morton's respect. "Rather drastic" was an understatement. In banning deferred dividends, the Armstrong laws terminated not only the most successful product in Equitable's history (80 percent of the Society's insurance in force was in tontines) but also the main source of income and profits. Tarbell complained to Morton, "[W]hile they are trying to make the companies better for the policyholders, they are really making the companies much less secure, and so much so in my opinion as to be unsafe." Reflecting years later on the transforming period between January 1905 and April 1906 — from the first shots in the fight for Equitable to the passage of the new insurance laws — the historian Burton J. Hendrick told an interviewer, "Of course, that resulted in a complete revamping of the whole insurance business. The days of Jimmy Hyde and Henry Hyde, and the deferred dividend and all that business — that was all wiped out."[10]

The insurance investigations and Armstrong laws had several immediate effects. One was that, to Hughes's surprise, they launched him on a remarkable career in public service. A few months after submitting his report, he was elected as reform governor of New York. Later, he was an associate justice of the Supreme Court, Republican presidential candidate in 1916 (losing by a sliver to Woodrow Wilson), secretary of state, and chief justice of the Supreme Court. His imprint on the life insurance industry was permanent. In 1945, forty years after the hearings, a New York insurance superintendent titled a section of a speech, "Armstrong Report of 1906 Still a Working Bible." As late as the 1990's, any serious discussion of insurance regulation included at least one mention of the Armstrong Committee.[11]

One effect of the Armstrong laws was that they depleted Wall Street's pool of investable funds. Without the large reserves of insurance companies' deposits in trust companies, Wall Street was more vulnerable to sudden downturns. A panic in 1907 left dozens of banks and brokerages insolvent or on the verge of collapse without ready reserves. J. Pierpont Morgan and the two other dominant bankers of the day, George F. Baker of the First National Bank and James Stillman of the National City Bank, improvised a last-ditch bailout by pooling funds from their institutions and other banks. (The creation of the Federal Reserve Bank created a new reserve system that largely took the place of the old insurance and trust company arrangement.) The 1907 panic might well have severely damaged Equitable and some other big insurers had it not been for some creative regulators. Bond prices at the end of 1907 were so depressed that the value of the Society's assets, which under the new system had to be carried at market value, was smaller than liabilities. The New York Insurance Department solved the problem by allowing insurers to appraise their bonds by averaging in not only the depressed 1907 prices but also the high prices of bonds at the end of 1906. The "thirteen-month year," as it was called, was the first, but hardly the only, demonstration of the insurance department's policy of satisfying the public interest by both keeping insurers solvent and attending to the needs of consumers. So austere and novel were some Armstrong statutes that the department, under the pressure of industry concern that companies might be destroyed, decided to delay full enforcement, in some cases for many years. The new

caps on securities holdings were not entirely imposed for a decade, and The Equitable was not legally mutualized for almost two. This flexible paternalism — rigorous regulation broken by occasional begrudging concession — would be repeated many times.

The situation that Paul Morton faced was precarious. Equitable's business was terrible. New sales collapsed from $307 million in force in 1904 to $88 million in 1906 and $73 million (less than half the maximum set by the new law) in 1907. In June 1905, the face value of policies sold by the Woods Agency in Pittsburgh was $1.5 million; in the same month a year later, it was $200,000. Voluntary policy surrenders by Equitable policyholders totaled tens of millions of dollars a year.

New York Life and Mutual Life were in no better shape. Revelations in the hearings had damaged them as badly as the well-publicized fight for control had harmed Equitable, and the racers lost their dominance in the industry. Prudential Life and Metropolitan Life, the two big industrial companies, were not affected and overtook them in size and sales volume. Meanwhile, a number of new life insurers appeared. The smaller insurers formed a national association, the American Life Convention, to lobby against state regulations that made start-ups difficult (for example, by requiring insurers to set aside the reserve against the first-year premium entirely in the first year). The big companies' trade group, the Association of Life Insurance Presidents, successfully fought the new, small companies in some eastern states, but the West became a haven for new companies. Between 1905 and 1912, the number of American life companies more than doubled from 112 to 250 as the racers' market share declined substantially.

There were other, internal problems. High costs due to loading and over-sanguine underwriting were making Equitable noncom-

The golden anniversary in 1909 was celebrated by a convention of agents and employees.

petitive among peer companies. In 1906, according to chief actuary Joel Van Cise, the Society's ratio of expenses to premium income, 19¼ percent, was 10 percent higher than many competitors'. In an effort to trim costs, Morton decided to install the system of branch agencies run by salaried managers that had been used successfully at New York Life for more than a decade. (Existing general agencies were grandfathered for the careers of their general agents. A few were subsequently permitted to remain as general agencies; the Woods Agency was not converted until 1942, fifteen years after Edward Woods's death.) At the same time, citing the Armstrong laws' restrictions on sales expenses, Morton cut average first-year commissions to 45 percent from the 73 percent that had been reached during the fat years of the tontines. The new controls on loading, a 13 percent cut in the dividend that made some Equitable policies noncompetitive, and lagging sales stimulated massive attrition in the agency

force, which between 1904 and 1907 declined from 10,000 to 2,800.[12]

If the general agents were angry about the loss of business, agents, and commissions, they were furious about the termination of the general agencies. No longer could they pass on their agencies to their sons; no longer would they control sales practices in their regions. They transformed the group that had opposed Hyde in 1905 into an organization called the General Agency Association. Bitterness and invective sear the pages of its minutes, which have been preserved in the Equitable Archives. Relations with the Home Office, and with Morton and Gage Tarbell in particular, were terrible. At one point Morton went so far as to warn Edward Woods, the president, that he would turn against the group if it "was maintained as an offensive and defensive alliance against the Society."[13]

Tarbell, fierce as ever, carried the Home Office's fight for a year; but in 1907, exhausted and apparently not pressured by Morton, he resigned to head a real estate development in Garden City, Long Island. Anybody who had thrived as he had under the success and loose regulatory scheme of older days was sure to be unhappy in a time of plummeting sales and morale. As he departed, he wrote his old colleagues of his pride in having played a part in "organizing and building up one of the greatest selling agencies that the country has ever known." He remained a director of the Society. Morton took over personal supervision of agencies in the West, while George T. Wilson, who had handled foreign sales, managed the East.[14]

When the branch office system went into effect in 1908, it was deeply resented by many general agents. A year later, Morton, in his keynote speech at the Society's golden anniversary celebration, briefly stepped away from the mood of celebration to issue a clear warning to agents:

> *The Equitable has always been considered as the "Agents' Company" and I want it distinctly and definitely understood that it is still the Agents' Company, but my construction of what is best for the Agent is that which is best for the policyholder…. [I]t is the policyholder who is the company…. This Society was organized for its policyholders. They must always be the first to be considered in the conduct of its affairs.*[15]

By 1909 the agents who had endured the tough times had to be content with the results of four trying years, during which Equitable had regained their and the public's trust. By 1908, policy terminations were down to one-third what they had been in 1905; in 1909, new business rose above $100 million. Although sales commissions were lower, the agents voted with their feet, and the agency force was up to 5,000. Costs dropped, income rose, and

An Equitable trustee under Ryan and Morgan, Judge Morgan J. O'Brien.

public confidence recovered. Assets grew by one-fifth to $479 million, and Equitable paid out $50 million in dividends to policyholders at a rate three times higher than in 1899. The New York Insurance Department, in a report that reads like a calm evaluation of a recovery from a nervous breakdown, declared that the hard times were over: "The department notes, with approval, that in this, The Equitable Life Assurance Society's jubilee year, such Society is no longer chiefly interested in large totals and the volume of its business." William Alexander told Vice-President William Day: "The history of the Society during the past five years represents a period of rehabilitation. The life insurance companies had just weathered a great storm. The Equitable was the chief sufferer…."[16]

Grover Cleveland died in 1908. The next year, the aging Thomas Fortune Ryan began to sell off portions of his empire. There is no record of these transactions in the Equitable Archives, but according to J. Pierpont

Morgan, Ryan sold some of his Equitable shares to Edward H. Harriman, who had stubbornly pursued him for years and who still hoped to create an international railroad and financial center. Harriman controlled one of the largest trust companies, Guaranty Trust, and continued to aspire to control of the National Bank of Commerce in a time of increasing consolidation of financial institutions. With the deadline for insurance companies to dispose of their stock in other institutions having been postponed to 1911, Equitable still owned a large share of the Bank of Commerce stock. Control of the Society, therefore, was attractive to Harriman even beyond the appeal of its vast assets. Whether the transaction would have been permitted by the New York Insurance Department is questionable, but Morgan, skeptical of Harriman's intentions, stepped in and asked Ryan to sell him his remaining Equitable shares at his purchase price plus interest. When Harriman died in 1909, Morgan (by his account) purchased his Equitable shares from his estate and gained a controlling interest.

Morgan later explained that he bought The Equitable because he wished to prevent the Society from again becoming a financial football: "I thought it best to have that stock where there was no danger of it being divided up into small lots." This explanation was not widely believed at the time; Morgan already had considerable sway at Mutual Life and New York Life, controlled a network of trust companies, and was popularly regarded, like Ryan and Harriman, as a financial pirate. It also was true that gaining control of Equitable was a means to dominating the National Bank of Commerce. Yet his stated prophylactic concerns must be given credence, since his hands were tied by the Armstrong laws and Ryan's five-year trust agreement, which was in effect until 1910. Morgan kept his hands off and further stabilized Equitable. He offered equal shares to his two

banking competitors and friends, George F. Baker and James Stillman (each turned him down but later bought one-fourth of Morgan's shares), and the three of them cooperated on an arrangement for joint control of the Bank of Commerce. This gave the trio and their banks control over almost two-thirds of the bankers' balances on deposit in New York. As for the Bank of Commerce, a prime target of Harriman's attempts on Equitable, in the 1920's it was merged into Guaranty Trust, which later merged with Morgan's bank, J. P. Morgan & Co., to form Morgan Guaranty Trust.[17]

When the trust arrangement expired in May 1910, Morgan took steps that continued to woo the public's support for the Society. He renewed the agreement with only one change, the addition of a clause promising to mutualize the Society. And when new trustees were needed, after briefly considering Baker and his own son J. P. ("Jack") Morgan, Jr., he followed the advice of his partners and appointed two people whom he trusted but who were regarded as more independent — George Perkins, who knew the insurance business, and Lewis Cass Ledyard, one of his lawyers. He reappointed Judge Morgan J. O'Brien, who was influential in Albany, where a mutualization law would have to be legislated. As Equitable recovered, Paul Morton's health failed. He was in such poor condition in late 1910 that when the agency department tried to give a new policy a well-publicized launch by selling him the first contract, the medical department not only refused permission but also sent a doctor to warn Mrs. Morton of her husband's declining condition. In January 1911 he died suddenly of a heart attack. The senior Vice-President, William Day, stepped in temporarily while the board awaited instructions from Morgan.

At that, a small group of wealthy men that included George Gould and John D. Rockefeller approached Morgan about purchasing his Equitable interest. Morgan

William A. Day continued Morton's reforms and introduced group insurance.

turned them down. Although many observers expected Morgan to name Perkins as Morton's successor, he left the decision entirely to The Equitable's Board of Directors and refused to return from England for the board meeting. Even the trustees declined to intercede except to suggest that the new President have a strong background in insurance. At the board meeting on April 20, 1911, the directors approved a mutualization plan drawn up by Ledyard and, ignoring a request by the insurance superintendent not to name a successor until the plan was in place, elected Vice-President William Day as the Society's fifth President.

Equitable had survived. Under the ownership of Thomas Fortune Ryan and J. Pierpont Morgan — two financial figures who were widely distrusted by the public, yet men who better than most people understood that the Society above all needed stability and public support — it had been led by Grover Cleveland and Paul Morton, sometimes against the criticism of its agents, until it was well on the way to recovering from the crisis of 1905 in a new shape and, as we will see in the next chapter, with a new type of product.

Born in Illinois in 1850, William Day became an attorney and, briefly, a politician (for a while he was mayor of Champaign) before heading to Washington and governmental work. Thanks to a tour in the quasi-judicial position of auditor in the Treasury Department, he claimed the title Judge. He later served in the Interstate Commerce Commission and Justice Department, where he supervised several difficult antitrust cases (including the Northern Securities suit) and a wide variety of other vexing problems, among them land purchases for the Panama Canal and investigations of reports of mistreatment of native Alaskans. In 1905, Morton, who had met and was impressed by Day during the 1890's, made him his first appointment to Equitable as head of the scandal-ridden Controller's Department. Before long he was Morton's chief troubleshooter.

Ironically, this career government lawyer had a deeper feel for the subtleties of marketing than his predecessor, whose job had been to haul the Society's head back above water. Discovering that some tactlessly worded letters had been mailed to policyholders, he issued an executive order demanding, "We must never fail to remember that *The Equitable never loses its temper*, and that every letter which it receives is entitled to a prompt, courteous reply." And despite his background in technical law, Day knew what to say to encourage sales agents. Soon after his election, he promised a visiting delegation of agents that his goal was to return Equitable to the top in sales volume. "Supply the Demand!" became his motto.[18]

Despite these gestures toward high volume, disputes between the general agents and the Home Office did not end. In 1911, they banned salaried agency managers from membership in the General Agency Association. A year later they set up an uproar after Day further trimmed agency overhead. The association's executive committee complained about "the more or less antagonistic and unsympathetic attitude of the officers to the committee, indicating a failure to recognize that the honor of the Society concerned the agent as much as the official." Day fought back by recommending that general agents voluntarily convert their agencies to branch offices and by recruiting as the new vice-president for agency operations a man who had never worked at Equitable, John B. Lunger, who came from Travelers Insurance. The idea backfired on Day. The agents received Lunger with such suspicion that, in order to curry favor, he approved several new policies that they had requested but that the actuaries had opposed. A disability insurance policy introduced in 1918 was an immediate disaster and was quickly withdrawn after only three years.[19]

The fires of dissent eventually were quenched by the return of business and by time. Between 1908 and 1912, forty-three of the 150-odd general agencies were converted to branch agencies; another twenty-three had been converted by 1923. By the late 'twenties, general agents became so rare that they were referred to as "Dodo Birds." The General Agency Association became a fraternal, self-help organization. Its minutes show that in place of fierce debates with Home Office executives, meetings were taken up with the singing of an alma mater, skits and jokes, prizes awarded for high sales performance, and educational seminars in salesmanship organized by Edward Woods. In gratitude for the general agents' new spirit of cooperation, Day began to refer to the association as "the backbone of the Equitable army" and, more frequently, as "the Old Guard" — a name inspired by Napoleon's famous personal elite unit. For a while in the 1930's and 'forties, when the most senior salaried managers were allowed to join, it was the organization's official name. In 1945, when the number of general

Soon after Paul Morton's death, Day (seated, in bow tie) meets with the General Agency Association, which he called the Old Guard.

agents was down to a handful, membership finally was opened to all agency managers. The official name became the General Agents and Managers Association, although it was always referred to as the Old Guard.[20]

As the Home Office restructured the agency system, it wrestled with mutualization. No insurer had been converted from a stock to a mutual organization; nobody even knew how to accomplish it. The Ledyard plan, which was passed into state law in 1911, was not satisfactory. Once stockholder legal challenges were dismissed by the courts, the highest hurdle was calculating a fair financial value for the stock. While Morgan owned a controlling interest, about 200 shares were scattered in small lots among a dozen other stockholders, including James Hyde, the Henry Hyde estate, various members of the Alexander family, Chauncey Depew, George Perkins, and the Protestant Episcopal Trust for Aged Clergymen.

The event that hastened mutualization was a disaster. Before dawn on January 9, 1912, an employee of Café Savarin accidentally dropped a lighted match into a wastepaper basket. When the first employees arrived, flames were licking out of the upper windows of the Equitable Building. Soon the iron columns failed, and the roof crashed down through the lower floors. Six alarms went out to fire compa-

nies as far away as Brooklyn, but the whole building went down, killing a fire chief and five employees of tenants and injuring at least twenty people. (Equitable paid the medical expenses of the injured and paid off the mortgage on the fireman's house.) The fire brought the financial district to a halt, and trading on the New York Stock Exchange had to be suspended because runners could not make their way between offices. Equitable itself paused only briefly. At 11 o'clock Day sent a telegram to 200 newspapers announcing that it still was in business. This was a brave hope, since some $300 million in negotiable securities lay inside a safe in the burning building. Out in the field, the agents spontaneously organized an energetic sales campaign that announced to policyholders and prospects that Equitable still was breathing. When the embers finally cooled, about all that remained intact were the huge basement vault, the securities safely inside it, and the John Quincy Adams Ward statue of Henry Baldwin Hyde. A few singed timbers were carried off to a carpenter to make gavels, with small commemorative plaques, to present to the Board of Directors and general agents.

T. Coleman du Pont, a partner in a family gunpowder and chemical business in Wilmington, Delaware, decided to branch off on his own as a real estate developer and purchased the site of 120 Broadway. With $20.5

Henry Hyde's statue (top) somehow survived the great fire of January 1912 that destroyed his building and brought Wall Street to a halt.

A massive new Home Office rose from the ruins.

T. Coleman du Pont.

million in financing from Equitable (in the form of loans and purchases of stock in the building's parent company), he began building a massive new Equitable Building. Designed by the architect Ernest R. Graham, it opened in 1915. Despite the name of the new structure at 120 Broadway — a name that is still in use — the Society neither owned nor dominated it, and in fact remained in it only for a decade. Equitable leased only two entire floors, half of two others, and a vault in the basement. It was the largest office building in the world (as late as 1961, the only building that had more rentable office floor space was the Empire State Building). Filling the block and stretch-

ing thirty-nine stories straight up from the sidewalk, it had six miles of marble-floored corridors, 1.2 million square feet of rentable space, and room for 15,000 workers. New York's mayor called it "a veritable municipality." The bulky building so dominated its plot and, in fact, the entire area that it stimulated the adoption of the country's first comprehensive zoning resolution, which, passed in 1916, required upper floors to be set back at a rate of one foot for every four feet of height.[21]

The Equitable Building brought Coleman du Pont into the Society's circle. He once said of himself, "I like conceiving, planning, organizing, systemizing, getting a project established successfully. Then I want to start something else." Having built the world's largest office building, he sold his large interest in the family business (as it turned out, on the eve of its great success during World War I), and bought the majority interest in Equitable from the estate of Pierpont Morgan, who had died in 1913. The price was the same as Morgan's and Ryan's, plus interest — a total of $4.4 million. Du Pont placed his Equitable stock in the hands of trustees and negotiated a plan for mutualization with Dwight Morrow, a partner at Morgan's bank. Under the plan, Equitable paid du Pont $2.8 million in cash and provided another $2 million by relinquishing a portion of the dividends on stock it held in the Equitable Building. The plan was approved by the courts, most policyholders, and the Insurance Department, and all but twenty-three of the 1,000 shares were turned in by May 14, 1918, the deadline of the stock purchase agreement. Mutualization was not perfectly legal until 1925, as there were many details to iron out. But as of 1918, the Society functioned as a mutual insurance company controlled solely by its customers. The final victor in the nasty war for Equitable was the average policyholder.[22]

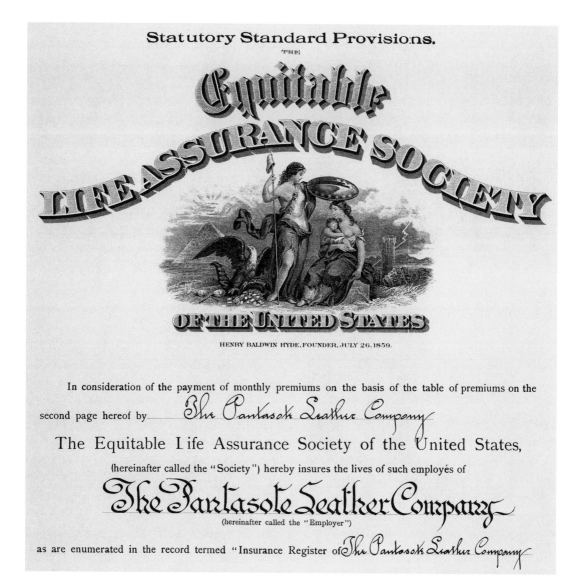

Statutory Standard Provisions.

THE

Equitable
LIFE ASSURANCE SOCIETY
OF THE UNITED STATES

HENRY BALDWIN HYDE, FOUNDER, JULY 26, 1859.

In consideration of the payment of monthly premiums on the basis of the table of premiums on the

second page hereof by *The Pantasote Leather Company*

The Equitable Life Assurance Society of the United States,

(hereinafter called the "Society") hereby insures the lives of such employés of

The Pantasote Leather Company

(hereinafter called the "Employer")

as are enumerated in the record termed "Insurance Register of *The Pantasote Leather Company*

*The first U.S. group insurance policy was issued by the Society to Pantasote Leather Co. in 1911.
Many other insurers thought group insurance a big mistake.*

CHAPTER IX

A NEW EQUITABLE

With the forced demise of tontines due to the 1906 Armstrong laws, Equitable lost its most successful and profitable product. If it were to continue to survive, much less grow, it would have to develop new lines of insurance policies. It chose two radically different strategies. One was to create a new line of intricate, high-premium, high-commission individual participating life insurance policies with savings components to sell to wealthy people. Developed by Edward A. Woods and other urban general agents with a base of well-to-do prospects, and designed by Home Office actuaries, these policies included partnership insurance, annuities, methods for making charitable donations, and alternative schedules for paying premiums and collecting benefits. This was a logical development for Equitable, which had been founded in part on the idea of selling to the middle and upper classes, and whose high sales commissions encouraged agents to sell large policies.

The other strategy was entirely contrary: to sell a large volume of low-cost nonparticipating insurance to a working-class clientele. The idea was encouraged by Woods and a few others at Equitable who were deeply concerned that the Society was shutting itself off from the broad market. Woods was sure that what he called "the present emergency" — Equitable's high lapse rate among policyholders and its startling attrition rate among agents — was in part due to the public's impression that premiums simply were too high. He insisted that if only Equitable would cut premiums on its most basic policy, term insurance

(which, unlike ordinary, whole-life insurance, offered pure protection and no savings component), it would tell the world that life insurance was not just for the wealthy. But since the premiums, commissions, and profitability of term insurance already were low, Woods's proposal found few supporters.[1]

Woods was stimulated by competition from low-cost term insurance sold by organizations to the rapidly growing population of working-class people in Pittsburgh and other factory towns. This was not Equitable's traditional market. Like many of the other mutual and stock companies with large sales forces founded in the 1840's and 'fifties, the Society historically had little interest in the working-class market, or even in selling term and other low-premium policies to the middle class. The blue-collar market was handled by two types of organizations. One was the small cooperative or fraternal benefit society, which had no reserves, little capital, no actuaries, and usually no agents. Instead of charging level premiums, a cooperative society assessed policyholders a small sum on the death of another policyholder. In 1870, these societies sold less than 1 percent of life insurance; but twenty-five years later, in the midst of the greatest wave of immigration and industrialization in American history, fraternal and other cooperative organizations were responsible for 55 percent of the $10.5 billion of life insurance in force in America.

These operations had a higher rate of failure than companies like Equitable, with large reserves and sales forces, largely because they dealt with special groups instead of the vast population. Their business began to decline around the turn of the century as a different type of organization selling low-cost term insurance to workers — the industrial life insurers, of which Prudential Life and Metropolitan Life were the most successful — rose to prominence. Originated by an act of British Parliament in the 1870's to provide social benefits to the masses of impoverished factory workers, industrial insurance was sold door-to-door by agents working on low commission who came around weekly to collect small premium payments. Because the collections were made against a debit account established when a policy was sold, industrial insurance also was known as debit insurance, and an agent's territory of a block of tenements or a street of two-family houses was called a debit. Prudential and Metropolitan specialized in selling industrial insurance to the large, rapidly growing population of blue-collar workers who manned America's expanding factories and railroads.

The demand for these types of insurance increased with the improvement of workers' incomes and lives in the last part of the nineteenth and early part of the twentieth centuries. According to a survey of mill laborers in 1875, only one out of 397 families spent money on life insurance. They had little choice: all but a tiny proportion of their earnings was committed to food, clothing, and housing costs. But during the next four decades, money available for nonsubsistence items in working-class families grew from about 10 percent to about 25 percent of their income. By the early twentieth century, one historian observed, life insurance had become "an essential part of the American standard of living." According to a nationwide survey taken in 1919 of 13,000 low- and moderate-income families, almost 90 percent spent money on life insurance. Of all nonsubsis-

tence household items, only soap and medicine were used by more families than life insurance, and only automobiles, bicycles, and undertakers cost more.[2]

An insurance executive looking to expand a range of products did not need opinion surveys to realize that the market for low-cost protection was growing. By 1900, Prudential and Metropolitan had come from nowhere to be the fourth and fifth largest insurers, after the three racers. When the racers declined in the shadow of 1905, the two industrial companies overtook them to become the largest insurance companies in the world. Paul Morton was determined to develop products for this market; he had known it well during his long career in the railroad business, one of the largest employers of manual workers. He began to look around for ways to enter it.

When James W. Alexander had been shown a British railroad's proposal for a group insurance policy with a payroll deduction plan, he was extremely dubious. "If this thing does materialize," he told James Hyde, "it will be the first time I have ever seen a proposition to do life insurance by wholesale turn out to be practicable." He decided to implement a similar plan only if an American competitor came up with one. Nobody did. So thoroughly was the British railway plan erased from Equitable's institutional memory that when Morton first learned of it in 1908, his source was a prospectus from an English insurer that had accidentally fallen into his hands. Intrigued, he sent his chief assistant, Henry L. Rosenfeld, to Europe to study it and some other innovations.[3]

A keenly analytical former agent as well as a Progressive with a deep and abiding concern for the social welfare of workers, Rosenfeld enthusiastically scoured Britain and Germany for industrial and other worker-oriented insurance programs. He returned with stacks of

Though he had his doubts about group insurance, Henry I. Rosenfeld (above and below) helped launch it.

reports and prospectuses concerning payroll deduction plans, pensions, insurance for home mortgages, and accident and health policies. Morton, impressed, set up a new department, Equitable Industrial Branch. He installed Rosenfeld as its head and sent him to Germany to investigate the advanced workmen's insurance programs that had been established there, including discounted coverage for groups. Morton, meanwhile, was proclaiming that the new Equitable's future lay in part in insurance for working people. "There is a much greater sphere of usefulness, in which I hope to see The Equitable do its full share," he announced at the Society's golden anniversary dinner in 1909. "That sphere is to give protection to the people who cannot afford to carry a big line of life insurance."[4]

Rosenfeld was less excited by group insurance than by a British scheme he had discovered on one of his trips for insured mort-

gages on private homes for workers and middle-class people. It was two products in one: Equitable would loan the money at market rates and secure the loan by selling the mortgagee a life insurance policy on the amount of the loan. Henry Hyde had proposed a similar idea in 1891, but with no result. Since then, only the Prudential and a company in Philadelphia had sold insured mortgages in America, although they were popular in Britain. So Rosenfeld's first program as head of the Industrial Branch was to put in place the nationwide Home Purchase Plan, which provided mortgages for homeowners who took out life policies whose beneficiary was the Society. By 1923, Equitable had loaned $40 million in Home Purchase Plan mortgages, ten times as much money as it had out in conventional mortgages.

Despite Rosenfeld's doubts about group insurance, Morton and his chief assistant, William Day, insisted on founding a group program. The Society was not inexperienced with the concept. Between 1902 and 1908, Equitable provided term insurance for 315 employees of the United Cigar Store Co. and for 600 of its Home Office employees. These plans were essentially individual term insurance policies tacked on to company savings plans, with the death benefit shared by the workers' beneficiaries and the sponsoring companies. The most unusual and controversial feature of these plans was that, in order to save costs, the Society did not require applicants to take medical examinations.

Based on this experience and on their conviction that labor relations were changing, Morton and Day sensed that a demand for group insurance would surface and grow. Businessmen were telling them of their frustrations with their workers, who, no longer placated by an old corporate paternalism best symbolized by annual handouts of Christmas turkeys, were listening seriously to union organizers. To hold off unionization, many companies were seeking out benefit plans to provide their workers. Day and Morton were sure group insurance policies would meet this demand. Day described the situation from the corporate point of view when he said, "Group insurance is a phase of the economic and social tendencies of the day for just relations between employer and employed." And from management's point of view, "just relations" meant a peaceful relationship between labor and management without labor unions.[5]

The first corporate application for a group policy came in October 1910 from Montgomery Ward, whose 3,000 employees were threatening to form a union. George R.

William J. Graham pulled group insurance into shape.

Durgan, the company's attorney and chief official on employee relations, laid out his needs to several insurers. The policies must provide annuities for retired employees and their survivors and also offer death and disability benefits; and expenses must be no greater than 4 percent of payroll costs. Rosenfeld warned Durgan that with such low premiums, the plan would be unprofitable, but Day instructed Equitable's Insurance Committee to develop a contract. To manage the project, he assigned a new officer who had been brought in from the outside, William J. Graham. Rosenfeld was not selected because, besides being unenthusiastic about group insurance, he was politically weak inside The Equitable, as in 1905 he had briefly favored James Hyde in the battle for the company's control.

After six months of work, the committee came up with a plan. Equitable would provide term insurance, with no savings component, on an "ordinary" level-premium basis for groups of at least 100 people at a 5 percent discount from the usual premiums. Costs would be controlled in three ways: by issuing a single policy for the entire group (rather than a policy for each member), by waiving medical examinations, and by selling most policies through salaried agents rather than commissioned agents. In May 1911, the Board of Directors approved the contract at the strong urging of Day, who had recently succeeded Morton as President. Ironically, the first modern group insurance contract was sold not to the company that had commissioned it but to another company. As negotiations with Montgomery Ward continued, the Pantasote Leather Co., of Passaic, New Jersey, signed on. Its treasurer, Eugenius Outerbridge, sat on Equitable's board and Insurance Committee and was so impressed by the contract that he had Pantasote purchase not only a group life policy but also a group health policy for its employees. Another five companies bought group contracts from The Equitable before Montgomery Ward finally signed up in 1912.

The insurance community agreed that group insurance was a sure disaster: "a lot of nothing" declared an Equitable lawyer. New York Life cautioned its employees that while the idea might seem theoretically sound, "Group insurance is the kind of star that it does not pay to shoot at." Many old-line insurance people blamed the idea on Day's short experience in the industry and what they scorned as his capitulation to the schemes of wild-eyed social reformers. Many of these criticisms had to do with the way group policies would be sold, for the system here was decidedly an alternative to the traditional one. For the first time in its history, Equitable was committing itself to sell insurance outside the agency force. Though Home Office employees were allowed to sell insurance, most marketing had always been through agents. Equitable

Pantasote hired priests to explain group insurance to workers.

had spent half a century building a high-commission sales force to sell relatively large, savings-intensive policies to middle- and upper-income individuals. Whether many agents really wanted to sell group insurance at the 10 percent commission schedules necessary to make the premiums attractive to companies — commissions one-fourth or less those of regular sales — was an open question. But there was a clear sense that simply by developing a product for alternative distribution, Equitable was engaging in heresy. Day (like Morton before him) already had tense relations with many agents, and group insurance only added to them. So while Equitable invented group insurance in America, internal opposition to sales outside the agency force by many (but by no means all) agents, general agents, and agency managers stalled the serious expansion of group insurance at Equitable for more than fifteen years.[6]

Another cause for alarm in the industry was that in eliminating medical examinations, the Society betrayed insurance values. The American Life Convention, the association of smaller, less well-capitalized insurers, claimed group insurance was "a menace to legal reserve life insurance," but William Graham argued that a checkup would be a waste of money and time; anybody healthy enough to

Actuaries did their work with mechanical calculators and key-punch cards. This photograph was taken in 1916.

hold down a job by definition had to be healthy enough to qualify for a life insurance policy. The dispute became public, with politicians, newspapers, and magazines joining the fray on the side of providing low-cost coverage for average working people on the simple, practical grounds that Graham proposed. "[Y]our pay check is the health certificate you need," editorialized the *Saturday Evening Post*.[7]

But Graham did have a medical screening test in mind. It was one not for the workers themselves but for the environment in which they labored. There was nothing new about insurers measuring environmental factors; they had long assigned risks according to residences and jobs, for example, by charging higher than usual premiums on policies sold to people who lived in swampy areas or served in the military. But after the turn of the century, the study of working environments had become extremely sophisticated. In 1903, the Actuarial Society of America published a compendium of mortality statistics for ninety-eight physical characteris-

tics and occupations, among them "height below 5 feet," "laborer," "has had gout," "wine or liquor seller, abstainer," "wine or liquor seller, non-abstainer," and every type of job around railroads. Using these data, actuaries developed risk expectations that raised or decreased the "rating," or the age against which the premiums were calculated. For instance, men who packed cement were rated ten years older than their chronological ages because of the clouds of dust involved that filled their lungs.[8]

To investigate work sites, Equitable set up its own Safety Engineering Department under Conservation Engineer Lew Russell Palmer, an electrical engineer and former all-American football player. He assembled safety records for every conceivable job and living area. As an early president of the National Safety Council, he advised railroad, automotive, and aviation engineers on improving safety in transportation. The environmental safety assumption was validated during the terrible 1918–19 influenza epidemic, when mortality rates among workers covered by group contracts were considerably lower than those of people covered by individual policies.

Other clients followed Pantasote and Montgomery Ward: Studebaker, the automobile manufacturer, with 10,000 employees; B. F. Goodrich, the tire maker, with 18,000; and the Union Pacific Railroad, with 35,000. By 1918, group insurance, which had inspired so much doubt only half a dozen years earlier, was so widely accepted that Equitable was facing stiff competition from several other insurers. Once, the Society even stimulated competition in order to open up a new territory: when Canada's insurance superintendent told the Home Office in 1919 that the Society could not sell group insurance there until a domestic company offered similar policies, Equitable invited some of Sun Life's actuaries down to New York for a crash seminar on the new product. Before long, Sun and Equitable were selling large group policies to Canadian corporations and Canadian subsidiaries of American businesses.

As the group insurance business expanded, three things became clear. First, the wide range of variables — including the safety of the workplace and the number and age of the workers — made the design of group life policies (and health policies that often accompanied them) a demanding and complicated exercise. One actuary who began working on group contracts in 1930, J. Henry Smith (later an Equitable President), remembered, "It was just catch-as-catch-can. Group insurance was truly developmental through that period of time. *Experimentally* developmental."[9]

Second, group insurance often successfully satisfied the businessman's need to assuage labor demands and improve workplace morale. In a speech to an insurance trade group, Eugenius Outerbridge, speaking from the point of view of management,

Lew R. Palmer, Equitable's safety expert (above center and below).

reported that group insurance satisfactorily dealt with what he called "an unexplained restlessness and constant shifting of men." Despite a relatively short work week and a program of paying bonuses, his company had suffered from a 35 percent annual turnover of its workforce. Then Pantasote decided to provide group policies. In order to educate the mostly immigrant Greek and Hungarian workers about group plans, Outerbridge had posters made in their languages and recruited priests to address workers' meetings. Still, the workers were apathetic; because the policies cost them nothing, they thought they must be worthless. Attitudes changed when the first check was issued to a worker who had broken his collarbone during a weekend baseball game. Waving the check, the man rushed out of the office into the factory yard and shouted that the company had indeed paid a $27.50 doctor's bill for an injury suffered on his own time. Within three years, Outerbridge reported, the factory's turnover rate was down to 15 percent. Other industries and other workers were not so accommodating, and their labor troubles often were not so easily settled, especially when unions were organizing; but group insurance did seem to have a settling effect on many labor-management conflicts.[10]

The third point about group insurance was that, through it, Equitable improved cash flow and its image at a time when both had been lagging. Harkening back to the old social service, missionary tradition that had been interrupted by the struggles of 1905, Equitable promoted itself and group insurance not just as sound business operations but as genuine expressions of the purpose of a mutual life insurance company. Group insurance policies, said Rosenfeld, were "justified in fullest measure as public service propositions." Cardinal James Gibbons of Baltimore endorsed Equitable's group policy for the Union Pacific Railroad as "the practical putting into effect of the principles of Christian charity." Equitable's advertisements carefully pursued these themes. One showed a factory in which an executive dressed in a suit hands an insurance policy to a worker wearing a shop apron; the caption reads, "Cooperation Pays." At around this time, between 1917 and 1919, the Society further enhanced its public image during World War I when it waived the usual prohibition against the payment of death benefits to men in battle, and helped finance the war effort by purchasing $90 million in U.S. and Canadian war bonds. The value of these efforts to restore Equitable's good reputation after the time of troubles could not be quantified, but it was important.[11]

From Equitable's first group policies in 1911, totaling $403,000 in coverage, the business blossomed industry-wide. During the war, the federal government provided group policies for the military and for wartime civilian employees. Other insurance companies followed the Society's lead. By 1925, several had sold a total of 12,000 policies with $4.2 billion in coverage. The competition was intense.

Rate wars lowered typical monthly premiums from $1.05 per $1,000 of coverage in 1911 to $.85 in 1914 and $.59 in 1921. Worried that rate wars would weaken the companies, the New York Insurance Department set minimum group premiums. In 1926 Equitable and fifteen other insurers formed a trade organization, called the Group Association, which set group insurance rates.

William J. Graham was the driving force behind group insurance at Equitable. Raised in the Midwest, he became an independent actuary and was sometimes called on by Woods to run seminars for his agents in Pittsburgh. After a stint as an actuary at Northwestern Mutual Life, Graham consulted midwestern insurance regulators conducting an independent review of the large companies at the time of the Armstrong investigation. Convinced that only the bad news was coming out of New York, he wrote a series of articles favorable to the companies that he collected in a book titled *The Romance of Life Insurance*. Rosenfeld recruited him to be an agency manager in Chicago and, in 1912, to come to New York. A strong-willed, brilliant, often arrogant salesman, Graham closed the agreements with Montgomery Ward and other big clients, including Standard Oil of New Jersey, whose business he brought to Equitable through a campaign that included a visit to John D. Rockefeller to discuss how group insurance improved human welfare. As Graham demonstrated his skills and jealously guarded his power, Rosenfeld was shunted aside to supervise the remains of the European business and, later, to supervise farm loans. In 1920, he left Equitable to go into the investment business.

Rosenfeld and Graham later had a furious quarrel that continued for decades over who was responsible for group insurance. In the early 1950's, George R. Durgan of Montgomery Ward, which had been the original client, heard

One of group's strongest proponents was Edward A. Woods (here with his staff), who helped free it from Home Office infighting.

that Graham was writing his memoirs and politely asked for some credit, although Graham was loath to give any. The truth is that Paul Morton and William Day laid the groundwork by having the vision to take Equitable in a new direction, Rosenfeld provided the crucial information and social conscience, Durgan defined the client's requirements, and Graham was the marketing genius.

Curiously, in the 1920's, the company that started group insurance lost its leadership position and even came close to getting out of the business altogether. The reason for this ambivalence was that many general agents and agency managers, and their representatives in the Home Office, could not reconcile themselves to a product that appeared to be competing with individual insurance and tak-

ing commissions out of their pockets. Yet some general agents from industrialized areas — most prominently Edward Woods — backed group insurance completely. They were certain that group insurance would make up in volume what it lost in first-year commissions, and that a group sale to a corporation would stimulate individual insurance sales to its employees. Yet their long-term vision was not shared by most agents.

The infighting had begun when group insurance was launched. President Day kept it under control until some of his best and most loyal assistants went off to duty during World War I. He suffered a heart attack in 1919, and while he was out of the Home Office the leadership vacuum was filled by two ambitious Vice-Presidents, J. V. E. Westfall, an auditor, and Alfred R. Horr, an accountant. They

Individual life insurance continued to be marketed using the traditional security theme.

jointly built their own empire by currying favor with the conservatives in the agency force. Graham, in his memoirs, described their attitude as thoroughly lacking in vision: "not looking for trouble, and not looking for opportunities that would mean more work, more care, and more responsibility." The head of the Agency Department, Frank H. Davis, had no interest in new products. "Our greatest problem between now and 1950," he declared, "is not so much to improve our product but to give wider distribution to a product already sufficiently perfected to serve human needs." When Day returned and discovered what Horr and

Westfall had been up to, he fired Horr. But Westfall remained and found a way to put group insurance under Davis, who dispatched Graham on a long assignment to Europe and raised group premiums to noncompetitive levels. In 1925, Equitable fell to a distant third place in group volume.[12]

Equitable Insurance in Force, 1899–1959
(in millions)

YEAR	INSURANCE IN FORCE	
	INDIVIDUAL	GROUP
1899	1,054	n/a
1909	1,335	n/a
1919	1,944	325
1929	5,403	1,357
1939	4,741	2,194
1949	7,381	6,698
1959	14,580	19,773

When Edward Woods learned that Equitable had lost a group insurance plan because its costs were twice those of other proposals, he came to New York, stormed into Day's office, and demanded to know what was going on. Day turned the problem over to his troubleshooter, Vice-President Thomas I. Parkinson, who had worked on the government's wartime insurance operation and saw a strong future in group insurance. At Parkinson's instigation in 1925, Graham was brought back from exile and restored to authority. Group insurance was further assured in 1927 when, at about the same time, Day chose Parkinson as his successor and the Woods Agency sold a policy to a steelworkers union local at a U.S. Steel mill near Pittsburgh. Four years later, Equitable group policies with a total face amount of $90 million were covering 58,000 U.S. Steel workers, and Parkinson was predicting that group insurance would outstrip individual insurance.

Varieties of standard group insurance began to appear slowly. Since the early days of group insurance, there had been speculation about providing pensions (or what insurers called group annuity contracts). The first corporate pension plan was created by American Express in 1875, and before long many railroads were using the idea to attract and keep talented employees (and, as with group insurance, to hold off unions). Although Equitable had a simple annuity plan for its officers, it was not enthusiastic about entering the field. In 1919, Equitable applied to the New York State Insurance Department for permission to write group annuities, but Graham had second thoughts and withdrew the application. Concerned about the actuarial problems of insuring a group of elderly retirees, he decided that the Society should limit its role to what he called the "social insurance service" of consulting corporations on the actuarial aspects of their self-insured plans. Interest at other companies also was sporadic until 1921, when the federal government revised the tax code to encourage pensions. That year, Metropolitan Life issued the first group annuity. The internal battle over group insurance did not encourage Equitable to follow suit.

Enter Edward Woods. In 1927, he asked for an Equitable group annuity plan for his agency to issue to agents and employees as a part of the upcoming fiftieth anniversary of the agency in 1930. After almost a year of work by two actuaries, the contract was approved by The Equitable's Board of Directors and the insurance department. (Unfortunately, its originator was not around to see it; Woods died at the age of sixty-two in November 1927.)[13]

Other agencies began to catch on to Woods's insight about group insurance. In 1931, the Society had over half the contracts written by the largest insurers. As the group insurance, health, and annuity business grew in the late 1920's and early 'thirties, Graham established an agent-training program. To help, he invited Gage Tarbell, by then an old man raising chickens and Guernsey cows in his hometown of Smithville Flats, to return to Equitable to impart some wisdom and, as Graham put it, "to help inspire Equitable agents [with his] indomitable energy and vigorous personality." Tarbell went back on the road once again, touring the country to visit agencies, and joining the top agents on an ocean cruise to Nova Scotia. Pausing briefly one day, Tarbell took Graham aside and gave him a piece of advice that seemed to summarize Equitable's phoenix-like recovery from the disaster of 1905: "Take advantage of your opportunities as they arise."[14]

"A workshop" William Day called the new Home Office across from Pennsylvania Station.
Its handsome lobby served as Equitable's auditorium.

CHAPTER X

PRESIDENT PARKINSON

B y 1920, only five years after moving into the new Equitable Building at 120 Broadway, the Home Office outgrew its space and spread out into the city in seven other buildings in Manhattan and Brooklyn. President William Day and the board agreed it was time to consolidate the administration in a new, company-owned headquarters. Day often spoke of Equitable's need for "moral fiber" and its "sacred trust," and his architectural expression of that ethic was simple and pragmatic: "What we need is a workshop that can be expanded to meet the Society's requirements for a long period of years."[1]

The workshop's very location, three miles from Wall Street, at 393 Seventh Avenue at 32nd Street, was itself symbolic of the Society's move away from high finance. So was the delicacy, compared with the pile of marble downtown, of the new twenty-six-story building across the street from Pennsylvania Station. The only touch of luxury was the lobby in which, under a high-vaulted ceiling engraved with gilded renderings of Equitable's protective goddess symbol, there lay a set of white marble steps. Yet even that was functional, for the lobby was the company's auditorium, and the steps served as Day's podium when he addressed the staff. Consistent with his vision of a more modest Equitable, Day decided that the building would not be named after the Society. (Today the building is called 11 Penn Plaza; the handsome lobby has not been altered.) As for the second Equitable Building on Henry Hyde's original site at 120 Broadway, the Society eventually sold its interest to John Hancock and a real estate company, though for many years the great structure housed an Equitable agency.

Another symbolic gesture was that when the Society moved to the new building in 1925, it left the statue of Henry Hyde behind in a storeroom. His kind of leadership seemed as out of style as an intimate relationship with an investment bank. But after ten years in exile, the statue was retrieved and placed in the new building's lobby by order of Day's successor, Thomas I. Parkinson. The move made sense. There were similarities between Hyde and the equally energetic and domineering Parkinson, who also tied Hyde's record for longest tenure as The Equitable's President, twenty-five years.

Born in Philadelphia in 1881, Parkinson went straight from high school to the University of Pennsylvania Law School, where, although one of the youngest members of his class, he graduated with honors and was twice elected class secretary. He started out at a Philadelphia law firm, one of whose most important clients was a 150-year-old life insurance company for Episcopal clergymen. As he worked on its legal matters, Parkinson found insurance appealing. But when he approached one of its officers and asked about being appointed an agent, the man brushed him off: "You won't do, not the type," Parkinson remembered. Perhaps he was referring to Parkinson's Irish heritage and Roman Catholicism, but the pugnacious Parkinson delighted in repeating the brusque rejection long after he had became Equitable's Chief Executive Officer.[2]

Though seemingly ornate today, the 393 Seventh Avenue building was restrained for the 1920's.

After moving to New York City, Parkinson went into private and then public practice. He advised the committee investigating the notorious Triangle Shirt-Waist Co. fire of 1911, in which 146 workers were killed, and worked on the resulting stringent new fire, building, and labor laws. His specialty was the demanding science of drafting laws. He served as counsel to several important legislative committees and was appointed the first official draftsman of the U.S. Senate. At Columbia University Law School, he taught courses and presided over the legislative drafting research department, which worked on workmen's compensation statutes and a new charter for New York City. His legal work introduced him to life insurance during World War I, when, as a major on the staff of the army's judge advocate general, he drafted the legislation for the military's first group insurance plan.

Parkinson caught President Day's eye in 1920 when he was doing consulting work for Equitable. Day — himself a former government lawyer — hired Parkinson to serve as a troubleshooter within the Society. Parkinson continued teaching at Columbia Law School and served as its acting dean in 1924–25, but his time was increasingly taken up with some of Equitable's most intractable and nagging dilemmas. Parkinson's first assignment was to close up Equitable's business in central Europe. Although foreign agencies had ceased writing new business, many policies remained in force. The postwar inflation (so steep that Equitable spent more on postage stamps for letters to foreign policyholders than it earned on premiums) led the Society to decide to sell off all European assets and policies and recover its deposits in government securities. In 1921, Parkinson traveled under harsh conditions to Germany, Hungary, and Austria, where he bought up thousands of policies and recovered almost $5 million worth of securities that Equitable had left on deposit. (The only target to elude Parkinson was a packet of railroad bonds worth $100,000, which eventually surfaced in a bank in Hamburg after the next world war.) After he liberated $2.2 million from one bank, an Equitable vice-president cabled him, "SNAPPY WORK TOMMY YOU ARE A PEACH."[3]

Back home, Parkinson was nominally assigned as Vice-President for Foreign Agencies but spent much of his time on legal matters, the most significant of which was completing the Society's mutualization. Although Equitable had been functioning as a mutual since 1918, the New York Insurance Department refused final approval until the Society changed certain relatively small features of its corporate structure and bylaws. Negotiations became so unproductive that Parkinson retained Charles Evans Hughes, then in private practice, as Equitable's outside counsel with the hope that his reputation would sway the department toward a compromise. The tactic worked. Some differences were settled, others were set aside for later negotiation, and the Society finally became a legal mutual in 1925.

As he labored on these assignments, Parkinson gained influence inside the company. In 1922, he impressed actuaries by convincing Day to drop the costly disability plan. Three years later, he pleased Edward Woods by saving group insurance from destruction. In 1926, Day appointed him as ranking Vice-President. Day, worried about his health, retired on short notice in October 1927 and recommended that Parkinson be named his successor. He assured a director:

"[H]e is not only a man of the greatest uprightness and of brilliant legal attainments, but is a very remarkable executive also. All these qualities are enhanced by his physical strength and his youthful energy...." The board promptly confirmed Day's choice. Day died six months later.[4]

Parkinson's election stimulated an exodus of officers who had opposed group insurance, including J. V. E. Westfall and Frank Davis, many of them for Penn Mutual Life Insurance Company. Parkinson set to work improving his strained relations with the field force. He expanded sales goals, enlarged the force, and often spoke before agents' groups. The agents loved him. Although initially shy about public speaking, he came to enjoy the spotlight. Short, stocky, with a bubbling personality and twinkling eyes, a compelling voice, a quick mind, and a sharp memory, he dominated all situations in which he was thrown. A capable manager, he solidified his power by replacing many of the departed officers with lawyers who had been his students at Columbia. His chief assistants were men in his mold: Glenn McHugh, the head of real estate, was once described as having "persistence almost inhuman"; of Sterling Pierson, the general counsel, it was said, "His hobby is work."[5]

Equitable was in such good shape when Parkinson took over that one director, Joy Morton, warned him that, given the inevitability of economic cycles, hard times surely must be at hand. So they were; in 1929 there began the Great Depression. Parkinson greeted bad times with apparent equanimity. At the end of 1930, in a brave speech titled "Insurance Knows No Depression," he announced, "I am ready to take any kind of cut in volume, if by doing so better service may be rendered to the people of the country." From the field came cries of anguish over lost commissions and dried-up business. A group of agents in the

Thomas I. Parkinson around the time he became President. He steered Equitable into a range of new investments, some of them bold for their time.

Woods Agency complained that while policies with a face value of $25,000 or more had been usual in the 'twenties, during the depression a $10,000 case "was almost the occasion for an agency celebration."[6]

    Worried about runs on insurance companies, the federal government in 1933 banned policy loans (other than to pay premiums) as well as cashing in policies. Parkinson established a $78 million reserve against potential losses, but even that amount was not enough; several programs were losing so much money that he had to end them. The worst failures were in Equitable's large home mortgage and farm loan businesses. Due to the depression and drought, in late 1933 one-quarter of all the residential mortgages and half its farm loans were behind on interest payments. The once very successful Home Purchase Plan of insured

Glenn McHugh.

mortgages was terminated, but the farm loan program was carried on. Between 1931 and 1938, the market value of the Society's farm mortgages fell from almost $200 million to $71 million, and it foreclosed on loans to 6,000 farms with a total of 1.1 million acres. State and federal laws protected most debtors from quick foreclosure. Equitable's special relief committee ruled on defaults on a case-by-case basis, usually leniently. When the Society's agent for handling farm loans in the plains states failed, Equitable quickly created its own field force to negotiate with banks (many of which were themselves failing), farmers, tenants, and receivers, as well as to maintain properties and buildings acquired through foreclosure. As the drought ended and the New Deal introduced liberal government farm loans, Equitable rebuilt its agricultural mortgage program.

Like Henry Hyde before him, Parkinson thrived in challenging times. He roamed from problem to problem, asserting himself (sometimes dogmatically) with a mastery of technical details and a ferocious competitiveness, which even his most self-confident directors were hesitant to challenge. As a lawyer, he took special interest in handling complex legal problems. In the early 1930's, 850 policyholders filed suits challenging the value placed by Equitable on insurance policies sold in pre-Revolutionary Russia. The Society's lawyer, John W. Davis, advised Parkinson to offer a settlement, but Parkinson rejected compromise, angrily muttering, "I often feel and at moments like this I express concern over compromising and its effects on the mettle of the Bar." By 1944, Davis had steered most of the cases to satisfying ends in the courts, but the remaining eighty-three suits were fought stubbornly by the plaintiffs until Davis finally convinced Parkinson to settle for $15,000. Parkinson's daring had paid off, for New York Life's settlements in similar cases had come to millions of dollars. In another instance of Parkinson's legal decisiveness, in 1944, after the Supreme Court (in *U.S. v. South-Eastern Underwriters*) had reversed the seventy-five year-old rule laid down in *Paul* v. *Virginia* that interstate insurance sales were exempt from federal oversight, within a week he had a proposal for legislation to return regulatory control of insurance to the states. In 1945, Congress substantially wrote the *Paul* rule into law in the McCarran-Ferguson Act.[7]

But it was in the area of investments where Parkinson devoted an unusual amount of attention and energy. Like his legal strategy, his investment program was contrarian, controversial, and often successful. Equitable needed a minimum net investment yield of 3 percent and was easily meeting that need during the 1920's. During the early years of the Great Depression, the Society's yield plummeted by more than one-third to just over $3\frac{1}{2}$ percent. But in time, because the market for new bonds had dried up, many corporations were forced to offer higher rates on their loans, and this helped Equitable and the other big insurance companies. In 1938, Charles W. Dow, the manager of Equitable's Industrial Securities Investment Department, began a $650 million program of loans to sixty industrial companies, most of them through private placements of corporate bonds.

The Equitable took its own path concerning investments in railroads, many of which were going through reorganization and even receivership. The conventional wisdom among many investors was to avoid railroads altogether, but beginning in 1938 Parkinson went his own way. The Society became the largest creditor of four of the largest lines in the country, including the Pennsylvania and the Atchison, Topeka & Santa Fe. When criticized for these investments a decade later, Parkinson snapped back that most of them had showed profits: "I said profits and I mean profits in the till."[8]

World War II transformed the investment environment in two ways — one a setback for Equitable, the other a success — that largely determined the Society's investment policies for two decades.

The setback was the collapse of government bond interest rates. During World War II, large quantities of low-interest war bonds were sold in seven Liberty Bond drives to help finance the two-front war. Sixty percent of the war's expense was covered by the sale of these securities. To support the bond market, the

U.S. Treasury Department continued a program, begun during the depression, of subsidizing bond prices by promising to buy war bonds back at the original price. By "pegging" bond prices at high levels, the government also pegged interest rates at low levels, for prices and yields go in opposite directions. And the yields on war bonds were low — about 3 percent for long-term bonds and under 2 percent for short-term bonds. As a regulated, mutual financial enterprise dependent on public opinion, Equitable had no alternative to buying war bonds in large quantities and, by the end of the war, bought $2 billion worth.

The insurance industry's holdings of government bonds increased from 15 percent of assets in 1940 to 46 percent in 1945. War bonds were available in a range of maturities. Most insurers bought relatively high-yielding long-term bonds, but again Equitable took its own path, this time by concentrating on low-yielding short-term bonds. Parkinson and his advisors were willing to accept the lower yield in exchange for flexibility. Anticipating that interest rates would rise after the war, they wanted to be free to move funds quickly into new investments. Given the current low yields, this bet on the future seemed safe enough. Unfortunately for Equitable, the government continued to peg bond prices after the war, justifying the policy as necessary to stimulate the economy. Between 1946 and 1951, yields on short-term government bonds dropped below the wartime levels to less than 1½ percent. Other insurers still had large investments in high-yielding long-term bonds, but Equitable was forced to scramble for attractive returns. It needed at least 3 percent; in 1946 it got only 2½ percent.

If pegging was a setback, the growth of Equitable's pension business was the success story of the war years. This occurred because of another wartime policy. In an anti-inflation

step, the federal government in 1942 imposed a war-time freeze on salaries and an 80 percent tax on excess profits (as defined by governmental commissions). To trim their tax exposure, companies and individuals searched for tax-deductible expenses. After Congress passed a statute confirming tax deductions for employers making deposits in qualified pension plans and granting tax deferrals for individuals who were members of them, money began to pour into group and individual annuity contracts and pension plans. Between 1938 and 1946, the number of corporate pension plans grew from 515 to 7,000. Equitable, one of only a handful of insurance companies in the field, saw its group and individual annuity business triple, and by the end of the war the Society had one-third of all group annuity contracts. This success produced a windfall of investable money; the difficulty was finding a place to invest it profitably in the poor economic climate. Equitable's in-house legal advisor to the Society's investment departments, Warner H. Mendel, would later speak of "the compulsion to broaden our investment base induced by large considerations received from group and individual pension business between 1940 and 1946." The problem was how to build that base in light of the pegging of interest rates.[9]

One investment area that Parkinson would not consider was the stock market, despite attempts by regulators to persuade the insurance companies to invest in common stocks. As yields from government bonds fell, New York Insurance Superintendent Shelby Cullom Davis had urged the life insurance industry to "break its bondage to bonds" and look to common stocks, which insurers were permitted by insurance law to purchase until they comprised 2½ percent of assets. Davis even hinted that he would be willing to increase the limit. But Parkinson and other

*This French poster from the late-nineteenth century shows an entire city of
Equitable Buildings from around the world.*

Hyde's Home Office at 120 Broadway, shown here in the 1890's.

THE CITY OF NEW YORK - SHOWING THE BUILDING OF
THE EQUITABLE LIFE ASSURANCE SOCIETY OF THE UNITED STATES.
Nº 120 BROADWAY.

A Currier & Ives print from the 1870's shows the giant Home Office
at the hub of New York's business district.

Equitable's third Home Office, near Pennsylvania Station at 393 Seventh Avenue,
was the company's headquarters from 1924 to 1961.

insurance executives attacked Davis' proposal as irresponsible, even vaguely sinful. The memory of the wild speculation in the 'twenties, followed by the terrible stock market crash of 1929, had convinced many Americans that common stocks were by definition unsafe. In addition, because the value of common stocks varied from day to day and their dividends from year to year, insurance people worried that equities could not satisfy the traditional obligation of a life insurer to match assets against the known liabilities of guaranteed death benefits and projected dividend payments. Since those liabilities were long term and set, bonds of medium to long maturity with fixed yields were, with real estate investments, considered to provide the most predictable match.[10]

With the uncertainty of the stock market and a weak government bond market, Equitable's postwar investment policy was limited mainly to real estate and corporate securities, both large, growing areas hungry for capital. Between 1945 and 1948, the company engaged in a mammoth shift of its investment portfolio into those areas. While the insurance industry as a whole pruned 14 percent of its government bonds, the Society eliminated 60 percent, or $1 billion worth. In March 1947 alone, Equitable turned in $200 million worth of U.S. Treasury notes. This extraordinary shift in policy would be termed by a student of insurance company investments as "a concentrated disposal program." But a later head of Equitable's investments, Grant Keehn, would look on it more accurately: since the proceeds were immediately transferred into new investments, the Parkinson program, Keehn said, was nothing less than "the great conversion."[11]

What Parkinson brought about was the transformation of Equitable's investment portfolio. The $1 billion reaped from the sale of government bonds, plus another $750 million derived from group annuities and other prod-

The first insured mortgage was called the Home Purchase Plan.

ucts and from sales of other assets, in the late 1940's were invested, sometimes in large amounts and innovative ways, in securities, real estate, railroad rolling stock, and mortgages. The nation's demand for large amounts of capital was great, and — at a time before the appearance of large pension plans — the main sources of that capital were The Equitable and the other big, old mutual life insurance companies that, over the previous ninety or hundred years, had accumulated billions of dollars in assets requiring investment outlets.

And so between 1946 and 1950, Equitable, in its search for healthier returns than its weak portfolio of government bonds could provide, energetically threw itself into a wide variety of large, dramatic, and sometimes risky projects. In so doing, around that time the Society ventured into several new territories. It became the country's largest provider of farm loans and residential mortgages. It built

The Home Purchase Plan was succeeded by AHO in the 1940's.

a major airline and saved a Texas wildcatter's empire. Through the technique of leaseback financing, which it innovated, it was a major source of funds for railroads and shopping centers. And the Equitable also rebuilt a major city, Pittsburgh.

Equitable became the most important private lender of farm and residential loans by consciously targeting the dominant institutions — in farms, the federal government; in mortgages, local banks — and aggressively selling against them with a more flexible line of products.

While the Society's Farm Mortgage Department could not match the interest rates offered by government land banks, which were subsidized by the U.S. Treasury, beginning in the early 1940's the department did provide more flexible, liberal terms than it, the government, and other lenders had previously made available. Its new contracts allowed farmers to make payments "in any

amount at any time if funds were from farm income" and to make prepayments into a reserve fund on which they could call if they had trouble in the future. Equitable also took ingenious advantage of its need and ability, as an insurance company, to make long-term investments. When farmers began to ask for longer terms than the five- to ten-year loans that banks wrote, Equitable negotiated cooperative arrangements with local commercial banks. The banks covered the first short term of the loan, provided the necessary on-site service and approvals, and shared fees and commissions with Equitable, which then picked up the next twenty- to thirty-year term. In this way, Equitable got the business and forged close relationships with the banks. It was a powerfully effective program. "There is nothing a federal agency has to offer that we cannot do," boasted an Illinois banker who worked with Equitable. Between 1947 and 1967, the government's share of the farm-loan business dropped from 40 to 25 percent while insurers' increased from 15 to 25 percent.[12]

Called the Approved Mortgage Plan, the Equitable's farm-loan system was copied by some insurance companies; others, realizing that they could not compete, withdrew from the farm-loan field altogether. Equitable's investment in farm loans more than tripled between 1946 and 1959, from $61 million to $193 million, an increase almost five times faster than the growth of other insurers' farm programs. By 1967, Equitable had $747 million in outstanding farm loans.

While it was developing into the leading insurance company in farm loans, Equitable also was becoming the largest insurer to provide residential mortgages through its new home-mortgage program, Assured Home Ownership Mortgage (AHO). It was unique to The Equitable. Revived in the ashes of the Home Purchase Plan in 1940, AHO became one of the Society's very largest investment areas; by 1958, The Equitable's commitment to residential mortgages totaled $1.7 billion.

The appeal of mortgages as investments was simple: at a time when a government bond yielded, at best, 3 percent, bank mortgage rates on residential homes ran far higher, at 4 or even 5 percent. As millions of soldiers and sailors returned home from the war to raise families, the demand for homes blossomed. If The Equitable could devise a way to offer services to homeowners that banks could not provide (in the same way that it had undercut the federal government's dominance of farm loans), it stood to reap healthy investment returns. And if insurance sales could be tied in to the mortgages, the income from premiums might be substantial.

The AHO system accomplished all that. It was devised by Glenn McHugh, head of Equitable's real estate operation, the City Mortgage Department, whose field force consisted of the salaried representatives managing the empire of farms. In AHO, a City Mortgage representative issued a mortgage to buy or refinance a residence at a nationwide rate as much as 1 percent below those offered by most banks. The condition was that the mortgagee also buy a whole-life insurance policy for the amount of the mortgage that was sold by an Equitable agent. The insurance policy guaranteed the loan while providing additional funds, through inside buildup, to pay off the loan before its contracted maturity. The total outlay by the mortgagee was about the same as that for a bank mortgage. The mandatory tie-in allowed commissions for agents and attractive returns for Equitable (so long, of course, as its mortgage rates were higher than market interest rates). The tie-in infuriated many banks that lost mortgage business to Equitable, and also irritated some state insurance regulators,

yet it survived legal tests. Of other insurance companies, only Prudential had anything like it, and its tie-in life insurance policy was a term contract with no inside savings component to be applied against the mortgage principal.

AHO succeeded because Equitable offered extremely competitive interest rates. Laurens Bruno, a career Equitable agent and agency manager, looked back on a time in the 1950's when Equitable was offering a national rate of just under 5 percent:

> *In metropolitan New York, the prevailing bank rate was 5–5$\frac{1}{2}$ percent and AHO was a really good deal for the homeowner. In Detroit and Chicago, where the bank rates were 6 percent, it was only necessary to make a reasonably good presentation, and the homeowner had an offer he couldn't refuse. On the west coast, interest rates were 7 percent and the plan was a virtual giveaway.*

California, which had the nation's highest interest rates, accounted for more than one-fourth of new AHO business.[13]

The best-selling product in the Society's history since the tontine, AHO was a success both as an investment and as an insurance contract sold by agents. Between 1946 and 1959, the City Mortgage Department expanded from $78 million (4 percent of Equitable's assets) to $2 billion (19 percent). The face value of AHO-related insurance contracts meanwhile increased from just over 2 percent of Equitable's insurance sales to 17 percent; the 2,000 percent growth rate was five times larger than that of any of the company's other products. By 1959, there were second thoughts about AHO as the advantageous spread in interest rates ended, but since it had become the foundation of many agents' careers, the debate over terminating it (as we will see in chapter 14) was long and divisive.

One of the more volatile investments of the 1950's was TWA.

While mortgages were the fastest-growing investment area after World War II, Equitable also continued to finance businesses aggressively, sometimes in unusual ways. Among the investments in the 'forties were $100 million to Gulf Oil, $90 million to R. J. Reynolds Tobacco, $75 million to American Tobacco, $40 million to Trans World Airlines, and hundreds of millions of dollars to railroads staggering out of the Great Depression.

Because Equitable needed higher interest rates than most insurers, which still had large inventories of high-yielding war bonds, Parkinson was hungry for corporate finance business. Yet as an anecdote about one of these large loans shows, he could not appear to be too hungry and risk-prone. In 1947, when Gulf Oil was expanding into Kuwait, its president, Colonel J. F. Drake, came to New York prepared to borrow $50 million each from Equitable and Metropolitan Life. Parkinson offered better terms, so Drake gave all of the business to the Society. Anticipating criticism for stealing business from a competitor, Sterling Pierson, Parkinson's chief aide, explained to the New York Insurance Superintendent that the decision was Drake's: "I can say to you very frankly that Mr. Parkinson went far out of his way to indicate to Colonel Drake that we had no selfish interest in taking the whole deal."[14]

Under Parkinson, Equitable also became the largest financier of a dynamic but problematic new business, the commercial airline industry. When C. R. Smith, president of Equitable's client American Airlines, said that insurance companies "should have credit for their major part in bringing about the jet revolution" in commercial airplanes, he was referring first to Equitable, which sometimes was the only insurer to participate in an airline's issue of bonds or preferred stock. By 1964, the Society held almost one-fifth of the total funded indebtedness of U.S. airlines — $279 million in all, or about one-tenth Equitable's industrial bond portfolio.[15]

Equitable's first big airline financing was a $40 million loan to Trans World Airlines in 1945. A year later, despite a pilots' strike and the grounding of faulty planes, it provided $20 million to American Airlines. While the Society backed other airlines, including Eastern and Braniff, its closest — and, at the same time, most trying — relationship with an airline was with TWA. Between 1945 and 1960, the Society made or revised loan agreements with TWA some ninety times, often in reaction to recurring crises at the airline (some of them stimulated by its unpredictable majority stockholder, Howard Hughes). In 1947, Parkinson became so concerned about TWA that he forced the airline's owners to agree to put the airline's stock into a voting trust if TWA failed to meet its repayment schedule. Although the trust was never needed, a flurry of lawsuits in the 'sixties eventually forced Hughes out.

Another flamboyant creditor of Equitable's was Glenn McCarthy, a Texas oilman whose risk-laden, energetic, and often successful

Howard Hughes.

Another difficult client was Texas wildcatter Glenn McCarthy.

Supervising the McCarthy loans at Equitable was Warner H. Mendel. A brilliant Columbia Law School alumnus who was crippled by polio, he had come to Parkinson's personal staff in 1933 and then moved on to become Equitable's legal counsel for investments. Once the weaknesses in the McCarthy empire were unveiled, Mendel browbeat the wildcatter into handing control to Equitable. The hotheaded McCarthy took this so poorly that he physically threatened Mendel. The stock was placed under the control of Equitable officers through a voting trust, and Mendel became president of the oil company and vice-president of the hotel. For several years he split his time between New York and Houston until Equitable sold off the Shamrock and the oil operation.

B esides direct loans, Equitable engaged in real estate development both as promoter and in a new type of financing, which it pioneered, called the sale and lease or, more commonly, leaseback.

Since well before the Armstrong laws, New York insurance companies had been prohibited from owning property for investment outside of their own offices, although the rule was eased slightly in 1938, when New York first allowed insurers to invest in low- and middle-income apartment houses. In the 1940's, Equitable built two apartment complexes in Brooklyn and the Bronx, Clinton Hill and Fordham Hill, that totaled sixteen buildings and 2,400 apartments. After long delays caused by wartime shortages of building materials, the projects, which eventually cost $28 million, were completed in the early 'fifties and sold at modest profits. Equitable also began work on a small housing project in Cedar Rapids, Iowa, where, after the collapse of agriculture during the depression, it owned thousands of acres of unused farmland; but this development produced only a few houses before it was ended.

style of doing business was summarized in his sobriquet, King of the Wildcatters. In the late 1930's, Equitable made a half-dozen loans to the McCarthy Oil & Gas Corporation with the proviso (insisted on by Parkinson) that an oil engineer be retained to keep a close watch on McCarthy's activities. McCarthy made some oil strikes and, helped by more loans from Equitable, created a successful petroleum and chemical operation. He borrowed more than $30 million from Equitable against his businesses to develop real estate. The centerpiece was the huge Shamrock Hotel in Houston, which featured a swimming pool the size of a small lake. This elaborate project began to unravel when Equitable's oil engineer discovered that McCarthy had significantly overvalued the security he had provided for the loans.

Fordham Hill, one of Equitable's first apartment complexes.

In 1946, Safeway Stores, a grocery chain based on the West Coast, came to Equitable for loans to free up its capital for expansion. Safeway asked McHugh, at Equitable, to buy their properties outright and then lease them back. This was illegal at the time. Parkinson, despite weak support by the insurance industry, convinced the Insurance Department in 1946 to allow insurers to own a limited range of commercial real estate for investment purposes. In 1947, Equitable invested almost $25 million in a long list of leaseback projects, including twenty-one Safeway stores, several Sears Roebuck and Sun-Ray Drug stores, the Merchandise Mart in Chicago, Filene's in Boston, and Bonwit Teller, Alexander's, and Macy's in New York City. Sometimes Equitable purchased only the land under the store — for example, the property under New York's flagship Bonwit Teller — and rented it back; often it bought the land and the building itself for leaseback. Before long, the Society expanded into baseball stadiums, theaters, shopping centers, hospitals, service stations, and factories. In 1954, it financed almost half of Conrad Hilton's $111 million acquisition of the Statler chain of ten hotels. The leaseback technique also was used by Equitable to provide financing for railroads strapped for cash at just the time, during the Korean War, when they were in demand to expand their fleets of freight cars to carry military supplies. The Society paid $130 million to purchase 18,850 freight cars and 207 diesel locomotives, which it then leased to six railroads. Although Equitable had helped the railroads out of their problems in the 1890's and 1930's, few people could have anticipated that the Society would itself own a locomotive, much less almost 19,000 pieces of rolling stock.

As striking as these investment initiatives and innovations were, the biggest and most dramatic investment made by Parkinson involved real estate in a city that had long played a crucial role in The Equitable's history. This was the reconstruction of downtown Pittsburgh in the $150 million Gateway Center project, which came to be called Pittsburgh's Renaissance.

"Our Dear Old Smokey Pittsburgh," as Andrew Carnegie had called the city, was in trouble, and the famous Golden Triangle at the confluence of the Allegheny, Monongahela, and Ohio Rivers was deeply tarnished. In the words of a local journalist, by the late 1930's it was "an unmanageable assortment of railroad trestles, freight yards, warehouses, manufacturing and secondary businesses, third-class taverns and rooming houses, and 'skid row' streets" — all this blackened with industrial soot and occasionally knee-deep in mud after floods swept down the rivers. An officer in the agency that would rebuild the city with Equitable's assistance, the Allegheny Conference on Community Development, did

Equitable used the leaseback to finance railroads.

not overstate the problem when he said, "In the mid twentieth century the eyes of the country were upon this city as it sought to rid itself of smoke, floods, and physical ugliness."[16]

In the early 'forties, local businessmen and politicians, convinced that the deterioration was dragging down the entire region, began to talk among themselves about the possibility of a downtown redevelopment. Led by an unusual tandem of very different men who between them had a lock on political and economic power in the city — Richard King Mellon, the patrician patriarch of the banking and oil family, and Mayor David Lawrence, one of the great old-time city bosses — the city's business and civic elite formed the Allegheny Conference. To bring pressure on the city and state governments to pass clean-air laws, the conference organized public protests in which its members walked through the streets in gas masks and wrote "Smoke Must Go!" on city buses. After pushing an urban redevelopment law through the state legislature, it began the radical redevelopment project by tearing down ninety-three buildings on twenty-three acres in downtown Pittsburgh and building anew. Because there were no federal or state urban renewal funds at that time, the enterprise would have to be funded entirely by the private sector. Enthusiasm for renewal increased in the spring of 1946 when the old station for the Wabash and Pacific Railroad (which had been founded by George Gould, Equitable's suitor of half a century earlier) caught on fire, crumbled into a wreck, and lay smoldering while the property insurance companies debated liability. That embarrassment propelled a delegation of Allegheny Conference leaders east to New York in search of major financing. While the Mellons and other leading families had donated land and money, the project would require substantial institutional backing, and that meant going to one of the big life insurance companies.

On July 8, 1946, four discouraged representatives of the Allegheny Conference were standing on a Manhattan street corner after having been turned down by their first candidate. One of the men, Wallace Richards, the conference's secretary, remembered that he and Thomas I. Parkinson were fellow members of an association of successful people born in Pennsylvania. They took a cab to The Equitable and, by exploiting the Pennsylvania connection, soon found themselves in Parkinson's office. Parkinson had hoped to build apartments in Pennsylvania but had been stopped by a state law banning insurers from developing real estate. Now, after the delegation told him of their hopes, he said that if the law could be changed, he would be open to developing apartment buildings. The proposal fit not only his need for large, potentially fruitful investments but also his appreciation of the publicity value of serving as an agent of social progress. And, of course, Equitable had enjoyed a firm relationship with Pittsburgh since 1880, through investments like the recent $100 million loan to the Mellons' Gulf Oil and through the great Woods Agency, which had placed tens of thousands of Equitable life or group insurance policies or

David Lawrence and Arthur Van Buskirk at a groundbreaking.

Pittsburgh's Golden Triangle in the 1940's was a pile of rusted railroad tracks and skid rows.

mortgages with Pittsburgh citizens. It seemed appropriate to cement the relationship with an effort to revitalize the city. As one of Parkinson's successors, James Oates, would later say, "There is a connection between the investment by the people of Pittsburgh in Equitable insurance, and the use of those funds for the good of the community."[17]

Gateway Center was Parkinson's great act of *noblesse oblige*. It was his pet project, and — like Henry Hyde with one of his buildings — he demanded total control over it. He and his personal assistants conducted most of the planning in conjunction with the chairman of the Allegheny Conference, Arthur B. Van Buskirk, a high official in the Mellon interests who soon was elected to The Equitable's board. Because Parkinson was so deeply

involved, the project moved along rapidly and at times daringly. Pittsburghers later would speak with awe of several tough decisions — "leaps of faith," local newspapers called them — by Parkinson that pulled the project over what had seemed impossibly high hurdles. For example, Parkinson decided that Equitable would buy all the land and be sole developer of the entire project, office buildings as well as apartments in a total of eight new buildings to be built over several years. It was a vast commitment; the initial three buildings were projected to cost $40 million and had 1.1 million square feet of office space, yet no tenants had been signed up. Still, Parkinson insisted on going ahead and signed many contracts. True to his optimism, nine Pittsburgh companies made commitments. Two of them,

Financed by The Equitable and built between 1950 and 1969, Gateway Center transformed the city.

Westinghouse Electric and the Mellon National Bank, had long, close relations with Equitable. Another tenant was the Woods Agency, whose agency manager, Lawrence C. Woods, Jr., a friend of Richard King Mellon's, served both on the Allegheny Conference and on the board of the Pittsburgh Regional Planning Association and sometimes acted as a go-between.[18]

Parkinson's aplomb seemed limitless. When an Equitable director, George V. McLaughlin, protested that the project violated a New York law banning insurers from committing an excess of funds to a single investment, the former law professor explained that what looked like one project was in reality three developments, since each building was a distinct legal entity. When negotiations over

the lease contracts were slowed to a halt by a nitpicking Equitable lawyer, Parkinson quickly replaced him with someone more flexible. When the original rents turned out to be too low, Parkinson went to Richard King Mellon and asked for an increase. When lawsuits challenging the legality of the whole project held up the demolition of the ninety-three existing buildings on the property, Parkinson instructed the authority to go ahead and knock down the buildings anyway. As for the choice of builder, Parkinson decided to retain, on a cost-plus basis and without competing bids, the same developer and contractor with whom he had worked on the Brooklyn and Bronx projects, City Investing Corp. and Starett Brothers and Eken. McLaughlin protested loudly. Some policyholders filed suits against the project; all were dismissed, although the most stubborn of them hung on until 1966.

Such was Parkinson's personal involvement that the printed program for the banquet at the time of the groundbreaking in 1950 carried his photograph and the caption "A Great Project Needs a Great Builder." The ceremonial dirt was dug by twenty-two shovel-wielding children who had Equitable policies. The first three buildings in the Gateway Center, completed early in 1954, were cruciform towers that seemed revolutionary to most viewers. If some architectural critics thought them bland, it was because, due to Korean War shortages, the specified nickel-alloy stainless steel had to be replaced by a chrome alloy of irregular sheen, which gave the buildings' exteriors a checkerboard appearance. Over the next fifteen years, Equitable put up another six buildings at a cost of over $100 million. Some architects had hoped for a uniform style throughout the center, but the diversity remains exciting, although the visual focus of the Golden Triangle has shifted to the taller, more modern buildings built in the city's "Renaissance II" development in the late 1970's and early 'eighties. (One of the livelier stories about the Gateway project concerned architects. A leader of the Allegheny Conference was Edgar Kauffman, head of Pittsburgh's largest department store and owner of a dramatic rural house, Fallingwater, designed by Frank Lloyd Wright. Kauffman wanted Wright to design the twenty-acre park on the point near Gateway. Unfortunately, Wright's preliminary plans showed an ugly combination of spires and doughnut-shaped buildings and little space for people. Kauffman was so embarrassed that he hid the plans under his desk.)

If the critics were correct about anything concerning the Gateway Center, it was their prediction of financial problems. Parkinson's projections of a 4 percent net yield and an occupancy rate of 95 percent proved excessively sanguine. The demand for office space was not as great as expected, rents were relatively high, and overhead was large because much undeveloped land had to be carried on the books. There was some discussion in the mid 'fifties, after Parkinson's departure from Equitable, about pulling out, but the Society instead sold some of the land to the state and to a local telephone company, leased a large plot to Conrad Hilton Hotels to build an 800-room hotel (financed largely by Equitable), and constructed a three-deck underground garage. The Gateway Center finally was out of the red in 1958, but the net return did not exceed 3 percent until 1960, when Building 4 was completed and Equitable's investment reached $91 million. That year work started on an office building for both IBM and U.S. Steel. The last buildings to be completed were an apartment complex called Gateway Towers, a medical center, and finally, in 1969, an office for Westinghouse. By then the Society's investment totaled approximately $150 million (almost 40 percent of the real estate portfolio), from which it was earning 6 percent.

Although Parkinson was properly criticized for personally leading Equitable into an overconcentration of its assets in one project, the Gateway Center was widely defended as a visionary commitment and the sort of worthwhile project that could be undertaken only by a large mutual insurance company, with its large assets and blend of social commitment and financial goals. In the decade between the groundbreaking and the first profits to Equitable, Gateway returned downtown Pittsburgh to a central position in the region's life; by 1961, 10 percent of the people employed in the metropolitan area worked in the center. After Building 4 opened in 1960, a Pittsburgh newspaper editorialized, "Again the Equitable Society is to be congratulated on the foresight which brought on this big, brilliant project."[19]

Equitable's commitment to the Gateway Center in turn benefitted the company behind it. In 1959, a Pittsburgh-based Equitable agent, in an article for an agents' magazine on how to increase sales, gave a piece of advice referring to one of Parkinson's successors: "get Mr. Oates to build a Gateway Center in your community — that will help." Twelve years later, the new manager of the Equitable agency, Robert Jones, stumbled upon another testimonial when he approached a city resident:

The Equitable and Pittsburgh were synonymous. My first sales call was on a man who lived in Gateway Towers who had called about buying an annuity. I went over to his apartment and began my usual talk by telling him about The Equitable. He interrupted me and said, "I live here in a building that The Equitable built. I worked at Westinghouse and have an Equitable group insurance policy. You don't have to tell me anything about The Equitable." [20]

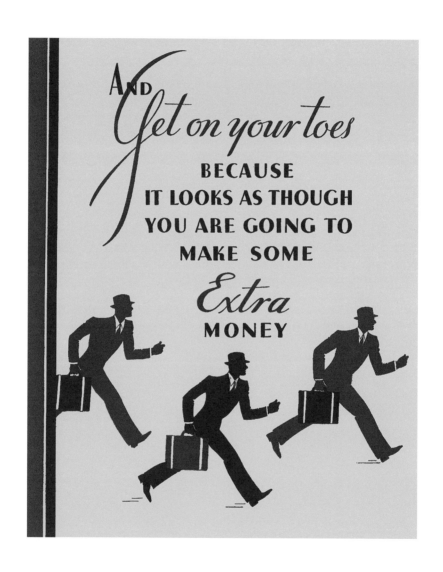

*An Equitable brochure for agents in the 1940's introduced a new product with
the traditional Home Office exhortation: work harder and the rewards will follow.*

CHAPTER XI

BEYOND POLICY PEDDLING

A s Thomas Parkinson asserted himself over investments, he also was attentive to Equitable's marketing programs. He esteemed Henry's Hyde's theory of a large, aggressive commissioned sales force supported by heavy promotion from the Home Office. As the economy recovered in the late 1930's, he ended the depression-era disciplines by reemphasizing sales volume, recruiting agents, and instigating huge sales campaigns, many of them named for him. His goal was to have Equitable representatives everywhere in the country. As he put it, he wanted "an agent at every crossroad." By the late 1940's, the Society had more than 10,000 agents. An agent who started out in the 'forties, Donald Bryant, Sr., recalled Parkinson's encouragement:

> T. I. Parkinson would always at "Par for Parkinson" gatherings make the point, "We want an agent at every crossroad in The Equitable," and that meant we were willing to have a lot of part-time agents, because when he said every crossroad, he meant every crossroad.

About half the agents were part-timers. Bankers, housewives, lawyers, clergymen, accountants, schoolteachers, football coaches, real estate agents, and others of good local reputation filled many of these niches in towns and small cities. Many sold only a half-dozen or a dozen policies a year, but they kept Equitable's flag flying.[1]

Supporting many of the agents was the highly popular and easily sold Assured Home Ownership program. AHO had been established as an investment, but it became, in the words of one agency officer, "a manpower acquiring policy." By the mid-1950's, as many as half of Equitable's agents were selling AHO insurance in tandem with the mortgages provided by the Society's real estate representatives. Some district offices sold little else. Clarence Metzger, the chief of training and advertising after William Alexander's retirement in 1935, came up with illustrations that got new agents selling AHO policies within only two months. One tool was a set of architects' plans, commissioned by Equitable, of modern, low-cost houses that was distributed to prospects, many of whom had only dreamed of owning their own homes. Another, more sophisticated sales tool explained the economics of an AHO contract. Metzger, an alumnus of the Woods Agency, had a genius for expressing complicated ideas effectively on simple charts. Sitting with the client and one of the graphs that Metzger had designed, an agent could demonstrate how the dividends earned by the AHO insurance policy would help pay off the mortgage well ahead of its maturity.[2]

Such relatively sophisticated sales techniques, based largely on the needs of the prospective client rather than on selling for selling's sake, gradually came into use beginning in the 1920's. The story of the evolution of life insurance sales from its earlier style, called policy peddling, pulls together many features of life insurance and financial history.

Clarence B. Metzger.   *Florence E. Shaal.*   *Frank M. Davis.*   *William W. Klingman.*

The nineteenth- and early twentieth-century tradition of the commissioned life insurance agent was often described in nearly mythological terms. The agent was a hearty, entrepreneurial type living out the Horatio Alger dream of the self-made American. "How a Young Man Without Capital Can Make His Fortune," ran the caption on an Equitable advertisement recruiting new agents, and Edward A. Woods kept the following slogan handy in his notebook: "There is no business in which it is possible for a man without capital to achieve such a financial success as in life insurance." The life was characterized as one of heroic drama and challenge. *"Will you do it?"* asked the headline of a brochure for a sales campaign. The year was 1911, but it could have been any time in Equitable's history to date. Likewise, Equitable Banner Month, in December 1915, was designed around a great pennant on which a star was sewn for every sale — 4,962 stars from 1,624 agents in all — and which was presented with due ceremony to William Day at the Society's annual convention at the Waldorf-Astoria Hotel.[3]

The myth, however, did not prepare young agents for the disappointments of regular rejection. "We meet with our little disappointments," hopefully reported an Equitable agent, Florence Shaal, "but the rejoicings over successful cases would do your heart good." Woods told his agents if they made twenty-one sales calls a week, they should have fourteen interviews, and that those interviews should produce two applications for insurance. And of those two applications, both might be turned down by the underwriters in the Home Office Actuarial Department as poor risks for health or financial reasons. Until 1962, agents worked on commission from their first day with Equitable. Their expenses were paid and, after 1913, they were permitted to draw advances against their income at a rate of $35 a week. Yet the compensation could be extremely low. By one estimate, in 1916 the average first-year agent earned only $160. Attrition was startling: half of all life insurance agents who were licensed in 1915 dropped out of the business by the end of the year. Conditions improved, but not much; in 1939 four out of every ten agents with more than five years of service had average incomes of less than $2,500.[4]

"Will you do it?" therefore, was a challenge about each agent's entire career, not only a particular sales campaign. The agents who succeeded — who answered yes throughout long careers — were people of unusually vigorous, sanguine temperament and bulletproof confidence. They usually had a deep faith in life insurance (which sustained them in times of rejection), a strong but appealing personality (which got them in prospects' doors), and a simple, methodical selling technique (which helped them close sales).

The immense, exuberant Frank M. Davis rose rapidly through the ranks and reorganized the Chicago territory, increasing sales 500 percent in five years, and went to the Home Office as head of the Agency Operations Department. On the wall of his office hung his credo: "The world makes way for a man who knows where he's going," but in person he was more likely to recite sentimental poems and humorous rural bromides like "To hell with poverty, we'll kill a hen." Davis spoke of life insurance like a religion. After his father died, a $7,000 policy was all that kept a roof over his family's head. "This made a profound impression on me," Davis said, "and left me in a state of mind to advocate life insurance to other people with my whole heart and soul." He would tell recruits, "If you don't think you're in the best business in the world, I don't want you to work for us." He once stopped off in a store to buy a phonograph, was impressed by the young salesman, invited him to lunch, and converted him. "Before we had got to the dessert he was an enthusiastic recruit," Davis recalled.[5]

Other agents were equally adept at making it all sound simple. William Washington ("Wash") Klingman, of St. Paul, Minnesota, reduced life insurance sales to a formula that he often recited to his agents and trainees: "Forget policy terms; forget premiums; think only of protection! That's what you're selling these people — protection against want!" William E. Bilheimer, a general agent in Little Rock, Arkansas, and a former YMCA physical education teacher, was known as the "Billy Sunday of life insurance" for his fervent faith in the gospel of protection. Such was his passion for Equitable that he was known to telephone his superiors whenever he had a good idea, even at two in the morning. Despite these excesses of enthusiasm, Bilheimer (like most other successful agents) staked as much on preparation and teamwork as on inspiration and solo performances. He developed a meticulous training program for his agents, with detailed personal supervision and an instruction manual.[6]

Pick Embry: master of "eyeballing" and maker of agency managers.

It was Bilheimer who enlisted and trained the king of the old-time, policy peddling life insurance agents, Ayelette Moarning ("Pick") Embry, manager of the Kansas City agency from 1924 until 1948 and mentor for many of the managers who dominated the field force into the 1980's. In 1910, Embry was running the meat department in a grocery store in Atkins, Arkansas, and trading horses on the side, when a coffee wholesaler he knew showed up, announced he was an Equitable agent, and asked Embry to join him. "I laughed him out of the store," Embry remembered. His friend kept after him, and Embry decided to test himself in a trial run with a neighbor. When the prospect said he had no interest in buying life insurance, Embry replied that it was for the better, anyway, since the man probably would not pass the physical. That sparked the neighbor's interest. Not wanting to be labeled as unqualified for anything, he was dickering with Embry over the

Embry long after his mule-riding days.

premium for a $1,000 policy when his wife appeared and forced him to sign up for a $5,000 policy. The lesson, Embry later said, was no different from the one he had learned while selling groceries and trading horses:

> *If you can make a fellow think that he can't get this thing you're trying to sell him — that it's not going to be so easy for him to get it — you'll find out that he'll get awfully anxious to try to acquire whatever it is…. When he finds out that it's hard to get, he'll immediately tear the buttons off his shirt trying to get it. Life insurance isn't anything different.*

That was Embry's first sales call and his first sale. "Well, that kind of convinced me that it could be done," he reminisced, "but we failed on the next three guys, so we didn't have such a big day after all." Undiscouraged, he collected the commission and signed an agent's contract with Bilheimer in April 1911.[7]

The going was slow: besides the lower premiums charged by the fraternal societies, he had to contend with the poor publicity of the 1905 scandals and a revival of religious fundamentalism. Embry remembered in an oral history in 1955, "[L]ots of people absolutely thought that buying a life insurance policy was dealing in blood money or against their religion." He had one Bible-read-

ing farmer sold until, just as he was picking up the pen to sign the application, lightning struck a nearby dogwood tree. But in his first year he sold enough insurance to win a vacation in the Thousand Islands.[8]

Embry's technique was to fit into his community, target his prospect, and apply his considerable skills of persuasion. In his early days, he rode around his rural territory on a mule, stopping off at farms to help his neighbors with their plowing or chickens, or hitching the mule to a hay wagon and climbing up on the buckboard for a chat. Somehow the conversation worked its way around to financial protection. Once the farmer showed a little interest, Embry pulled Equitable's rate book out of his hip pocket, turned to a policy description, put his face in the prospect's, and commenced selling. A younger agent, Robert Wenzlaff, described Embry's technique:

> *Embry did what is called "eyeballing." You see it in Texas, Southern Illinois, and Missouri. Have you ever seen a picture of Lyndon Johnson talking some poor Senator into voting his way? That's eyeballing. When Pick Embry stood there making his point, his eyes got wide and never blinked. It was almost like his eyeballs were popping out. He eyeballed you down until you lost your will to resist. It took somebody big to make it work. It was like arm-wrestling. Basically it was a form of intimidation.*

As to what he said while the prospect was locked in his sights, Embry made no pretensions about a scientific approach: "Back in those days, you know, all of our sales were made on sentiment. We didn't have any programs or any of this high-falutin' distribution to the beneficiaries…. It was sentimental — strict, pure, and simple."[9]

When Embry visited unfamiliar territory, he shifted his technique from one of intimacy to one of showmanship. This was a long tradition. When Gage Tarbell was out in the field in the 1890's, he arranged to enter a new town in a conspicuous fashion — say, by riding on a white horse behind a marching band. Once noticed, he visited the leading citizens and offered them a year of free insurance in exchange for endorsements. Embry was not above engaging in similar tactics — for example, getting off the train and renting the handsomest car he could find, which often was the mortician's black hearse.

Such tactics struck the next generation of agents as crude. One of them, Donald Bryant, Sr., who knew Embry well, looked down on his salesmanship as mere "policy peddling":

> There were all kinds of gimmickry to selling life insurance and there was a lot of fear of the Lord, a lot of quotations about the Bible, a lot of appeal to the emotions, a lot of crying went on at the sale, etc, etc. And that was the way it was sold. It wasn't sold on logic. It wasn't sold on tax and figures. It was sold on emotions…. I think what we've got to give some creditable thought to is that this business is so good and so foolproof, it survives that kind of thing by those kinds of people.

Yet emotionalism never went out of style. Bryant himself was remembered by people who worked with him as a master of eyeballing and weeping on cue.[10]

But in his own way and for his time, Pick Embry was a sophisticated marketer. He was an early proponent of the technique of financial planning called programming, in which the agent determined the prospect's financial needs and then built a program of insurance around them. Programming began as a defensive strategy against Social Security. The insurance industry vehemently opposed the New Deal's proposal for government old-age insurance (and later fought its expansion), but

once Social Security was instituted in 1935, Embry and other alert agents found a way to turn it to their advantage. Social Security, they told prospects, offered only "the floor of protection" — the foundation but not the roof of a personal insurance portfolio. From information provided by the family and government Social Security tables, the agents filled out formulas to illustrate family need based on the breadwinner's income. One formula was:

> $NEED = C + 1 + \frac{1}{2} + \frac{1}{4}$
> Cash to cover immediate expenses
> + 1 year's income
> + $\frac{1}{2}$ year's income per year until children are grown
> + $\frac{1}{4}$ year's income for widow after children are grown

After the policy was sold, a good programming agent kept checking back with prospects and offering suggestions for enhancing the program around changing needs.[11]

Salesmanship was no less important in programming than it was in old-time Bible-thumping, but it had to be more subtle. "It was just need-based selling as against policy peddling," said Wenzlaff, who learned programming from one of Embry's protégés, Warren V. Woody, and later headed agencies in New York and St. Louis. Wenzlaff continued:

> You can establish the need. The skills come out of establishing the want. Prospects want to have insurance. You just want to get them to want it a little earlier. We must put up with a human being's resistance to talking about death. I used to tell the agents I was training to say this to a prospect: "If the good Lord had decided to make an angel of you last night, and if you could look down and describe how much income your wife and family should have, what would it be?" Most people are afraid of death. Make them angels.[12]

Because the needs-based approach of programming required more skill and knowledge than policy peddling, the job of the district manager, who in the Hyde system was charged with recruiting and training new agents, became crucial. Pick Embry was unusually creative in how he trained his district managers. Wenzlaff looked back:

> *He made the district manager system work the way it was designed to be used. The district manager system must be used competently, otherwise it's very expensive. Embry made sure district managers were active and not just sitting on their butts. He had them hire only qualified agents, and then he made them work with new agents in the field on split commissions and show them how to sell.*

To induce district managers to do their jobs properly, Embry dangled an inducement: if they performed well he would arrange for them to become agency managers on their own. Since successful agency managers made more money than anybody in Equitable (including the Society's presidents), Embry's challenge was appealing and effective. And once he had placed them in agencies, Embry personally trained them in their new jobs. At least sixteen of his district managers in Kansas City went on to head agencies; half a dozen of them were presidents of the Old Guard.[13]

Though not a protégé of Embry's, Smith Ferebee was another colorful agent with a large following in part because he was a colorful and, occasionally, outrageous character. A Virginian who before joining Equitable had made and lost a couple of fortunes, Ferebee was a pioneer in activities that are now called extreme sports. He won a large bet by swimming a mile with his hands and feet tied, participated in endurance contests in trap shooting and golf, and once made a cross-country tour of golf courses by airplane, stopping off every several hundred miles to play a round. After becoming an Equitable agent and then a district manager in the Woody agency in Chicago, Ferebee served as Equitable's manager in Richmond, Virginia. While growing wealthy selling insurance, he also became the kind of manager who, like Embry, is as much remembered for his personal influence on his agents as for his own vivid personality. One of Ferebee's agents, James Gurley, echoed what has long been said by many other agents of their mentors: "Everything I have in the world, except my wife and four children, I owe to Smitty Ferebee."[14]

Programming was a minor reform compared with the gradual evolution of scientific salesmanship and training programs under the patronage of Edward Woods. Equitable had been attentive to training and education since its early days, when Henry Hyde gathered general agents for seminars. In the summer of 1902, the Home Office sponsored what may have been the first systematic program for potential agents. One hundred twenty-five students were recruited from colleges and divinity schools for a month-long internship in the Home Office that ended with an elaborate dinner at which Gage Tarbell led them in a pledge of allegiance to Equitable. The program was repeated for several years.

Meanwhile, in Pittsburgh, Woods was becoming convinced that insurance sales was

J. Smith Ferebee.

not merely an extension of an individual's personality but rather a science to be learned by qualified people. Woods's career as an insurance reformer began in 1894, when he was twenty-nine. He stood up at an early convention of the

Edward Woods at the time he helped found the CLU program.

Dr. Solomon S. Huebner.

National Association of Life Underwriters (NALU), the agents' trade association, and accused the industry of tolerating agents who engaged in such abhorrent practices as rebating premiums and "twisting" customers away from other agents. Pithily describing these agents as "the basis of all the evils this association has anything to do with," he told the convention, "if you cannot eliminate a certain class of men from our business, we are wasting our time." NALU soon backed anti-rebating laws in nineteen states.[15]

Woods made his general agency into a laboratory for insurance sales techniques. At the turn of the century he created an intelligence bureau that conducted demographic surveys and other research on insurance issues and propagated innovations by other researchers (for instance, a system developed in 1903 by John Marshall Holcombe, an instructor of insurance at Yale, for estimating the economic value of a human life by capitalizing earning power over the years). Around these techniques Woods developed a system of team selling, in which younger agents went on sales calls with district managers. "Joint selling is profitable to all. Half a loaf is better than none," Woods lectured his agents. Woods tempered his theorizing with traditional motivational prods. To agents who complained, he sent a brochure he had written titled *The Kickers*, which invited them to reflect on whether their problems were of their own devising; to those who did not demonstrate the requisite positive attitude, he provided another brochure, *The Will To Be Cheerful*. He backed up these publications with a regular series of training programs; his way of celebrating the agency's forty-fifth anniversary in 1925 was to hold a two-day marathon of seminars and lectures.[16]

Woods was sure that the large attrition rate of new agents was due not to recruits' personal defects but, rather, to weaknesses in the agency system. He contemptuously used the word *sieve* to describe the typical agency's haphazard recruiting operation, which simply hired all comers without any evaluation and sent them out on sales calls with minimal supervision until they proved their incompetence. Woods was sure that things could be improved by hiring capable men and women, training them well, and enforcing high professional standards. To attract college graduates, Woods lobbied for industry-wide, standardized academic training somewhat similar to that in a graduate business school. In 1915 he spent $10,000 of his own money to publish a textbook on life insurance by Dr. Solomon Stephen Huebner, who was teaching one of the first college-level insurance courses at the Wharton School of Finance and Commerce at the University of Pennsylvania. That same year, Equitable, pressed by Woods,

Dr. John A. Stevenson.

pulled together his and Huebner's ideas into a training system called scientific salesmanship, which combined market research, education, and recruiting in an effort to improve agencies and sales. All along, Woods said that the key was strong leadership: "If you can get supervisors, you can get men all right," he told a trade group. "If you can find out how to train the supervisor, I think the agency problem can take care of itself." In 1917 Equitable began training district managers in the art of recruiting and providing them with forms on which to rate potential agents on their appearance, character, intelligence, and other qualifications.[17]

In 1917, Woods was elected president of NALU and chairman of its new committee on scientific salesmanship. That year he helped found the Carnegie Bureau of Salesmanship Research, affiliated with the Carnegie Institute of Technology, in Pittsburgh. The Carnegie Bureau and the Association of Life Agency Officers (an association of insurance sales managers and officials that he also headed) founded an insurance school with forty-three students and seventeen staff members. Later, Woods helped found a pilot program for training agents at the University of Pittsburgh. Woods believed that, at the least, the academic program would attract college graduates to insurance sales while screening out unqualified candidates in the classroom before they made expensive mistakes in the field.

The Carnegie Bureau's director was Dr. John A. Stevenson, formerly a professor of education at the University of Illinois. In 1920, Equitable hired him as the first full-time training officer at any insurance company. Stevenson founded the Society's first systematic training

operation, the Cashier Training Program, which provided a thorough introduction to the business of life insurance by placing new recruits in the Society's 100-odd local administrative offices. After a nine- to twelve-month tour in a cashier's office, the employee went to the Home Office for a two-week orientation with the rest of the class, and then was assigned to the Home Office or another cashier's office. Most of these cashiers stayed on the business side, while others became agents. As Stevenson developed these ideas, he wrote three books on salesmanship in a series of insurance texts, published by Harper & Brothers, that also included volumes by Woods and Huebner.

All this activity led to the foundation, by Woods, Huebner, and others, of the American College of Life Underwriters, in Philadelphia, and the creation of the Chartered Life Underwriter (CLU) designation. There was a tension between, on one hand, Huebner's academic conviction (bolstered by colleges and business schools) that the program must be rigorous if the degree were to have any meaning; and on the other hand, the insurance industry's desire that the CLU not be too difficult to earn. Concerned that the college would be a diploma mill, Woods took Huebner's side, though not uncritically. When Huebner proposed a reading list of twenty-three books, Woods warned him he was going too far; he himself had been unable to get through them all. Huebner reluctantly agreed to cut the reading list in half.

When the time came in the fall of 1927 to get the National Association of Life Underwriters to back the college, Huebner was in Japan, which probably was a good thing, since he was not about to compromise further. At the NALU convention, Woods assured the many doubters, "[M]y friends, we cannot make this a cheap degree. If you are going to make it a cheap degree,… college men will laugh at you, you are going to ruin the whole thing…." Woods ultimately agreed to a compromise by approving a second, less demanding degree. (Huebner was furious about it when he returned to America.) When the District of Columbia, where the college was chartered, refused permission to call the CLU a degree, it came to be termed a designation. Huebner was elected as the American college's first dean, Woods as the founding president (Woods died before the college opened its doors in 1928). Of the first twenty-two students, sixteen were college graduates, nine were Equitable agents, and six were from the Woods General Agency.[18]

Biographies of agents who started out in the 1930's and 'forties are stories of ambition, mobility, determination, and sheer hard work. Successful agents worked seven days a week, often a dozen hours a day; to make themselves known in their communities, they volunteered for local church, community, and fraternal organizations; they earned their CLU designations by studying Huebner's and others' texts in their occasional free moments and taking examinations; and all this time they looked and waited for opportunities that came their way through networks of friends and acquaintances in the agency force and Home Office.

In 1927, Joseph Beesley came out of DePauw University, in Indiana, with a degree in business administration. He learned about Equitable from a form letter sent by the Society's recruiting department and started out in the Cashier Training Program in Columbus, Ohio. From there he went to Phoenix and, later, Syracuse as cashier, spending his evenings studying for the CLU exams and selling insurance door to door. He passed his tests and, after six years in Syracuse, went as assistant cashier to the Home Office. He made his fifth move in fourteen years when he transferred to Chicago as cashier in 1940. Five years later he returned to Syracuse as agency manager, and in 1952 he was called back to New York at a sizable pay cut

to serve as Field Vice-President for the New York metropolitan region.

In the 'thirties, Laurens F. Bruno became an agent in Chicago after working in administrative jobs in the Home Office. He met Beesley, who inspired him to try sales and study for the CLU. When Beesley was transferred to Syracuse in 1945, Larry Bruno asked to be taken along. He and his wife packed their young daughter and skimpy furniture into their car and drove to Middletown, New York, where he opened a district office of Beesley's Syracuse agency.

Bruno then tried to make himself visible in the community. The rule of thumb (as passed down to a manager of a later generation, Robert S. Jones) was, "Buy yourself a big home in a good neighborhood, get to know your clients, join a country club, and be active." In Middletown, Bruno joined two country clubs, the volunteer fire department, the Kiwanis, and the Presbyterian church; he chaired a fund drive for a local charity; and he helped organize a local agents' association. Bruno had two broken-down agents and one raw one in need of hand-holding. But he also had a tremendous asset, which he called "one of the strongest tools any agent could wish for": a list of local Equitable policyholders who had been "orphaned" when the agents who had sold them their policies either retired or moved on. The orphans had lost contact with Equitable, and now Larry Bruno tried to adopt them. He conscripted several agents, including a few from West Point and other nearby military bases. With the fresh recruits tagging along as apprentice trainees, he visited the orphaned policyholders to ask if they were happy with their policies or wanted

Joseph L. Beesley.

changes. Soon those agents were working on their own, as he went about the district manager's job of hiring and training another three or four agents a year. By the time Bruno left in 1949 to manage the agency in Albany, his Middletown district was the second most successful in the region. After three years in Albany, Bruno moved on to run the Boston agency from 1952 to 1963. He lost his job in a conflict with a regional Vice-President, refused another transfer, to Fort Wayne, and became a successful agent in his own right. He finally retired in 1983.[19]

For the depression-era generation of college graduates looking for meaningful work, insurance sales had broad appeal. In 1939, Richard Hageman, a young Ohio State alumnus, was in his fourth year as a salesman in his father's shoe store in Dayton, Ohio, when he met an Equitable district manager. The manager, Hageman remembered,

> became acquainted with me and began unfolding to me the story of The Equitable and the story of the life insurance business. He told me about renewals and commissions and write your own ticket, earning whatever you're worth, work as hard as you want to work, be your own boss[,] all of the wonderful ingredients of this great career of ours.

Hageman passed this on to his brother, who became an Equitable agent. Six months later Hageman was an agent, too. Soon he succeeded his mentor as district manager, and four years later, in 1947, he became the Cincinnati agency manager.[20]

Another new agent was Coy Eklund. Forced to drop out of the University of Michigan during the Great Depression because of lack of funds, he polished rolling pins for 35 cents an hour at a woodware factory. After an acquaintance who owned a local department store advised him that the best career a young man could have was to be a life insurance agent, Eklund applied to New York Life but was told that, at nineteen, he was too young. He took a job demonstrating kitchen utensils. One night in 1937, a mailman who was a part-time Equitable agent promised to buy a set of pots and pans if Eklund would purchase a life policy. Eklund agreed. Eklund was sufficiently impressed to go back and ask for a job. He liked it that the business concerned finance and therefore seemed important. Anyway, he told himself, "it's got to be better than rolling pins." A couple of weeks later he met with The Equitable's local district manager. It was the turning point in his life. "[A]fter two hours I went out of there just walking two feet right off the ground, I was an Equitable agent," Eklund remembered. "...[I]n two hours [he] stimulated me and inspired me and reassured me, sold me on the life insurance business, like nobody it seems could." That afternoon the new Equitable agent sold his first policy, to his fiancée.[21]

Returning to college, Eklund sold insurance part-time as a student. After he went off to the army, like all Equitable agents in the military, he received an occasional letter from Clarence Metzger guaranteeing him a job after the war. Eklund had thought his insurance days were over, but the correspondence changed his mind:

> Clarence Metzger kept writing letters to me all through those four years. He never let me go.... And he followed me so religiously and it meant so much to me that I recruited agents over in France and brought them back here all ready to go. I had nine agents virtually under contract before they got back to these shores. When I was writing letters back and forth, I was determined I was going to come back to The Equitable.

When Eklund returned to America in 1945, he went straight to New York and the Home

HOW EQUITABLE'S ABLEST WOMAN AGENT WON SUCCESS IN INSURANCE

Mrs. Florence E. Shaal, Who Makes More Than $10,000 Year, Talks With Eleanor Ames.

Stepped From Home Into Business Office; in Six Years Has Made Department Pre-eminent.

By Eleanor Ames.

During the recent noteworthy conference of the managers and agents of the Equitable Life Assurance Society, held at the Hotel Savoy in New York, a certain rather small, extremely well-gowned woman, with a noticeably bright, smiling face and a vivacious manner, attracted much attention.

Sometimes she was in earnest conversation with President Alexander or Mr. Gage Tarbell. Again she was cordially greeting some prominent Equitable man from the West or the South. Always she was being sought out and greeted. Evidently she was a woman of much distinction in Equitable circles.

"Who is she?" asked one not well acquainted.

The one addressed looked amazed. "Don't you know her?" he would ask. "Why that is Mrs. Florence E. Shaal of Boston, the cleverest woman in the insurance business to-day. Has organized and built up a woman's department that's a wonder. Has sixty women agents working for her and makes over $10,000 a year. I thought every one knew our Mrs. Shaal.

"She's got lots of us men beaten to a standstill, but we're all proud of her."

Those who know Mrs. Shaal through the newspapers know her chiefly as a woman who makes $10,000 a year. Filled as it is with clever and capable women, Boston has not many feminine wage earners whose annual salary will approach that figure. Nor has America, in fact. So from an earning standpoint Mrs. Shaal is a most interesting woman.

However, when you meet her and know her, you decide that the fact that her income is $10,000 is not the only remarkable thing about her. In very many ways Mrs. Shaal is an unusual woman.

If she hadn't been she could never have stepped from her drawing room into an office, having no more idea of business than a child, taken up a business of which she knew next to nothing, except that she might succeed in it, and in six short years have organized and made successful a department which has no equal in America's insurance circles.

Necessity the Spur.

In the case of Mrs. Shaal, as in the case of many another brilliant business woman, it was necessity which drove her from the home to the office.

There came a time in her career, after a breakdown of her husband's health, that she realized the money was going out far faster than it was coming in to the household, and that she had a young son whose education must be completed, and whose career in life must be mapped out. "I'm going to work!" she announced. Her family and friends stared.

The youngest of a large family, brought

Florence E. Shaal of Boston.

Office, where he was given a district managership in Detroit. Two years later, at the age of thirty-two, Eklund was appointed manager of a newly formed "scratch" Equitable agency in Detroit. [22]

The agency force, unlike the Home Office, was almost entirely a male preserve. As everywhere in the country, women did not attain positions of authority in Equitable until the 1960's and 'seventies. But since the turn of the century they had been the backbone of the Home Office's clerical organization. According to the U.S. census, the country's clerical workforce was 40 percent female in 1880, 77 percent in 1900, and 92 percent in 1920. The population of Equitable's stenographers and typists followed the same pattern. Yet, although Equitable's symbol was a female shielding a family in need, men continued to fill almost all sales and management jobs. In any year between 1900 and 1960, less than 5 percent of the agency force — fewer than 500 women, most part-timers — was female. This pattern was typical of life insurers who sold to white fam-

Early women agents, including: (above) Ray Wilner Sundelson, Lizzie Law, and Sarah F. Jones.

ilies, where most economic decisions were made by men; but in insurance companies that specialized in selling to African-American families, whose mothers and wives made many economic decisions, most agents were women.[23]

The name of the pioneer Equitable female agent is not known, but the first one to make her mark was Bertha Straus of Pittsburgh, whom Edward Woods assigned in 1893 to canvass Jewish communities. At that time, female policyholders younger than forty-nine were subject to a surcharge on life insurance and tontine policies because of reported high mortality rates in childbirth. But in 1895 Gage Tarbell learned that

women's life expectancy actually was a year or two greater than men's and convinced Henry Hyde to equalize premiums. The Home Office and several large agencies subsequently developed internal "women's departments" of female agents for selling mainly to female prospects. The best-known women's department was in Boston and run by Florence E. Shaal between 1899 and 1909. Having started out, as she put it, as "an absolute novice, with a desk, a bottle of ink, and a bunch of applications," she became manager of a sixty-person operation that had its agents, doctor, and lawyer, all of them women. In 1902, Shaal's department alone wrote more insurance than all Equitable agencies in New Hampshire and

The widows and orphans security theme was constantly brought up to date in vivid, often emotional advertisements.

Vermont. Shaal was elected as the first female vice-president of the national agents' organization, NALU.[24]

A few agencies were managed by women but had mostly male sales forces. One was a New York City agency founded in 1896 by Ray Wilner Sundelson, who said it helped that her first name sounded like a man's. Up in Vermont, Alice C. Hammond worked a snowy, mountainous district with a team and driver. Of her, the *Burlington Free Press* wrote, "It shows the progress that is being made all the time in the different avenues of the business when a young lady is capable of taking a set of papers and starting for a rural district to adjust a claim against an insurance company." The numbers of female agents dwindled in the 1920's, when social norms changed to push many women back into the home. There was a brief revival during the Great Depression, when some women came to work in agencies for family financial reasons, and during World War II, when many men were away at war (Equitable's first female officer, Grace W. Jordis, was appointed in 1944). But from V-J Day until the 1970's, very few female agents came into Equitable.[25]

The irony of a largely male institution producing and selling products tailored toward women was not entirely ignored. At the time of Equitable's seventy-fifth anniversary in 1934, a proposal arose to elect a woman to the Society's Board of Directors, but it was derailed by William Alexander, a committed chauvinist. A few years after Alexander's retirement, Lawrence C. Woods, Jr., Edward Woods's nephew and the head of the Pittsburgh agency, urged President Parkinson to place a successful family woman on the Board of Directors. It was only fair, Woods said: "Life insurance was created and developed largely as a protection for women," and more than three-quarters of all life insurance benefits were payable to them. Parkinson replied that the prejudice was too great to overcome. That kind of change, it seemed, came as slowly to Equitable as it did to the society at large.[26]

The agents, male and female, were supported by a large Home Office promotion budget. Print and radio advertising were minimal for years because the general feeling was that the best advertising was the word-of-mouth endorsement of a satisfied policyholder, and the way to bring that satisfaction was to provide a well-prepared agent and a high dividend. An agency newsletter in 1945 described the year's dividend payments not as simple financial transactions but as "Two and A Half Billions of Publicity." Otherwise, anything that helped agents was presumed to help Equitable, and that included calendars, blotters, pencils, brochures by the hundreds, and

The Garden of Security at the 1939 World's Fair.

customized form letters. The Personalized Letter Service had a library of form letters for agents: Letter D-13 described ways to insure the life of a boy; Letter D-6 focused on how policies could be used to pay tuition; and Letter D-18 was directed to women "who have seen the generation before them grow old without growing independent."[27]

Occasionally, advertising campaigns promoted specific agencies. In 1948, Parkinson's son Courtney approached his father with a proposal for a campaign in rural and small-town newspapers to support the "agent at every crossroad" marketing strategy. Although young Parkinson had a skimpy background in advertising, his father and the top aides approved the idea. The ads, which ran in more than 600 weeklies around the country, aimed at sup-

The insurance guarantee has long been a strong selling point.

porting local agents by publicizing Equitable's national reputation as an investor that underwrote the country's infrastructure. "Insurance Dollars Helped the Cattle Get to Market" was the headline on one advertisement showing cattle being loaded onto a railroad car financed by Equitable. As with many of Equitable's advertisements, the names of local agents and agencies were run in the text. The response to the tie-in campaign was encouraging, and Equitable increased its budget to over $500,000 a year.

Most promotions and campaigns were directed toward helping agents in the field, but there remained some energy for old-fashioned broadcasting of the Society's name. The problem was finding the right image. Financial measurement, along the lines of the "Strongest in the World" idea of the Hyde era, went out of fashion at the time of the 1905 scandal. Any claim that even hinted at profit-seeking was deemed inappropriate to a beneficent, missionary enterprise. The word profit, banished from advertising in the late nineteenth century, was not used even in internal communications. ("Serving on the Equitable board was my only experience with a non-profit that was doing things that other people were doing for profit," said a director of a later time, Francis H. Burr.) The term "surplus" remained the all-purpose catch-all for financial strength, including both capital base and profits, and it was often used internally. But externally, instead of emphasizing financial strength as Hyde had done, Equitable under Parkinson relied on the theme of "security," which by implication encompassed both the old "widows and orphans" and the "strength" themes. At the 1939 World's Fair in New York, Equitable had an exhibit called the Garden of Security, where in a quiet park setting were displayed many of the Society's symbols, including a statue based on the Protection Group.[28]

Babe Ruth was an Equitable spokesman for many years. Second from the left is Arthur H. Reddall, Equitable's long-time advertising director.

Endorsement by famous policyholders was another theme of advertising, though instead of nationally known preachers, Equitable now used sports and business heroes, whose names and faces were publicized in posters, recordings, and occasional print advertisements. William Graham was especially aggressive in promoting group insurance by listing the giant companies and well-known individuals who held Equitable

Agency head Ray Dolan, Joe DiMaggio, and board chairman John Fey at an Equitable major league event.

group insurance policies. One of those individuals was the man who became one of Equitable's chief spokesmen in the 1930's, George Herman ("Babe") Ruth. The connection between Equitable and the greatest sports star of his time was not that surprising, given the Society's long involvement with baseball dating back to the 1860's. Besides fielding teams that played in industrial leagues, Equitable employed star ballplayers as spokesmen. The first was Mickey Cochrane, a catcher for the Philadelphia Athletics, who in 1931 signed on to endorse Equitable annuities. Cochrane was well known, but the real coup was Babe Ruth, who became an Equitable spokesman in 1932.

Ruth had come to Equitable somewhat unwillingly. His profligate life off the field had been tamed by his new wife and Christy Walsh, a sportswriter who was his agent, promoter, and financial advisor. They convinced Ruth to deposit the earnings from his many promotional activities in Equitable annuities. Whenever Ruth tried to get his hands on the money to pay his gambling debts, Graham (whom Ruth respected well enough to call "Chief") found a way to discourage him, usually by calling in Walsh or Mrs. Ruth. One time when Walsh dragged him to the Home Office

to make a large deposit, Parkinson appeared and effusively congratulated Ruth on his great good luck in having Equitable look after his future. "Yes, I guess so," Ruth answered. "There's no doubt I'm lucky. There is also no doubt that you have my $35,000."[29]

Ruth agreed to promote the Society's policies for a fee, which his advisors instructed Equitable to place in his annuity. Sometimes he appeared for Equitable in person or on posters, but on one occasion he recorded an endorsement that was sent to agents to play for their prospects. The recording took much longer than anybody had anticipated because Ruth was unable to pronounce *Equitable*, which came out *Ekitable, Ee-QUIT-able,* and even *wikt-able.* "I just can't get that," Ruth complained to Graham. It took him a day of practice before he could pronounce the name correctly and make the recording.[30]

Equitable's successful relationship with Ruth helped the Society to be chosen in 1947 to manage major league baseball's first pension plan for players, coaches, and trainers. The work was glamorous but also had its surprises; for instance, when the group department learned to its horror that two insured teams flew to a game on the same airplane, the league imposed a requirement that teams travel separately. As the leagues enlarged, the business was dispersed to several insurers, although the Society retained a share of the major league pension business as well as group life and health insurance for teams. In the 1980's, Equitable was active in the effort to raise money for former ballplayers who had retired before pension plans were begun. The company sponsored old timers' games and helped establish a foundation, the Baseball Assistance Team (BAT).

Equitable's most famous promotion campaign was a weekly radio program, *This Is Your FBI,* that it sponsored with the endorse-

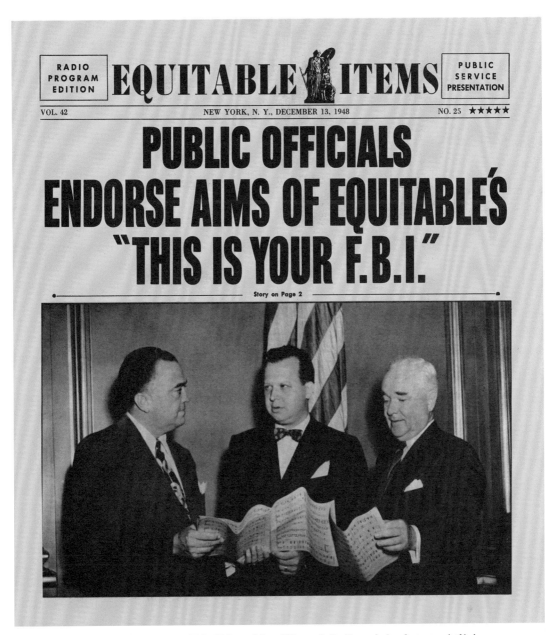

RADIO
PROGRAM
EDITION

EQUITABLE ITEMS

PUBLIC
SERVICE
PRESENTATION

VOL. 42 — NEW YORK, N. Y., DECEMBER 13, 1948 — NO. 25 ★★★★★

PUBLIC OFFICIALS ENDORSE AIMS OF EQUITABLE'S "THIS IS YOUR F.B.I."

Story on Page 2

J. Edgar Hoover, Van Cleave, orchestrator of "the FBI march," and Thomas I. Parkinson during the program's third year.

ment of the FBI's head, J. Edgar Hoover. In 1944, CBS Radio, without Hoover's permission, began producing a weekly drama, *The FBI in Peace and War,* that was criticized by parents and teachers as unsuitable for children. Hoover decided that the FBI itself should produce a show that would more accurately represent the bureau's real work, and he asked Equitable to be the sponsor. Although

the cost was steep at a projected $700,000 a year, Parkinson believed the new show would help Equitable's image as a provider of financial security. The chief appeal was the tie-in with Hoover, the personification of American security. Perhaps the most famous and respected person in the country, he was regarded as the man who had rid the country of hoodlums and Nazi spies.

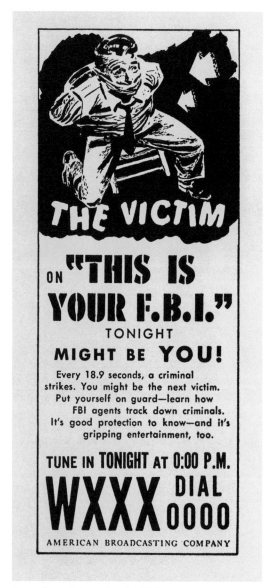

A sample newspaper ad for the FBI show.

This Is Your FBI had its debut on Friday, April 6, 1945, on the NBC Blue Network (soon to become ABC), where it ran for eight years. The series consisted of thirty-minute dramatizations of true stories introduced personally by Hoover and Parkinson, whose message was that their two institutions protected the American people. The show's motto was, "To your FBI you look for national security… and to the Equitable Society for financial security." Parkinson echoed that theme in his introduction to the first show: "In nearly every form of security other than the services rendered by your FBI, Equitable considers itself your partner and your friend. Our business, too, is safeguarding the security of the American family." Equitable's commercials were tributes to American businesses that Equitable insured or invested in, including the Pennsylvania Railroad, the textile industry, and the thousands of newspapers that carried agents' advertisements.[31]

The show's plots concentrated in a docudrama style on the meticulous labor of FBI work and, by implication, of insurance companies. In the first show, for example, two special agents identified a Nazi spy by systematically checking 5,000 baggage declarations and handwriting samples. The scripts were crisp and tense, the acting solid. *This Is Your FBI* started out on 178 radio stations and by the end of the third season was broadcast over 233 stations to an estimated 18 million listeners. Often it was one of the five most highly rated shows in the country. Agency managers and agents (many of whom had at first been dubious about the show's merits) raved about the prestige that the show brought them and Equitable. One veteran agent who made cold-call sales in rural areas reported to Parkinson that if mentioning "The Equitable" drew a blank, all he had to do to win a prospect's full attention was to say "FBI." Equitable also became identified with the show's pounding theme music — *da-da-da-da-dupp-dada* — adapted from Prokofiev's *The Love for Three Oranges* and soon to be known widely as "the FBI march." Of the Society's successful sweep into network radio, the editor of *Best's Insurance News* wrote, "The Equitable Society has pioneered a new field in selling life insurance, a field that many other life companies would do well to explore."[32]

The show was controversial. Although its directors and writers worked hard to follow Hoover's orders to deglamorize the lives of criminals and FBI agents, *This Is Your FBI* was criticized for exposing its large audience of children to violence. Equitable's advertising director, Sam Shope, and the FBI quickly put together an educational program sponsored by Equitable called the Better Citizenship Bureau, which sponsored anticrime seminars in urban high schools, at which special agents and policemen made presentations and students were asked to sign a pledge that they would obey the law. Some 10,000 teenagers participated at the first seminars in five eastern cities. In another step to defuse the criticism, one segment was broadcast from the middle of a convention of 5,000 New Jersey schoolteachers.

By 1949 the show was costing $1.1 million a year (the equivalent today of approximately $9 million, twice Equitable's 1993 advertising budget). Equitable withdrew as sponsor in 1952 partly due to the lingering internal debate about violence but mainly because agents protested that radio was losing influence to the new medium of television. By 1959, five years after Parkinson's retirement, all Equitable's nonprint advertising was on a televised series of dramas about great Americans called *Our American Heritage*, which the Society produced in cooperation with *American Heritage* magazine.

Feisty Tom Parkinson took on the New Deal, the insurance industry, government monetary policy, and the New York State Insurance Department. Though he won more battles than he lost, his last one was not successful.

CHAPTER XII

THE STORM FIGURE

I n the spring of 1947, J. Edgar Hoover invited Parkinson to present the graduation speech at the FBI Academy, and as they marched to the podium to the staccato beat of the FBI march, Equitable's President found himself in the spotlight that he had been attracting.

He had not always been so eager for publicity. In 1932 he had quietly turned down Franklin Roosevelt's offer of a cabinet position largely because he opposed the President-elect's plan to devalue the dollar in order to try to springboard the economy out of the Great Depression. And for several years thereafter he had ignored policyholders' pleas to publicly oppose the New Deal's tax-raising and inflationary policies. Appalled though he was by inflation and its degrading effects on financial values, Parkinson held his tongue because, as a student of the history of life insurance, he was acutely aware of how much the Society's welfare depended on avoiding controversy. He told his colleagues that Henry Hyde had scared away many prospects when he publicly opposed William Jennings Bryan and the inflationary free silver populists of the 1890's. He was not about to build on the same mistake and attack a sitting president. "The future of our business depends on public confidence," he said. "In this matter of public confidence, life insurance owes a debt of obligation to those governmental agencies which represent the public."[1]

Yet in the late 1930's, Parkinson became less circumspect and assigned himself the gadfly role as the insurance industry's — if not the country's — leading and increasingly strident critic of high taxes, government-induced inflation, and what he called "a crooked combination of the two." An insurance periodical observed, "When the life insurance industry needs defending, President Thomas I. Parkinson, of the Equitable Life Society, will always come to the front." He was encouraged by the warm responses to his public appearances. The newsreel camera and radio microphone especially liked his spunk, and he in turn came to like the media's attention. After he introduced the first broadcast of *This Is Your FBI*, an agent wrote him, "They tell me that the 'mike' frightens a great many men half to death but you appeared just as much at ease as when you are talking to your Equitable friends." He made speeches around the country, wrote articles for insurance magazines, and for a while substituted for the syndicated financial columnist Merryle Stanley Rukeyser (father of the financial commentators of a later generation, Merryle and Louis Rukeyser). He wrote and had Equitable mail anti-inflation educational brochures to its 2.5 million policyholders. By 1945 he was such a public figure that New York Mayor Fiorello La Guardia identified Parkinson as a possible successor. Parkinson was tongue-tied for one of the few times in his life; eventually he said he was not interested.[2]

To him the villains were, first, the politicians in the Roosevelt and Truman administrations who created and continued the policy of pegging bonds, which he excoriated as inflationary; and, second, bankers who, he claimed, supported pegging because easier credit brought them more business. Parkinson was a

"We Can't Walk Out on 78,000,000 Policyholders!"

AN OPEN LETTER
TO THE BOARD OF DIRECTORS
OF THE LIFE INSURANCE ASSOCIATION OF AMERICA

GENTLEMEN:

On December 8, 1948, the resolution reprinted on this page was proposed to you. This resolution would have added your support to the many economic leaders who are alarmed by the inflationary effect of current monetary practices . . . and who are convinced that these practices urgently need a comprehensive review by a competent and unbiased commission.

Such an examination would obviously be in the best interests of those provident men and women who own life insurance policies. Their policies were bought with the intent of providing their beneficiaries with an income of definite purchasing power at maturity. Today's life insurance proceeds, you will have to agree, signally fail to accomplish the purposes for which they were contracted as recently as 20, 10, or even 5 years ago.

This crisis constitutes a major challenge to all who are entrusted with the safeguarding of life insurance funds.

That you felt it expedient to reject this resolution, on the grounds that it constituted a criticism of the Government's current monetary policies by the life insurance business, seems to us to be unwarranted timidity contrary to the tenets of good citizenship. In a democracy, the life insurance business, friend and bulwark of the Government in peace or war, has a duty to speak up with sincere and honest criticism whenever opposition is felt. To do less is tantamount to a betrayal of the trust and confidence of 32 million American families who have faith in life insurance.

I shall continue, therefore, to urge upon every member of the life insurance fraternity and upon the general public, the pressing need for re-examination of our Federal Reserve System's currency and credit policies. Certainly the ideal way to conduct such an appraisal would be through an impartial monetary commission. We can't walk out on 78,000,000 policyholders!

FAITHFULLY YOURS,

Thomas N. Parkinson

PRESIDENT.
*The Equitable Life Assurance Society
of the United States*

THE REJECTED RESOLUTION

RESOLVED: That the Board of Directors of L.I.A.A. adopt the following statement of policy with respect to the current monetary problem:

The members of the Life Insurance Association of America, noting the continued inflation of our money supply and the decreasing purchasing value of our dollar, now declare for the guidance of our monetary authorities that the policyholders of our life insurance companies are suffering more detriment as the result of current monetary policies, and particularly the Federal Reserve System's support of the Government bond market, than they would be likely to suffer from any decline in the market price of Government bonds if that support were ended. In support of this declaration, attention is called to the fact that while the total life insurance in force in this country has increased from $117 billions in 1940 to approximately $200 billions at the present time, the purchasing value of the $200 billions now in force is approximately $114 billions.

We also join in the recommendation which now has the support of many individuals and organizations that a Monetary Commission be created to review the field of currency, credit and related matters in the light of present day problems.

Parkinson's challenge to the insurance industry.

director of the Chase National Bank, Equitable's traditional banker, but tension was building between Equitable's large intrusions into banks' usual territory through its Assured Home Ownership mortgages and its large corporate financings. Yet Parkinson was unmoved. Sylvia Porter, a financial writer, described Parkinson's assault on the banks as "a wow of a fight going on today in the most rarified circles of American finance... our billion dollar insurance companies versus our billion dollar banks." While the American Bankers Association was holding its annual meeting in Detroit in 1948, Parkinson arranged to give an antibanker speech to a Detroit organization, and bankers who had appointments with him sometimes found themselves waiting for long periods in his lobby.[3]

Why he went public to such a degree must be guessed. There may well have been a mix of personal and tactical reasons having to do

with his own extremely confident temperament, his concern about the government's economic policy, his frustration at the insurance industry's inclination to avoid any controversy, and — in the 'forties — Equitable's quandary after it made such a large commitment to short-term bonds. But whatever the reasons, his pronouncements made him a standout in an industry that, since 1905, had been very cautious in the way it presented itself to the public that purchased its goods and to the government that regulated its business. Such behavior stimulated the leading insurance trade newspaper, *National Underwriter*, to describe him as "a storm figure in the business because of his views on inflation control." Where he led, the industry did not follow. His vociferousness pleased few insurance executives. While the industry enthusiastically joined doctors in successfully opposing Truman's national health plan in 1950, officers at other companies generally preferred quiet negotiation with government to public arguments. In 1950, the board of directors of the Life Insurance Association unanimously defeated his motion for a resolution attacking bond pegging because they did not want to appear to be critical of the government. Calling the industry association "timid and inconsistent," Parkinson took out fullpage, signed advertisements in the insurance press that shouted, "We Can't Walk Out on 78,000,000 Policyholders!" Other insurance executives warned that he was inviting trouble. "If Mr. Parkinson is right he is awfully, awfully right," editorialized a trade magazine, "but if he is wrong, stand by to pick up the pieces."[4]

Parkinson sometimes found himself fighting what he thought were the industry's battles singlehanded. One of his more dramatic campaigns was his attack on a tax law in 1950. The question of how governments could tax insurance companies had long been controversial. Some states taxed income from premiums, although mutual insurance companies argued that the premiums were not theirs to be taxed but rather money held in trust for their policyholders. Another system began to be used in the early 1920's by some states and the federal government: they taxed the return on investments after deducting the amount set for reserves. But in the 1940's — thanks to pegging — government bonds were yielding less than the reserve rate of 3 percent, and insurance companies were paying no federal taxes at all. In 1949, the Treasury Department proposed a stopgap tax law that would lower the reserve exemption retroactively to 1947. While most of the rest of the insurance industry refused to oppose the legislation, Parkinson railed against what he called unconstitutional taxation and marshalled a large letter-writing campaign by policyholders. Appearing before the Senate Finance Committee, he put on another of his shows. Reported a trade magazine, "It was Parkinson... who provided fireworks, as had been expected." He won and the tax bill died, but his reputation in the industry was lowered another notch. Equitable and the New York State Insurance Department frequently found themselves at loggerheads over even small points in audits and in negotiations over new contracts.[5]

Parkinson attracted the attention of other regulators. Representative Emanuel Celler, chairman of the powerful House Banking Committee, criticized Equitable's investment program as unsuitable for a life insurance company; insurers "privately gobbled up" loans that lay in the province of commercial banks. Parkinson defiantly testified before Celler's committee that a life insurance company's duty was solely to its clients and policyholders, and it needed a decent income in order to provide its services to policyholders at moderate cost. Some of this was for show; Parkinson and Celler regularly met privately over quiet lunches. In any

case, no legislation followed. Parkinson trusted Celler sufficiently to propose that the Treasury Department hand over the government's monetary policy to Congress, which would then issue $10 billion

Douglas Southall Freeman.

worth of 3 percent "national emergency bonds" to life insurers and savings banks — but not, he added, to commercial banks. None of this happened, and pegging finally was ended in 1951 when the Federal Reserve and the Treasury Department agreed that the Fed henceforth would set monetary policy. Interest rates on government bonds rose, taking all market rates with them. But by then, Parkinson's role as the nation's financial troublemaker was permanent.[6]

In 1952, feisty Tom Parkinson turned seventy-two and began his twenty-fifth year as President, tying Henry Hyde as Equitable's longest-serving chief executive. At the banquet celebrating his silver anniversary, Douglas Southall Freeman, an Equitable director and the biographer of Robert E. Lee, toasted Parkinson: "It is enough for us to say, it is our pride to say, that you have done what you have because you have been unflinchingly, unswervingly, yourself."[7]

He had been himself — inspiring, pugnacious, dogmatic, at times truculent if not arrogant, and regularly and contentedly controversial. And despite his cries of government-imposed doom, in the years since the Great Depression, he had presided over one of the most financially robust eras in Equitable's history. Individual and group insurance sales were booming, and investment yields of residential mortgages and corporate financing had been improving steadily since their nadir in 1946. The success was not all his (or anybody else's) doing, for the 1940–52 period witnessed one of the highest consumer savings rates ever; the war brought a dramatic economic recovery and offered limited opportunities to spend money, and during the next ten years the economy improved even further as Americans concentrated on rebuilding their lives and homes after a generation of instability.

In terms of building capital, this was one of the best periods in Equitable's long history. In the thirteen years since the end of the depression, between 1940 and 1952, Equitable's capital base increased fourfold from $107 million to $426 million. By comparison, over the next twelve years, through 1964, capital would less than double to $718 million. And over the next *thirty* years, between 1952 and 1982, it would only triple to $1.4 billion, and that figure is distended at least one-third by inflation.

In a few other ways, the second half of the Parkinson regime was admirable. In 1948, for example, he noticed new tax legislation that appeared to affect the handling of estates. Deciding that agents should be informed about it, he created a special Home Office organization of legal and financial specialists to be a resource for the agency force, the Special Services Division. In 1951, to keep an eye on financial policy in Washington, he hired a personal economic advisor, Reynolds Nowell. In part to improve Equitable's public image after its bitter opposition to national health care, he had Equitable develop the first private major-medical health policy, first issued in 1951 as the In-Hospital Major Expense Policy.

And Parkinson pushed the Society's Medical Department into new, pioneering fields. Historically, it had consisted of a few doctors and nurses who advised underwriters on the approval of applications. But in the 1930's it established its own cardiovascular unit, and its doctors published research in

medical journals. In 1953, the department was divided into three parts: the Bureau of Medical Selection focused on the new problem of adjusting actuarial assumptions around the new antibiotics; the Bureau of Medical Research, headed by Norvin Kieffer, produced medical texts and conducted research (it developed a drug for the treatment of tuberculosis, Equilite); and The Equitable's Bureau of Public Health created and ran a health education program.

Yet in other and important ways, as a manager Parkinson clearly had stayed on for too long. Equitable seemed to be running on automatic pilot, and not very well at that. Despite its financial successes, it was in desperate need of definition and reorientation in its image, its operations, and its products. "Equitable was just *big* — huge, a whale," said a man who in 1951 was an agent for New England Mutual, a competing insurer, Richard H. Jenrette (who later would become an Equitable Chief Executive Officer). Arriving as the new Personnel Director in 1953, Edward A. Robie found an institution that called itself "Mother Equitable" but that, in the last days of the Parkinson regime, often was "paternalistic in a very autocratic sort of way…. It was not that everything was in a mess. It was that almost everything needed improvement, coordination, and forward planning."[8]

In his first twenty years Parkinson had been an able manager, sensitive to his subordinates, encouraging of teamwork, planning, and the promotion of capable, imaginative young officers. But after he became a public figure — and especially after his heir apparent, Sterling Pierson, died in 1949 — he retired to his office with a small bunch of advisors, led by a capable if secretive and cautious officer, Raymond H. Weins. "Kingmanship" was how many described Parkinson's remote management style in the years after World War II. When he appeared in the Home Office lobby in the

Sterling Pierson.

morning, the elevator starters shooed people out of the way so that he could rise, solitary, to the executive floor. To a young agency manager in Detroit, Coy Eklund, Parkinson was no more than a "very articulate, proud, and impressive" individual who ruled by fear: "Everybody quaked when Parkinson approached." He required each department to report directly to him, trusted few subordinates, and did nothing to develop a successor or new talent. The Home Office ground to a halt at his desk. A rising actuary, J. Henry Smith, would say of Parkinson:

> *People who did grow, began to grow, got cut off at the knees over and over again.... He operated as a one-man company with inadequate development of the company's structure and management. He simply did not bring enough young people into increasing responsibility.*

Discouraged, many of those talented people moved on to other companies.[9]

Half a century earlier, the reign of the Hydes and the Alexanders had been ended by board members and public officials who distrusted their empire building, defiance of public opinion, and nepotism. Now another reign would end for many of the same reasons.

Though nepotism was not the most important of these concerns, it was the most visible and the one that first tripped up Parkinson. He had two sons. The elder was Thomas I. Parkinson, Jr., a lawyer at a prominent New York firm that did considerable work for Equitable. His younger brother, Courtney V. Parkinson, though inexperienced in adver-

tising, was placing hundreds of thousands of dollars worth of company advertising and was being paid by Equitable to distribute the texts of his father's antigovernment speeches to newspapers and magazines.

In June 1950, in two circular letters to the Board of Directors, George V. McLaughlin, a board member, protested what he saw as favoritism in Parkinson's handling of advertising through his son and also of Gateway Center contracts, which had been assigned without competitive bids. A crusty banker who saw himself as Equitable's conscience, McLaughlin had crossed swords with some of the most powerful people in the state. He had been state banking commissioner under Governor Alfred E. Smith and New York City police commissioner under Mayor James J. Walker, who fired him because he refused to end police raids on gambling dens run by Walker's friends. McLaughlin was head of the largest bank in Brooklyn and had protected the Brooklyn Dodgers from outside takeover. A fellow director described him as "seldom sitting mute but never dull; wrong but never in doubt." One thing never in question was McLaughlin's distrust of Thomas I. Parkinson, whom he thought arrogant. Parkinson replied to McLaughlin's charges in his own memorandums. In accordance with an Armstrong law mandating that documents pertinent to an insurer's business be sent to the New York State Insurance Department, copies of the exchanges were delivered to the superintendent.[10]

The department was then engaged in one of its triennial examinations of Equitable, this one for the three years ending December 31, 1950. The regulators were trained to examine insurance companies as thoroughly and skeptically as Charles Evans Hughes had back in 1905, and to look at them from the point of view of policyholders. An insurance superin-

George V. McLaughlin.

tendent of the 1940's, Robert E. Dineen, once pointed out that while there were many trade groups representing agents and insurance companies, "The most inarticulate group in the whole picture is the public, the consumers. I concede it to be my responsibility to make their welfare my first job." A sign that his department was functioning properly, he went on, was that a triennial audit always found something wrong. Just how much the regulators modeled themselves on Hughes was indicated by an anecdote told by Equitable's General Counsel Davidson Sommers. When a new lawyer in the department's Life Insurance Bureau asked its director, Julius Sackman, for material to introduce him to his job, Sackman handed over a copy of the Armstrong Committee's report. And when the employee reported that he had finished, Sackman instructed him to read it again. Sackman himself was meticulous. An Armstrong law required that a "substantial" number of a mutual insurer's directors own insurance polices with the company. When the examiners found in its 1947 audit that ten of the thirty-three directors did not own Equitable policies, Sackman demanded that every director buy a policy. The "technical legal issue" was insignificant, he wrote in his report: "as a matter of sound policy, substantially all the directors of a mutual life company, such as the Society, should be policyholders of the Society." By 1950, only two directors did not have policies — but Sackman continued to press the point.[11]

Yet, despite its appearance as adversarial, the relationship between insurers and their regulators could be subtle and flexible. It also was

permanent. Parkinson appeared at retirement dinners for insurance superintendents; and at Sterling Pierson's funeral there appeared a delegation of six officers from the New York Insurance Department, led by Julius Sackman.

The audit proceeded into 1951. In June the chief examiner, John Byrne, called Superintendent Alfred J. Bohlinger's attention to George McLaughlin's complaints, plus two new charges: Equitable had been funneling legal business to firms in which some board members were partners; and Parkinson, in his memorandums, had misled Equitable's board about the relationship with his son's advertising agency. When Bohlinger confronted Parkinson, the President seemed not to take the charges seriously. Of the nepotism issue, all he could do was speak vaguely of the "father and son angle." The superintendent then availed himself of his authority over the companies that he regulated to call the board's executive committee to a meeting in his office. Very soon thereafter, the board terminated the contract with the Parkinson advertising agency, retained a former judge to review assignments to law firms, and resolved that the board approve contracts in excess of $50,000. It also passed a strict bylaw banning nepotism in the hiring of employees and retention of consultants and law firms. As the Equitable board was responding so quickly to his wishes, Bohlinger asked state Judge William Mertens, Jr., to further investigate Parkinson's recent behavior.[12]

All this remained behind the closed doors of the state Insurance Department and Equitable's boardroom until late January 1952, when the story of the relationship with the Parkinson advertising agency was leaked anonymously to the *New York Journal-American's* financial columnist, Leslie Gould. Gould wrote five accurate, mildly sensationalized articles that attracted wide public notice and stimulated seven policyholders to file suits against directors for losses due, the complaints claimed, to nepotism and the Gateway Center project. (All of the suits eventually were dismissed or withdrawn.)

For the growing number of Parkinson's critics, the time seemed almost ripe for him to move on, yet few wanted him to have to be forced to depart at a time when he was under fire, and no suitable successor was on the near horizon. Weins had few admirers and the other Senior Vice-President, chief actuary Ray Murphy, was sixty-five. In August 1952, Parkinson was prevailed upon to appoint an officers' committee, chaired by Weins, to review administration. The board obviously did not trust management to take the assignment seriously because the next day it created its own committee. Indeed, the officers' committee spent its time debating minor issues before Weins was replaced by Charles W. Dow, Vice-President in charge of investments. While management stuttered, the directors' committee, chaired by Douglas Southall Freeman, addressed the succession question. Parkinson was aware of what was up and did not like it; at his silver anniversary dinner, he said he knew there was talk of a replacement to fill his shoes, but he was not thinking of leaving. His shoes, he said, were "tightly laced." But not long after, Freeman's committee decided to take day-to-day control of Equitable out of Parkinson's hands by giving him the title of Chairman of the Board, and appointing Ray Murphy as President. When Freeman brought this news to Murphy, he dramatically prefaced the surprise in his smooth Virginia accent by announcing, "The hand of the Lawd is about to descend upon you." Murphy was surprised — yet not so much that he neglected to ask what his powers would be. Freeman assured him he would have full power and added that one of his duties was to locate and name his successor.[13]

LESLIE **Gould:**   *Financial Editor*

Parkinson's Exit Still Leaves Many Questions Unanswered

The exit of Thomas I. Parkinson from the $6 billion Equitable Life Assurance Society, following revelations of nepotism, still leaves a few things to be answered.

These are:

1.—Who will succeed to the top spot in the country's third largest life company. The present president—Ray D. Murphy, who took over last year, is 66 and close to the retirement age.

2.—What is to happen to the directors, particularly the lawyer ones, who went along with Mr. Parkinson for so many years and some of whom or their firms collected large fees.

3.—What is to be the future policy as to counsel for borrowers. A substantial part of this legal service was done through the law firm in which a second Parkinson son, Thomas I. Jr., is a partner. The firm is Milbank, Tweed, Hope and Hadley, one of the biggest in the country.

Run By An Autocrat

4.—Will the State Superintendent of Insurance Alfred J. Bohlinger make public or pigeon hole the investigation and report on Equitable's management made by former City Court Justice William Mertens, Jr. Even Equitable directors—except possibly one or two—haven't seen this report, which goes into legal fees.

There is nothing wrong with the company, except that for too many years it was run by an autocrat. The company is sound financially and has made a good record in operations. While several political figures have been named as possibilities for the top job, including Gov. Dewey and Mr. Bohlinger, the idea may be novel—but why not someone who knows the insurance business and handling investments?

The insurance industry, while shocked by the turn of events, on the whole feels that a real public service has been performed in bringing the matter out. That in the long run it will be good for all parties.

Where there is questionable conduct, it should come out—whether it involves public officials or private business interests. The insurance companies are semi-public in that there are no shareowners in the great life companies. They are mutualized —run for the benefit of the policyholders. This is fine, but it can, as shown in this instance, lead to abuses and self-perpetuating management and directors.

Question of Legal Ethics

The case presents another question to the legal profession and the rather elastic ethics of that fraternity. Equitable's board of 33 includes nine lawyers, not including one judge. Some of these lawyers or their firms collected fees. One such lawyer-director, who has since died, gathered $150,000 in fees for representation in a utility bankruptcy. His fees should have been made a claim against the bankrupt and paid by the court, and not by Equitable. If they had been, they probably would have been substantially reduced.

It is a great honor to serve on an insurance company board. The job also carries with it public responsibility. This was not exercised by many of the Equitable directors. There were a couple of exceptions— George V. McLaughlin, as the insurance report brought out, was one. Federal Judge Knox was another. There were a couple more.

Parkinson's troubles were covered by a New York newspaper.

Judge Mertens submitted his report to Bohlinger on March 31, 1953. He confirmed the examiner's criticisms but added a new, serious charge of nepotism: during his examination he discovered that Parkinson had instructed his staff to send large amounts of legal work to the law firm where Thomas Parkinson, Jr., worked. Mertens had no complaints about the services rendered; but the issue, as with Courtney Parkinson's advertising commissions, was conflict of interest, which the Armstrong laws and subsequent legislation and rulings had barred at life insurance companies. Concluding that Parkinson was "untrustworthy within the contemplation of the insurance law," Mertens recommended that Bohlinger remove him as an Equitable officer and director.[14]

It was an extraordinarily serious charge. In late May, Bohlinger presented the demand to Parkinson. In negotiations through Parkinson's attorney, Theodore Kiendl, Parkinson agreed to step down. Bohlinger planned to announce his retirement in the report of the department's examination, which he would release in the autumn, but relented when Kiendl protested that Parkinson desired and deserved a graceful exit and was entitled to make his own announcement. Clearly, Bohlinger wanted to make an example of Parkinson; just as clearly, Parkinson did not want to be made an example of.

Compounding the problem were two major and unnecessary misunderstandings. First, while Bohlinger expected Parkinson's own announcement to be imminent, at least before that year's elections to the board, Parkinson intended to say nothing publicly until February 1954, when the new board would take its seat. What Bohlinger did not know was that Parkinson was up for reelection to the board that year. Second, Bohlinger perceived Parkinson's impending departure from Equitable as a "resignation," while Parkinson believed he would "retire" simply by not taking his seat on the board in February. While the directors agreed with Bohlinger that Parkinson had to go — they had no choice, for he threatened to go public with his revelations — they clearly did not appreciate the confused interpretation of what had been negotiated. The summer and early autumn passed without any announcement from Parkinson, although there were rumors. If the stories were true, editorialized a trade magazine, Parkinson's separation from Equitable "will be a distinct loss to the institution of life insurance." Such sentiments did not encourage the necessary forthrightness on Parkinson's part. At some point, Bohlinger discovered that Parkinson's name was listed on the ballots for the upcoming board election.[15]

Parkinson had made no announcement by October 28, 1953, when Bohlinger released the report on the triennial examination. He said nothing about Parkinson's agreed-on retirement and made only a brief reference to the Courtney Parkinson nepotism issue, which had been settled two years earlier. But the next day, in a press conference that he had called, Bohlinger described and criticized the relationship. Though conceding it was not illegal, he said, "I don't look with great favor on nepotism in any such institution as a great life company. I do not approve it." At that he announced that Parkinson — whom he described as "not a well man" — would resign from the board in February.[16]

Somebody other than Parkinson in this unwinnable situation would have interpreted Bohlinger's comments as offering an opportunity for a graceful retreat, but Tom Parkinson — fierce and proud as ever — would have none of that. He was outraged that Bohlinger had violated his understanding of their agreement, that the word *resignation* had been applied to his planned departure, and that he had been characterized as being in poor health. It was true that he was going into the hospital that day for a cataract operation, but otherwise, he believed, he was in good shape. In a written statement released from the hospital, he refused to resign, and in a letter to the board he stated that if someone had demanded a public announcement in June he would have made it. "At no time did I agree that the announcement of my retirement should come from the superintendent's office," he insisted. "The difference is not immaterial but fundamental, to me, to you, and to the Society." Parkinson and his friends refused to take his situation seriously: Bohlinger, they were sure, was merely ambitious for his job.[17]

This left Bohlinger with no alternative but to call a meeting of The Equitable's Board of Directors. Parkinson was sure the board would back him. At the meeting, on November 4, Bohlinger warned the directors

*Appointed as an interim CEO to succeed Parkinson,
Ray Murphy stayed four years.*

that he would hold public hearings if they
did not immediately let Parkinson go. "I cannot temporize with this, gentlemen," were
his parting words. After twelve hours of often
angry debate, at 11:30 that night the board
resolved that they would immediately
announce that Parkinson would leave
Equitable the following February. Though
couched in the language of retirement, the
resolution was accompanied by another
announcement that indicated otherwise. At
Bohlinger's request, the board passed a bylaw
that permitted future boards to drop a director
for cause. The implication about Parkinson
was painfully clear. It was a humiliating blow
to a proud man. In January 1959, Parkinson
had the satisfaction of having a state supreme
court justice rule that, just as Bohlinger had
said, he had done nothing illegal. Parkinson
died five months later.[18]

Parkinson's successor as Equitable's
seventh Chief Executive Officer was
a very different sort of man. The Society's
chief actuary, Ray Dickinson Murphy, was
described by a close associate as "a very
warm, gentle, and extremely bright person,"
and he often was underestimated by people
who, having worked under the acerbic
Parkinson, were given to mistake civility
for passivity.[19]

A descendent of William Bradford of the
Mayflower, and a Phi Beta Kappa at Harvard,
he was advised by his mathematics professor
to take his skills into actuarial work. While
bright and capable, he impressed his peers at
Massachusetts Mutual as insufficiently
aggressive; as one colleague remembered
him, he was a terrific second baseman on the
company baseball team but too much a gentleman for the rough-and-tumble play of the
insurance company league. At twenty-three
he was appointed chief actuary of the
Hartford Life Insurance Company. When it
was acquired by its reinsurer, Missouri State
Life, he declined the offer to move west and
joined Equitable in 1913. Murphy rose
through the ranks and in 1930 was appointed
Vice-President in charge of the Underwriting
Department. This was one of the Society's
hot seats; underwriters approved or disallowed
applications for policies sent in by agents,
whose commissions rose and fell on the
underwriter's judgment. Six years later, he
became the Society's chief actuary. An authority on actuarial theory and the author of
textbooks, Murphy also had a good, if quiet,
marketing sense and helped found the insurance industry's publicity arm, the Institute of
Life Insurance. Parkinson relied on him as a
member of his small cluster of advisors, and
when Murphy was named Executive Vice-
President in 1950, he and everybody else fully
expected that he would retire in the job.
Then came Parkinson's problems.

Murphy knew that Equitable was in trouble, and he had a notion as to how to begin to reform it. On the night of his election as President in 1953, he presented his management philosophy to a meeting of agency managers in New York. It was a philosophy counterpoised to Parkinson's. A manager who was present, Horace H. Wilson, summarized one part of the speech emphatically: "This he regarded as an institutional *team* responsibility in which his job was that of giving the *team* a chance to function." Murphy arranged for early retirement for Raymond Weins and, throwing out the one-man autocratic management scheme in which all department heads reported directly to the Chief Executive Officer, gave responsibility to the vice-presidents.[20]

His main assignment was to find a capable successor to himself. Some directors had their own ideas. "We'll have to get a good-sized name to offset the effects of the Parkinson affair," one board member told a journalist the day after the showdown with Superintendent Bohlinger. "Maybe the best idea would be some ex-general." But others who knew Equitable well were sure radical surgery was unnecessary. Wrote Leslie Gould, the financial columnist who broke the nepotism scandal, "There is nothing wrong with the company, except that for too many years it was run by an autocrat.... [W]hy not someone who knows the insurance business and handling investments?"[21]

Equitable, 1909–1959 (in millions)

YEAR	PREMIUM INCOME	ASSETS	SURPLUS
1909	53	479	8
1919	81	599	17
1929	235	1,179	57
1939	281	2,401	83
1949	600	5,255	308
1959	1,099	9,663	522

Murphy agreed. Two talented candidates were working at Equitable. One was the new chief actuary, Walter Klem. Although only a high-school graduate, Klem had great ability and knowledge of life insurance. But he also was dry, demanding, and uncharismatic (in a speech to agents, he went on at length to describe the blessings of interdepartmental conveyor belts). He was also supremely jealous of his prerogatives and could be secretive. Recalled Edward Monahan, the former Philadelphia Athletics pitcher who worked in the Controller's Department: "He protected the surplus of The Equitable. That was his surplus. You'd get only financial data from Klem, and only if he wanted to give it to you."[22]

The fact that agents and agency managers were suspicious of Klem — or any actuary — was neither new nor surprising. The cultures could not have been more different. A traditional actuary's job by definition was to be pessimistic, an agent's to be sanguine. As underwriters, actuaries cost agents commissions by turning down applications that, to agents, seemed perfectly safe. And actuaries, as a group, were not particularly good public speakers; they were not rewarded for presence, as agents often were, and they did not have the agents' tradition of morale-boosting speeches and correspondence. For many managers, the archetypal actuary was Klem, who underwrote so cautiously that an agent, Robert Wenzlaff, recalled, "We used to joke that if you had a pimple you wouldn't get a case approved." Klem, said one fast-rising manager, Coy Eklund of Detroit, was "the bane of our existence." Although Murphy favored Klem and refused to give the Old Guard a direct say in the choice of the new President, he was attentive to managers' opinions. He reluctantly decided against Klem and in favor of his other nominee, Charles W. Dow, the Society's fifty-three year-old chief of investments. Dow was liked by many agents in large part because he was not Klem; and by the directors because of the Society's generally successful investment portfolio.[23]

Early in 1956 the board elected Dow as President, the number-two job, with the understanding that he would continue to concentrate on investments; Murphy, now Chairman of the Board, remained in overall command. The plan was that after a year or so, Murphy would retire and Dow would take over. But Dow, encouraged by some agency managers, was eager to take over immediately. When he began taking responsibility for sales and agency relations, Murphy complained that he should be spending more time on investments. Dow then asked the board to accelerate the succession. Murphy, feeling betrayed, threatened to quit. In January 1957, the board requested Dow's resignation. He had been on the job for only eleven months. New York Insurance Superintendent Thomas Thacher made no fuss, but the second abrupt departure in three years of a high Equitable official was another embarrassment, further indicating that The Equitable was floundering.

This time the board conducted the search. It was chaired by Henry T. Heald, president of the Ford Foundation. Murphy nominated Klem, but the names of some of Equitable's outside directors were being circulated. Warren V. Woody, head of Chicago's largest agency, heard favorable comments about a director who was a local lawyer and businessman, James Oates. Woody asked Wenzlaff, who was one of his district managers and had done some work for Oates, to arrange a meeting. Over a lunch that included Wenzlaff and two other managers, Lee Wandling of Milwaukee and Smith Ferebee of Richmond, Woody asked Oates if he would allow his name to be considered as Equitable's next President. Oates indicated that he was open to the proposal. Woody and Ferebee, with Eklund and Arthur D. Hemphill, the agency manager in San Francisco, went to New York and asked Heald for a meeting. According to Eklund, their purpose was not to press the name of a nominee but to lobby against Klem. When the search committee next met, Heald suggested Oates, with whom he had worked when he was a university president in Chicago. The other members of the committee liked the idea. Meanwhile, Klem, unaware of the managers' lobbying efforts, was so confident he would be elected that, on the day of the board meeting, he and his wife moved into a hotel near the Home Office so they would be on immediate call. But Oates was selected and Klem was disappointed for the second time in two years.

By that circuitous route there came to Equitable the man who unified it and renewed its purpose by reorganizing its administration, its sales force, and its investment operation; and who introduced variable insurance products, separate accounts, and other tools that transformed the enterprise. When his successor, J. Henry Smith, spoke of Jim Oates, he would describe him as "a savior sent by Providence, I think, to set us back on the track that we had lost."[24]

Jim Oates in a characteristic stance at an Equitable meeting.
"He had the most amazing combination of abilities," said one board member.

CHAPTER XIII

THE PRIME MOVER

I n 1959, the third year of James Oates's Presidency, The Equitable Life Assurance Society commemorated its hundredth anniversary. The ceremonies were long and elaborate, for there was much to celebrate. One hundred years after Henry Hyde hung the banner out the window, The Equitable remained at the top of its industry as the third largest insurer in the world, trailing only Metropolitan and Prudential. A huge sales campaign had determined which agents would earn free trips to and seats at the celebration, mounds of customized souvenirs were handed out, and 25,000 copies of a history of the Society written by R. Carlyle Buley, a Pulitzer Prize-winning historian at Northwestern University, were distributed to agents, customers, and libraries around the country. (Five years later, Buley's expanded, 1,500-page, two-volume version of the history would be published.) A service of thanksgiving and celebration was held at the Fifth Avenue Presbyterian Church, now in mid-Manhattan in a building financed by Equitable. The guest of honor was eighty-three year-old James H. Hyde, pleased to be an Equitable man once again.

At Madison Square Garden, throngs of agents and Equitable staff members watched performances by some of the nation's most famous athletes and artists, participated in a special Equitable edition of the popular television quiz show *The Price Is Right*, and took in lectures on the state of the world by academics and government officials. The theme was Equitable's success through a century of rise

and fall. Yet the triumphal tone was broken when U.S. secretary of health, education, and welfare Arthur S. Flemming shocked his audience with the blunt warning that if private insurers refused to cooperate with the advent of mandatory old-age medical insurance, the government would go ahead and bring it about on its own. On July 26, the exact anniversary of the Society's legal incorporation, a clergyman prefaced the invocation with another stunning reminder of the ceaseless pace of change: James Hyde, he announced, had died that morning. The tributes duly paid, President Oates stood before a huge American flag and led the crowd in singing "God Bless America."

Even as Oates led the celebration, he was asking whether Equitable was prepared for its second century, and whether it was properly fulfilling not only its business responsibilities but also its social role as a traditional mutual life insurance company.

As the insurance industry's share of the savings market declined, it became more competitive. Equitable's share of new individual business among the fifteen peer companies was almost 8 percent in 1955 but dropped to just under 6 percent in 1957. Meanwhile, Equitable also was losing market share in a business in which it once had dominated — pensions ("group annuity contracts" in insurance terminology). At the end of World War II, Equitable was responsible for one-third of all group annuity plans sold by insurance companies. It had a larger pension business than most banks, and was selling half a billion dollars worth of group annuities annually. The

James Hazen Hyde.

pension field grew explosively after 1949, when the Supreme Court ruled, in the case of *Inland Steel Company* v. *National Labor Relations Board*, that pensions could be the subject of collective bargaining between unions and management. But the expansion of the pension business in the United States from less than $20 billion to almost $60 billion during the 1950's did not help Equitable and other insurance companies anywhere near as much as it did banks, which for a variety of reasons were able to provide plans with a better investment return. Between 1950 and 1960, insurers' proportion of pension plans was halved from 80 to 40 percent. Equitable itself lost 117 contracts involving 230,919 employees and annual premiums totaling almost $69 million. Worse, Equitable lagged behind other insurance companies as its proportion of the insured group annuity business fell to 4 percent. By the late 'fifties it had only a handful of new group annuity clients. "Instead of being the primary carrier," ruefully remembered a later Equitable President, J. Henry Smith, "we became an afterthought."[1]

During Equitable's times of trouble, the company's Board of Directors tended to bring in leaders from outside the ranks of its career officers. The first was Paul Morton in 1905; the third, eighty-five years later, was Richard H. Jenrette. The second of these imported leaders was Jim Oates. Besides bringing cohesion and purpose where there had been disorder and lurching, he and the people he placed in high positions introduced the new tools that Equitable would use to shape itself in its second century. Among them were separate accounts, which by segregating clients' deposits

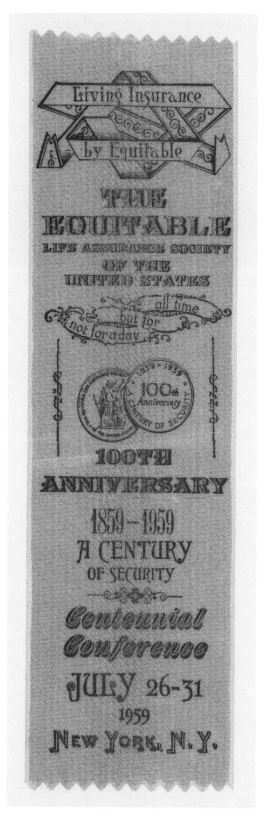

The centennial celebration ribbon.

The centennial celebration filled Madison Square Garden. James Hazen Hyde died on the exact day of the anniversary.

brought about the revival of the pension business and the introduction of a specialty as a
manager of other institutions' assets; the New
Epoch restructuring of the agency force, which
focused and disciplined sales; variable products, in which Equitable (marrying insurance
products to the stock market) had a product for
a new type of policyholder of the late twentieth century; and, finally, a corporate social
purpose that harmonized the Society's many
parts while fulfilling the traditional social
service, missionary function of a mutual insurance company. But what Oates best and most
comprehensively provided was his vital personal leadership. Davidson Sommers, his
General Counsel, observed:

> *I would say that the basic problem really
> was lack of leadership, more than anything
> else. And I can easily describe Jim Oates's
> contribution to The Equitable: he breathed
> new life into the organization.... [He]*

*breathed new life by his leadership.... He
had a mind that could see needs, a personal integrity that inspired trust, and a
charismatic personality that created confidence. Oates saw that The Equitable
needed to improve and to change.*[2]

Born in 1899, the son of a YMCA secretary
who became a general agent for Northwestern
Mutual Life, James Franklin Oates, Jr., was
raised in Chicago and educated at Princeton
and Northwestern University Law School.
He considered the ministry but followed law
and became a successful litigator in one
of Chicago's top firms, now called Sidley
& Austin, where he was a partner and close
friend of Adlai Stevenson, the two-time
Democratic Presidential nominee. In the 'forties he helped steer a local public utility out
of bankruptcy, became its president, and built
it into one of the largest power companies in
the Midwest. Along the way he was elected

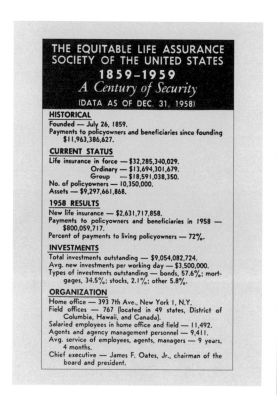

THE EQUITABLE LIFE ASSURANCE
SOCIETY OF THE UNITED STATES
1859–1959
A Century of Security
(DATA AS OF DEC. 31, 1958)

HISTORICAL
Founded — July 26, 1859.
Payments to policyowners and beneficiaries since founding
$11,963,386,627.

CURRENT STATUS
Life insurance in force — $32,285,340,029.
           Ordinary — $13,694,301,679.
           Group   — $18,591,038,350.
No. of policyowners — 10,350,000.
Assets — $9,297,661,868.

1958 RESULTS
New life insurance — $2,631,717,858.
Payments to policyowners and beneficiaries in 1958 —
$800,059,717.
Percent of payments to living policyowners — 72%.

INVESTMENTS
Total investments outstanding — $9,054,082,724.
Avg. new investments per working day — $3,500,000.
Types of investments outstanding — bonds, 57.6%; mort-
gages, 34.5%; stocks, 2.1%; other 5.8%.

ORGANIZATION
Home office — 393 7th Ave., New York 1, N.Y.
Field offices — 767 (located in 49 states, District of
Columbia, Hawaii, and Canada).
Salaried employees in home office and field — 11,492.
Agents and agency management personnel — 9,411.
Avg. service of employees, agents, managers — 9 years,
4 months.
Chief executive — James F. Oates, Jr., chairman of the
board and president.

"A century of security" was the theme in 1959.

chairman of the board of trustees of Princeton University and, in 1955, a director of Equitable.

Although Jim Oates did not become a clergyman, he always seemed to be in a pulpit, and his personal touch permeated the enterprise. Physically imposing and vigorous (according to one of his friends, people seated near him at an exciting football game had to watch out for their own safety), he exuded energy and also great sympathy. His successor, J. Henry Smith, characterized him as "a man of high spiritual content and character." When the dais collapsed at a gathering and people were spilled into a heap, Oates calmed the panicked crowd by leading them in the doxology of thanksgiving ("Praise God from Whom all blessings flow"). He ended one of his last talks to an Equitable audience, "Know all you can, love all you can, do all you can."[3]

Where Parkinson had aloofly refused to rub elbows with his subordinates, Oates welcomed contact. A few months after his arrival at the

Centennial souvenir medals were struck.

Home Office, he had his staff set up meetings with each department so that he could shake hands with all 7,600 employees. The time spent, he said, was well worthwhile because, he told a company magazine, "It would be difficult indeed for the head of a company to assist his business associates by isolating himself in a lonely office." This display of midwestern evangelism left the Society's more conservative officers and directors wondering what they were in for. "That sort of thing was *completely* overwhelming as far as the ordinary New Yorker was concerned," Henry Smith recalled. But those on the receiving end remembered Oates with affectionate respect. One morning he spotted a mailboy in the elevator and asked his name. "Bill McCaffrey, sir," the lad answered. His jowls shaking, Oates leaned over and confided, "Billy, you get ahead by *working hard*. Look at the fellow working next to you, and work harder than he does. That's how you get ahead." Thirty-five years later, McCaffrey (then Equitable's Chief Administrative Officer) said, "After that, whenever he saw me, Oates said it again: 'Billy, you get ahead by working *hard*.' Jim Oates was a class act and an inspiration."[4]

The hard-boiled old-timers who snickered about the handshake tour soon learned that there was more to him than a big heart and good cheer. His concern about people was deeply rooted in philosophical conviction, not just a good chief executive's desire to raise spirits in a demoralized institution. "I believe that man is a sacred personality," he announced in his first speech as Equitable CEO, "that he, the individual, is the important unit in life and the indispensable ingredient of business. No person or institution can trample on him." While Oates deeply sympathized with insurance agents — in a speech titled "The Dignity of Selling" he reflected on the "real isolation of people who must daily raise the painful topic of death with their clients" — he refused them special privileges. In 1960, he rejected a proposal by The Equitable's Agency Operations Department for a company-wide payroll deduction plan for buying insurance that would encourage Home Office employees to patronize Equitable agents. Oates explained that though the plan did not mandate that staff members purchase Equitable policies, the implicit sense of obligation would inevitably constrain their freedom. Managers, he said on another occasion and with characteristic intensity, "must have in their gizzards a sincere respect for the individual human rights of every employee.... [S]uch respect is a moral imperative." In the spring of 1958, less than a year after he was elected President, Oates issued one of the nation's pioneer statements of a liberal corporate personnel policy, *A Code to Work By*. Drafted by Personnel Director Edward Robie and described in its preamble as "a set of principles on which officers and employees of Equitable strive to base their relationships with each other," the *Code* established specific company-wide guidelines for fostering fairness, dignity, and decent working conditions. Six years before the 1964 federal Civil Rights Act, the *Code* banned discrimination based on factors "unrelated to ability."[5]

"He had the most amazing combination of abilities," recalled one of his directors, Lincoln Gordon, former president of Johns Hopkins University. "He was a natural orator, a natural raconteur, and also a man of great firmness and direction." His colleagues quickly discovered that Oates, in addition, was a driven, meticulous manager. "I'm constituted so that I'm happiest when I'm working," he once said. His assistants used such words as *ferocious* to describe his seventy-hour work week; one officer described Oates's mind as "like a steel trap." There also was amazement at his openness to change and experiment. Coy Eklund, one of his first assistants, noted in a journal in 1960 that Oates was a "springboard to the future" and drove people to "create a mood and practice of innovation." Twenty-five years later, recently retired as an Equitable CEO in his own right, Eklund recalled, "He turned this company around in the best sense of the word. He just gave us a lot of faith and confidence."[6]

Oates quickly decided Equitable was out of touch with developments in business and academic thinking, unprepared to change, and lacking a clear mission. He initiated several internal and external reviews. In an internal review of financial operations, an officers' committee determined that it was a mistake for Equitable to continue the traditional policy of mutual insurers of measuring success solely by sales volume. What was needed was the discipline of a bottom-line financial measure that indicated efficiency. The problem was that there was no room in the post-Armstrong Committee mutual insurance company tradition for focusing on the usual business measure of performance, which was profitability. The ideology of insurance fundamentalism, in fact, scorned any suggestion that the company's interests stood above those of policyholders. But Oates did succeed in establishing an internal audit department, the Cost Analysis and Planning Unit, which oversaw operations and engaged in long-range planning, and also in bringing in consultants to study the company and identify problem areas.

In one study, McKinsey & Company, the management consulting firm, looked at

Oates and his main aide, Chief Investment Officer Grant Keehn.

Equitable's often unsuccessful efforts, outside the Actuarial Department, to recruit and develop college graduates. For decades, most officers came up through the same system: they were recruited from New York City's top high schools, spent several years in an apprenticeship in a department, earned college degrees in night school on Equitable scholarships, and developed within one of the specialties — for example, investments, sales, or individual or group insurance — with little or no experience in other departments. While the system encouraged acquiring detailed knowledge of important areas in the business, it did not foster a company-wide outlook. There was not a career track for managers who could shape the departments into a common purpose. Addressing this problem, the McKinsey study stimulated the creation in the early 1960's of a new company-wide college recruiting and management training program.

Oates and his staff imported other new ideas. Some of them were stimulated by an outside study in 1958 and 1959 by a committee of professors from the Harvard Graduate School of Business Administration, who were brought in by Oates to study the Society's capability for innovation. Their report, submitted in May 1959, was a sharp critique of business as usual. One acute problem that they identified was an obsession at the Society's highest levels with legal concerns. Since every decision had to be run through what the Harvard team called a "forbidding gauntlet of administrative scrutiny and review" by state insurance regulators (a routine that had become an ordeal thanks in part to Equitable's recent history of poor relations with the New York State Insurance Department), the Society's top officers and directors were distracted by short-term regulatory concerns rather than concentrating on long-range policy. Agreeing that this bottleneck was stifling change, Oates increased the responsibilities of the vice-presidents and doubled their number to twenty-four; and, to improve dealings with the Insurance Department, hired Equitable's first General Counsel, Davidson Sommers.[7]

The Harvard Business School consultants identified another, possibly more dangerous, problem: people both outside and inside Equitable were ambivalent about the Society's identity and further development. In a public-opinion survey in which respondents were asked to say anything that came to mind at the mention of Equitable's name, only 6 percent were able to come up with a comment of any kind (as against the almost 50 percent who had responses to "Metropolitan" or "Prudential"). When the question was repeated to Equitable officers, the responses were more numerous but extremely vague, for instance, "Equitable is a very sound company" and "Equitable is a large, conservative company." The consultants concluded that "People at Equitable just aren't very clear as to what *kind* of business *is* Equitable's business." Those few who believed that Equitable had a unique identity labeled it simply as an individual life insurance company. This ignored the historical fact that the company had invented group insurance and for years had been a major force in it, and the economic one that Equitable was deriving one-third its premium income from group products. The reason for this anomaly, the consultants suggested, was that many Equitable officers were former agency managers or had otherwise come out of the agency force, which had little experience

with group insurance and, in fact, tended to oppose it. When those same officers were asked what changes or improvements should be made, most of them replied that the only concern was that minor tactical shifts in marketing were needed to respond to challenges by competitors. As for the Society and its products, many officers seemed to believe that life insurers had solved all their problems.[8]

The Harvard consultants advised that this climate of complacency not only detracted significantly from Equitable's ability to innovate but also reflected an unfortunate remoteness from changes in postwar American life. They recommended that Oates take marketing and product development out of the hands of the actuaries and put them in a new department. At the least, he should create a social research office in order to regain touch with Equitable's policyholders and reshape its identity. These criticisms were echoed by the Society's advertising agency, Foote, Cone & Belding.

The consultants found an enthusiastic audience in Jim Oates. As a university trustee and brother of a Princeton professor and administrator, Michael Oates, he respected academic thinking. He also was convinced that change was a fact of life, and that any institution that did not keep up with its environment and regularly clean out its system was flawed. But while Oates was enthusiastic about the Harvard report, some officers of long tenure did not embrace it. Serving as chairman of a committee evaluating it, Walter Klem produced a report defending actuaries and their consultative relationship with the field force: "Their effectiveness in developing and revising our services is self-evident. The Equitable's history is marked by many 'firsts' as a result of good work they have done along these lines." That was true, but the claim ignored the consultants' point that new tools were needed for changing times. Klem rejected the proposals for a new products department and a research office; these jobs, he believed, were being capably managed by his Actuarial Department. Oates, in no position to become entangled in a long war with Klem, compromised by forming an Office of Social Research in his own staff. It was charged with conducting research on insurance matters of day-to-day concern as well looking into the applicability of basic social theory to Equitable and life insurance.[9]

To advise and work with him, Oates also assembled a staff of experts experienced in various aspects of Equitable's obligations. Two were longtime Equitable people whom he brought into his office as personal assistants to advise him about insurance: J. Henry Smith, a calm, confident actuary with a strong background in group insurance; and Coy G. Eklund, a charismatic speaker, former agent, and former agency manager who reorganized the demoralized agency force. And to invigorate Equitable's investments and work with regulators he recruited two experienced officers who, like him, were in their fifties: Grant Keehn, a quiet, methodical investment banker, and Davidson Sommers, a genial but detail-oriented lawyer. Each of these four men would rise to become an Equitable President or Chairman of the Board.

These initiatives were backed by Equitable's Board of Directors, on which Oates had only recently served as an outside, nonmanagement member. He had their implicit trust. "[H]e was the kind of man you'd accept on the face of it," Smith said of this relationship. "Unless he did something totally wrong, you would just naturally like him and approve of him. He never did anything wrong, as far as the board was concerned."[10]

Although the board's size had been pared down, with more than two dozen members it could be an unwieldy body. Its members were talented but self-perpetuating. Oates complained mildly that it was Equitable's version of the College of Cardinals, but did little to change it. The board was his to appoint, but his only innovation was to seek able men outside New York City to reflect the country's geographical and occupational mix (like most corporate boards before about 1970, it contained no women or African Americans). Directors during Oates's tenure included Roger M. Blough, chairman of U.S. Steel, a Pittsburgh company; Neil H. McElroy, chairman of Procter & Gamble, in Cincinnati; and two university presidents, Robert Goheen of Princeton and Lincoln Gordon of Johns Hopkins. There were several permanent directorships for the occupants of various positions: the CEOs of the Chase Manhattan Bank, Equitable's longtime bank, and the Pennsylvania Railroad, for which the Society was the largest bondholder. The "doctor's seat" was always occupied by a prominent New York doctor, the "Mormon seat" by the president of the Church of Jesus Christ of Latter-Day Saints.

A few seats were held by prominent attorneys, with whom a lawyer like Oates (and Parkinson before him) had an easy understanding, and who had a better understanding than most other directors of life insurance's intricate regulatory problems and unusual statutory accounting system. From the 1920's into the 'fifties, the board's leader was John Lord O'Brian, an astute, well-connected attorney from Buffalo who had served in both the federal and state governments. He was succeeded by his protégé, also from Buffalo, Manly Fleischmann, who often represented the Society before state legislators and insurance regulators and also handled delicate chores. When Charles Dow was dismissed, Fleischmann was on hand to negotiate the financial settlement, draw up the press release, and explain his departure to agency managers. Besides lawyers, if any group seemed disproportionately represented on Equitable's board it was the alumni of Princeton University, largely because of the historic connections between the two institutions stretching back through Oates and several generations of Alexanders. Feisty George McLaughlin, who had pushed Parkinson so hard on several fronts, remained on the board into the 'sixties, but had less to complain about; he was a defense witness for Equitable in one of the suits concerning the Gateway Center investment, which McLaughlin himself had first challenged.

The most controversial director was John C. Knox, senior judge of the Federal District Court of the Southern District of New York. When his appointment was announced in 1948, Knox was criticized for opening himself to conflicts of interest, for as a director of one of the country's largest financial institutions, he inevitably would vote on financings and other concerns of corporations that might come into his courtroom. In 1954 and 1955, Knox refused to recuse himself from a policyholder suit against Equitable over the Gateway Center investments and even adjourned the case six times. Although his rulings were administrative in nature and the case ended up in state court, the Brooklyn and Manhattan bar associations made a point of declaring that a judge should not serve on an insurer's board. Knox heatedly denied any conflict of interest. The prohibition against a judge's involvement with businesses did not apply in his case, he insisted, because Equitable, as a mutual, was not a profit-making institution. Yet Knox had joined Equitable's board apparently not solely to do good but also to supplement his $15,000 judge's salary, which he often publicly criticized as insufficient, with director's fees. The Society paid directors $100 for each meeting they attended, and Knox was the board's most active member, attending as many as 100 meetings a year. The entrepreneurial Knox

Manly Fleischmann was the key outside director.

remained on the board until he reached the mandatory retirement age of sixty-five, by which time judicial salaries were raised to the more satisfactory level of $22,000.

Henry Smith once said of Oates, "He certainly produced a new direction for The Equitable." Oates was the first President since Henry Hyde to consciously articulate the enterprise's direction and mission. That mission was to be a custodian of people's money — in other words, a fiduciary. Oates's sense of duty was patriarchal. John Riley said:

> *He had almost a religious conviction about the role of life insurance in the American economy. In speech after speech, he held forth on the almost "sacred" relationship between the company and its policyholders. The fiduciary relationship was something never to be tampered with.*

I can hear him say, "All the people out there are entrusting us with their little premium payments every month or every year, and we have to guard them. If anything happens to their trust we are in deep, deep trouble. And nothing will happen as long as I have anything to do with it." It was almost like a sermon.[11]

While a fiduciary duty had long been implied in Equitable's advertising, never before had it risen to the level of a statement of clear corporate purpose. If there had been a single mission in the Society's first century, from the early days of Henry Hyde to the last days of Tom Parkinson, it had been to make Equitable the biggest — or at least "the strongest" — insurance company as measured by sales volume, insurance in force, or surplus. But Oates, while attentive to financial measurement, expanded the mission to explicitly include specific responsibilities that, until then, had been only tacitly assumed as included in a mutual life insurer's job. In retreats with officers, he developed an eleven-page, single-spaced mission statement, distributed on the last day of 1960. Its title was a mouthful: *The Fundamental Purpose, Business Objectives, and Implicit Goals of The Equitable Life Assurance Society of the United States*. Yet its message was succinctly conveyed by the opening statement, which married ethical purpose to technical expertise:

The purpose of the Equitable Society is to provide on a scientifically sound, demonstrably fair, and economically attractive basis, mutual insurance protection against financial hazards which people encounter because of disability and uncertainty as to length of life.

The statement went on to address the unique mix of private and public interests that constituted a mutual life insurance company. One article said that Equitable was "a private public service enterprise which is highly competitive but which cannot measure its success in profits and which is managed by those who cannot enjoy many of the financial rewards of the proprietor."[12]

Determining the mission was the first step. Oates went further and struggled to rally The Equitable's people around it. After involving officers in the development of the statement, he published a management manual (Equitable's first) based on the mission. Titled *The Chairman's Long-Range Plans* and referred to as "a framework for planning," the manual laid out the duties of the Society's specialized departments within the context of the mission statement. It went into so much detail about operations that his subordinates, worried that it might fall into competitors' hands, asked that it be kept confidential. But Oates, characteristically opting for openness and inclusiveness, insisted that the manual be distributed widely. He told the board,

I believe the most important benefits that will arise from our planning efforts will be in helping a manager at any level to see the whole of the organization and to understand the contribution that he is making in the achievement to our common goals. To do this we must communicate our plans, risky as that may be.

There had been too much secrecy and specialization; now it was time for the Equitable community to talk openly among themselves and reach mutual agreement.[13]

Through such steps, Oates succeeded in sweeping out much of the tense, defensive, and demoralized feelings of the last years of the Parkinson regime and in opening the institution to change. Spirits revived to their old level. Davidson Sommers, arriving from the outside, was skeptical about the talk of the "Equitable family," but he was quickly won over to admiration of the company and its culture under Oates. "There was a feeling of congeniality and collegiality inspired by Jim Oates," he told an interviewer. "In the past, change had been pushed upon people, but under Oates there was an openness to change." Unity would not come as easily or as totally as Oates (or Sommers) wished, and Equitable would continue to wrestle with the fundamental problems inherent in its mixed identity and specialty-intensive organization. Outside circumstances and seemingly intractable financial problems would prevent Equitable's surplus and capital base from growing at their old rate. But innovation bubbled. During Oates's dozen years as CEO,

Equitable developed the ambitions, staff, aptitudes, and tools that took it toward the end of the century. Separate accounts, a new sensitivity to consumers' concerns, variable annuities and, later, insurance, and large money-management and pension businesses — all came about or were launched in the Oates years. These developments were expensive, and not all of them were successful, but they and the new climate brought purpose and cohesion to a company that had been stagnating. After Oates retired in 1969, Sommers told him simply, "You were the prime mover of it all."[14]

Grant Keehn, a banker, was brought in by Oates to reform investment policy.
He challenged one of Equitable's top-selling insurance programs.

CHAPTER XIV

REVIVING INVESTMENTS

O ates quickly addressed the low investment yield that was holding back the
group annuity area, which some people saw as
the future of life insurance. He soon hired two
experienced men to manage the investment
and legal sides of the problem, which in all
their facets constituted many of the challenges
faced by The Equitable and life insurance in
general during the late 1950's and the 1960's.

To run investments, he needed an officer
who was widely and deeply experienced in the
field and especially in equities. Oates believed
that common stocks had to be part of the
investment portfolio if the Society were to be
competitive with other financial institutions.
After a long search (during which no Equitable
employees were considered) Oates offered the
job of Senior Vice-President and Chief
Investment Officer to Grant Keehn, president
of First National Bank. Keehn also was elected
to the Board of Directors. Raised near Chicago
(where he had known Oates slightly), Keehn
attended Hamilton College and Harvard
Business School, where, at the age of twenty-
one, he graduated first in his class in 1923.
Starting out at Goldman, Sachs & Co., he
worked in the investment and banking business
and eventually became a high officer of First
National. After it merged with the larger
National City Bank to form First National City
Bank (now Citibank), Keehn assumed the number two job of president. He was beginning to
plan his retirement at the time Oates called.

In a talk to agents several years later,
Keehn explained why he had accepted Oates's
offer. First, he was impressed by Equitable:

"Here was a truly great company — a company
with an outstanding record of success behind
it." And he was swayed by Oates's enthusiasm
and ambitions to change and update the enterprise: "He outlined to me, as only he can do, his
hopes, aspirations, and plans for the further
growth, development, and improvement of our
great institution. It was an exciting, stimulating
and challenging program." Keehn assumed
charge of all investments, including real estate,
but Oates asked him to go further and oversee
Equitable's general economic situation — a job
that until then had been in the hands of Walter
Klem and the Actuarial Department. Though
somewhat reserved in personality, Keehn was
able to assert himself with his thorough knowledge of corporate finance, his integrity, and his
warm sense of humor. He and Oates were
almost the same age and shared many interests
(for example, each chaired his college's board of
trustees) as well as an optimistic outlook on
America's economic future. From the start it was
clear that Keehn was Oates's right-hand man.[1]

With the investment position filled by one
imported senior officer, Oates then set about
searching for another one, a lawyer of comparable pedigree, to work to bring deregulation
and to smooth the jagged relations with the
New York State Insurance Department. Oates
found Davidson Sommers, Vice-President and
former general counsel of the International
Bank for Reconstruction and Development
(better known as the World Bank), which had
played an important role in reviving the postwar economy through cross-border loans.
Sommers' job had included delicate negotia-

Davidson Sommers was the third newcomer in a top position.

tions with the U.S. Treasury Department and foreign governments. At fifty-four, Sommers was four years younger than Oates and Keehn; like them, he was a midwesterner. He took the job, he said, largely because friends assured him that, in Grant Keehn, he would be working with one of the very best investment people in the country. His title was Senior Vice-President and General Counsel and, like Keehn, he was elected to the board. Gregarious, persuasive, and flexible, Sommers quickly took on a variety of duties.

If the installation of an outsider as Chief Executive was a wake-up call to the Equitable family, the fact that he imported his two top aides from other institutions was (as intended) a shock to the entire system. Another aspect of his choices signaled just how serious Oates was about revitalizing the organization. Because they were virtual peers and because he intended to remain CEO until mandatory retirement, their jobs clearly were to change the institution, not to be groomed to take his place. Their removal from succession politics

therefore liberated them to freely challenge the shibboleths of Equitable in particular and mutual insurance in general.

It worked to everybody's advantage that they performed such a difficult task as gracefully as they did. Still, they did not always succeed in changing their colleagues' approach; for example, in using profitability as a measure of success. On his retirement in 1973, Sommers explained his frustration over the stubborn resistance to an enlightened use of the bottom line: "I do not see why The Equitable should not be as profit-conscious, though not as profit-motivated, as a stock company. For a mutual company, this can be a form of consumerism." Sommers and Keehn also were taken aback by the infighting and hierarchical thinking they encountered. Noticing an absence of the kind of dialogue that he knew in banking, Keehn persuaded Oates to sponsor quarterly interdepartmental meetings to allow officers to vent their concerns and educate one another about their work. At the first meeting, Keehn was surprised when senior people dominated the agenda, controlled the podium, and ignored their juniors. He took Oates's assistant, Coy Eklund, aside and insisted that the meetings be opened up. Meanwhile Keehn, concerned that Equitable had a habit of thinking about investments only in the long term, was introducing modern investment theory, including the "new money" standard of measuring success by comparing yields on reinvested recent income.[2]

Sommers, for his part, faced a difficult management challenge. Because of the importance of regulation in daily insurance operations, insurance companies were unique among American financial institutions in having large law staffs. While few banks or investment firms before the 1970's had more than a handful of attorneys, Equitable, forced by the insurance industry's stringent regulatory environment, had a staff of seventy lawyers. They were divided into three distinct, jealously guarded domains. The smallest was headed by Vice-Chairman Robert L. Hogg, a former congressman who was the Society's chief lobbyist and representative to the insurance industry. Then there was the large Investment Law Department, which handled the detailed paperwork on loans and financings; it was headed by Warner Mendel. The third group was the Insurance Law Department, headed by Leo Fitzgerald, who had resisted all efforts to merge his department with Mendel's. Both Mendel and Fitzgerald were annoyed that Sommers was placed above them. After Fitzgerald died of a heart attack while returning on a train from an Equitable meeting in Florida, Sommers tactfully assuaged Mendel's feelings and freed himself for larger policy issues by naming him General Solicitor in charge of all day-to-day legal work. It was an ideal arrangement for Sommers, a pragmatic, policy-oriented lawyer, as described by one of his colleagues, Jule E. Stocker: "He could see the forest as well as the trees. He could see the leaves on the trees. He could see the whole panorama beyond the forest." This sweeping perspective, which Oates and Keehn shared, would often be called on during the challenging years that lay ahead.[3]

The poor organization and personal antipathies among the lawyers seemed to typify the entire organization. "I don't think they were in much more disarray than The Equitable in general," Sommers recalled. "What had happened was that The Equitable had had for ten years managerial trouble. Not financial trouble. Parkinson stayed too long.... [H]e ran the place as a one-man shop." Oates, Keehn, and Sommers quickly acted to remove the residue of Parkinson's quirks and prejudices. One of them was his antagonism toward bankers, whom he had often left to languish in the lobby to await his summons to his office. To show that Equitable was eager to cooperate with commercial and investment bankers, Oates organized receptions and dinners so the heads of big banks and Wall Street firms could meet Keehn in his new position (of course, many bankers already knew him well from his old job). In his speeches at these events, Keehn made it clear that he was eager to be conciliatory, jotting these notes as cues:

Helpful to us, Helpful to You.... Basic Point — Want and need and use best effort to have close friendly active working relations.... When there is business we want to see it.... NEW EQUITABLE.[4]

In the Home Office and with agents, Keehn, like Oates, also spoke of a "new Equitable" in which its specialties worked together toward a common end instead of fighting each other in costly turf wars. Investments and agency work had often been presented as mutually exclusive, if not antagonistic, but Keehn worked hard to explain that they were interdependent. For example, in 1959, to explain the significance of the Society's relatively poor investment return, which was seventeen basis points (0.17 percent) below the average of fourteen peer insurance companies, he told agents that since each basis point was worth approximately $1 million, Equitable was $17 million behind in the competitiveness of its insurance policies; that $17 million, he said, could increase policyholder dividends by 10 percent, making them the largest in the industry. By clearly linking investments to sales, Keehn demonstrated Oates's point that cooperation would make Equitable a more productive institution.[5]

The chief worry about low yields was that they were causing the slow death of the group annuity (or pension) business, an area in which Equitable had pioneered and had a large proportion of assets. Although

Equitable's market share was slipping, it continued to lead insurance companies in the specialty, thanks to its sales force and an aggressive public relations campaign that featured a national touring road show of presentations to companies and advisors. Insured group annuity plans still had a following among small companies because they demanded less supervision by company officials than bank plans, which were managed in trust funds. However, larger corporations, which were more likely to have well-staffed personnel departments, overwhelmingly preferred bank plans because they offered returns as much as one-fourth higher — 5 percent as against less than 4 percent for insured plans. The Society struggled gamely by cutting the amount of necessary paperwork and offering innovative contracts, yet it still could not compete against the high interest rates offered by banks. At the end of 1958, an Equitable officer who specialized in group annuities, John M. Hines, gloomily ended a memo summarizing this downward spiral: "We have maintained a vigorous and progressive approach in meeting the changes, demands, and needs. We have, however, seen the trusteed business grow far more rapidly than the business placed with insurance companies." Under such restraints, he concluded, it was impossible to stem the flow of clients and market share. This was a startling, even frightening admission considering that group annuities accounted for almost 40 percent of the Society's reserves and $275 million in annual income.[6]

Trusteed bank plans enjoyed tax and other regulatory advantages. To secure its eroding beachhead, Equitable initiated a counterattack on these fronts. The tax question came first. While some states taxed income from insurance premiums, since 1941 the Internal Revenue Service had been taxing insurance companies on their net investment income beyond the amount needed for reserves. In the 'forties, Equitable paid no taxes because, thanks to pegging and Parkinson's investment policies, there was no net investment income. But when interest rates rose in the 'fifties, there were taxes to be paid. Because income from trust funds was not taxed, pension plans placed with banks went tax-free. By one estimate, every ¼ percent paid in taxes by an insurance company meant another 7 percent in increased costs for a pension fund. This detracted from insurers' ability to compete with banks.

The actuary in charge of group insurance, Raymond M. Peterson, became so frustrated by this discrepancy that in the summer of 1951, as a private citizen, he complained about it in letters to the chairmen of the Senate Finance and House Ways and Means committees. Soon he and Ray Murphy talked the two main insurance trade groups, the Life Insurance Association and the American Life Convention, into addressing the issue. As chairman of the insurance industry's pension committee, Peterson, with the help of Hogg and Walter Klem, lobbied Congress for eight trying years before a reform tax law was passed in 1959. Over the next three years, the government cut life insurance taxes by $50 million, and the tax discrepancy was trimmed though not eliminated.

More controversial yet was the question of investing in equities. Trusteed bank pension plans were allowed to buy all the stocks they could, and they thrived in the bull market of the 1950's, when common stocks appreciated at an annual rate of more than 10 percent. But under the Armstrong laws' prohibition against insurers' distracting themselves with other businesses, insurance companies were historically barred from buying common stocks. The law was liberalized in 1951 to allow common stock purchases up to 3 percent of assets; in 1957, the limit was raised to 5 percent or one-half the surplus, whichever was smallest. The

City Activities with Dance Hall

AMERICA TODAY
Mural series by Thomas Hart Benton, 1930-1931

Collection of The Equitable

City Building   *Steel*

Coal

Instrum

The Atlantic Cable Projectors
Painting by Daniel Huntington, 1894-1895

Collection of New York Chamber of Commerce on loan to The Equitable

Equitable director Cyrus W. Field (second from right), promoter of the first transatlantic telegraph cable,
with his colleagues in the project at their initial planning meeting in 1854:
(left to right) Peter Cooper, David Dudley Field, Chandler White, Marshall O. Roberts,
Samuel F.B. Morse, Daniel Huntington, Moses Taylor, Cyrus W. Field, Wilson G. Hunt.

City Activities with Subway

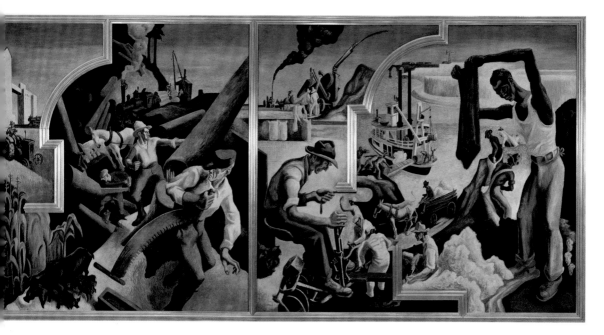

Midwest   *Deep South*

wer

Changing West

Grover Cleveland

Former President of the United States
Equitable Trustee, 1905-1908
Painting by William McGregor Paxton, 1906

Collection of The Equitable

problem was not entirely one of regulation, for few insurers took significant advantage of the new rule; Equitable's common stock holdings in 1958 consisted of only one-fifth of 1 percent of assets. Of the twenty-seven employees in the Investment Department at the time of Grant Keehn's arrival, six concentrated on railroad investments, fourteen on industrial bonds, and none on common stocks.

Common stocks were unpopular as an investment for two reasons — one technical, the other marketing. The technical problem was that, due to their market-driven values and dividends (and generally unlike fixed-income investments, bonds and mortgages), the value of stocks varied from day to day. These short-term fluctuations meant both that common stock assets could not be predictably and precisely matched against the known long-term liabilities of insurance policies, and that surplus, or capital base, could not be precisely fixed. The marketing problem of common stock investments struck to the heart of the historic appeal of life insurance. The 1950's were only a quarter century or so after the 1929 stock market crash, which was well within the lifetime of most Americans. The stock market, therefore, was hardly regarded positively by the risk-averse consumers who were most likely to purchase life insurance. Believers in "the gospel of protection" wanted above all else a guaranteed return based on safe investments. That meant fixed-income investments rather than stocks, which were both variable and reminiscent of bad times. So long as clients were risk-averters, so, too, were insurance companies' investment departments.

Banks, meanwhile, were free of regulatory prohibitions against investing funds under their management in stocks, and many of them took advantage of the rising stock market of the 'fifties when managing pension plans. When General Motors placed its huge pension plan with several banks in the early

'fifties, it stipulated that no more than one-half the assets be invested in common stocks. Before long that restriction was regarded as cautious.

As an increasing number of pension plans chose the trust structure managed by banks, insurers came to the hard realization that while their individual policyholders feared risk in the portfolios backing their whole-life policies, their corporate clients were willing to trade some security for higher yields. Sommers described the situation concisely:

> [F]ixed income made sense in the whole-life part of the business as it then was in a non-inflationary world. The company's obligations were fixed, and balancing these by investments fixed as to principal and income was a prudent course. But the corporate pension business was moving in a different direction. Corporations saw their pension costs growing and wanted their pension assets to have a chance of growing, too, even if that meant that the corporations themselves would have to bear the risk of losses.

These needs were best met by trusteed bank pension plans, which could put funds anywhere. If Equitable wanted this business, it would have to find a way to offer the same services to its group annuity clients before they disappeared.[7]

The Equitable's new top officers did not share the insurance industry's traditional wariness of common stocks. Oates even included in the company's new mission a statement to the effect that investment in equities was a sound idea. Before Keehn arrived, Oates had attempted to sway Walter Klem and his advisors by setting up a diversified "phantom" portfolio that tracked the stock market; though the portfolio did well, Klem was not convinced. Only when Keehn appeared was a stock investment program put together. Over the first five years, the value of the stock portfolio grew by 16 percent, which was superior to the performance of the Dow Jones industrial average. By the end of 1964, the program was worth almost $215 million, slightly less than Equitable's real estate holdings but still less than 3 percent of the total portfolio.

That was an improvement, but a pension client still could not take full advantage of any good new investment opportunity. That was because, by law, insurers had to pool all their investments — good, bad, and indifferent — in their general accounts, which, by law, consisted mostly of bonds and mortgages, with only a small fraction of assets available for common stocks. The best a client could do was the best that Equitable's only investment account, the general account, could do. Such a large pool of investments in such an old, large company was bound to have a few low-performing ones; in fact, older and larger insurers tended to have lower yields than newer, smaller ones. In The Equitable's case, the portfolio in the late 'fifties included many excellent corporate bonds; some left-over Liberty bonds and other government notes; the then poorly performing Gateway Center investment; other new projects that Parkinson had taken on; agricultural and residential mortgages; leasebacks on real estate and railroad cars; a vast number of securities of America's faltering railroads; and many others. In order to become more competitive in the pension business, the company had to be able to free pension funds on deposit from this drag on return imposed by the limitations of insurance law. Insured pension funds had to offer the same opportunities for gains and losses from investments that were offered by bank trust funds.

The way to bring this about was to change the law so that pension funds could be segregated from the general account. Sommers' top priority was to improve relations with the New York State Insurance Department and its chiefs, especially the demanding head of the life insurance division, Julius Sackman. The official who introduced new subordinates to their jobs by assigning them to read and reread the Armstrong Committee's report, Sackman outlawed any project that hinted of overconcentration of assets. When the Society planned to put up a new headquarters office building in Chicago, Sackman — concerned that Oates was ambitious to build a Henry Hyde-type empire in his hometown — insisted that Equitable sell the old building it replaced rather than rent it out. When Equitable bought two plots in New York near the Time & Life Building, which it had financed, with the intent of building on them — one for the new Home Office, another for a rental property — Sackman insisted that one be sold because, he said, Equitable was taking too large a risk in the neighborhood. It made no difference that the neighborhood, which included Rockefeller Center, was one of New York's most desirable areas. Then, when Equitable submitted the plan for the Home Office, he told the company to chop four floors off the design in order to cut building costs. (When it was opened in 1961, the new forty-two story Home Office at 1285 Avenue of the Americas, designed by Skidmore, Owings and Merrill, was the largest building in the country occupied by a single company.)

When Sommers learned that regulators were hard on Equitable because, during Parkinson's regime, the company had been uncooperative, he decided to be accommodating. He promised Sackman that he would keep him well informed of the Society's plans. As Sommers described his strategy, "You don't have to kow-tow to the department. You just have to be open with them." He began to seek regulators' approval for changes that would improve the yields on group annuity plans. One was a new accounting system, called the

The new Home Office (foreground) at the time it opened, with the Time & Life Building to the right and Rockefeller Center just beyond.

investment year method (IYM), in which the yield on a deposit to a plan was credited according to the year in which it was made, rather than averaged in with the yield of the entire plan. Once approved by the Insurance Department, the IYM increased returns for new group annuity policies by more than 20 percent. The IYM was not sufficient for sponsors of pension plans who wanted investment accounts segregated from the general account. Manly Fleischmann led an insurance industry

effort to gain approval for trust accounts for insured plans, but it was sunk by the banking lobby and regulators' concerns about the safety of common stocks.[8]

With that, Fleischmann and Sommers proposed that New York adapt a practice already in place in Connecticut, which Fleischmann privately called "a trust in disguise": an insurer would be allowed to establish accounts separate from the general account. While the general account would continue to consist of Equitable policyholders' own money backing insurance liabilities, the separate accounts would serve as investment pools for the clients' own money to be managed by Equitable in ways specified by the clients. If allowed, the separate account would be a watershed in the insurance industry. With it, Equitable and other insurers would no longer be just in the business of managing money for their policyholders. With separate accounts, they could be money managers for third parties, including pension plans, and invest in any area.[9]

The banks organized another lobbying campaign, but this time the insurance department expressed no opposition. The insurance companies were prepared and, once, alertly caught the bankers in a trap. An officer of an upstate bank testified before the state legislature's insurance committee that he welcomed competition from insurers, so long as everybody played according to the same rules in the same "ball park." One of those rules, he went on, was that an insurer administering a group annuity plan must exercise the same fiduciary duty as a bank trustee for a pension plan. Jule Stocker chased down a pension trust agreement from the officer's bank and discovered a clause that exempted pension trustees from most usual fiduciary obligations short of willful misconduct. When Oates testified before the committee, he produced the agreement, read the clause, and announced with relish, "I would be happy to play by the rules of that ball park." Approval of separate accounts then sped along quickly and was finalized in 1963. The state's approval still was required for each account and its investments, but at least Equitable and other insurers could compete with the banks. In the 'sixties, Equitable set up eight separate accounts, some concentrating on common stocks, others on other types of investments.[10]

Tensions between insurance companies and banks had existed since the turn of the century, when each side first invaded the other's traditional territory, with insurers offering mortgages and savings banks selling life insurance. Later, Thomas I. Parkinson's aggressive investment policies included private-placement corporate loans and Assured Home Ownership residential mortgages. All the same, relations between Equitable and its bankers had remained cordial until the dispute over separate accounts. Concerns about potential conflicts of interest later led Equitable to bar bankers from its Board of Directors and to forbid its own officers to serve on banks' boards.

There continued to be internal disagreements about new investment policy. While Sommers and Keehn had intended separate accounts primarily as flexible vehicles for pension plan investments in common stocks, should pension customers desire them, Walter Klem demanded that stock portfolios be capped at half pension plan assets. Sommers was stunned: "Actuaries, like the Insurance Department, were still working under the atmosphere generated by the crisis of 1905." But Klem no longer had control over investment policy, and he was ignored. Because the bull market soon ended, the concentration on common stocks was short-lived, but from this start in group retirement plans, separate accounts went on to be the mechanism for Equitable's expansion into a range of new products, including variable annuities and variable life insurance.[11]

The effort to improve investment performance reached into the Assured Home Ownership program. Launched as an investment to fill the need for decent yields in the "pegging" years around World War II, AHO had also become Equitable's most successful insurance product and an important part of many agencies. By the mid-1950's, AHO business was expanding by $100 million a year and had become a central part of the business of many agents and agencies. Unique to The Equitable and relatively easy to sell, thanks to the highly competitive interest rates the Society offered on residential mortgages, AHO provided an excellent means to launch a new agent's career and to introduce a new prospect to Equitable's other products. One of the most successful agents was a former door-to-door encyclopedia salesman, Bob Wolf, in Pittsburgh, who, because of his background, was not afraid to pick names out of telephone books and go out and make cold calls. Whole districts devoted themselves almost exclusively to AHO.

While AHO mortgages were both competitive and profitable in the 'forties, they became an investment problem during the 'fifties because their mortgage interest rates were not allowed to rise with market interest rates. By the latter part of the decade, AHO no longer was a good investment for Equitable, since it sidetracked a large portion of the investment portfolio into relatively low-yielding mortgages from higher yielding investments elsewhere. AHO, in other words, was being subsidized by the rest of the Society's investment portfolio. "[I]n effect, Equitable had put its investment policy into the hands of its agency department because agents had a first call on all investment funds," Davidson Sommers later said. "No other major company had an arrangement like that." Sommers had other concerns about AHO. One was that its mandatory tie-in probably would not survive a legal attack. Another was that it was subverting the agency operation by placing the emphasis on marketing mortgages, rather than marketing life insurance. AHO, Sommers concluded, was harming the entire company: it was "eating into The Equitable like a cancer.... [T]he AHO program was going to poison the whole institution."[12]

Oates gave Keehn authority to address the AHO issue. In a report to Oates in 1959, he laid out how heavily subsidized AHO was:

> [I]n recent years residential mortgage has absorbed not only all the funds arising

Jule Stocker helped get separate accounts approved.

> from repayments on residential mortgages, all funds provided by net additions to ordinary life reserves created by AHO business, all funds arising from net additions to ordinary life reserves created by all other ordinary life business, but in addition funds generated by the net additions to the reserves and other liabilities created by group annuity business, other group business, supplementary contracts, dividend accumulation, etc.

In the previous four years, some $273 million had been channeled to AHO from other investment programs. The result was that the amount of new money available for investment had been reduced by almost 20 percent, or $85 million.[13]

But as strongly as he opposed AHO as an investment, Keehn did not underestimate how important it had become to many parts of the agency force. AHO, he told Oates, was "an important, basic, and integral feature of the

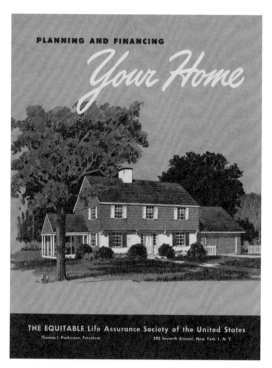

AHO began life as a profitable Equitable investment program.

sales program.... It has become a fundamental element in Equitable's philosophy of business. There are large numbers of our personnel dependent on this business." Such a quandary struck to the core of the historic tensions between the agency force and the Home Office. Gentle handling was required.[14]

In his first few weeks on the job, Keehn increased AHO interest rates and introduced a plan, devised by Manly Fleischmann, to end the mandatory tie-in by allowing mortgages to be insured by other companies. Then, in January 1959, Keehn decided to address the problem head-on at the agency managers' annual winter meeting in Boca Raton, Florida.

For an investment officer to speak frankly to the sales force was a bold step. Since the days of Henry Hyde, their functions had been regarded as mutually exclusive, even though investments provided a sizable portion of the income that provided policyholder dividends. Investment people had often spoken to agents

gingerly, apologetically, and even patronizingly. ("Perhaps I am emphasizing an activity which seems remote from your daily experience and contacts with life insurance," Treasurer Meredith C. Laffey told agents in a brochure on investments in 1928. "It is, however, like a small unit of vital machinery concealed far below decks on a great liner.") So it should not have been surprising that before Keehn went to the managers' meeting, he received plenty of advice from old Equitable hands. One was Warner Mendel, who forwarded a list of topics that he thought Keehn should either avoid or emphasize. This list survives with Keehn's penciled comments. Mendel first told Keehn that the managers wanted to know what Keehn's job was. "Yes," Keehn scribbled in the margin. They also wanted to learn how his policies would affect their interest, "which of course is the interest of the Society." Apparently, Keehn disagreed with Mendel's interpretation; he wrote "no." Finally, Mendel advised, "Your intentions as to AHO will be awaited with great eagerness. This is money in the bank to the managers and their agents." Here Keehn again jotted "yes."[15]

No matter how strongly he felt about AHO, Keehn had no intention of starting a wasteful war between the Home Office and the agency force. But sharing Oates's ideal of the insurance enterprise as a unified entity composed of mutually dependent specialists, neither was he going to dodge or gloss over the issue. And so he confronted the agency managers directly and tactfully.

Aware that he was facing a hostile audience that had already learned through the Society's grapevine of his opinions about the product, Keehn smoothed his path by opening his speech with a self-deprecating joke. He likened himself to the town drunk who smokes in bed, starts a fire that burns down the hotel, and then tells the judge that not only was he not drunk but the bed was on fire before he got into it. As the laughter subsided, he carefully referred to Jim Oates as a personal friend and then got to work asserting the mutual dependence between the agents and the Investment Department. "This rate of return on our investments is a vital thread woven through the whole fabric of our competitive position in the industry," he said (as he remembered in a reconstruction that he dictated from memory a day or two later). "It is an essential element in our cost and hence affects importantly your ability to sell our product. We must strive to improve it." By *"we,"* he said, he meant all of Equitable's investment-related departments, plus the man in charge: "We includes me, Grant Keehn." Keehn's courage, charm, and concern for the Society defused a potentially dangerous moment, and the agency managers received him openly. Relieved, Oates wrote him, "I certainly liked your speech. I am so proud and happy. Thanks!"[16]

In a long, confidential memorandum to Oates that included twenty-two charts and graphs, Keehn later described AHO as "one of our most serious problems" and concluded, "Basically, the need is to make the investment program less captive to the requirements of AHO." Careful to consult with officers in the Agency Operations Department, Keehn recommended that sales volume be capped while AHO be gradually closed down. In September 1959, the executive committee of the most senior officers, the General Policy Committee, cut AHO sales by one-fourth, to $300 million a year, and replaced the uniform national interest rate with a system of regional rates at parity with local bank rates. As AHO sales predictably slumped, Equitable's overall sales volume for the year dropped by 3 percent — the first decline in new business since 1945. But the Society's investment yield increased from 3.7 to 3.8 percent. The next year, Equitable cut back some more until the amount loaned was

half the 1957 level. Further and deeper slices in AHO ensued.[17]

The AHO issue split the company. John W. Riley, on the sidelines of the argument as head of the Social Science Research Office, remembered "a bitter internal battle." In the field, many agency managers had thrown their agencies into AHO, but a few disliked it. One, Warren V. Woody, limited the number of AHO policies sold out of his big agency in Chicago. One of his district managers, Robert Wenzlaff, remembered:

> He would not allow district managers to let agents do more than one-third of their business in AHO. Probably 90 percent of the agency managers would have voted to keep AHO, but he thought it was a giveaway of Equitable assets. We got mad at him, but what he was doing was egging people on to their full potential. He was making men out of us. He could help people see the best in themselves.

Woody was unusual in opposing AHO. "This was really a traumatic experience for some agents and agencies," recalled an Agency Operations officer at the time, Joseph L. Beesley. Managers of agencies that had depended on AHO tried unsuccessfully to persuade Oates and Keehn to return interest rates to their previous, below market-rate levels.[18]

In the Home Office, investment people and actuaries opposed AHO, while officers in the agency departments tended to favor it. An investment officer, Ralph Hardison, became so insistent that Equitable increase its mortgage interest rates to market levels that the head of the AHO operation, R. O. Brown, lost his temper at him and shouted (as Hardison recalled), "God damn it, Hardison, I am tired of hearing of this. It will be done over my dead body. I don't want to hear any more about it." Oates's assistant, Coy Eklund, whose agency in Detroit had been successful with AHO, complained so vigorously about criticisms of the program that Oates twice told him that he would brook no further disagreement.[19]

The tension was obvious in January 1960, when Grant Keehn returned to Boca Raton to once again address the managers. This time, he offered no jokes; the session, he said, would be "a workshop talk." He explained, "I'm handling it as kind of a family conference to discuss a family problem." He told the agents he understood their problems, but he had also sat in on a few unsuccessful presentations to group annuity prospects who had gone elsewhere in search of higher yields. Equitable still ranked fourteenth among the fifteen peer companies in the area of investment yield. "We're in a long-term distance race with our competition and the other horses are running, too," Keehn continued, using language that agents, competitive types of people, were sure to appreciate. "If we're going to catch them we are going to have to do a better job on each lap, which means we're going to have to do a better job each year on our new investments than they're doing." The last of his cue cards for this speech reflects his optimism that the AHO issue would not be seen as a factional fight: "This is a job that will take a little doing — but working together I believe we can get it done." But Keehn had second thoughts. He crossed out "I believe" and wrote, "I am sure."[20]

Keehn was too optimistic. The dispute over AHO was hardly the first between the agency force and the Home Office, but it was more than a conflict over policy. It was, as he himself had said, "a family problem" stirring up the old fundamental disagreement concerning the priority of the agents and sales within the Society. Now, in attempting to link the interests of both operations, he threatened a deeply held conviction, at least among agents and managers, that Equitable's essential identity lay in its agency force. "The Equitable has

been strongly keyed to the field [since] way back from the days of Hyde," observed a long-time agency officer, Leroy E. Long. "It has come down through all the generations of management...." An agency manager, Calvin D. Kanter, expressed the same idea slightly differently: "[T]he managers of this company over the years have been the strength of this company.... The field managers and agents are the people that have done it." Such ideas seemed unrealistic to Keehn's colleague, Davidson Sommers, who was struck by how many non-agency officers shared the credo that Equitable was an agent's company. "I never thought that was either a good idea or a fact," Sommers said in his oral history memoir. "I thought Equitable was running things too much for the benefit of the agency managers, who were a powerful group." As to why the "agent's company" label stuck, Sommers ventured an explanation:

> I think there was a tradition in The Equitable, to a certain extent it still prevails, as in most insurance companies and many private businesses, to talk in somewhat unrealistic terms. I thought they were trying to make the agents feel good. It was part of the effort to recruit and to bring agents up to an adequate level.[21]

Try as Keehn did to shape a single identity by struggling to get the agency force to see how dependent they were on investment success, unity did not come easily. AHO was still around, though at a much reduced level, in 1967 when Coy Eklund, by then the head of the Agency Operations Department, wrote a memorandum to Oates opposing continuing AHO cutbacks. The issue, he told Oates, was fundamental to Equitable's identity, because it could be either supportive of agents or supportive of investments. There was no middle ground, he said:

[I]t is clear that we have a classical example of the situation in which two elements of the organization, each striving to serve company goals, can achieve them respectively only at the "expense" of the other. Investment considerations may urge the curtailment or even the abandonment of AHO business in the current period.... But it must be made equally clear that to curtail or abandon AHO involves "costs" to the company's strategic program aimed at building a productive resource of successful agents upon whom we can rely for the quantity and quality of production satisfying to the company over the long pull.

The Society could not have both high investment yield and a substantial expansion of the sales force, Eklund went on. Equitable's future lay with sales and the agents. Should AHO be terminated in the interest of bettering investment return, he predicted, more than 1,000 agents would leave the company.[22]

But AHO was terminated. Districts and agencies that had specialized in it were broken up during the 1960's, and many agents left insurance (Bob Wolf would find a new niche placing group annuities and pensions). To plug the gap with a highly competitive product that inexperienced agents could sell fairly easily, the Society introduced new coverage for small groups called Circle E Group Insurance, but it did not succeed nearly as well as AHO. AHO's body was

barely warm in 1969 when it was finally eliminated because inflation had pushed interest rates above the limits of state usury laws. On the occasion of giving his business papers to the Equitable Archives in 1971, Keehn said that eventually ending AHO was the most important of his accomplishments at the company.

In 1964 Oates assumed the position of Chairman of the Board and CEO, and Keehn was elected President. (Walter Klem, passed over for the third time, retired.) Oates avoided formally delineating most of his and Keehn's duties because, he wrote, "To do so would introduce an undesirable rigidity and artificiality into the management structure and be inconsistent with the nature of the two offices." Keehn used somewhat less formal language to describe the symbiosis, telling a reporter, "I may have a somewhat louder voice, but Oates is still the boss. When he's away I'm the boss."[23]

As for investment returns — the issue that had stimulated the arrival of separate accounts and the cutting back of AHO — between 1959 and 1968, Equitable's net investment earnings increased by one-fourth, from 4 percent to 5 percent. That was the fourth largest increase among peer companies. The return on new money reached over 6½ percent. The slide in group annuity contracts ended in 1963, and over the next five years, using separate accounts, new pension business increased almost six-fold.

With a blend of traditional salesmanship, modern social science, and charisma,
Coy Eklund founded Equitable's modern career agency force.

CHAPTER XV

THE NEW EPOCH

As Equitable was overhauling the investment program, it was transforming its agency force, which had been stagnating in the Parkinson years.

Historically, agency managers had been permitted great freedom to hire whomever they wished. Under Henry Hyde's marketing strategy, the Society provided policies to agents to retail in ways they thought best. "The view was that the policyholders should be the *agent's* policyholders, not the Home Office's," former Equitable Vice-Chairman Harry D. Garber has said of the system in the mid- and late-twentieth century — though the same rule applied to previous decades. The Society's sales success often rode on the strengths and weaknesses of the local manager. Observed an Agency Operations official, Leroy Long, the manager "kind of rose or fell, in a way, with the organization which he built up." Yet there was a widespread feeling in the agency force in the 1950's that the Home Office was not providing enough support and discipline.[1]

The crux of the issue was Parkinson's "agent at every crossroad" marketing policy. Since many of those crossroads could not support full-time agents, the policy meant that half Equitable's 10,000 agents were working odd hours. This huge part-time force, consisting of local lawyers, accountants, clergy, teachers, and housewives, was responsible for as much as one-fifth of new sales. The system's advantage was that since many of these agents were already well connected in their communities, agency managers did not have to expend much energy and time getting them established. The

Home Office portrayed part-timers as worth emulating. For example, in 1951 an Equitable agency magazine devoted several laudatory pages to the "dual career as entrepreneur and life underwriter" of a part-time agent, Estel Hawkins, of Steubenville, Ohio. After starting out as manager of the cigar department in a department store, Hawkins became a part-time agent, bought a delicatessen on the proceeds of his Equitable commissions, and eventually became a full-time agent.[2]

The disadvantage of the system, which was noticed more in the field than the Home Office, was that, since most life insurance companies had mostly full-time, career agents, Equitable suffered under a reputation for having an unprofessional agency force. Agency managers were sensitive to such criticism, which often was thrown at them by managers at other companies competing for the same prospective recruits. Parkinson's retirement left the "agent at every crossroad" program in place but under review. The agency managers coalesced around their organization, the Old Guard, to influence the Home Office to develop a more professional, full-time force.

The basic agency structure was the distinctive three-tiered one established by Henry Baldwin Hyde: agency manager, district manager, and agent. There remained a handful of general agents, but almost all the 100-plus agencies were run by managers accountable to the Home Office, who were paid nominal salaries but earned large incomes from overrides on their agents' commissions. The district managers also were salaried and received overrides. Their main job was to recruit and train a handful of new agents a year — "getting men, getting them to produce," according to an agency manager and supervisor, Joseph L. Beesley. It was a grueling job. Many district managers washed out and went back to selling full-time.[3]

Their motivation, as in the days of Pick Embry, was the opportunity to do well enough to qualify as an agency manager, which (long before the rise of extremely successful individual agents) was the best-paid job in Equitable except for the top Home Office executives. Manager development was strictly internal. Leroy Long, who worked in Agency Operations for more than half a century, from 1926 to 1979, could not remember even one manager who had started out with another insurer. Agency managers, successful or not, often were offered jobs in the Home Office at salaries below their earnings in the field. The appeal of a Home Office job was that it offered a modicum of national power and visibility and was a challenge to the very ambitious. Two Equitable CEOs in the 1970's and 'eighties, Coy Eklund and John Carter, started out as agents and worked their way up through the ranks.

The biographies of three agency managers of the 1950's and 'sixties — Warren V. Woody, Don Bryant, and Calvin Kanter — show that rising through the agency system demanded a blend of skill, hard work, connections, and good luck.

Warren V. Woody was a high-school football coach in Sterling, Kansas, in the 1920's when Pick Embry induced him to try selling insurance part-time to his players' families. In eight months he earned $8,000, the equivalent of more than $70,000 today. He decided to switch over to selling insurance full-time. Woody got the full Embry treatment: careful

Donald L. Bryant, Sr.

training, meticulous supervision, a district managership, and the promise of an agency if he worked hard. As a district manager, he recruited former athletes and coaches, like himself, because he thought they had the proper appreciation of teamwork and self-discipline. He was extremely successful and, through Embry's influence, got an agency first in Baltimore and then in Chicago, where he built one of the great Equitable agencies. He built a power base within the Society, was elected President of the Old Guard, and made a small fortune in life insurance sales. He was remembered by one of his agents, Robert Wenzlaff, with the mixed respect and affection of a former army recruit talking about a fierce-looking but warmhearted drill sergeant:

> *If you ever wanted to have a guru, W.V.W. would be the best one. He saw something in me I didn't see in myself. He told me I'd be independent in six months, and I was. Then he made me a district manager. He told me I had an obligation to show other people how to overcome their own fears and become successful, too. He was the most soft-hearted, sentimental person I ever met, but he had a deceiving facade as an SOB to cover it up. He used to tell us, "There are the technical rules; my rules are tougher." He was exacting in his expectations and gave us very detailed instructions.[4]*

Every successful agent was challenged and advanced in a different way. Donald L. Bryant, Sr. (his son, Donald, Jr., became a successful agent in his own right), was introduced to Equitable on the night of the eighty-first anniversary of its official founding, July 26,

1940, when he purchased his first life insurance policy from a friend in Mount Vernon, Illinois. The friend was overjoyed; because it was the Society's anniversary, the sale qualified him for an honor club, The Equitable's Loyal Legionnaires. After Bryant went off to war, the agent supplied his family with soap, meat, butter, and other rationed goods and regularly wrote him to report about the home front. Bryant was so impressed by his agent's loyalty that, after the war, he became an insurance agent. Bryant went into a vast agency in southern Illinois managed by another Embry protégé, Fred Holderman, who kept in touch with and motivated his agents by Western Union. Holderman assigned Bryant as district manager in two weak districts, one after the other, both of which he revived. After three years he decided he should know more about agency administration and volunteered to be Holderman's assistant agency manager at a large cut in compensation. He soon was appointed agency manager in St. Louis, where he stayed for many years until 1969, when he was elected president of the Old Guard. Partway into his term, Bryant was called to a job in the Home Office.

The third of these agency managers was Calvin D. Kanter, of Chicago. The son of a Sears, Roebuck salesman, he worked his way through college in a photography store. He was heading back to that job after returning from Korea in 1954, when his fiancée's cousin, a district manager in an Equitable agency in Chicago, introduced him to life insurance and its financial rewards. When Kanter asked if he could make as much as $5,000 a year, the cousin replied that if he paid attention, he would earn at least $10,000. "[I]t was like a revelation to me. I thought bank presidents made that," Kanter remembered. His start was slow, since his family had already bought all the insurance they needed from his cousin; but Equitable loaned him $50 a week, his dis-

trict manager shared commissions with him, and in his second year Kanter earned that $10,000. He looked back, "So I began to realize, 'I can do this.' And it was like the skies were opening." Eight years later he was Equitable's sec-

Calvin D. Kanter.

ond youngest agency manager. At his first managers' meeting, he had another revelation in a poker game with a group of old-timers from the Pick Embry school:

Then, if you didn't have grey hair, you just weren't an agency manager.... I was thirty-two years old. And they were cigar-smoking, heavy drinking, card-playing guys. And after our meetings, we would sit around to all hours of the night and smoke cigars and play poker and drink. So I got into this game and these fellows were — they were devilish and they were cruel. I mean, when it came to poker you had to make your way. So I got myself together and I got into this poker game and, one way or another, I survived. And that was all I could do. The next day, Lee Wandling came up to me and he said, "Kid, you're gonna be okay. I can tell by the way you play poker."[5]

The oldest problem in the life insurance business was agent attrition, which ran as high as 50 percent for first-year agents and 25 percent for more experienced agents. These rates had applied to the entire life insurance industry since the middle of the nineteenth century. Equitable had been addressing it for decades, but with little effect. Year after year, about half of all new agents and one-fourth of all agents left the business after an extended and expensive training period.

One reason for poor retention was that getting established as an agent usually took two or three years; ordinary whole-life insurance was difficult to sell to people whom the agent did not know. It helped if the agent could find a niche market. Between 1940 and 1969, when it finally was ended, one niche product was an Equitable residential mortgage in the Assured Home Ownership program.

Besides AHO, agents found a specialty in group insurance. To provide group insurance with independence and prestige within the company, Oates placed it in its own department headed by a respected and successful agency manager and former Old Guard president, Horace Wilson. Agents who went into group sales found that with its infrequent sales and intense competition, it could be more demanding than individual sales, even in industrial centers, like Pittsburgh, where Equitable's agency was well established. In 1951, six years after it was converted from a general agency, Lawrence C. Woods, Jr., stepped down as agency manager to become a full-time agent and was succeeded by Mark Higgins. Woods and Higgins worked for years to place or maintain group insurance policies with many of the big local manufacturers as well as the Pittsburgh Pirates baseball club and the University of Pittsburgh (Equitable also loaned the university money against the collateral of its famous Cathedral of Learning). Group insurance was not every agent's cup of tea; it demanded large amounts of time to negotiate and sell a contract, and then came time-consuming quarterly meetings with policyholders. Yet for a certain breed of agents, it was a good business that often led to a sizable number of individual life sales to people in the group desiring additional coverage.

In an article that he wrote for an agents' magazine, Higgins emphasized the differences between selling the two types of policies:

Being an insurance advisor to companies is not a once-a-year job when a dividend is delivered, but it is a once-a-week job fifty-two weeks a year. In other words, you have to work hard to earn your commission. I find you cannot leave too much of the work up to the insurance company or the first thing you know you are out of the case and someone else is in. You have to live with your cases more than ever before, keep up to date with everything going on, expand your knowledge, and truly be an insurance advisor to your clients.

Higgins advised his readers to develop a high profile and take advantage of Equitable's reputation as an investor in local projects, although, living in Pittsburgh, he admitted had an advantage that few agents enjoyed.[6]

Besides encouraging specialties like AHO and group insurance, the Agency Operations Department in the Home Office attempted to increase agents' productivity by providing special training and support. After World War II, the Society held a two-week seminar in Highland Park, Michigan, for fifty district managers who had shown an aptitude for becoming agency managers. In 1948, Parkinson founded a Home Office think tank called the Special Services Division, headed by Gordon K. Smith. It conducted research on estate planning, tax questions, and many other concerns (the chief exception was legal issues) and offered advisories in memorandums and at traveling seminars. Retitled the Advanced Underwriting Unit, the operation grew from a staff of four in 1951 to 180 in 1969 as it established branch offices across the country. It even developed an information-gathering operation called the Competitive Information Assistance Unit, whose special interest in competing insurers was reflected in its initials, CIA. In tandem with the increasing complexity of insurance and the American economy, these research programs gradually affected the typical agent's daily routine. Recalled a long-time Equitable agent, Eugene D. Badgley, "Many and many a man who had been selling insurance over the kitchen table began to realize the possibilities in business insurance, in estate planning, fringe benefits, and pension trust, this kind of thing."[7]

Another approach to the problem of retaining agents was to offer them better compensation either in commissions or in benefits. Contracts between agents and Equitable (which were identified as even-numbered "editions") underwent dramatic changes. The Eighth Edition Contract, introduced in 1922, established a scale of commissions and a loan program for new full-time agents, but little else. In 1941, the Tenth Edition Contract continued the loan program and added a small package of insurance and retirement benefits, the size of which was keyed to sales performance. The loan fund was expensive for Equitable to maintain — financing charges alone ran as high as $3 million annually — but it seemed to help agents get started. Yet one feature of the loan fund was very unpopular: dropouts were exempted from paying back the loans while successful agents were liable. There were widespread complaints that it was unfair to penalize the people whom Equitable claimed it wanted.

All those programs helped some agents at one time or another, but not the sales force as a whole, and the attrition rate did not diminish. Agents and agency managers tended to blame the Home Office. Speaking of Equitable in the tense 'fifties, Coy Eklund (who then managed an agency in Detroit) referred to "a somewhat mediocre agency force" and depicted the relationship between the Old Guard and the Home Office as one of "persistent confrontational antagonism." The

complaints poured in from agents and managers: agency offices were poorly furnished and in shabby districts; financial assistance was too little; underwriting was too rigid; paperwork moved lethargically; and products were not imaginative or consumer-oriented.[8]

What all this came down to was that The Equitable, as it neared its centennial — though justifiably proud of its innovations in products and investments — appeared to have fallen behind in adapting to agents' requirements and consumers' concerns. Harry Garber remembered what it was like when he joined the Actuarial Department in 1950:

It was a sleepy business — a very structured, simple business. Premiums and cash values had not changed between 1910 until just before I arrived. Premiums did not vary with the size of the policies. There were no niches with different risks —

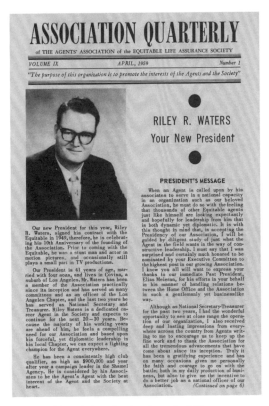

The Agents' Association stirred up fears of rebellion.

everybody paid the same rate by age wherever they lived, whether they smoked or didn't smoke. We did not even know what the costs for policies of different size were. It was the ultimate of risk-sharing.

Some of this was due to cautious regulators. While companies based in other states were doing well with adjustable whole-life insurance, in which premium rates decreased as face values increased, the New York Insurance Department ruled that adjustable whole-life discriminated against holders of small policies. Yet agency managers and agents who wanted to sell these policies often blamed the actuaries in the Home Office for the regulators' conservatism.[9]

Extreme caution also guided relations between the Home Office and the field, except in the language of complaints. "[A]t that time the Old Guard was hammering on that, hammering on that, hammering on that," remembered Don Bryant of the fierce debate about financial support. Some managers concentrated their fury on the requirement that successful agents repay their start-up loans. Richard Hageman, manager of a big successful agency in Cincinnati, looked back: "It irritated managers that our representatives were not really and truly able to devote themselves solely to becoming professional life insurance people."[10]

When the Old Guard complained, the Home Office paid attention. It derived its influence largely from agency managers' positions as chief distributors of Equitable policies and from their financial success. "The Old Guard's power was the power of persuasion," Wenzlaff (a former Old Guard president) said, perhaps with some understatement. "We were not there to assassinate anybody in the Home Office. But we may have succeeded in pointing out flaws or mistakes that affected the image and goals of The Equitable." What made the Old Guard especially potent was the stability of its leadership, which often outsur-

vived the tenure of Equitable's officers. The nine-man executive committee was a self-perpetuating group of more senior agency managers, many of them from the old Embry Agency in Kansas City, who usually met in secrecy and kept in constant contact with Home Office executives and with key members of the Board of Directors. Another former president, James B. Gurley, described the Guard in the three decades after World War II as "a very close, cliquish, and clannish group, an old-boy network — a kind of Tammany Hall." And he characterized its leader, that poker-playing heir of Pick Embry, Warren Woody, as "one of the finest politicians not to have become a politician."[11]

As attentive as the Old Guard was in attending to the needs of agency managers, many agents feared that it did not place a sufficiently high priority on representing their interests. The story of efforts by agents during the 1940's, 'fifties, and 'sixties to organize an agents' organization on a par with the Old Guard is a little-known chapter in Equitable's history.

In 1946, a Pacific Mutual Life agent in Atlanta, Nola Patterson, began publication of an industry-wide monthly newsletter for agents titled *Life Insurance Reveille*, which she called "The Voice of the Agent" and in which she attacked the power of managers (whom she labeled "company spokesmen"). A handful of Equitable agents were active in the *Reveille*; some allowed their names to be run in its pages. There was not much sympathy in Equitable's Home Office. "She is the type of agent who becomes disgruntled over practically everything, and likes to stir up other agents to take part in her crusades," agency head Vincent ("Deak") Welch complained about Patterson to the Society's General Counsel, Sterling Pierson, in 1947.[12]

In 1948 and 1949, two groups were formed by Equitable agents: the Agents' Association, which was based in Boston, and the Underwriters' National Association, centered in Chicago. Their initial specific protest was that Equitable, unlike many other insurers, did not offer agents a disability insurance policy. When the founding members were harassed by their agency managers, Underwriters' National filed a complaint with the National Labor Relations Board, which in 1949 arbitrated a settlement whereby Equitable, while refusing to recognize the two groups officially, agreed not to restrain agents from joining them. That was little comfort to agents, who, fearing retaliation by managers or the Home Office, rarely signed their names to articles in the groups' publications. The two groups merged in 1951 as the Agents' Association under the presidency of a successful Boston agent, Silas D. Wyman. In February 1951, in the first issue of *Association Quarterly*, Wyman explained that the body existed because the Old Guard was not meeting agents' needs; agency managers, "however well-intentioned, are, of course, an arm of management." By the end of the year the Association had 1,225 members across the country.[13]

"The purpose of this organization is to promote the interests of the Agents and the Society," the Association announced. What was clear from the beginning was that the agents were sure that their interests *were* the Society's interests. Years later, Newton Press, the group's president in the mid 'sixties and the longtime editor of the *Quarterly*, said of his activity: "Our heart was in The Equitable, which was why we were career agents in The Equitable. We were interested in improving the mix for the whole company. We were on the front lines. We knew what was happening." The *Quarterly* published comparative studies of insurance companies' benefit packages, products, and administration, and other issues that arose. Yet what pervaded the debate was a self-conscious conviction on the part of the agents involved that Equitable had lost its way and, distracted by Wall Street, was taking the agents of Main Street for granted. One agent complained, "After all, John Doe does not know Mr. Oates or 1285 Avenue of the Americas or how many billions the Society owns — he only knows Bill Smith, Equitable agent, in whom he believes and has confidence."[14]

The issue, then, seems to have been as much about recognition as compensation and benefits. Although Ray Murphy and Oates soothed feelings by meeting with Association officers and offering small compromises, the frustration was not assuaged. "The Home Office was very standoffish," Press remembered. "They had their own private club." But what the officers of the Agents' Association did not know was that the Home Office was keenly alert to — even frightened by — their activities. Within a few months of the *Quarterly*'s first issue, the Home Office, fearing that Equitable agents would abandon ship for other companies, held a secret, top-level re-evaluation of the agency force. It concluded that the army of part-time agents should be retained in part because they were less expensive to maintain than full-time career agents, but also because they were less likely to organize and undertake a job action. The agent contract was liberalized somewhat in 1951 to provide new benefits and an enhanced loan program for new recruits (the Association still had to buy a disability policy from another insurer). Although Wyman, Press, and other leaders of the Association thought their main complaints were reasonable and negotiable, the *Quarterly* ran a few provocative, unsigned letters that caused some nervous agency managers and Home Office executives to come to the unjustified conclusion that the Association was a hotbed of bomb-throwers. The manager of an agency in Boston, Laurens F. Bruno, went so far as to characterize the organizing effort as "this insurrection." Deak Welch and other agency officers became so fearful that their agents would be recruited by other companies that they reduced the number of agents in the industry's Chartered Life Underwriter training program; of the Old Guard's twenty National Honor Agents between 1941 and 1960, only six had the CLU designation. For the company that had played a crucial role in creating the CLU program in the first place, this was strange behavior.[15]

The Agents' Association was not helped by its internal conflicts. Radical members wanted to form a union to engage in collective bargaining with Equitable, while Wyman limited his aims to an agents' seat on Equitable's Board of Directors. Another issue was the elimination from the agents' contract of the "prior rights" clause, which prohibited agents from selling other insurers' products without Equitable's approval. Of the three goals, the first two were not realized, while the third was attained in the 1970's.

In the centennial year of 1959, therefore, Equitable's agency force was in a state of low morale. The agents and managers were divided over many issues, yet were united in feeling that the Home Office was inattentive to their concerns. Oates recognized that the agency side required leadership comparable to what he had provided for the investment side and began looking around for someone to bring change.

In August 1958, at the annual agency managers' meeting in Boca Raton, Coy Eklund, as president of the Old Guard, gave an electrifying stemwinder of a speech that he closed by repeatedly shouting, "Boy, do I feel good!" Oates, in the audience, became so excited that he leaped up and enthusiastically joined Eklund in the chant, and soon the whole group was in a happy uproar. At a later meeting,

Oates invited Eklund to his hotel room to discuss the state of the Society and especially the performance of the agency force. By the end of the meeting, he had asked Eklund to come to the Home Office as a Vice-President serving as his personal assistant to work on agency matters. That was the genesis of an innovative and influential program for recruiting and training agents that Eklund designed and implemented, and that Oates called the New Epoch. Calvin Kanter would later say, "John Kennedy changed the United States. Coy Eklund changed Equitable. And that was a new epoch."[16]

Coy Eklund, whose influence on Equitable's history would stretch into the 1980's, had enjoyed a fascinating life even before he came to the Home Office in 1959. Born in 1915 in Brookston, Minnesota, a logging settlement, he was raised near the cabin that his paternal grandfather built after emigrating from Sweden. His paternal grandmother was a midwife who delivered more than 3,000 babies. The family spoke Swedish; when Coy's father mastered his second language, it was Chippewa, taught him by friendly Indian neighbors. Coy's father was a logger and storekeeper, and his mother read aloud to the boy from an inspirational tract titled *Keys to Success*. Looking for new logging opportunities, the family moved to the Upper Peninsula of Michigan and settled in a new town of fifty-two residents that the Postal Service named Eklund, possibly because his father was postmaster. The town was too small to have a high school, so Coy boarded out in a distant town for $5.50 a week and returned home on weekends — "way out there in that desolation, that poverty," he remembered painfully — to work the family store, which was called the Oasis.[17]

The boy's great pleasure was school, but not because of the classes and books: "It had a *band*. That's all I enjoyed, that's all....

Expression, I could express myself." What he liked most about the band was not so much the music but its flamboyant leader, Lyle Atkins. In 1975, the year he became Equitable's President, Eklund reminisced about Atkins and his effect:

> *Have you ever seen somebody who can walk on a stage, and he just looked terrific and every movement of his body was like a cat, just lithe and appropriate? You know we just admired him. His showmanship was par excellence. You know, learning is in a large sense imitating, isn't it? You do intend to repeat that what you see.... And he was with me in all these years. He just stimulated the dickens out of me.*[18]

Eklund played the trombone well enough to finish second in the 1932 National Solo Contest in Chicago. He worked his way through a year at the University of Michigan by giving music lessons, baby-sitting, and washing dishes, but, broke, was forced to drop out. He did odd jobs and returned to school on a band scholarship at Michigan State, where he majored in police administration and led a busy dance group advertised as Coy Eklund and His Band: Purveyors of Fine Dance Music. It was there that he became a part-time Equitable agent, making his first sale to his fiancée. He specialized in offering $1,000 term policies to his fellow students in the student union; when they expressed interest, he marched them across the street to a doctor's office for a physical examination. He did well enough to buy his first car (from his district manager) for $75.

In the army, Eklund was shipped to Europe and served in the personnel department of General Patton's Third Army. He had opportunities to observe Patton interacting with troops, and was impressed: "I was right there and I caught the spirit. It was a contagious spirit. It was simply a spirit of winning.

That's all there was to it." From Patton he also learned some leadership skills, including the value of quickly rewarding outstanding performance. Patton carried a pocketful of Bronze Stars to hand out to the troops. "He always said, 'The shorter the time between the act, the meritorious act, and the recognition of it, the more effective is the recognition.'" After the war, Eklund went back to The Equitable and then to Detroit, where by 1958 he built the second largest of the Society's 105 agencies.[19]

Striking in appearance and demeanor, with an intense countenance and rigid military posture, Eklund was gifted with a persuasive ability that became the stuff of Equitable legends. In 1956, he and Laurens Bruno went to New York to present the field force's position in a dispute with Walter Klem over an aspect of adjustable whole-life insurance, which the New York Insurance Department had finally approved. Arguing the agents' case before Ray Murphy, Eklund made an emotional speech in which he predicted dire consequences for the Society should the agents not be allowed to meet the competition. The change went through. (Many agents of that generation were unhappy with Klem and other actuaries, but Eklund was remembered as being unusually skeptical.) Such incidents impressed Warren Woody, Fred Holderman, and other leaders of the Old Guard who were a generation older. They invited Eklund into their councils, and he accompanied them when they went to New York in 1957 to talk the Board of Directors out of electing Klem the new CEO.

In James Oates, Coy Eklund found a mentor and sponsor. At a banquet long after the older man had retired and the younger, at Oates's strong recommendation, had become Equitable's Chief Executive Officer, Eklund inscribed Oates's program, "To the Man who has meant most to me in my lifetime — Jim Oates, Jr.!" The intimate relationship that they forged in 1959 was founded on their similar charismatic personalities and their deep faith in life insurance. Master and protégé alike were ambitious, analytical midwesterners who were unhappy with bureaucratic caution, comfortable exerting power, and naturally driven to reshape their surroundings. Both were insurance fundamentalists convinced that they had been called to their jobs to preach the old-time gospel of protection and security — Oates by restructuring the company itself, Eklund by infusing salesmanship with a mysticism rarely seen in Equitable's history.[20]

The key to selling insurance, Eklund would say, was not just to have a good product; rather, the agent must be self-confident and able to imbue prospects with that confidence. This was not a new idea. It had been articulated in other ways by many preachers of the gospel of protection as well as by those clergymen who, a century earlier, had endorsed life insurance as a social boon. But Eklund expressed the idea more fervently than most people, often relying on his store of inspirational quotes. "It is the spiritual always that determines the material," he often proclaimed, his voice a hypnotic drumbeat, quoting the transcendentalist Thomas Carlyle. Any program or product that made that spiritual exercise easier and more effective for the agent was good for insurance sales and, therefore, good for Equitable.[21]

Eklund's missionary zeal, rhetorical powers, showmanship, and convictions can be gauged from a few excerpts from his speeches. Here is a paragraph from a talk, titled "Forward Together," that he gave at the January 1959 Equitable managers' meeting at Boca Raton, just after Grant Keehn dropped his first bombshell about AHO:

Believing always in what life insurance does, we come to believe most in what it is — a magical, mystical, financial instrument. It has the endurance of faith; it has the spirit of hope; it has the goodness of love. Life insurance is caused by love. A business founded on love must be a good business as well as a permanent one.

A theme of other Eklund speeches was that the business founded on love was a rigorous calling that demanded an elite corps of gifted, spiritually mature, disciplined workers. He could make insurance agents sound like the Marines. "This is a difficult business," he told an industry seminar. "It is for the few who are strong. It takes courage and strength. You've got to be determined and rugged to succeed in life insurance." It was his job to inspire them with his rigorous exertion of what he called "élan and éclat." He opened a talk to some agents in Baltimore with a quote from the French philosopher Ernest Dimnet, "The presence of superior men is a unique tonic." That was the launching pad for Eklund's peroration:

The presence of superior men is a unique tonic! That presence is here in this room tonight... an aura of achievement, a sense of high purpose fulfilled. I feel it in the air — and it's wonderfully invigorating, like being the winning pitcher in the deciding game of the World Series!

The occasion for this outburst was a gathering of some insurance agents who had earned their CLU certification. How they responded is not known, but if they were like many agents who heard him over the years, they were at least entertained, probably inspired, and possibly converted into lifelong followers. That is not an exaggeration. One of his staff members, Robert W. McCabe, recalled the effect of meeting Eklund just as the makeover of the sales force was being planned: "I'm saying this from the bottom of my heart, I felt like the original disciples must have felt when they first listened to Our Lord preach." Not since Henry Hyde had the agency force had such a charismatic leader.[22]

Coy Eklund being greeted by members of the Order of Excalibur at an agents' meeting.

Eklund believed all of it and shaped his life around it. He later related how, when he was an agency manager, he was reading Norman Vincent Peale's popular self-help manual *The Power of Positive Thinking* when he realized what his ambition was. He laid out that ambition in the book's margin: to be President of The Equitable Life Assurance Society. To get there, he developed a range of skills, some of them seemingly contradictory, for in some ways he was a radical, in others a traditionalist. He restructured Equitable's agency force with the assistance of two social theorists; yet he drafted peppy slogans for sales campaigns such as "There's Work to Do in '62," "A New Esprit in '63," and "Achieving More in '64."

When Oates in 1960 assigned him the task of reorganizing the agency force, Eklund might have depended solely on these time-proven methods and his own demonstrated interpersonal skills. Yet the New Epoch

reforms were largely based on academic research. Eklund's colleague was the Second Vice-President for Social Research, Dr. John W. Riley. A Harvard-trained former chairman of the Sociology Department at Rutgers University, Riley had been hired after a long search that began when Oates asked the advice of his brother Michael, at Princeton, who referred him to Robert K. Merton, a sociology professor at Columbia University. Expert both in applied research, which addresses immediate practical problems, and in basic research, which develops theories of human and organizational behavior, Merton was one of the country's most influential social scientists. Among his contributions were the research technique of the focused interview (the foundation of the focus group), an understanding of how influential ideas are disseminated, and several concepts that became part of everyday language, including "self-fulfilling prophecy" and "public image."

Merton headed the search that led to Riley.

Riley had a strong background in social and consumer research. During World War II, he had worked with fighter pilots to help improve their success rate and, after D-day, interviewed French citizens to determine how they would receive the Allies ("Some threw flowers, some were snipers," he reported). He had surveyed public opinion about a wide range of topics, including alcoholism, contraceptives, and television. And he had worked in the newly developing field of corporate social responsibility, which lay at the intersection of business and ethics, much like the ideology of mutual life insurance companies. Despite firm warnings that he was selling out — "You've been seduced by the capitalists," said one academic friend — Riley accepted Oates's offer to become, as Riley put it, "a kind of resident intellectual." Few if any American companies then had such a position.[23]

Eklund, who helped Merton with the search, got to work even before Riley arrived in 1960 by setting himself a rigorous program of reading in social science and designing projects in both applied and basic research. In a journal he kept at the time, Eklund enthusiastically referred to Riley and himself as a "two-span bridge linking academia (the world of knowledge) to ELAS (the world of affairs)." He ventured a description of the new Basic Social Research project (BASORE):

> *Vital Hypothesis: that through intelligent, imaginative study of research findings (literature), which might be called the "idea hunt," we (life insurance people) can develop practical and rational application of new knowledge directly in our operations — thereby securing "pay-off" not contemplated or regarded by the BASORE effort itself!*

When Riley arrived at the Home Office, he was astonished to find an insurance person who could speak his language. "It was a tour de force," he recalled in 1994. "This man had an analytical mind like I'd never seen before. He could do analytical problems in record time. He was a quick study and he was systems personified." Riley tutored Eklund about sociology, and Eklund tutored Riley about insurance. Advised by Merton, they threw themselves into the pioneering basic research program, whose purpose, according to Merton, was "to assist Equitable in arriving at fresh perceptions of ways in which it could take the lead in providing new services to the American people."[24]

Riley started work on an analysis of the 1960 census with an eye to identifying demographic patterns relevant to insurance. Another project was designed to introduce insurance executives to social theories that would help them rethink their institutions' images and public responsibilities. He organized seminars and edited publications, including a book on corporate social responsibility titled *The Corporation and its Publics* and a special issue of a professional journal on social research and life insurance. Not all these ideas came to fruition; some were too abstract for Equitable's use, others too long-range. After an agency officer told Riley that all he had to do to attract interest was to tell agents how to sell more insurance, Riley arranged for Equitable to sponsor a research project called "The Meaning of Death" that included a public opinion survey of American attitudes toward dying. The topic had long been taboo. Riley remembered: "People had never been able to talk about death before. They *thanked* us for the opportunity to talk about it. What we found was that people are concerned not for themselves — they know they are going to die — but for their survivors." Riley drew up reports and ran training programs for agents, who learned that they need no longer avoid directly mentioning death during sales presentations.[25]

Dr. Robert K. Merton.

As intellectually fascinating as it was, basic research was quickly side-tracked by immediate concerns, the most important of which was the agency force. Eklund, with Riley's and Merton's assistance, began a manpower research project to better understand attrition, career patterns, and productivity. Personal and sales data concerning 32,000 Equitable agents who had been hired since 1947 were sent to Columbia University for computer analysis. The results showed two patterns. First, by far the highest attrition rate occurred during agents' first four years; after that, agent retention improved dramatically. This suggested that an agent's career was not continuous from recruitment to retirement but, instead, had two very different stages. Second, the data showed that agents' productivity was correlated with such personal characteristics as an agent's educational level, age, and prior occupation; with this information, the analysts were better able to predict a new agent's success. "It was a brilliant, I say, a brilliant piece of research," Riley later said of Eklund's project.[26]

As the agent manpower data were being interpreted, Oates appointed Eklund head of the Agency Operations Department, where he quickly got to work making the changes that comprised the program that Oates called the New Epoch. Analysis of agent manpower results and his own experience convinced him that there were better ways to organize, select, train, and motivate people to sell life insurance successfully. In 1962, he told an insurance seminar at Ohio State University that improvements in this area were crucial if life insurance were to compete successfully against other products offering financial security: "Sales manpower is today the key requirement — the key challenge — for the whole industry...," he said. "We have got to find some better solutions to the building of substantial numbers of successful salesmen of life insurance or we will just lose this great market for thrift and protection by default."[27]

His solution had several features. One was the end of the Equitable's system of part-time agents. He was sure that a properly trained agency force of fewer than 4,000 full-time agents with the right backgrounds and aptitudes could outperform a force of twice that size consisting largely of part-timers. For this new, smaller agency force ("the Superior Sales Force of the entire life insurance industry," he styled it), Eklund provided a two-part structure that he called the segmented agency force. It addressed the discrepancy in retention rates between new and more experienced agents by organizing them in two groups. One, the Developing Sales Force, covered approximately the first four years of a career, when the learning

Dr. John W. Riley, a sociologist, worked closely with Eklund.

curve was steepest and attrition was highest. Each year was treated as a separate stage, much like each of the four years of college. In the second group, the Experienced Sales Force, were the alumni of the Developing Sales Force — agents whose overall attrition rate was lower and production generally higher. Both groups were closely monitored by the Agency Operations Department in the Home Office.

This tandem structure was introduced at the same time as the new Twelfth Edition agent's contract, which banned part-time agents and sales by non-agents, and laid out the four-year training regimen for the Developing Sales Force. In the first three years, a new agent earned a subsistence wage of $800 a month, plus bonuses and partial commissions on sales; the salary replaced the old system of loans that agents and managers had long objected to. The fourth year was a transition year to full commissions. Then the agent would move into the Experienced Sales Force. As the standard of agent success, Eklund introduced a measure called the production credit, in which sales volume was one factor. To boost professionalism, Eklund restored Equitable's support of the CLU designation. And to stimulate sales, he formed honor clubs for high production. Among the honor clubs he established were the Hall of Fame, the National Leaders Corps, and the Order of Excalibur. He had learned his lesson well from General Patton: a public award, Eklund said, was like a snowball rolling downhill; an award to one agent challenged other agents to perform better. It had to be that way, he said in long-familiar language: "People do not buy individual life insurance; it must be *sold* to them. And it must be sold hard, by skilled, effective salesmen, approaching prospects face to face and earnestly discussing additional protection in a very personalized way." Eklund vested the awards with mystical showmanship; initiation into the Order of Excalibur involved the passing of a ceremonial sword in a candlelit, Arthurian setting.[28]

Managers also received attention; Eklund raised their salaries, expense allowances, and benefits. He also supervised them closely, replacing them if they did not perform up to his standards. Said James Gurley, "He wasn't afraid to promote them and he wasn't afraid to fire them. You felt you had a chance, but you knew you were watched." Some independent managers of the old school did not fit into this more centralized agency system.[29]

To provide agents for this two-part agency force, Eklund created a national recruiting system. Until then, while the Home Office had provided some guidance, managers had used their own hiring standards, which could be subjective if not bizarre. Most managers relied on friends and relatives to provide referrals, some sent handwriting samples to a psychic in Kentucky for analysis, and one was reputed to be able to identify good prospects by the shape of their eyebrows and chins. Eklund was sure he could do better using a profile of an applicant's aptitude for insurance sales based on an evaluation derived from the agent manpower project. This profile, which he called the Relative Development Potential, rated the potential for insurance sales of 130 occupations cross-referenced by age groups. There were four categories, from no significant potential on up to high potential. Schoolteachers and coaches, for instance, were ranked low potential until they were thirty, medium potential from thirty to thirty-five, and high potential for older ages. And one group of forty-five occupations — including pharmacists, military officers, and writers — was ranked low potential until thirty and medium or high potential at older ages. The only category graded highest potential in every age group was "salesman," although some types of sales work were considered superior to others. Life insurance salesmen from other companies were ranked low potential in all age groups.

Eklund's motto for this massive restructuring and recruiting effort was "Increased Production is the Goal — Improved Manpower Is the Means." Exactly how manpower should be improved was, according to Riley, the subject of one of the few disagreements between himself and Eklund. Eklund believed that once Equitable identified and hired qualified applicants for agents' jobs, everything should fall into place given proper motivation, training, and entrepreneurial spirit. If there was attrition, it was because agents failed to live up to their capability. But Riley, the sociologist, was sure there were structural issues: new agents' success depended largely on their social relationships in the agency with district managers, the agency manager, and experienced agents; and the agency should be organized to enhance those relationships. This theory later was confirmed by research by Riley's assistant, Harris Schrank, indicating, for example, that agencies in which retired agents were available to assist younger agents had relatively low attrition rates.

To boost agents' spirits and keep the field force informed about policies and the Home Office, Eklund introduced new Equitable publications over which he exerted close editorial control. Through a number of symbolic gestures he made it clear that, as far as he was concerned, the agency force was Equitable's highest priority. For example, he directed that company publications always capitalize the word "Agent" and place it first in lists of jobs regardless of alphabetical order. Accountants and actuaries were amused or even angered, but agents loved it. In an end run around the Agents' Association, Eklund in 1969 established an agents' organization, the National Agents Forum, which eventually came to be the recognized voice of the agents, much as the Old Guard was the voice of the managers. While the Agents' Association collapsed, agents now could feel that they were receiving the attention for which they long had lobbied.

The New Epoch was an immediate success. In its first years, between 1961 and 1965, the number of agents taking CLU exams doubled, honor club membership increased by half, production of beginning and novice agents in the Developing Sales Force more than doubled, and overall sales climbed despite the shrinkage of Assured Home Ownership.

For decades, the vast company was run by many different agencies and departments held together by thousands of clerks and assistants. This photograph, taken in 1916, could have been taken at almost any time between 1900 and 1960.

CHAPTER XVI

"ONE COMPANY"

Since the time of the Civil War, The Equitable, as a pioneering national (and, for forty years, international) consumer marketing operation, had dealt with complex administrative problems that most other types of businesses did not face until the twentieth century. The day-to-day necessities of communicating between the Home Office and the hundreds of sales and cashiers' offices, of keeping track of millions of policyholders' records, and of moving piles of paperwork and money all demanded a massive, decentralized administrative system of offices around the hub of the Home Office.

The system was remarkably stable. It was structured around thousands of clerks, many of whom worked at the company for forty or fifty years, and a few tools invented in the late nineteenth century, including the typewriter, the vertical filing cabinet, the adding machine, the addressing machine, and the telephone. After carbon paper appeared in 1895, the next major advance in office technology was the first computer, which was installed in the 1950's. With the arrival of computers, which permitted further centralization of administration, the system began to change dramatically. Simultaneously, the company transformed its perception of itself and its role.

Before the computer, the system was a decentralized one. Policyholder information was recorded on index cards, called premium record cards, kept for each policy in each agency's business office, the cashier's office. Agents handled sales, cashiers handled business. The entire history of a policy was recorded on its card. "The premium record card was the Bible of The Equitable," remembered Don Finn, an Agency Operations official in the 1950's. "We operated as 100 little companies out in the field, because we had about 100 cashiers' offices." Despite the intimacy suggested by the name, cashiers' offices often were large, exceptionally busy operations requiring many people to send out bills and keep up the all-important premium record cards by hand. The biggest cashier's office in the 1950's, which handled administration for three bustling agencies in Pittsburgh, had seventy-six employees, including three tellers who took payments and paid commissions and benefits, still largely in cash. The cashiers' offices were treated as distant satellites of the Home Office, connected by telephone, telex, and an occasional surprise visit by an audit team, which would count the cash and check the bookkeeping. It was local and it was simple. "In the old days, we didn't know the Home Office even existed," recalled Howard Osman, who began work in the Pittsburgh cashier's office in 1954.[1]

When agents died or retired, more often than not their policyholders were "orphaned," that is, not reassigned to other agents for annual updates and the follow-up calls that often led to new business. Although dividends and death benefits continued to be paid, without agents, old policyholders were essentially relegated to insurance limbo. The solution lay in the power of automated data storage that, by making all records instantly available to both the Home Office and the cashiers' offices, would turn all those little dispersed local companies into one large administrative whole. Equitable's actuaries began to computerize policyholders' records in the mid-1950's, but the work was slow. When the Home Office moved in 1961 from 393 Seventh Avenue to 1285 Avenue of the Americas, the movers reported that Equitable had 7,350 employees, 7,159 filing cabinets, and only 525 business machines — this at a time when there were about 3 million policyholder files. But automation expanded rapidly in the 1960's.

Historically, all the paper was handled by an army of clerks in the Home Office and cashiers' offices. Of the 10,000 salaried employees in the 1940's, 'fifties, and early 'sixties, a large majority were assigned to process applications, evaluations, policies, and checks. In the mid-'sixties, 25,000 benefit checks were processed daily. Anybody unaware of how dependent the Society was on this army

learned the lesson in January 1966 when the first New York transit strike threatened to drag the Home Office to a stop. In the first week of the ten-day strike, Equitable spent an extra $1 million to keep essential personnel at their jobs by renting hotel rooms and vans. Chairman Oates and President Keehn walked to work while their limousines gathered up essential clerical workers. "If we fell behind substantially it would be like trying to dig ourselves out of a landslide," Personnel Director Edward Robie told a reporter.[2]

Like other New York City financial institutions, Equitable recruited its clerks from the graduating classes of the city's high schools, many of which assigned teachers to maintain relationships with personnel departments at insurance companies, banks, and the New York Stock Exchange. Every spring, Equitable recruiters went out to these schools with arm-

Walter Klem, who supervised the important CAPS computer project, shows Ray Murphy an early IBM machine.

loads of brochures and films. The selling points for Equitable were its size, its stability, its benefit program, and its long history of providing lifetime employment for dutiful women and men. Recruiters would report, accurately, that not even during the Great Depression had anybody been laid off except for cause.

The majority of the clerical staff in the Home Office were women. A typical employee was Peggy Ward. She was a senior at Walton High School in the Bronx, with four years of typing classes behind her, when Equitable's recruiter paid his annual visit in 1944. She went to the Home Office for an interview and aptitude and typing tests, passed them, and was offered and accepted a job in the Annuity Department at a salary of $17 for a five-day week. She was taken to a large room filled with rows of metal desks, was assigned a desk, and was trained by the woman she replaced, who was leaving to have a baby. (Before the 1970's, there were relatively few working mothers.) Her job was to process claims for beneficiaries of annuity policies. Each claim would take anywhere from a couple of hours to several months, depending on the policy and the circumstances. As she processed the claim, she might consult with an agent, and if she had to communicate with the policyholder or a beneficiary, she sent instructions to a clerk, called a correspondent, whose job was to write letters. Otherwise she was on her own until the standards were met and she made out the check.

Set production goals had to be met, so supervision and working conditions were strictly enforced by the observant male supervisor sitting in front of the rows of desks. Ward had to sign in every morning and be at her desk when a bell rang at 9 o'clock. There were short breaks for coffee and a brownbag lunch. The work day ended at 5 with another bell. "Everybody used to think the bells were crazy because it was like school," Ward remem-

Staff parties boosted morale. Peggy Ward is third from right.

bered. There was no time off for doctors' appointments or family problems, which were to be attended to over the weekend. Clerks had to observe a dress code determined by their departments; Equitable was liberal in this requirement, since other insurers required workers to wear company uniforms. "It was work," Peggy Ward recalled in 1994, "but it was a wonderful place to work." There were benefits — an annual two-week vacation, dinner dances, Christmas parties, and summer outings — and the satisfaction of having steady work at decent pay alongside a group of friends. "You wanted to come to work every day, it was like family," Ward remembered. "I always say that we were glad to live when we lived. We were so happy. We were not stressed-out the way people are today."[3]

In the 1960's and 'seventies, computer systems gradually took over much of the handling of paperwork. The first computers, installed in the 'fifties, were low-powered, magnetic-tape machines used for such simple jobs as billing, calculating payments of agents' renewal commissions, and creating tables for determining premium rates. Typically for most tape-drive office systems of the time, data could be accessed only in batches at scheduled times. A leap forward in flexibility and power came in the early 'sixties with the arrival of the

David Harris and his colleague Walter de Vries in 1955.

early disk-drive IBM computers. The Methods Research Department, headed by an imaginative technology-focused actuary, David Harris, developed a proposal for transferring all the data on premium record cards to disks and installing computers in agencies and cashiers' offices so that information would be accessible throughout the Society. This idea was the seed for the Society's Cashiers' Automatic Processing System, or CAPS. (After 1968, as cashiers' offices were renamed general services offices, the first letter stood for Computerized.) Walter Klem, in his last big job at Equitable, was in overall charge of the CAPS project when it was launched in 1962, and he ably oversaw it through the planning stage. After his departure in 1965, Harris and Harry Garber took over and developed the CAPS program into a new technology-driven operations area, the Systems Department. By the time CAPS became fully operational in 1972, it had absorbed well over the original $30 million budget and the efforts of 500 full-time employees, and was providing the first intimate tie between all of Equitable's insurance operations.

CAPS was largely in place in the late 'sixties when a series of studies was begun to determine how best to exploit the new system. The head of Agency Operations, Coy Eklund, intended that agents use computers wherever possible in sales and administration, for instance, in tracking orphans. Among the CAPS programs were a few for writing policy proposals, called "illustrations," for prospective policyholders. Illustrations reflected the variety of premium rates, commissions, and other relevant financial data. In the pre-computer era, this flexibility had been crimped by limited calculating power; Howard Osman recalled that the rate book carried by agents in the 'fifties was approximately the size of a child's prayer book. But with the coming of computers, premiums and commission rates became more numerous, rate books grew to thousands of pages, and illustrations proliferated. One of the new CAPS programs, the Personalized Electronic Proposal Service, turned out 40,660 computerized policy illustrations in its first year, 1965.

But there also were growing pains. The field force went into an uproar when a new system for paying commissions, which was expected to save $400,000 a year, delivered the checks several days late. And some agents wondered if the hours saved by putting together policy illustrations by computer paid off; the old system was laborious, but it gave agents plenty of time and opportunity to get to know and win the trust of their prospects. Like every other company struggling with automation, Equitable learned that it was subject to events beyond its control. In November 1965, a massive power failure blacked out New York City and stopped the computers. After that and the transit strike, Equitable moved its computers and many of its service offices to locations outside the city.

Despite those problems, CAPS and the other computer projects came to revolutionize Equitable in two ways. First, they increased efficiency by making large amounts of data more quickly accessible to more people. Second, and perhaps more important in the long run, in opening up those new or larger channels of communication between departments they broke down many of the barriers surrounding the old fiefdoms of the specialties. For the first time since Henry Hyde, high executives in the Home Office sensed that, with some reorganization, they might be able to coordinate and standardize performance around company-wide goals. James Oates knew as well as anybody how important this development was, even though he was by nature a humanist and not a technocrat. "It is ironic," he wrote, "that the machine is forcing cooperation and an acceptance of mutual interdependence when men — though recognizing the evils of 'little empires' and allegiance only to one's own specialty — have heretofore failed to adequately attain these goals."[4]

The problem at The Equitable was not that all those "little empires" were inefficient, poorly run, or staffed by unqualified people. Many of them had engaged in rigorous self-scrutiny, had good internal controls, and implemented efficiency measures. Rather, the trouble was the lack of coordination of goals and standards throughout the company. Harry Garber, who would head a reorganization effort, described

Harry Garber laid out the new matrix organization.

some of these problems as endemic to a business with a population of experts:

We haven't thought much about it, but we have tended to be a functional company, and in a functional company you rise to the top of your ability and don't need people who are management specialists. We are still at heart a kind of functional organization. The bad thing is that it's very hard to get anything done here.... This is probably an affliction to some degree of the insurance enterprise. It tends to require all these particular kinds of specialists.[5]

The narrowness that Garber referred to can be seen in two examples. The first is the management training program for college alumni set up in the early 'sixties. Although the purpose was to impress upon talented young men and women Equitable's respect for their intelligence, the trainees still had to satisfy humbling requirements not imposed on their friends in training programs at banks and industries — for example, low pay and an obligation to sign in each morning. Trainees became discouraged, and the program did not survive the 'sixties. The second example of the balkanized system of the "little empires" was the lack of interdepartmental coordination in two crucial functions, underwriting insurance applications and processing death claims. Each demanded close interaction among three separate departments, yet one of them, the Medical Department, was located on a different floor from the other two. In many other tasks, decisions involving two or more departments often required plodding negotiations between their heads. In the words of an officer in the company's Advanced Underwriting think tank, Neil M. DeVries, the whole process of decision making was not so much a coordinated system as "an older, more comfortable system of proposal and response."[6]

Oates was able to speed things along by applying heavy doses of his charisma, but even he could not be everywhere. His successor, J. Henry Smith (who became President in 1967 and CEO on Oates's retirement in 1969), did not have the advantages of a dominating personality or — because he was regarded as an interim President — of unquestioned power. Smith, who had worked in Equitable's trenches for three decades, was even more impatient than Oates with the languid diplomacy of decision making. He was astonished that department heads were so wary of dealing directly with each other that they insisted on coming to him for his personal approval of their programs. Smith complained, "They weren't being very adult, they weren't being very sensible, and they weren't willing to consider the other fellow's point of view to try to produce a singleness of purpose." Frustrated, Smith established a goal that he called the One Company Concept and held regular meetings at which he insisted that department heads make decisions by consensus.[7]

The one area where Equitable actually was "One Company" — personnel policy — was controversial. With Oates's support, Edward Robie developed the Society's first open, equitable, and consistent company-wide personnel policy. Robie was certain that fairness was crucial not only to efficiency but also to the Society's cohesion, morale, and public image: "Most managements underestimate the degree of information and concern about the reputation of the company that there is throughout the organization," he said. His rules were attacked as excessively rigid by officers who wanted the freedom to run their departments as they pleased. But despite these complaints, Oates and Smith supported Robie's rules in the name of the ideal of corporate unification.[8]

Smith's push toward management reform and the arrival of computers stimulated the first

Ruth S. Block established the regional service centers.

substantial rethinking of the traditional operation inherited from Henry Hyde. The internal studies were headed by David Harris and Harry Garber, who, having created the computer systems from scratch, were familiar with collaborative, innovative work to create new communications systems. In 1969, they set up five interdisciplinary task forces to examine and improve systems development. This group decision-making process was fraught with tension. One task force imploded immediately, and two others lasted only a few meetings. The first meeting of the task force on computers was described by Ruth S. Block, its chairwoman, as "one of the most personally agonizing experiences I ever had." But the process ultimately succeeded by forcing people to make decisions on which they previously would have waffled.[9]

After these long, painful internal discussions, in the early 'seventies, Garber laid out a new management structure based not on specialized functions but on principles described variously as line organization and matrix organization. Instead of bunching all specialists (say, systems development people) in one function-focused group, it distributed them through the company in various departments (group annuities, health insurance, and so on). With the power centers of the old specialties thus whittled down, Equitable in 1973 set up its first company-wide insurance operation.

To reform management within the matrix, Harris appointed Second Vice-President Ruth Block to head a task force called the Regional Operations Planning Group to study how work flowed among the Home Office, the agencies, and the cashiers' offices. She was then to put into effect a new Equitable-wide administrative system. There were three goals. One was to establish Equitable's first planning operation, which would result, for example, in distinguishing insurance sales from such long-range marketing strategies as determining future consumer demands. "This activity of setting objectives had never existed," Block said. "Nobody had ever used the word *marketing* before." Another goal was to save money. Block successfully offered prizes to induce department heads to break old habits and cooperate with each other. She found that with each award for outstanding performance, a department head became less intransigent and more willing to innovate.[10]

Black agency managers in the mid 1980's:
(left to right) Frank Russell, Jr. (Troy, Michigan);
Alphonso Carlton (Washington, D.C.); Collier St. Clair
(Atlanta, Georgia); Hyde Anderson (Baltimore, Maryland);
Sidney Levy (Tampa, Florida); James Obi (New York,
New York); William Green (Indianapolis,Indiana);
Clarence Wright (Washington, D.C.); and Carroll Carson
(Wilmette, Illinois).

The third goal, intended to facilitate accomplishing the other two, was to end the ancient divisions between the sales and business sides by breaking down the walls between the agents and cashiers. The cashiers' offices were gradually closed down in the 'seventies, and their duties were split between agencies, the Home Office, and six new regional service centers, all connected by computers. The first regional service center opened in Fresno, California, in February 1976, and was followed by others in Des Moines, Iowa; Charlotte, North Carolina; Columbus, Georgia; Milford, Connecticut; and — the last, in 1979 — in Colorado Springs, Colorado. Installation was swift and pragmatic; the Milford office was initially located in what had formerly been the lingerie department of a department store. As the system shifted from local to regional service centers, Block and her staff trained or retrained more than 2,000 employees, relocated more than 1,500 people, hired another 600, installed hundreds of computer terminals, modified more than fifty computer systems, and redesigned Equitable's nationwide telephone network. When it was up and running, the program required one-third fewer than the 3,250 people who had been doing administration in 1975 and saved about $30 million a year, while allowing a closer watch on agency expenditures and projections.

The "One Company" goal was helped by efforts by Oates and his successors as CEOs, Smith and Eklund, to give Equitable a unique identity through visible corporate purpose. This program revived and modernized the nineteenth-century image of the mutual company as a benevolent business enterprise. Traditionally, Equitable as an institution had not been active in charitable events outside of subscribing to war bond drives. From its early days, the company had argued that life insurance itself was an agent of social benefit through its provision of protection and savings, and that Equitable had done more than its share by developing new types of insurance, by distributing dividends, and by making socially beneficial investments.

But Oates, like many business leaders of the 1960's, believed that his company had to participate more fully in solving the nation's problems. In the 1960 mission statement, the section titled "Corporate Citizenship" affirmed that "to effectively sell and distribute growing volumes of life insurance, Equitable must be a good and respected corporate citizen and the public must be aware that it deserves such a stature." Later, in a speech at Columbia University, Oates laid out the assumptions underlying his conviction that good social policy is good business:

> These are that (1) every business enterprise operates to meet human needs through the use of capital; (2) human needs change as social values change; and (3) business succeeds to the degree that the changes in social values are recognized and the resulting new or changed human needs identified or served.[11]

To Oates this was an expression of his unified view of life. Said Robie, "I think it speaks of the nature of the man that he felt that any action one took needed to be guided by principle." For the first time in its history, Equitable, under Oates, engaged in direct financial giving despite criticism for donating policyholders' money. At its centennial the Society donated $1 million to the National Academy of Sciences in Washington to build a new science wing carrying Equitable's name (the wing now houses the academy's main conference center).[12]

John W. Riley, the in-house, one-man think tank, helped Oates further hone his vision. "One could call him the conscience of the organization, and also the idea man in

social responsibility," J. Henry Smith sympathetically said of Riley. Framing the issue for the company in the 'sixties, Riley asked, "Where and how does The Equitable Life Assurance Society of the United States fit into the larger society of the United States?" To some extent, the answer was out of Equitable's hands. In 1962, the Kennedy Administration invited Equitable and several other corporations to assume leadership positions on the Committee for Equal Employment Opportunity. Oates and Riley took special interest in the program's Committee on Youth Employment, which enhanced work opportunities for young people from racial minorities. Five years later, Oates led the insurance industry to form the Committee on Social Responsibility and then commit $1 billion to pay for housing, jobs, and community services in inner-city areas. (The fund later was doubled to $2 billion.) The money, $172 million of which came from Equitable, was spent in 227 cities in forty-two states, Washington, D.C., and Puerto Rico, to provide 31,000 jobs, 63,000 low- and moderate-income housing units, and start-up funding for minority businesses. Equitable's activities ranged from a $2.7 million loan to a group of 5,000 black doctors to build a 256-bed convalescent home and medical complex in Washington, to a $7,000 grant to a street gang to open an automobile repair shop in Brooklyn. The Society also helped 5,200 low-income families buy homes in more than a dozen cities nationwide, financed the construction of 1,000 low-rent apartments, and — working through a subsidiary, The Equitable Life's Community Enterprise Corporation — invested $1.4 million in minority-owned businesses. The Society's Office of Community Assistance provided emergency programs and worked with youth groups in the Bronx. Financially these were small parts of Equitable's activities, but in other ways they shaped its image in the 'sixties.[13]

Meanwhile, Equitable — like almost every major institution — had to clean its own house in racial matters. The company had an excellent record of nondiscrimination where Roman Catholics and Jews were concerned, largely because of Thomas I. Parkinson, a Catholic who had suffered some prejudice and sympathized with others who suffered more. Oates put an equal opportunity policy in effect in *A Code to Work By,* and spoke loudly in favor of integration, which he had brought about at the Chicago Bar Association as its president in the 1940's. When he retired from Equitable at the end of 1969, almost 20 percent of the Home Office's employees and 15 percent of the Society's employees around the country were African American or Hispanic. *Black Enterprise* magazine would call Equitable one of the best companies in the country for African Americans to work for.

Integration, however, did not come easily. Six months after he arrived as Equitable's President, Oates asked the head of the Agency Operations Department, Joseph L. Beesley, how many black agents The Equitable had. Beesley told him there were none, because there was no interest in writing policies for African Americans. "Let's get some," Oates told Beesley. Beesley passed Oates's wish on to some agency managers, but the response was unenthusiastic. A few weeks later, Oates asked Beesley how many blacks he had contacted. When Beesley answered that he had made no approaches, Oates formally ordered him to hire a black agent. Several black agents were hired, some of whom became district managers. Supported vigorously by Oates and one of Beesley's successors as head of the agency force, Coy Eklund, Equitable ended its ancient prejudicial underwriting and sales restrictions, and in 1965, at Davidson Sommers' insistence, several years before it was required by law, Equitable removed the "race" identification

National Urban League chairman Coy Eklund and the organization's president, Vernon Jordan.

line from insurance applications. In the late 'sixties, the company initiated a marketing program aimed at African Americans. And in 1969, Oates chose the Society's first black director, Clifford Wharton.[14]

For an establishment figure, Oates could sound quite radical. He spoke of "the social revolution going on about us," approved of picketing substandard schools and apartments, and endorsed birth control, which then was as controversial as abortion would be in the 1990's. He ended his farewell speech to the insurance industry with a characteristic expression of faith in the mission of life insurance companies to better society:

> *Somewhere, someone is developing a process which will save our rivers; and the insurance industry will, in ways yet to be discovered, make it possible for him to prove that it will work. Somewhere a child is wretchedly sick; our industry is working on ways to help provide the attention he requires and deserves. Somewhere a family is finding it impossible to secure an economic foothold; our industry must do its part to show the way.*

Oates went on to quote Albert Schweitzer: "I don't know what your destiny will be, but one thing I know; the only ones among you who will be really happy are those who have sought and found how to serve."[15]

His successors as CEO, Henry Smith and Coy Eklund, shared his commitment. Smith chose Equitable's first female director, Eleanor Sheldon, and oversaw the appointment of the first black agency managers. As a leader in the New York Urban Coalition (and, after his retirement, as New York City's director of social services), he became prominent as a spokesman concerning urban problems. Eklund, as Agency Operations head and, later, Executive Vice-President and Chief Executive Officer, played the most important role in breaking down old restrictions. If Oates's opposition to racial discrimination was founded on conviction, Eklund's was due in part to his experiences as a boy in Minnesota, where his dentist was a black man and one of his neighbors was an imposing Chippewa chieftain named Bear Grease. (In the 1970's, Eklund and his father produced a book on the Chippewa language.) Eklund advised each agency manager to hire at least one black agent. When the head of the only agency in Wyoming protested that there were no African Americans in his state, Eklund jokingly replied, "Import some."

By 1968, there were seventy black agents and seven black district managers, but no black agency managers. That March, Eklund invited five black district managers to meet with him and other Agency Operations officers. According to people who attended the meeting, the mood was tense until Eklund announced that the company would establish and work toward numerical goals. He committed Equitable to an affirmative action program whose goal was by 1972 to have 250 black agents, ninety black district managers, and ten black agency managers, and to establish a black advisory council. The agreement that came out of this meeting was later known by black Equitable agents as the Emancipation Proclamation. The first black Equitable

agency manager, appointed later in 1968, was LeRoy Beavers in Los Angeles. A nephew of the chairman of the board of Golden State Life Insurance, a predominantly black insurer in California, Beavers had been an Equitable

LeRoy Beavers.

agent for several years. When word got around that he had quadrupled his income and that, almost simultaneously, a black district manager had won a national manager's award, interest by African Americans in Equitable's agency force improved noticeably.

There also were increasing concerns about the small number of women in the agency force and Home Office. While there continued to be several hundred female agents, female agency managers all but disappeared. As for the Home Office, Ruth Block said of Equitable's attitude about the advancement of women during the 'fifties, "[T]his was not a supportive environment. This was not an environment that was trying to help me grow or blossom." Block herself stubbornly plowed on and was fortunate to be assigned to the CAPS computer project, which — new and innovative — was more oriented toward performance than traditional social status, and she went on to be Executive Vice-President and head of all insurance operations and the highest ranking woman in the life insurance industry.[16]

Yet few women rose as high as Vice-President until the 1970's, when Eklund became the most vociferous proponent in Equitable, if not the insurance industry, for equal opportunity, or what he called Coming Right with People. His conversion was radical. As an agency manager, he had even refused to hire male agents whose wives worked outside the home, but his friends in the civil and women's rights movements converted him. During his tour as CEO between 1975 and 1983, Eklund brought an unprecedented number of women and minorities into high ranks. By May 1978, Equitable had twenty-eight female and ten black or Hispanic officers as well as four female directors; by his retirement in 1983, there were sixty-seven female officers. Outside the Society, he was chairman of the National Urban League, a board member of women's and Indian groups, and a well-known spokesman for corporate social responsibility. He told an admiring *Time* magazine business columnist, Marshall Loeb:

> *To cater only to the maximization of profits is to invite corporate doom. In this country, we've developed corporate enterprise by reason of the will of the people. The only way that we will continue to have the support of the people who enfranchised us is to perform in ways that are socially desirable. If we do not, somebody will blow the whistle on the whole corporate enterprise system.*[17]

While many of his stands on social concerns were ahead of their time among businesses, Eklund was not afraid to identify them as Equitable's positions (for example, the 1978 Equitable annual report included a photograph of Gloria Steinem, the controversial feminist editor of *Ms.* magazine and an Equitable policyholder). During his tenure as CEO, Equitable's annual reports and advertising evoked the century-old theme that the company provided necessary social benefits for individuals and America as a whole.

An assertive consumer movement swept across America beginning in the late 1960's. Consumerism favored individual rights and self-actualization and opposed the autocratic authority of large institutions. As an enterprise in a consumer business, dependent on public trust, Equitable inevitably had to be sensitive to the movement's issues. Inside Equitable, Eklund established programs for consultation with employees. In one, called the Rotating Advisory Panel (RAP) program, he met with small groups of minority and female employees and middle managers. There also were larger open meetings. These were vigorous engagements; at one session in 1974, 650 people submitted 709 written questions.

In 1972, Donald L. Bryant, Sr., the former midwestern agency manager then working in the Corporate Relations Department, produced a list of ninety-four concerns that consumers had expressed about life insurance. One was environmentalism, which at times influenced Equitable's choice of industrial companies to invest in. Another was racial equality, which set standards for Equitable hiring. A third concern was male chauvinism, which led the Society to reluctantly drop one of its oldest advertising slogans, "The Man from Equitable." Other issues that arose in the survey led Equitable to make several substantive innovations, including writing insurance contracts in everyday language, adding ten-day "free

Coy Eklund embracing longtime employee Mario Lluria at The Equitable Hispanic Achievement Awards in 1979.

looks" at policies, disclosing a policy's costs, and providing toll-free telephone consultations with insurance advisors. The company, however, did not act on an intriguing suggestion made in 1972 by a public relations staff member, Andrew R. Baer: the Society, he argued in a memorandum, needed a rigorous self-evaluation, and the most thorough way to undertake it was to examine its status as a mutual company and consider the disciplines of the free enterprise system as a publicly-owned stock company. "While it is doubtful that we would ever take such a step," Baer commented, "we think it would be a good exercise, and would help us in the evaluation of our present organization." As enthusiastic as Equitable was for new ideas, nobody seems to have taken seriously Baer's proposal for debating what he called "nonmutualization." (Twenty years later, necessity would bring about what came to be called demutualization.)[18]

Consumerism helped stimulate a revived corporate identity through advertising. Oates was unusually concerned with and sensitive to advertising as a way for Equitable to present itself and its concerns to the world. As soon as he arrived at the Home Office, he began to speak about the Society's various constituencies of clients, which he called its "publics,"

The population indicator at the 1964 World's Fair exhibit.

and about the need to address them clearly and directly. This certainly was not a new challenge for an organization that had a long history of finding ways to appeal to a variety of audiences — including purchasers of insurance policies, their beneficiaries, homebuyers, and companies in need of financing. Equitable's advertising agency, advised by Riley and Robert Merton, developed advertising and promotional campaigns to present the Society to these audiences and to the public at large as a huge but humane and reliable financial institution in touch with the needs of the average American. One project was the exhibit for the 1964 New York City World's Fair. Rather than put on something elaborate, like its expansive Garden of Security exhibit at the 1939 New York Fair, the Society developed a display that reflected a tool of life insurance, demographics, in a way that could both educate and excite people. As an indicator showed America's increasing population, on an adjacent, large map of the United States, lightbulbs flashed or dimmed when people were born or died. John Riley remembered, "People from Louisiana would cheer when they got a baby in Louisiana, and when somebody in Utah died there would be a sigh."[19]

The subtle message of the exhibit was that Equitable was a reliable, caring institution that balanced large populations and individuals. This was one of the themes of the Society's extensive print and television advertising campaigns in the 1960's and 'seventies — a time that saw an imaginative, large-scale effort to clarify the Society's identity. When Riley was appointed head of the new Corporate Relations Department, he took control of public relations, advertising, corporate giving, urban affairs, and internal communications and worked to have Equitable speak with a single voice. He also insisted that in the future public relations should be supported by focus groups of policyholders and other tools of social science. Riley's assistants were two young men of strikingly different backgrounds. William McCaffrey, who had had a memorable encounter with Oates in an elevator, had started out at eighteen as a messenger hunting down insurance applications in various departments, a job known as app chaser. As McCaffrey slowly worked his way up — he would have twenty-six jobs in thirty-nine years — Equitable put him through college and business school. Riley's other assistant was Harris Schrank, who had simultaneously earned a law degree and a doctorate in sociology at Yale. McCaffrey, who knew everything about Equitable, was in charge of getting things done; Schrank, the academic, was in charge of research.

Except for the early days and the period of *This Is Your FBI*, Equitable had lived with smaller advertising budgets than most of its peer companies, and had put most of its budget for promotion into sales aids for the agency force. But after Riley was put in charge of corporate relations, with the assistance of Equitable's ad agency, Foote, Cone & Belding, he studied the Society's advertising assumptions with the idea of undertaking a multimedia institutional ad campaign not to sell a particular product but to present a likable, memorable image. One thing that was clear to all concerned was that the old Protection Group image, featuring the Goddess of Protection, remained an effective summary of Equitable's identity. Foote, Cone had already endorsed it as the sign that Equitable was "tender as a mother, historic, a friendly giant." The ad campaign of the late 'sixties and early 'seventies took different routes to the same purpose of promoting the caring, protective giant. One of the longest-lived radio campaigns was built around the phrase "Living Insurance," usually including the names of local agents. To promote the agency force, one campaign was built around the theme The Protectors; another,

Demographics was the theme of Equitable's exhibit at the 1964 World's Fair.

Dedication; and a third, which ran in *Ebony* magazine, featured black agents helpfully telling prospects, "I'm glad you asked that question." (About 10 percent of the advertising budget in the late 'sixties and the 'seventies would go to black-oriented ads.) To attract prospective young policyholders and agents, a campaign in about 100 college newspapers used witty cartoons on the problems of young adulthood drawn by Charles Saxon.[20]

But the main target audience consisted of well-paid, married men in their twenties through forties. To reach them, Equitable advertised in *The New Yorker, Sports Illustrated*, and other high-demographic magazines, and also published a series of instructional fitness pamphlets in coordination with the President's Council on Physical Fitness and a line of posters of sports heroes. A few of these ads combined high technology and personal service by describing how the Society's new computers helped agents tailor policies to individual situations. Others referred to social concerns about which Equitable had taken stands (one ad showed a photograph of urban children over the caption, "Who cares if these kids become dropouts?"). Equitable's slogans varied, but the theme always was one of caring: "Helping People Build a Better Life" or

"In this anxious world... Equitable offers a corner of security."

A campaign that accounted for one-fourth of the advertising budget during the 1960's was directed not at prospective insurance clients but, rather, at businessmen in need of corporate financing. At first glance, the ads seemed to be recruiting agents. Their only message was a list of the qualities expected of an Equitable agent. But the subtle message was to identify the Society as a high-quality company by assuring potential clients for financing of its demanding personnel standards. The campaign was so low-key that the Internal Revenue Service denied Equitable a tax deduction for the costs of recruiting investment business. When Riley and Schrank told Robert Merton about the disagreement, he responded with a question that at first seemed surprising but that led the IRS to change its mind. Schrank remembered:

> *Bob asked us, "How in fact does the investment process work?" I was startled that such a sophisticated man could ask such a seemingly naive question. I figured it was obvious that investments were made to optimize rates of return. But since Bob thought this was worth exploring, I dutifully set out interviewing investment people. They told me that social factors — relationships, corporate reputation — were more important to the investment decision than just the rate of return. Merton's "naive" question was in fact brilliant. It enabled us to establish a sociological argument describing how our advertising supported investment operations.*

Making the point that high-quality corporations would perceive the Society as undistinguished if its ads blatantly promoted the availability of investment dollars, Schrank, Merton, and Riley convinced Equitable's lawyers to file an appeal. The IRS eventually reversed its ruling and allowed the tax deduction.[21]

Hair.
It's not the style that counts,
it's what's under it.

Equitable is looking for people who have what's under it to fill management or professional positions in: Actuarial Science, Investments, Systems and Operations Research, Marketing and Sales Development, Insurance Administration. For the facts, check the alphabetical listing in this Annual, see your Placement Officer, or write John P. Riley, Manager, College Employment, The Equitable Life Assurance Society of the United States, 1285 Avenue of the Americas, New York, N.Y. 10019. An Equal Opportunity Employer, M/F.

THE EQUITABLE

In a gentle way, you can shake the world.

THE EQUITABLE

For a free 18" x 24" poster of this advertisement, write: The Equitable, Dept. A, G.P.O. Box 1170, New York, N.Y. 10001

The memorable advertising campaigns of the 1970's emphasized individual personalities and security needs. The Albert Einstein ad (top) was a favorite in college dormitories.

To reach a broader, more general audience, Equitable returned to television with a large campaign on what became a memorable theme. Recent consumer research had noticed two striking shifts: the public's awareness of Equitable's name was decreasing, and so was the average age of policyholders. Foote, Cone proposed a new television campaign with a distinctive thrust to run on shows favored by the target audience of men in their twenties and thirties. Radio advertising was eliminated and print advertising was tailored to complement the TV advertising campaign. The new campaign, based on the theme "There's Nobody Else Exactly Like You," consisted of seven gently humorous commercials showing how differently people performed activities such as bowling, dancing, and playing softball. Some people were awkward, some fluid; each had her or his individual style. The message that unique personal traits and needs are worthy of notice — and were attended to by Equitable — was not new (for instance, personal choice had been an appeal of tontine policies). But when it was revisited in the 'seventies, it hooked into the growing consumer movement by giving a tender personal face to an institution widely regarded as being large and impersonal. In a companion print campaign in college newspapers and other periodicals, the theme was portrayed by images of famous individuals — among them Albert Einstein, whose flowing white locks exemplified the idea that a great mind may lie behind a countercultural appearance. Gandhi, Babe Ruth, and Martin Luther King, Jr., were among the other subjects. Tens of thousands of poster ver-

sions of the ads were given away, and the Society's campaign became a popular decorative motif in college dormitories and offices.

The "Nobody Else" TV campaign began in the 1970 World Series and moved on to college and professional football and pro basketball. Recognition of Equitable's name doubled in five months and quadrupled in fifteen. Among the target audience, name recognition increased by a factor of five and remained at that level after the campaign ended in 1974. In the mid-'seventies, new versions of the campaign were devised to address a new target audience that included the growing number of working, independent women. One of these commercials showed a lonely young woman recently arrived in a new city but still under the continuing attention of her hometown Equitable agent. This story line, which would have been inconceivable in consumer advertising a decade earlier, was part of a larger campaign that included advertisements in *Ms.* and *Redbook* and publication of a pamphlet, *Life Insurance... Women Speak Their Minds,* that was distributed to more than 100,000 women.

Financial problems cut the advertising budget by 40 percent in 1975, and the familiar "There's Nobody Else Exactly Like You" campaign lingered on in a reduced form. It was terminated in 1978 (along with almost all the ad programs) after President Eklund decided that the money would be better spent on agency operations. With that, thirty years of broadcast advertising campaigns, based on various versions of the classic themes of security and social concern, came to an end.

"I often wonder why people don't like change," said J. Henry Smith, the CEO in the early 1970's.
"I don't like being anchored to one principle or one style."

CHAPTER XVII

DIVERSIFYING

J ames Oates stepped down as The Equitable's Chief Executive Officer at the end of 1969. In his twelve years at Equitable, he had reinvigorated the staff and agency force, refocused its management, and expanded and liberalized its public image. During his tenure, assets had grown by almost half to $13.5 billion, annual insurance sales (in face amounts) had doubled to $5.7 billion, and capital had increased by almost three-fourths to $1 billion. The $2.5 billion in dividends paid out to policyholders during the twelve years of the Oates regime was three times greater than the value of all the dividends paid out in Equitable's first 100 years.

But for all these and other signs of health at Equitable and, generally, across the life insurance industry, at the end of the 1960's it seemed to some observers that the business might have matured to the point where rapid growth was behind it. Between 1860 and 1900, when the great life insurance empires were built, premiums had increased eighty-fold — twenty times faster than the four-fold increase in American national income. Over the next thirty years, from 1900 to 1930, life insurance premiums increased ten-fold, two and a half times faster than national income, which again increased four-fold. But between 1930 and 1950, premiums for the first time grew more slowly than national income; while national income tripled, life premiums only doubled. Still, life insurance did exceptionally well between 1950 and 1965 as measured by another indicator, the proportion of the country's personal disposable income that went to pay premiums for whole-life insurance. In those years the proportion increased by one-fifth, from 2 percent to almost 2½ percent. But then it fell until in 1975 it was below 2 percent, where it remained into the 1980's. In other words, between 1965 and 1975 America apparently trimmed its budget for traditional individual life insurance — for insurance companies, the most profitable type of policy — by one-fourth.[1]

One explanation put forward for this proportionate decline is that it was only apparent: due to improved mortality and better yields on investment portfolios, insurers reduced rates by about 15 percent between 1965 and 1975, from $14.40 to $11.41 per $1,000 of face amount for a twenty-five year-old man. (These figures were not factored for the steep inflation of the 1968–1982 years.) That accounts for more than half the 25 percent decline. As for the remaining 10 percent, traditional life insurance was facing unprecedented competition. Some of the most intense rivalry came from within the insurance industry itself, which was growing rapidly, becoming more competitive, and offering a wide range of low-cost (and, for Equitable, relatively low-profit) term and group insurance policies. Group insurance, increasingly offered at the job as an employment benefit, had become a huge business. At Equitable, ordinary life coverage took a century to reach $15 billion in face amount; group took only forty years and surpassed individual insurance, by face amount, in the late 'fifties. Competition also came from individual and group pension plans. Industry-wide, annuity considerations took twice as large a

share of disposable personal income as traditional life insurance.[2]

And traditional individual life insurance
also faced heightened competition from other
types of financial products marketed aggressively by banks, securities firms, and other
financial institutions. These products included
such new or newly popular instruments as
money market funds, certificates of deposit,
unit investment trusts, high-interest savings
accounts, and mutual funds, many of which
offered (or at least projected) yields above the
dividend rates of whole-life policies, albeit
without the guarantees that only a life insurance contract could provide. This competition
began soon after World War II. While total
household savings increased fourfold between
1945 and 1964, deposits in commercial banks
increased two and one-half times, deposits in
savings and loans built almost thirteen times,
pension funds grew twenty-one times — and
the portion of life insurance policies considered
as savings only doubled.[3]

But it was not until the late 1960's that
many Americans strayed from the time-honored
conviction of life insurance fundamentalism
that life insurance was a unique product
whose main value was to offer protection.
They came to think of life insurance as one
of many available savings, even investment,
instruments. The turning point can be dated to
the years 1967–71. In 1967, *Consumer Reports*, an
influential advisory magazine that usually limited its concerns to automobile and appliance
purchases, told its readers that whole-life insurance was a poor choice as a savings instrument
and that instead they should buy term insurance and invest the money that they had saved
on premiums in other instruments. Over the
next four years, there first appeared the two
financial magazines that would most influence
investment decisions for decades to come,
Institutional Investor and *Money,* plus two new,
simple, and flexible consumer investment

instruments, the money market fund and cash
management account, that provided flexible,
relatively high-yielding investments that consumers could easily understand and administer.

Spotting these trends, Francis H. Schott,
Equitable's Chief Economist, in 1968 told the
company's General Policy Committee, the top
management committee, that American consumers were becoming more independent and
knowledgeable about personal finance, more
demanding of short-term performance, more
eager to share in a sponsoring institution's profits through higher dividends, and more open to
group insurance. There was, he wrote, "an
unmistakable trend toward a collective as
against the individual approach to security
even within the private sector." He warned
that insurance companies would make a serious mistake if they did not venture into new
areas: "It could be that the industry might be
attempting to resist economic and social forces
beyond our control in seeking an excellent
performance in traditional fields alone."[4]

Later, two Equitable officers summarized
the challenge in plain language. Said former
Chairman of the Board Davidson Sommers,
"The market was shifting from the person living
in an ivy-covered cottage and needing a $5,000
policy to a much more sophisticated market
very much influenced by business needs, estate
planning, and the tax benefits of life insurance."
And Mel H. Gregory, a head of Agency
Operations, looked back on the time before the
transition of the late 'sixties and 'seventies with
wistfulness (and some exaggeration): "That was
the old Equitable. We made 8 percent and spent
only 4 percent. It was another world. We never
had a crisis to manage."[5]

While these changes were surfacing, Oates
was choosing his successor. The main
candidates were two men who had served as his
personal assistants. President J. Henry Smith, a
sixty-one year-old actuary and veteran of group

insurance, had succeeded Grant Keehn in 1967. Coy Eklund, younger by seven years, was head of the agency force. They were very different in background and personality. Among the people whom Oates asked for advice was John Riley, who recommended Eklund. He recalled telling Oates, "Coy has a vision, he has energy, he has leadership qualities, he's got time on his side. Henry is shy, not a charismatic speaker, solid as a rock, a brilliant actuary, and probably knows far more about the theory and philosophy of insurance than Coy Eklund." Oates replied, "I believe everything you've said about Coy but he's not ready. It's Henry's turn."[6]

When Oates told Smith he wanted him to be CEO and Chairman of the Board and Eklund to be President, Smith surprised him by demurring. This would move Eklund too quickly, Smith told Oates; Eklund needed seasoning. So with the tacit understanding between him and Oates that, if all went well, he would be succeeded by Eklund when he retired in several years, Smith became President and CEO, Davidson Sommers Board Chairman, and Eklund Executive Vice-President with a general assignment to supervise agency operations and become familiar with other departments. Smith and Sommers worked out the same kind of harmonious relationship that Oates and Keehn had enjoyed. (Oates, after retiring in 1969, returned to Chicago to practice law and chaired the federal government's Jobs for Veterans Committee for Vietnam War veterans, while Keehn retired as Vice-Chairman of the Board in 1971 and moved to Washington State; both men died in 1982. Sommers retired as Board Chairman in 1973 and later served as a consultant to the president of the World Bank, engaged in a number of charitable activities, and was a member of a law firm. He was still thriving in 1995 at the age of ninety.)

James Henry Smith (he rarely used his first name) was the son of a Methodist clergyman who had a series of parishes in Maryland, Delaware, and Virginia on the Delmarva Peninsula. He later credited his childhood mobility for preparing him, as an insurance executive, to resist the comfort of the status quo: "I guess the early upbringing I had, when we moved about from town to town every three years or so, got me accustomed to change," he told a reporter at the time he retired as Equitable's Chief Executive Officer in 1975. "I often wonder why people don't like change. I don't like being anchored to one principle or one style." He did well in mathematics and was steered by one of his college professors toward actuarial work. In 1930, an Equitable agent helped him get a $1,500-a-year job at the Home Office reviewing applications for group policies. Smith, a modest, humorous man, liked to say that he got the job only because the agent happened to be trying to sell a group insurance policy to a clergymen's organization in which his father was prominent, but that his influence had little effect: while the organization decided on an Equitable contract, the Society belatedly determined that clergy groups were too high a risk, and one of Smith's first assignments was to break the bad news to his father. After a few years without a pay raise — in fact, he suffered the 10 percent pay cut imposed on all Equitable employees during the Great Depression — Smith accepted a $2,100 a year job offer from the Travelers. Equitable hired him back during World War II when it needed experienced actuaries to work on the new group annuity contracts that were pouring in. As Smith rose through the ranks of group insurance as an actuary and manager, he liberalized underwriting and made a point of visiting and inviting comment from agency managers.[7]

Though sharing Oates's religious faith and social reform convictions, Smith expressed his values in a much quieter manner that, at first, may have disappointed agents and others who were used to the traditional gregarious booster-ism. He delighted in publicly poking fun at himself and his authority. "The trouble with being President," he once told an Equitable group, "is that while he never makes a mistake himself, he is responsible for everything that goes wrong." Benjamin Holloway, a real estate officer, recalled a retirement party for Smith in 1975: "Coy Eklund had given his usual ten minutes of flowery talk about how Henry was godlike in every way, [and] Henry got up and said, 'Coy, you have finally been able to stomp the last shred of humility out of me.'" Smith asserted his authority just as delicately. Appointing a subordinate to a new position, he wrote, "Without meaning to suggest a course of action...," and then gently laid out the options. In the early 'seventies, the young co-managers of an agency in Philadelphia, George W. Karr, Jr., and Robert Barth, invited Smith to speak at an awards banquet. They were surprised when he accepted and amazed by his modest behavior when he arrived. Discovering that his hotel room was not ready, Smith joined his hosts in their room, where he contentedly plopped himself on a bed and chatted while they dressed for the banquet.[8]

A major worry was the Vietnam War "guns and butter" inflation, which began in 1966 as the federal government juggled fiscal policy to pay for both the war and a massive program of social reform. From the hindsight of the double-digit rates that came later, the 6 to 8 percent inflation of the late 1960's was a blip on the screen, but at the time it seemed devastating. Henry Kaufman, the financial forecaster, remembered how fearful these shocks were, beginning in 1966 with a sudden spike in interest rates from less than 5 percent to over 7 percent: "I must tell you, when that credit crunch occurred in the summer of that year, conditions were more taut than when the prime rate hit 21½ percent in the early

'eighties." Market interest rates were so unpredictable that banks, for the first time in American history, unfixed their rates and required loan customers to accept adjustable ones that floated against the prime or another rate. President Nixon's wage and price controls briefly halted inflation, but in 1974, during the first Arab oil embargo, it rose to an astonishing 11 percent — a level unprecedented in peace-time. The consumer price index more than doubled between 1967 and 1979.[9]

The time was a critical one for a life insurance company. The newly high, volatile interest rates were eroding the value of invest-ments based on long-term fixed-rate bonds and mortgages — the two core investments in a life company's portfolio. Many consumers were shifting from an ethic of risk aversion to one of risk tolerance, living more on credit, and looking for higher returns on investment instru-ments among the new generation of products invented by financial institutions. The new rule of thumb was not to seek safety but to "chase yield." Banks and securities firms developed more intricate savings and invest-ment instruments offering ever more flexibility and higher interest rates. The awkward word *disintermediation* was invented to describe how individuals and businesses, in unprecedented numbers, were borrowing against life insurance policies at low rates imposed by state insurance laws, or moving funds from other accounts managed by institutions, in order to put money into higher-yielding accounts under their own management. The wave of disinter-mediation first appeared in the late 'sixties and swept through the country during the 'seventies, when insurers' share of American financial assets dropped from almost 30 percent to 20 percent. Some one-fifth of Equitable's policyholders borrowed heavily against their individual life policies and invested the loans elsewhere at rates higher than the dividends they had been getting. In

Henry Smith, his back to the camera, chairs a meeting of his close advisors in the early 'seventies: (clockwise from Smith) John W. Riley, David H. Harris, Morton D. Miller, Richard Hageman, Frank H. Briggs, Eli Ferguson, Edward A. Robie, Thomas F. Murray, Coy G. Eklund, Earl Helsel, Reynolds Nowell.

1974, Equitable policyholders took out $100 million in loans against their policies.[10]

The revolution in personal finance triggered innovations in life insurance. The Equitable was positioning itself to meet the demands for more flexibility and higher yields by developing new products. As Schott put it, "We no longer told them, 'This is what life insurance is and it is good for you.'"[11]

The pressures of wholesale disintermediation and the resulting deregulation also pushed and pulled Equitable into an expensive but necessary program of diversification into new businesses, some of them far afield from its traditional work. Diversification and subsidiaries had been banned by the Armstrong laws' prohibition against owning stock in businesses unrelated to life insurance. In 1969, the New York State legislature amended the insurance law to permit insurers to form holding companies and create subsidiaries. The so-

called Ruebhausen law, drafted by a lawyer and Equitable director, Oscar Ruebhausen, set some restrictions: the subsidiaries had to be in areas whose business was ancillary to insurance; their total cost could be no greater than half the company's surplus or 5 percent of assets, whichever was less; and their liabilities could not involve the general account. Equitable quickly set up The Equitable Life Holding Company and started looking around for opportunities to diversify in areas related to the Society's normal investment and insurance activities.

By 1970, there already was a subsidiary project underway that fit the times and the impetus toward diversification. This was variable life insurance, a policy that was part insurance, part investment. It derived its name from the fact that the value of benefits, above a guaranteed minimum death payment, varied with the changing value of the fund of common stocks or bonds backing the policy. While traditional whole-life insurance offers the policyholder participation in the performance of the insurance company's general account, which consists largely of long-term bonds and mortgages, variable insurance (which went on the market in 1976) instead of participation is undergirded by separate accounts consisting of common stocks, short-term bonds, and other investments from which the policyholder is free to choose. Variable life was a new thing for The Equitable in another important way: variable life provided Equitable with a new and substantial source of income — fees paid by policyholders.

Variable life insurance offered quite a lot to meet the new environment of the early 1970's. It was flexible, it involved common stock investments (which usually are a better hedge against inflation than bonds), and it had the traditional advantage of an insurance product: a tax-deferred capital gain, which mutual funds could not offer. The appeal of variable products was not lost on Jim Oates. In his farewell speech to the insurance industry in December 1969, he proposed that insurers provide "a financial program which offers the individual client the opportunity to participate, not merely in the certain accrual of a death benefit, but in the venturesome accrual of an investment goal." The public seemed to agree, at least in theory, for in an Equitable-sponsored survey of attitudes about financial institutions in 1973, almost 60 percent of the respondents expressed interest in insurer-sponsored investment plans and in variable insurance.[12]

Variable insurance had been around for almost two decades, though not in the form that Equitable eventually developed. The first variable product in America was the variable annuity, introduced in 1952 by the Teachers Insurance and Annuity Association, a mutual insurance company founded by Andrew Carnegie to improve the financial security of college and school teachers. Allowed by regulators to sell variable annu-

ities so long as it limited its market to educational institutions, TIAA formed a subsidiary, the College Retirement Equities Fund. Prudential Life began selling variable annuities in 1959, but only after a long tussle to gain permission from New Jersey's insurance department. Equitable decided to enter the individual variable field, first with annuities and later with life insurance.

"Variable life was something the Equitable did extremely well," Harry Garber looked back in 1993. "If we hadn't done it, no one would have." The assignment to develop variable products was given to Vice-President Harry Walker, an actuary at Equitable since 1931. A small, quiet man of great determination, Walker defended variable insurance on three fronts — against regulators, against opponents in the financial services industry, and against doubters at Equitable.[13]

The first step was the variable annuity, an individual retirement plan whose income was derived from stock investments held in separate accounts. After variable annuities were allowed by New York insurance law, they had to be approved by the federal Securities and Exchange Commission, which regulated securities transactions. In 1969 Jule Stocker, of Equitable's legal staff, drafted a sample prospectus and sent it to the SEC in Washington, D.C. The son of a Polish immigrant, a Phi Beta Kappa at Harvard College, and in the top five of his class at Harvard Law School, Stocker had had a long career at a Wall Street law firm before coming to Equitable as head of special projects and troubleshooter for Davidson Sommers. After a wait for the SEC's response, Stocker received a telephone call at 12:30 one day in December 1969. He was told that the SEC was not approving Equitable's application and that it would tell him why at a meeting that afternoon in Washington. Stocker found Walker at lunch, and they raced

With Harry Walker in charge, Equitable was the first insurer to develop and market variable life insurance.

to the airport. The SEC staff insisted that Equitable's plan could not go forward without substantial changes that would set the project back by at least a year. Instead of heading back to New York, Stocker dug in his heels and, over the protests of the Society's Washington lawyers, demanded an immediate audience with the SEC commissioners, who instructed the staff to meet with him again. Changes to the prospectus were negotiated the next day, and the document was redrafted and approved. In 1970, Equitable introduced its line of individual variable annuity policies, which turned into a pleasant success.

Harry Walker was by then involved with a proposal for variable life insurance. While Equitable would be the first insurer to sell variable life insurance in America, it did not invent the idea. Products somewhat like it had long been available in Europe, although they worked more like investment pools than life insurance policies. The first American to try to develop this idea into an insurance policy was an actuary at New York Life, John

Fraser. He was sure that if variable life were to pass the scrutiny of government regulators and find a public market, it would have to be much less like an investment instrument and much more like a traditional life insurance policy, with a schedule of level premium payments and a minimum death benefit. Yet the policy still would be very different from an ordinary life policy: the policyholder would be free to choose the investment backing the policy; the policy would pay no dividends and have no minimum cash value; the value of the death benefit (above the minimum) would vary with the value of the assets that supported it; and the assets supporting the policies would be located not in the general account but in separate accounts.

J. Henry Smith was intrigued by the idea and appointed a task force to investigate. The task force approved, and in September 1972, taking advantage of the new Ruebhausen law, Equitable created The Equitable Variable Life Insurance Co. (EVLICO), whose President and CEO was Walker. Yet variable life insurance was not wholly welcomed at Equitable. Executive Vice-President (and, beginning in 1973, President) Coy Eklund believed that because the values of common stocks were not guaranteed, they should not be mixed up with life insurance, whose historic chief appeal was the provision of guaranteed protection. He worried that variable life, designed by actuaries, would lead agents astray from their main line of work. He complained in an oral history a decade later:

> *It was horrendous to think about all of this. Here we were again, distracting our life insurance professionals, who knew how to sell life insurance, with a thing that predicates on the performance of common stocks, a portfolio of common stocks, which to me was anathema. I didn't want to put our agents in the securities business, to state it simply.*

While he believed that actuaries had a valuable role as "the caretakers of the financial well-being of the institution," Eklund thought that they had too much, and agents too little, say about product design. He recalled with some bitterness how, during an officers' retreat in the early 'seventies, he asked Smith for time to discuss new products, and Smith replied, "Coy, leave that to the actuaries."[14]

On the opposite side of the variable life issue was another veteran of the agency force, Donald L. Bryant, Sr., then in the Home Office heading much of Equitable's diversification program. "I had seen our group annuity business go out the window to the banks until we came up with the new money concept, the investment year method, and separate accounts," he looked back. "The point with variable insurance was to get individual life insurance into separate accounts so we could use the same methods. But Coy was a traditionalist when it came to life insurance. In fact, the whole industry was pretty much against it." Bryant was exaggerating only slightly. The president of Prudential privately counseled Eklund to stay out of variable life; and Metropolitan Life's chairman, Gilbert W. Fitzhugh, warned that variable life would shift vast sums of money from the traditional home for a mutual insurance company's assets — bonds and mortgages — into investments that served the needs only of speculators. Where, he asked in 1971, would the average American acquire a simple mortgage? "I think it would be a tragic mistake. They would really sell these [policies] like hotcakes, but it's going to come back to bite us if it happens, and I hope it doesn't." Such critiques were exploited by the mutual fund industry, which fervently opposed variable life as an incursion on their territory.[15]

According to Bryant, he and Eklund met at the Home Office one Saturday afternoon to try to change each other's mind. In what

Bryant would call "a four-hour knock-down-and-drag-out argument," each tried and failed to swing the other around to his position. Eklund's doubts finally were erased when he became convinced that there would be a fixed, guaranteed minimum death benefit that applied regardless of the value of the investment, and when Smith agreed to limit policy face amounts to a minimum of $25,000, a large amount at that time, thereby effectively restricting the market to people with high incomes who were likely to understand the risk of the stock market.[16]

Getting regulatory approval for variable life insurance was a more intractable problem: were variable life insurance policies securities or insurance products? If the former, they had to be registered as a security with the Securities and Exchange Commission in Washington. The SEC was inclined to believe they were securities. For Equitable, this was not a minor issue, since SEC restrictions would greatly modify its marketing system. Securities laws limited total sales loading to only 9 percent, well below insurance agents' usual 50 percent first-year commissions. The laws also severely restricted the use of policy illustrations, which for decades had been important sales tools used by insurance agents. Equitable, New York Life, and a few other insurers pressed the SEC for exemptions. In hearings and meetings with SEC staff members and commissioners, Fraser laid out the complicated technical argument, while Walker described the general idea in lay language. After Fraser died, New York Life stepped back, leaving Equitable as the leader of the group, with Davidson Sommers chairing the industry committee. Henry Smith, who was committed to variable insurance, set up a new Equitable task force headed by Walker and including Bryant, Stocker, and Harry Garber. In 1973, SEC Chairman William Casey, in his last decision before retiring, granted the exemption.

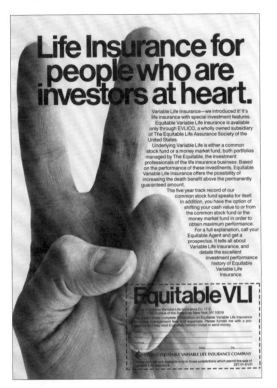

Life Insurance for people who are investors at heart.

Variable Life Insurance—we introduced it! It's life insurance with special investment features. Equitable Variable Life Insurance is available only through EVLICO, a wholly owned subsidiary of The Equitable Life Assurance Society of the United States.

Underlying Variable Life is either a common stock fund or a money market fund, both portfolios managed by The Equitable, the investment professionals of the life insurance business. Based on the performance of these investments, Equitable Variable Life Insurance offers the possibility of increasing the death benefit above the permanently guaranteed amount.

The five year track record of our common stock fund speaks for itself. In addition, you have the option of shifting your cash value to or from the common stock fund or the money market fund in order to obtain maximum performance.

For a full explanation, call your Equitable Agent and get a prospectus. It tells all about Variable Life Insurance, and details the excellent investment performance history of Equitable Variable Life Insurance.

Equitable VLI

This advertisement for variable life insurance reflects the changing consumer focus from protection alone to investments.

Two years later, however, as Equitable was preparing its first variable life contracts, the SEC changed its mind and withdrew the exemption. At that, every insurer except Equitable revoked its SEC filing. Working alone, criticized by other companies, Equitable stubbornly fought on. By a process that Jerome Golden, Walker's chief assistant, described as "chipping away at a block and ending up with sales load," the Society's actuaries and lawyers convinced the SEC staff that there was a way to fit variable insurance under federal securities regulation while satisfying newly adopted state regulation. In October 1975, the SEC granted the exemption to Equitable with the understanding that agents selling variable life would pass examinations required for securities salesmen and use cautious hypothetical scenarios when making sales presentations. (One of the three approved scenarios projected a bleak situation in which there was no gain whatsoever.)

All this time, Equitable, with the cooperation of the New York State Insurance Department, was engaged in the grinding job of convincing the legislature of virtually every state in which it intended to sell variable life insurance to pass laws allowing and regulating it. The first license was granted by Kentucky, and while several western and southern states soon followed, populous states straggled in; it took four years to win a license in Illinois. When Equitable finally started selling variable life insurance in New York, in September 1976, the Society ran a full-page advertisement in the *New York Times* announcing, "Once there was only life insurance. Now there's variable life."[17]

These rapid changes in product design and operations in the 1970's were paralleled by shifts in Equitable's investment operations, most dramatically in real estate. The company had long backed construction of new buildings in many large and medium-size cities, usually through mortgage loans. As in Pittsburgh, these projects could transform cities. In 1957, it financed St. Louis' first downtown office building since the Great Depression. That project led to others with the same developer, Raymond Wittcoff. He recalled, "Given a new face, the city was revitalized. The Equitable was acclaimed as the prime mover in financing a series of projects that transformed the area, and proved to be sound investments." Wittcoff worked closely with Equitable's growing real estate department, was a trustee of the company's real estate investment trust, and became a director of the Society in 1980.[18]

In the late 1960's and 'seventies, real estate became attractive as an investment because, unlike bonds, its value tended to increase with inflation. With the securities markets weak, this hedge was extremely attractive to many investors. Equitable launched a program of making equity real

Chicago's City Front Center was one of Equitable's large developments. This is the NBC Tower in the center.

estate investments for, and in joint ventures with, third parties, including pension plans. One new mechanism was The Equitable Life Mortgage and Realty Investors (TELMARI), a publicly owned investment trust for third-party real estate investments. Its stock was owned by Equitable and other investors. TELMARI was launched in 1970 in a suc-

cessful public offering managed by Goldman, Sachs & Co.

TELMARI and the general account's rapidly growing real estate operations were run by Robert Schlageter, Benjamin D. Holloway, George Peacock, and George Puskar. Their large national operation, based on the old City Mortgage Department, worked through five regional and thirty-four divisional offices. The company's real estate business was changing quickly. It continued to make substantial mortgage loans, for example, to Chicago's City Front Center and Detroit's Renaissance Center, to a midwestern chain of twenty-five day-care centers, and to Hilton for the first new downtown hotel built in New York City since 1936. But in the early 'seventies, Schlageter and Holloway, convinced that real estate was undervalued, lobbied to have the Society shift its emphasis from mortgages to direct investment for itself and as an asset manager for pension plans. Some members of the Board of Directors were nervous, but the idea went through, and the Equitable Real Estate operation was founded in 1973.

The real estate people were enthusiastic and ambitious. Between 1972 and 1977, the company's property ownership in whole or in partnership with other institutions more than doubled from 4½ percent of investments to almost 11 percent. As of November 1977, the real estate portfolio included 368 properties valued at a total of $1.1 billion, including thirty-six shopping centers and eight office buildings in New York City, some Holiday Inn and Hilton hotels, the Wells Fargo Bank Building in San Francisco, and a half interest in the Tishman Speyer Realty Co. In the largest real estate transaction in Equitable's history until then, the Society, in partnership with its real estate operation for pension plans, Prime Property Fund, purchased nine shopping centers in Michigan and Minnesota for $360 million. *Business Week* wrote in 1977 that Equitable's and the other big insurance companies' new involvement in equity real estate was "probably the most significant development in the real estate industry so far in this decade." Holloway, who had come up through the City Mortgage Department in Richmond, Virginia, succeeded Schlageter as head of Equitable's real estate departments and became one of the most powerful people in the field of institutional real estate. Later, Equitable as a rule of thumb put half its new investments into real estate.[19]

The real estate investments helped fill the vacuum left by the collapse of the railroads in which Equitable had been so interested for almost three-quarters of a century. Two old favorites, the Pennsylvania Railroad and Chauncey Depew's New York Central Railroad, were merged in 1968 to form the Penn Central Transportation Co., which had 40,000 miles of track in sixteen states. Two years later, Penn Central filed for bankruptcy, citing $4 billion in liabilities. The largest bankruptcy in American history, the collapse of the Penn Central deeply affected the value of Equitable's assets, since the Society was one of the largest of the railroad's seventy major creditors with $143 million in bonds, equal to 1 percent of Equitable's assets and almost 8 percent of the railroad's debt. The bondholders' committee, which largely handled the reorganization, was chaired by Equitable's Deputy General Counsel, Richard Dicker. After eight years of heated disputes over the value of the Penn Central's properties, a reorganization plan was negotiated in 1978. The bondholders received their value in cash and stock; the railroads were shed (to create Amtrak, Conrail, and Metro-North, among other new lines); and the remaining oil, real estate, and other holdings remained under the Penn Central, of which Dicker became chief executive.

The arrival of these new investment policies, like the push for variable life insurance, reflected the environmental shift during the inflationary years from long-term to short-term investment thinking. The 100-year bonds of the Pennsylvania and other railroads were inconceivable in the new day of spiking interest rates. The shift provided a level of energy and daring on a par with that of Thomas I. Parkinson. Wittcoff described the new attitude as it was expressed in real estate:

> *In the past, insurance companies made mortgage loans, and the kind of person who did it was fairly removed from the entrepreneurial type. Joint ventures and equity ownership had different kinds of problems and required different sorts of people. It required more than sound judgment. It required flair and imagination, and those are not easy to come by.*

In order to attract and hold this kind of person, Equitable found it had to change its approach to compensation from a salary system to one offering incentives and bonuses. In 1978 Eklund, by then Equitable's CEO, established the Society's first incentive compensation plan.[20]

While real estate investing was clearly a part of usual insurance operations, some other subsidiaries formed in the 1970's seemed to test the rule that they at least be ancillary to an insurer's main business. As Donald Bryant, who oversaw much of the diversification, observed wryly, "The word *ancillary* can be rather broadly interpreted." One of the first subsidiaries was a computer software company, Informatics, a consultant on Equitable's CAPS system that was acquired in 1970. Since Equitable needed computer programmers and data processors, Informatics was indirectly linked to Equitable's main business. So was the Student Life Funding Corporation, which financed life insurance premiums for college and graduate students and evolved into a larger personal-credit operation. The justification for forming Equico Lessors, which leased and financed various kinds of equipment, was that it provided an *entrée* for agents; for Equitable Environmental Health, it was that group insurance and annuity clients needed advice on work-related environmental problems. Equico Securities, which held a seat on the Philadelphia Stock Exchange, was intended to save some of the cost of commissions paid to outside brokerages for securities transactions; another subsidiary, Equico Capital, was the channel for Equitable's investments in minority-owned businesses.[21]

Bryant was the point man for the largest and most complicated subsidiaries, including EVLICO, an operation in Canada, and a property and casualty insurance company. When Henry Smith called him from St. Louis to the Home Office in 1969, Bryant was manager of the largest Equitable agency west of the Mississippi and the newly elected president of the Old Guard. The quiet, subtle actuary and the emphatic master of old-fashioned salesmanship seemed an odd couple, but Smith entrusted Bryant with some big duties. One was corporate relations, first as Riley's associate and then, as Riley prepared for retirement, as operating head. In February 1973, Smith assigned Bryant as a one-man task force to develop ideas for new insurance projects. Working alone over the next five months, Bryant drafted a proposal for more than a dozen diversifications. He looked back, "My idea was that there were potential markets out there that were not being served, even if they were not our usual upper middle-class markets — although there was some internal debate about that." Some of his proposals horrified insurance traditionalists who believed that Equitable's chief calling should continue to be to offer ordinary life insurance protection for upscale families. But Bryant disagreed, citing surveys that indicated that the clientele was more diverse than most people imagined — and that an even larger market lay untouched.[22]

Some of his ventures carried old businesses into new forms. Equitable, which had long offered group health insurance, set up an early health maintenance organization on Long Island with more than 600 doctors and seventeen hospitals, and later bought an HMO in Albuquerque, New Mexico, and a nursing home company in Texas. There also was the first foreign subsidiary in half a century, Heritage Life, in Canada. And then there were two new initiatives, the variable life operation, EVLICO, and a property and casualty insurance company.

Heritage was Equitable's first reach across a national boundary in eighty years. When talk of a Canadian operation began in 1969, some officers preferred to open a branch, but the board wanted a sizable company because peer companies had large operations there. Since Americans were tightly restricted in their ability to purchase existing Canadian insurers, Equitable had to go through the expensive procedure of creating a new operation; the price was $25 million by the time the doors opened for business in 1975. Since there already was a Canadian insurer called Equitable Life (which had taken over many of the old policies when the Society departed in 1921), a new name had to be chosen. After some consumer testing, Heritage was chosen because it meant the same in French and English — no small advantage in fiercely bilingual Canada. While the start-up costs were high, Bryant and his advisors were sure Heritage would succeed over the long run, and also serve Equitable as a laboratory for new sales and marketing ideas. By 1979, Heritage had about $100 million of insurance in force, but was losing money.

The Canadian company had many supporters, but Bryant's proposal to take Equitable into property, fire, and casualty insurance for homes and automobiles set off an intense internal debate. For years life insurers and property insurers had been going about their business in different ways and with very different cultures. Life insurance was a relatively low-volume business of hard-to-sell products selling at high commission and requiring a limited amount of post-sale service. By contrast, property and casualty was a high-volume, low-commission business whose products were fairly easy to sell because many were mandated by law, but demanded considerable post-sale service because they involved damage claims. Property insurance had suffered in the 'sixties due to extensive damage by large hurricanes, but was recovering to profitability in the early 'seventies. Several of Equitable's peer companies, including Prudential and Metropolitan Life, were developing property and casualty lines, which led Equitable to look into it as a defensive measure. There also were positive reasons for moving into the field. Group insurance clients were asking for group property and casualty policies to offer their employees as benefits. A trend toward consolidation in insurance retail sales into what were called "one-stop financial security services" was benefitting multi-line insurance brokers at the cost of Equitable agents. And some agents and agency managers believed that property insurance would be a good product, like the old Assured Home Ownership, for recruiting new agents and helping them become established.

Yet support for expanding into property insurance was well short of unanimous. Board members with experience in the field opposed it, as did the Agency Operations Department, whose head, Ray Dolan, went so far as to warn Eklund that the property and casualty line would undermine and might even destroy the agency force. Eklund argued that property insurance would not fit into Equitable's culture; career life agents said they had no interest in spending their evenings and Sundays inspecting dents in auto fenders.

Eklund's opposition was so firm that the normally placid Henry Smith turned on him in a planning meeting and accused him of never having been open-minded about the idea. (Smith later telephoned from his home to apologize to Eklund.) Although Smith himself was not enthusiastic about property insurance, he was eager to take advantage of the powers granted by the Ruebhausen law to expand into new areas, and he believed Equitable could make the best of the opportunity.

Bryant recalled the debate: "This kept moving forward inexorably, even though somewhat slowly and with a lot of mixed feelings and with a lot of intense feelings." The agency managers seemed to like the idea. In a survey of the Old Guard in 1973, only eight of 171 respondents were opposed, forty-seven were moderately enthusiastic, and 116 were highly enthusiastic. When Bryant attempted to assuage some opponents by agreeing to sell only group property and casualty insurance, agents and agency managers asked for — and got — an individual line. In August 1973, the company decided to go ahead. It paid $35 million for an existing property and casualty carrier, Houston General, renamed it Equitable General Insurance, and, after cutting some of Houston's agencies, kept the Houston General people in charge. As a concession to Eklund's concerns, the line was started as a pilot program in seventeen western states. Despite reports of better agent retention and productivity, and despite the Old Guard's continuing support (in a survey in 1977, three-fourths of the members surveyed said it was a good idea), property and casualty continued to generate controversy. Perhaps these complaints might have faded if the business had come up to financial expectations, but, buffeted by high claims rates and problems getting premium increases approved by state insurance departments, Equitable General averaged almost $10 million a year in losses while absorbing $78 million of Equitable's capital. Bryant was confident that the business would turn around when it went nationwide in 1978 or 1979, yet expansion came slowly and criticisms did not end.[23]

Even before 1970, Equitable had felt the pressure of competition for assets in the flourishing field of pensions and group annuities, which by 1967 was valued at $100 billion. While the group annuity business had improved during the 'sixties thanks to improved investment yields, clients complained that the company was not responding quickly enough to the changing interest rates that prevailed during the inflation. "Employers were seeking more flexibility in benefit design and contribution timing, and wanted a more immediate reflection of mortality, expense, and investment experience in their account balances," recalled Dr. Joseph J. Melone, an author of a textbook on pensions and, in the 1990's, Chief Executive Officer of The Equitable's life insurance company.

The Equitable and other insurers responded with pension product modifications, such as deposit administration and immediate participation guarantee plans. What this generation of products had in common was that each iteration had less guarantee and more immediate reflection of actual plan experience. What this meant in turn for the insurers was lower risk charges and lower margins, i.e., lower profits and contributions to surplus. In short, the pension business was moving very rapidly to a pure asset management business. This trend stimulated much internal debate about the future of the pension business.[24]

Some at Equitable believed the company should serve only as a consultant to companies and plan sponsors, but a task force in 1969 recommended that Equitable remain a major player in the pension business with two definite goals: "(1) Growth of assets under management, (2) Growth of total purchase payment income and new business production." And, the task force added, Equitable must be prepared to meet clients' increasing demands for flexibility and high yields. Once Henry Smith was assured that the business was being run by people he trusted, he gave his approval.[25]

Besides traditional defined-benefit corporate pension plans, there was a growing business in so-called thrift plans, in which contributions were defined, and in which employees, rather than their employers, decided how the investments were made. Originating in oil companies in the 1950's as stock purchase plans, thrift plans became popular supplements to defined-benefit retirement plans. By 1973, thrifts were in place in almost one-fifth of American companies and half the largest ones. The Society's first big thrift plan, for the American Dental Association (ADA), illustrates the intense competitiveness of the pension business at that time. For two years, a committee of the ADA considered forty proposals from banks and insurance companies for the right to market retirement plans to the association's 83,000 members and their employees. With an estimated $1 million in initial fees, plus later fees and, potentially, tens of millions of dollars of assets to manage, it was an appealing prospect. However, Equitable did not become involved until early in 1967, when the ADA selection committee was about to meet in Chicago to draw up its short list

James A. Attwood.

of finalists. After an agency manager in Indiana heard about the competition from his dentist, he alerted Warren V. Woody, who was able to wrangle an interview with the committee. Scheduled for ten minutes, the meeting ran to an hour and a half until the committee agreed to delay its selection for two days to allow Equitable to submit a formal bid. The proposal was put together at the Home Office, but a blizzard cut off air travel and, in a time before efficient facsimile machines, all Equitable could do was have a local Group Department officer trudge through the snowdrifts and make a sketchy oral presentation without supporting documents. Once the airports were opened, Grant Keehn and other Home Office executives flew out and made a full presentation. Equitable won the contract and set about marketing the plan.

The next year, again in a tight competition, the Society won the retirement account for the American Bar Association. While their main competitor, a bank, proposed a nonguaranteed pool of low-yielding corporate bonds to back the plan, Equitable guaranteed a minimum 8 percent return for seven years. It was a sizable bet on future interest rates and on Equitable's ability as a money manager to get high returns. If market rates dropped below the guarantee, Equitable would face a negative spread. The Group Department was willing to take the risk in part because of the many thousands of lawyers who might refer their own clients to Equitable, in part because high interest rates seemed there to stay.

In 1969, Procter & Gamble told Equitable and other insurers that it wanted to buy annuities for its top executives and lock in the interest rates for several years. When neither the investment year nor the participation guarantee method provided yields competitive with those offered by other companies, the actuary handling group annuities, Harrison Givens, devised an even more flexible, short-term system of calculating rates. Called the opportunity money method, it allowed Equitable to base yields on new investments made over extremely short periods of time using funds deposited by the client. After some debate at Equitable, it was presented to Procter & Gamble and the sale went through.

Givens further honed the opportunity money method and the standard group annuity contract into what came to be called the guaranteed interest (or, sometimes, investment) contract, or GIC. The first GIC was a five-year contract sold in 1970 to a $40 million plan for employees of the Federal Reserve System. By 1972, GICs made up 3 percent of the Society's new business, due largely to an energetic executive in the Group Department, Leo Walsh, who worked closely with Givens. That year, Walsh was appointed head of the new Pension Department by the head of Group Operations, James A. Attwood. Four years later, the GIC was Equitable's most successful product in terms of gathering new assets, while the new subsidiaries in variable life insurance and other areas on which so many hopes had been placed were disappointments.

President Coy Eklund at an Equitable meeting in the late 1970's with (left to right) Senior Vice-President Donald R. Kurtz, Vice-President Franklin Kennedy, and Executive Vice-President Carleton D. Burtt.

CHAPTER XVIII

EKLUND TAKES OVER

A fter two years as President, Coy Eklund became Chief Executive Officer at J. Henry Smith's retirement in 1975. For the position of Chairman of the Board, considered a largely ceremonial and advisory job, Smith and Eklund nominated and the Board of Directors elected John T. Fey, former president of the National Life Insurance Company and the University of Vermont. Smith soon was appointed New York City's human resources administrator and commissioner of social services, which put him in charge of the city's $4 billion welfare program.

In his first speech to agents as CEO, Eklund likened Equitable to a jumbo jet with a new pilot. Smith, he said, had gone back into the passenger compartment and had given command to his former copilot. Eklund advised that he might make some adjustments to compensate for changing winds, but he never would put the aircraft on automatic pilot. Such language came easily to Eklund, who styled himself Equitable's "namer of things." He enthusiastically invented slogans for almost every service and function, going so far as to call the Society's employees Equipeople. (Henry Smith once teased him about this predilection by referring to a birthday cake as an Equicake.) If Eklund's showmanship and loyalty to Equitable remained intact, so did the social ideals that he shared with his predecessors Smith and James Oates. During his seven-year tenure as CEO, dozens of minority and female officers were appointed, and the company had close relationships with civil rights organizations. Eklund himself served as national chairman of the National Urban League.[1]

As Eklund's jet pilot metaphor made clear, he was no less inclined to take charge as CEO than as head of the agency force. To anyone exposed to his personality and the numerous accounts of his management style in action, the most succinct characterization was *commanding* (although Eklund himself bristled at the adjective, which he felt implied that he was imperious). Of course, The Equitable enterprise had usually placed a premium on vigorous personal leadership and expected its Chief Executive Officers to (as Henry Baldwin Hyde put it) "jam things through." But so comfortably did Eklund, like his mentor Oates, wear his authority that he rarely had to assert it forcibly. "Coy had a magnetism that nobody had," said Robert Barth, a Philadelphia agency manager who knew him well and admired him. Respect for him was intensified by the widespread awareness of his devotion to the Society and its agency force, his optimism, and, not least, his analytical acuity, which often steered him in surprising directions. "Coy was brilliant at looking at a problem and turning the kaleidoscope slightly to see it differently than anyone else," remembered Nancy Green, who worked closely with him in Equitable's Corporate Relations Department.[2]

His work ethic was legendary. Every night, Eklund's staff gave him a packet of memorandums and other documents, which he read on the way home to Connecticut. Every morning he arose early, sat down with his single cup of

#41

Jim Attwood. SEO.
Harry Gerber. EVP.   Re: Complaints.

    I am not satisfied with The way we have been handling complaints. We have an excellent process for dealing with the specific case (Paul King has always done a first-rate job) but I feel The responsible line officers are not even seeing (or hearing) what goes awry so that the basic nature of the problems may be escaping us.

    What we want above all is to know The problems That cause complaint so That we can deal with their root causes, rather Than only with their individual solution.

    For a test period, I am seeing all complaints that come to me and Then referring Them directly to HDG if they are Ind. items. I will expect him to pursue each case to a proper disposition with ultimate advice to me. Also, I would be confident That he will deal with any endemic problems effectively. (We seem to have some.)

                  Thanks.

cc DLB.

                  CVE
                  7/30/78.

An action memo by Coy Eklund on the subject of handling complaints.

coffee for the day and a spiral-bound notebook, and, in one draft, wrote brief memorandums to his subordinates. Some were as crisply authoritative as an operations order for an infantry campaign, others were simply brief queries about some technical aspect of one of the many specialized departments. When he reached the office, his secretary photocopied and distributed these notes, which Eklund called action memos; everybody else called them spiralgrams because of their format and quick delivery. Action memos, he said, were "a means of keeping us all focused." Once in the hands of their recipients, the memos stimulated flurries of meetings, research, and reports. The same decisive attention to detail went into the three collections of tips on management and etiquette that Eklund compiled and distributed. *Some Leadership Skills to Think About* listed forty-four aptitudes for better leadership. *I Like These! (Hope You Do)* was a forty-nine page compilation of inspiring quotes. *Reminders for MC's*, a guide to organizing gatherings, laid out such hints as "Always put name tag on right shoulder — never on left," "Always say dais, never dias, as so many do," and "Always move promptly to quell interfering noise, wherever!" If Eklund sometimes seemed to overdo it, he usually was forgiven. Said Robert Wenzlaff, an agency manager who worked closely with him:

> He served under Patton in World War II, and I don't think he thought of himself as anything other than a general. The objective was to accomplish the task whatever the cost. He was too much of a dictator, in my opinion and others', yet he had liberal social views. He seemed to have a split personality. But Coy had so many pluses that we could put up with a few minuses.[3]

Eklund surprised nobody by focusing on the agents. While Metropolitan Life and other peer companies were shrinking their agency forces during the 1970's, Equitable's grew from 4,707 to 7,104. In 1974, the company put into place the 14th Edition Agents' Contract, which had two significant features. First, it eliminated the prior rights clause barring agents from selling other insurers' policies without the Home Office's permission. Eklund and other agency veterans believed the clause offended their agents' professional commitment to place the needs of their clients above other concerns. This commitment was required by the pledge signed by all Chartered Life Underwriters as well as expected by the growing consumer movement in the United States. Second, the new contract provided an expensive benefits package for commissioned agents similar to the one granted to Equitable's employees, with life, health, dental, and disability insurance, plus investment plans and a pension plan twice as large as the agents' previous one. In granting commissioned agents the seemingly contradictory rights to sell other insurers' products and to enjoy the benefits of salaried Equitable employees, the company once again emphasized the core importance of the agency force. According to Eklund, these changes were not stimulated by competition with other insurers for recruiting and retaining agents; rather, the motivation was to enhance agents' professionalism and satisfy the demands of consumers.

As Eklund settled into his new job, variable life insurance, which he had once opposed and now backed, was introduced to the market. But agents were not interested in it. Harry Walker's task force had predicted that variable life would constitute 3 percent of the Society's new business in its first year and 20 percent by its tenth year. After variable life finally was approved by the Securities and Exchange Commission in 1976, it seemed hardly likely to come near meeting either goal. "EVLICO management has been learn-

Harrison Givens (left) and Leo Walsh, the GIC's designer and marketer. "The confidence in Givens was very strong."

ing that the world is not clamoring for our product," reported the subsidiary's president, Karl M. Davies, in his 1977 report. The world, he explained, included Equitable agents and state regulators as well as the general public. "It is not much of an exaggeration to say that nobody has even heard of variable life insurance."[4]

The timing for the debut of a product intimately associated with the stock market could hardly have been more unlucky. The early and mid-'seventies saw a sustained bear market and, simultaneously, high interest rates that attracted investors to bonds. An Equitable-sponsored public opinion survey of consumer attitudes about financial institutions in 1973 found that only 7 percent of the respondents thought stockbrokers and mutual fund companies were dependable, and 50 percent thought common stocks very risky. According to a study by the New York Stock Exchange, the investor population had stopped growing in 1970; in 1978, the exchange gloomily reported, "There is no indication that this trend has been reversed."[5]

"Variable life is now taken for granted," Alan Grant, a veteran of EVLICO's marketing department, reminisced in 1994, when it was the top-selling form of life insurance. "But back then we did everything we could to get agents to sell it." Equitable sold only 1,200 variable life policies in the first year. John O'Hara, head of EVLICO's Human Resources Department in its Long Island headquarters, recalled how each morning he saw an underwriting officer stride optimistically down the hall to the mail room to pick up policy applications, only to return discouraged and empty-handed. EVLICO's hard-driving sales manager, Ralph Solomon, and his staff futilely roamed the country trying to drum up support among the agents and managers, who complained about the SEC-imposed low commissions and limits on illustrations. Explained Lester Lovier, who also was working for EVLICO, "Agents tend to go with the most competitive product in the portfolio, and they are very sales illustration-driven." Grant recalled the field force's bored reaction:

I can remember going out on a road show in 1976. We had ten pounds of marketing material per agent. I think the agency managers sent the agents to the road shows so they could get a free lunch. At one show, I walked down the aisle and saw a manager sitting there reading some materials on bonds! It was a slow start.[6]

It did not help that the training program for selling variable life was so cautious that instructors spent much of their time detailing the risks involved and the intricate workings of a variable life contract. "It was like requiring a car salesman to know everything that's going on under the hood," Harry Garber said. "Eventually, we switched to just telling them what happens in a variable policy, and it started to sell." Sales increased 50 percent in 1979 when the stock market made a modest recovery, but it was too little. As part of a company-wide cost reduction program, EVLICO was shrunk and pulled back into the Home Office, although it remained a subsidiary.[7]

If variable life was a disappointment largely due to the poor environment for common stocks, another new line — the guaranteed interest contract (GIC) pension product — was doing extraordinarily well in part because the same environment produced high interest rates. The GIC fit the needs of many pension plans for high yields at minimal risk, and it exploited the traditional strengths of Equitable's investment departments.

The GIC was largely in the hands of two bright, market-oriented, demanding men — Leo M. Walsh, head of Equitable's pension operations, and his actuarial advisor, Harrison Givens. Walsh arrived in 1950 fresh from Regis High School, one of New York's top Catholic secondary schools. He started out in the mail room and, after a two-year leave

for military service, returned to Equitable and took only five years of part-time study to earn his bachelor's degree from St. John's University in night classes funded by Equitable and the GI Bill. He rose through the Group Department. In his 1966 performance review, his superior, Givens, wrote that Walsh's work ranged from "quite satisfactory" to "excellent," and that Walsh hoped to lighten his routine workload so he would have time to write a guide to underwriting, contribute to a textbook on pensions, and develop new pension products for small companies. Walsh worked on the new thrift and GIC business as it was born in the late 1960's and early 'seventies. Walsh was the person for the job of building assets with a new product; he told his colleagues and staff that any business that was not growing was dying.[8]

At Walsh's side was Harrison Givens. "The confidence in Givens was very strong," said Harry Garber. "He was the most imaginative product guy that I ever knew at the Equitable." Givens' view of an actuary's job was very different from that of Walter Klem and other cautious protectors of surplus. As Givens described the job in a recruiting brochure, it was part technician, part marketer:

The principal role of the actuary here is architect and guardian of financial integrity for insurance services. In part this responsibility requires evaluating monetary risks and providing adequately for them. A less obvious part is identifying the changing pattern of the public's needs and desires, and designing insurance services to meet them that are attractive, useful, and economical, bearing in mind the highly competitive character of the life insurance industry and of alternative vehicles for savings and security.[9]

A Yale math major, William Harrison Givens, Jr., entered Equitable's actuarial training program in 1946 and, like other trainees, served a long apprenticeship rotating among several departments. He did well and served tours as a personal assistant to Klem and Oates. After a spell as officer in charge of special research and product development, he went into the Group Department. Although Givens had initially favored the Society's limiting its pension work to consulting, he came to be the GIC's chief designer and also its most enthusiastic cheerleader. He was gifted with a commanding personality, a dazzling intellect, and a charming collection of interests (he spoke fluent Latin and French, was an amateur boxer, and once astonished a colleague by complimenting him for his use of the pluperfect subjunctive in a routine memorandum). People readily followed him. Actuarial colleagues were impressed by his creativity and ability to improve the draft of any document that came across his desk, whether a contract, a marketing brochure, or a pricing memorandum. And outside the actuarial departments, business and sales officers who had fought with Klem and other extremely cautious actuaries found Givens' openness and flexibility refreshing. Walsh remembered him this way:

> *Harrison Givens was in many ways my mentor. When I gave a eulogy at his funeral in 1985 I said he was my father in the business community. He always had about ten projects going at a time. Usually, one out of twenty that he worked on was brilliant. He was the leader of the actuarial community. He was on the cutting edge. Many actuaries were trying to preserve tradition, but he did not observe tradition for tradition's sake.*[10]

Givens designed the GIC to meet the demands of potential clients, and Walsh sold it. They were a dynamic pair — smart, imagina-

tive, competitive, and extremely self-confident. Between them, they built Equitable's new group annuity business into a giant. In 1974, according to *Institutional Investor*'s survey of the pension business, only one money manager picked up more new pension accounts than Equitable, which had almost $500 million in new business. New clients included Bendix, Du Pont, Continental Oil, Allis Chalmers, Armco Steel, and the Budd Company. In 1975, group annuity considerations totaled over $1 billion, the Society won almost $200 million worth of contracts from competitors, and Equitable's total pension assets grew by 20 percent to $9.75 billion. Not all of that growth was due to the GIC; Equitable had become a large manager of nonguaranteed accounts for pension funds and other institutions. But the GIC received most of the credit. As J. Henry Smith told the Board of Directors in 1973, "Aggressive sales management and top-notch investment performance have combined to produce these rather spectacular results." The GIC seemed like a new wonder.[11]

Givens conducted the design and pricing of the GIC much as actuaries designed any insurance product, around assumptions about the expected behavior of the policyholder and the economic environment in an attempt to hedge risk. The product had to appeal to the marketplace and be remunerative for Equitable. The risk was Equitable's. The company accepted deposits, whose investment it managed, and guaranteed a fixed rate of return to the client at a contracted minimum interest rate that — it anticipated — would be lower than the yield on its own investment of the assets.

The challenge was to properly anticipate economic swings so as to establish contract lengths and set interest rates for GICs. In the early days of the GIC, Givens used three scenarios, or "paths," for the behavior of interest rates: stable for the life of the guarantee, and either up or down very slightly during the first few years of the guarantee and stable thereafter. To cut Equitable's risk, the pricing was conservatively based on the worst possible case. Since the results of the three paths were closest in eight- and nine-year cycles, GIC contracts ran approximately that long; during that time the contracts remained open and clients could make further deposits at the guaranteed rate. Over time, as concerns were raised in Equitable about the success of GICs and the volatility of interest rates, assumptions and calculations became more sophisticated and complex. The three path pricing model was replaced by a model in which interest rates could be stable or swing up or down ½ percent in each year of the guarantee. (The unprecedented inflation and interest rate volatility were optimistically assumed to be history.) Instead of three possible paths, there were now 2,187. Givens and his staff calculated the probabilities of any of these paths occurring, and of their profitability. The guide for the GIC came to be called the 2,000-case pricing model.

As with other insurance products, volatility had to be contained on both the liability and the asset sides so that they would match and minimize the insurer's risk. At first, assets backing GICs were in the general account because, by New York insurance law, separate accounts could not be guaranteed. Those assets consisted mainly of long-term, high-yielding, fixed-return corporate bonds and mortgages. These were two areas in which Equitable's investment departments had been unusually successful for decades. Regulatory approval was obtained to permit a guaranteed separate account for GICs, Separate Account 9, whose portfolio consisted largely of fixed-return investments and was designed to provide a close match between assets and liabilities.

On the liability side, Givens assumed that a law of averages would apply to ensure stability and balance Equitable's risks, for two reasons. First, he believed that interest rates would not vary by more than 1 percent a year. If the wide range of possible investments all had approximately the same yield, they would balance each other out. And second, thrift-plan clients — the millions of individual workers themselves — would make their choices independently rather than be herded by the plan's trustee, by an employer, or by investment advisors toward another investment. Some limitations were imposed; for example, clients initially were not permitted to move money to other GICs or to Treasury bills and other government securities. All in all, however, contract holders were given considerable latitude, and this flexibility added to the product's appeal without, it seemed, adding to Equitable's risk. At the end of the contract, clients would be free to collect their money and transfer it elsewhere, but Givens was sure that many of them would roll their funds over into new Equitable contracts. He summarized this conviction in a GIC business plan: "[W]e have assumed that any investment bias resulting from individual participants' investment or transfer elections is likely to work in our favor, and have ignored such effects in our study."[12]

For those familiar with the 2,000-case pricing model, Givens' theory was extremely impressive in its analysis and seemingly built-in checks and balances. So sure were Givens and Walsh of its originality that its details were carefully hidden from other insurers — and many Equitable people — by extremely tight security. Business plans were numbered and distributed to a very small group of people. In one meeting, Walsh physically restrained Givens from passing papers across the table to actuaries from another department. One name often absent from the distribution list was that of Francis Schott, whose job as Equitable economist included predicting interest rates and inflation. He feared they would increase during the 'seventies, but the quick success of GICs at first seemed to disprove his argument that fierce inflation inevitably would strike to the heart of the insurance business.

The GIC was appealing both in the sophistication of its actuarial theory and in its ingenious marketing, which emphasized the product's flexibility, high yields, and guarantees. "The guarantee was *very* important as a marketing tool," Leo Walsh looked back. The appeal of the guarantee reflected the widespread, historic trust in the solidity and reliability of life insurance companies. Givens cited that tradition in classic terms in a speech he gave to investment bank securities analysts in 1977:

> *Life insurance companies have been doing this continually — and exclusively — for the last 200 years.... These guarantees are of the same standing, in terms of the life insurance company's obligation, as every life insurance promise to a widow or orphan.... An interest guarantee, therefore, puts [sponsors'] minds to rest on meeting their investment assumption, and not only on current plan assets but, wonder of wonders, on future contributions, too, for the duration of the guarantee.*[13]

To complement the simplicity of the guarantee, and its uniqueness to the insurance business, Givens and Walsh labored to assure prospective clients — all those employees who were members of thrift plans — that a GIC was as simple, stable, and secure as an old-fashioned passbook savings account. (This, of course, was before the savings and loan collapses of the 1980's.) Walsh later spoke of this marketing approach:

> *The GIC is a good example of the value of the KISS formula: keep it simple, stupid. There was a sea change in the financial world. There were waves of investment decisions going through society. But the American people were driven by how a bank savings account worked, not how a bond worked. A savings account offered a guaranteed return, and that's what people wanted. The GIC was a savings account alternative offering individual choice and a guarantee.*[14]

It was important, therefore, that the GIC contracts be easily comprehended by Equitable's salespeople, plan trustees, and individual employees choosing from among several investment options. It was in drafting contracts that Harrison Givens was in his element. An actuary who worked with him, Gordon Dinsmore, said: "Harrison was a crusader that contracts should be short and elegant. He loved words. He cared much more than you would expect in a numbers guy." For example, rather than list all the many varieties and maturities of savings bonds, Givens bundled them neatly under the simple, familiar term "government obligations."[15]

While describing the contracts was relatively simple, determining their profitability was difficult. Many assumptions had to be made about the behavior of future interest rates, taxes, investment returns, the matching of assets with liabilities, Equitable's capital requirements, and the way rates would be credited to clients' accounts using the investment year, opportunity money, or some other method. A number of projections were made, some showing profits and others indicating losses. To some mystified insiders, this seemed to be not a particularly businesslike way to run an insurance product.

Another problem with the GIC was that it tapped Equitable's liquidity. A New York valuation law, intended to induce caution in investments, required that special reserves be taken from the surplus against liabilities that had interest rates higher than the 4 percent reserve rate. With interest rates on GIC guarantees rising far above that level, large reserves had to be set aside, and they strained the surplus. Because of this surplus strain and for other reasons, surplus declined from 6 percent of assets to 4 percent in 1974, when The Equitable suffered a net loss of $166 million. Financial pressures were unusually intense that year: there was a decline in the stock and bond markets; the Penn Central bankruptcy drove down the value of its bonds; demands for policy loans were high; and the costs of ongoing projects to automate and diversify the company were steep. As surplus strain appeared again in 1975, Equitable stopped selling GICs for several months. By the end of the year, the company and other insurers, also suffering from surplus strain, had succeeded in convincing the New York State Insurance Department to adopt a less rigid valuation law.

There were other regulatory concerns. After an Arkansas insurer offered extremely high guaranteed rates, Texas capped interest guarantees in annuity contracts. Givens, furious, warned a colleague that this was "a development of the utmost danger and concern for us.... If this situation should spread to other states it would be disastrous." Under industry pressure, the Texas insurance superintendent backed down. At around that time, the SEC was investigating whether some types of group annuity contracts were securities whose sale should be subject to federal regulation. Though the SEC did not regulate annuities, the insurance industry formed a study group on group annuity regulation on which Givens served as Equitable's representative.[16]

Always fiercely competitive, the pension business became even more cutthroat after the passage in 1974 of the sweeping federal Employee Retirement Income Security Act

Harry D. Garber was quietly concerned about GICs.

(ERISA), which imposed fiduciary obligations on pension plan sponsors and money managers. ERISA had the effect of making GICs extremely attractive due to the safety of their unique guarantees. Money flooded into the contracts; even banks bought GICs for their pension plans. As other insurers entered this growing market, Equitable, to attract new clients and keep old ones, became more flexible in negotiating terms. One feature was what Walsh called "this new, 'upward-only' modification guarantee." As of June 1974, whenever new guarantees for new clients were increased by at least ¼ percent to meet the competition, rates for old clients were ratcheted up automatically by the same margin, which later was raised to ½ percent. The ratchet, which until then had not been a feature of Givens' 2,000-case model, was intended to make Equitable's GICs more competitive in general and, in particular, to convince clients with expiring contracts to roll them over into new contracts rather than transfer their money to other insurers or banks. Transfers became a major worry as the size of the contracts grew into the hundreds of millions of dollars and as GICs provided increasing proportions of Equitable's assets, profits, and capital. As competition for pension dollars intensified and interest rates rose during the late 1970's, ratchets became retroactive subject to negotiation with clients.[17]

In terms of attracting assets, GICs were an astonishing success for Equitable. Between 1974 and 1978, the Society went from America's ninth biggest pension fund manager to the largest, with GICs making up half of Equitable's group annuity business (the other half lay in traditional investment management accounts). The $10.1 billion growth of Equitable's assets between 1974 and 1978 was entirely accounted for by pension assets, which increased by exactly that amount. Between 1969 and 1978, Equitable's group pension considerations grew sixteen-fold while its insurance premiums only doubled. By 1980, 40 percent of The Equitable's assets were GIC-related.

Yet as the business ballooned, there were questions about GICs. The sheer size of the new business, relative to traditional life insurance products, was staggering. "GICs were big contracts, and we went into big investments based on them, and we had no control over the violent fluctuation of interest rates," recalled John Jacobus, the Equitable lawyer who looked after pension-related legal matters. Risk was a serious concern. Delegated to study methods for hedging Equitable's risk, Jacobus developed amendments to the New York insurance law to permit the use of interest rate futures to hedge the risk of interest rate fluctuations. In the summer of 1974, the Society's Investment Planning and Coordinating Committee, chaired by Robert Hendrickson and including Givens, debated whether guaranteeing high interest rates would lure Equitable into taking on excessively risky investments. Robert Johnstone, Equitable's conservative Controller, questioned whether a product with an automatic upward

ratchet feature was the sort of thing that Equitable should be selling.[18]

In February 1976, President Eklund sent an action memo to Harry Garber, by then Executive Vice-President in charge of corporate operations: "We must become thoroughly reassured that 'pricing' of 'Guaranteed Interest' Pension proposals is sound, and over the long run profitable. How can this be done?" Garber responded in a three-page, single-spaced memorandum expressing worry about GICs. As an actuary and friend of Harrison Givens', he admired the theoretical elegance of the GIC design. But he worried that Equitable had insufficient control over the pricing and size of the business: "In the end, whether we make a profit and the extent of our profitability on a particular contract depends more on the movements of prevailing interest rates than on any management actions we can take," Garber observed. Apologizing for sounding pessimistic, he concluded by asking Eklund:

(1) Can we be reasonably certain that this product will be marketable over the long time span which I believe is required to assure profitable results? and (2) Even if we can have this certainty, do we want to be in a kind of business with this profitability pattern?

Garber clearly believed that the answer to each question was no.[19]

Garber had no further queries from Eklund about GICs at that time. Givens maintained that Garber did not fully understand the theory. Garber's concern was less with the theory than with the increasing flexibility that was being added to the product to stimulate and sustain sales at a rate that, he believed, would overly concentrate the Society's assets in GICs. Extremely bright and knowledgeable about insurance and many other technical matters, Garber was one of Equitable's top officers and had Eklund's trust and ear. Although Garber remained critical of GICs within the company, Eklund appointed him head of individual insurance operations in 1978 and the company's first Chief Financial Officer in 1979. Garber was not the sort of officer to lead an executive suite revolt over a questionable product; at awards dinners, he instructed young actuaries that their job was to work for the businessmen who ran The Equitable. He later said that he showed his memorandum to only a couple of people besides Eklund. Indeed, most people would first learn that he had been so harshly critical of GICs in a 1990 *Wall Street Journal* article about, among other things, the terrible losses that GICs had sustained for some of the reasons that Garber had laid out.

Asked about the internal debate over GICs, Eklund said that by 1976 it was too late to get out of the business. Though still relatively small, it was growing rapidly, was becoming solidly profitable, and was satisfyingly meeting the original purpose of building assets. In an interview in 1994, Walsh looked back:

> *Debate went on all the time. In the early years, a single sale to a pension plan that provided deposits as small as $100,000 a year was a major, major event, so we were surprised by how GICs developed in 1975 and '76. That kind of growth was scary. There was always a tug-of-war about how fast to grow. The right question to ask then was, "Why are we in it?" But the marketplace was absolutely exploding — it just grew astronomically.*[20]

At the time, Givens complained about the "hand-wringing and analysis." There was no problem: "It's O.K.," he assured other officers. But at times even Givens seemed nervous that GICs might be too successful. In 1975, he predicted to Francis H. Schott that by the end of the decade investments underlying GICs might constitute as much as half of Equitable's

assets; yet with contracts worth half a billion dollars expiring annually, should pension clients be lured away by competitors, Givens told Schott, "there would be a great liquidity problem." But then Givens shook off his doubts: the pension industry was maturing away from hypercompetition; and anyway, Equitable was securely covered by the competitive advantages of its contracts.[21]

Still, the feverish competition for GICs brought new concessions to clients. For several years, Equitable prohibited them from transferring deposits to government bonds and Treasury bills, but in 1978 other insurers began to open the option. Walsh was reluctant to go along, but Givens talked him into it. There seemed little risk, since government bonds usually had yields well below market rates. If Equitable could not do better than government bonds, Givens told Jacobus, it did not deserve to be in business. Within two years, this decision would come to haunt Equitable when an unprecedented interest rate climb drove Treasury bills to over 15 percent. "We were convinced that we had to do it to be competitive," Walsh later said, "but when interest rates spiked in 1980, it turned around and bit us."[22]

Until then, Equitable was in a position of unparalleled prestige as it dominated the pension business as thoroughly as, in earlier times, it had ruled the insured mortgage, group insurance, and tontine businesses. In 1977, the federal government was about to remove the tax exemption from the corruption-ridden $1.4 billion Central States Southeast and Southwest pension fund of the International Brotherhood of Teamsters but changed its mind when the fund was turned over to Equitable to manage. Explained a Labor Department official, "Our only requirement was that they settle on a recognized, independent financial manager and Equitable is as recognized and independent as you can get." It was an obvious encomium to the Society's pension accomplishments.[23]

As successful as the GIC was in gathering assets, there were financial concerns about the company as a whole. With $27.7 billion in assets in 1978, Equitable was twice as large as in 1969, yet its capital base had increased by only 4 percent. The ratio of capital to assets had been 7 percent in 1969 but had dropped below 5 percent in 1974 and was falling further.

The problem was high overhead. In the spring of 1978, Harry Garber, by then head of individual insurance operations, became worried that rising expenses would soon eat into policyholder dividends to such an extent that Equitable would be noncompetitive with other companies. He took his concern to the head of all insurance operations, James Attwood. In May, at a board meeting in San Francisco, they took Eklund aside and urged him to begin a serious program of cost reduction. Garber later came across a faded memorandum written in 1907 by Joel G. Van Cise to warn William Day that the surplus was being drained by high costs. Garber sent a copy to Eklund with a comment: "You will note that the world hasn't changed much in seventy-two years."[24]

Eklund instituted a cost-cutting and reorganization plan that he called More Profitable Growth (MPG). It was Equitable's first serious program of financial austerity since the Great Depression. One feature was the introduction of a new measure of success: Eklund removed the traditional taboo from use of the word *profit*. To speak publicly of profit in a mutual life insurance company was a shock to the system; to many old hands, it suggested that somehow the company's success was independent of that of the policyholders. The first time Eklund uttered the word at a board meeting, a director vigorously objected.

Eklund also took a bold step in investment policy when, in 1978, Equitable liquidated almost all the common stocks in the general account — half a billion dollars' worth ($3 billion worth of common stocks remained in separate accounts). The sell-off produced almost $60 million in capital gains. Eklund had three reasons for the sale. First, stock performance had been poor during the bear market of the mid-1970's. Second, there was the brake of the mandatory securities valuation reserve (MSVR), a government-mandated reserve fund against equities held in the general account as a cushion against the volatility of common stocks. And third, Eklund believed that common stocks were inappropriate for the general account because the only way to realize their full value, in order to distribute larger dividends, was to sell them. Fixed-income investments with fixed maturities, on the other hand, provided steady, predictable income. "Common stocks are simply not the type of assets needed in The Equitable's general account," Eklund told his officers in a memorandum.[25]

The most visible (and painful) step in the MPG program was the laying-off of personnel. Salaries and benefits had more than doubled since 1970 and accounted in 1978 for more than half the budget, above the ratio in peer companies. Eklund instituted a cutback of salaried managers and staff (only the agency force was excepted) intended to eliminate 550 jobs. While small compared with contemporaneous layoffs in other industries, the staff reduction had no precedent in Equitable. For decades recruiters had promised lifetime employment, and for decades the Society had made good on those promises. If ending lifetime employment seemed paradoxical in Eklund's personal history as an idealist, he explained that as CEO, his duty was to sustain the health of Equitable as a whole: "Corporate finance was coming into the picture — the concern for the financial well-being of the corporation," he later said. He personally approved each layoff.[26]

Nelson Broms.

The staff reduction would have been unpleasant at best even if it had been perfectly handled. Department heads, few of whom had any experience with such an assignment and little, if any, sympathy with it, unenthusiastically huddled in their offices to come up with names. While the goal was not reached, the response was tense and sometimes angry, with talk of organizing a union and the filing of an age-discrimination class-action lawsuit by former employees and the federal Equal Employment Opportunity Commission (Equitable settled the suit at a total cost of over $20 million). Eklund publicly defended the layoffs in language that appeared to conflict with his declarations about the priority of human values. Articles about Equitable in business publications pursued the "man bites dog" angle implied by a headline in the *Wall Street Journal*: "No More Nice Guy." After that, Eklund reportedly became thin-skinned about the press.[27]

Company morale suffered badly. More than fifteen years later, Equitable people who had lived through the staff reduction spoke of it in pained voices. "The Equitable turned a corner in 1978. I don't think any shock was as great as that one," said John O'Hara, an officer in the Human Resources Department. Ed Monahan, the former ballplayer and, later, Equitable Controller, looked back: "It would never again be the same, you could tell."[28]

The More Profitable Growth program also ended many of the subsidiaries that had been formed only recently. The diversifications were estimated to have cost $185 million in cash and lost investment opportunities, and several of the new businesses were deemed too small, too costly, or poor fits with Equitable's evolving new direction toward providing a wider range of financial services. Donald L. Bryant, Sr., disagreed and departed for early retirement in Florida. On Christmas Day 1979, Eklund sent Nelson Broms, head of the Equitable Life Holding Company, an action memo written with characteristic brio:

Action Memo #352, 25 December 1979
Re: Your ELHoCo Mission as of
Jan. 1, 1980.

During 1979, you had the primary mission (as CEO of ELHoCo) of disposing of "unwanted subs." You have made excellent progress toward this difficult goal and I am confident you will accomplish desired results within a short time. Until divestment is completed, you will represent me in managing subs not assigned to ELHoCo EVP's [executive vice-presidents] (Attwood & Hendrickson) by recent Executive Announcement. As an important new assignment I want you to....[29]

Equico Personal Credit, based on the old Student Life Funding Corporation, and the environmental health operation became inactive, and the computer software and Canadian operations were sold. TELMARI, the real estate investment trust, was later liquidated. For a while there was a plan to take the property and casualty operation, Equitable General, nationwide and sell property and casualty policies wholesale to insurance brokers, even to other insurance companies, to retail under their private labels. Backers of private labeling believed it would build sales volume, take advantage of Equitable's technical expertise, and trim the Society's exposure to risk in a highly volatile, low-profit marketplace. But Eklund vetoed the idea. Distribution of products outside the system, he said, would subvert the entire career agency force. "There's no such thing as an alternative distribution system for the Equitable," he would state in 1985. "We've got 10,000 agents out there. You can't replicate that in less than twenty to thirty years, and at huge expense." Late in 1981, Equitable sold most of Equitable General in two blocks, to Geico, the large automobile insurance company, and Tokio Fire and Marine, a Japanese insurer.[30]

In the meantime, to strengthen EVLICO, there was talk of marketing variable life insurance policies through alternative distribution channels. One of the more vocal proponents was Jerome Golden, Harry Walker's former assistant. Again there was no change and Golden departed in 1979. He looked back:

> They decided it was more important to keep the agents as exclusive sellers and simply wait for sales to build. Officers would appear at agents' meetings and say, "We will not market this product through stockbrokers," and everybody would applaud. That would have only been a small amount of the business, and it could have led to more business. It was too early in Equitable for alternate channels of distribution. They weren't ready for it.[31]

Besides EVLICO, the only subsidiaries formed in the early 'seventies to survive 1982 intact were the leasing, health maintenance, and securities operations, and Equico Capital, the minority investment company. Speaking of his program of closing down many of the subsidiaries that had been founded by his predecessor, J. Henry Smith, Eklund said, "Henry was a starter of things and I guess I was a concluder of things. I closed us out of most everything that we had gone into."[32]

Within two years of beginning his active effort to improve the bottom line, Eklund in 1980 announced that he wanted

Equitable to increase sales volume and catch Metropolitan Life and Prudential as the world's largest life insurance company. The Society, he said, should go "from bigger and better to biggest and best." He was at the podium at a national agents' meeting when a videotape appeared on the screen behind him and showed the Rock of Gibraltar, the symbol of Prudential Life, exploding to reveal Equitable's Protection Group. The message could not be more clear, but some people wondered if greater sales volume and improved profitability went hand-in-hand. Robert Hendrickson, the Chief Investment Officer, in a memorandum to Eklund tactfully referred to "a challenging dilemma for Equitable — viz., your aspiration to be largest in insurance in force (a *highly* desirable long-range goal) vs. a de-emphasis on sales in favor of increased earnings."[33]

The problem, Hendrickson explained, was that individual insurance alone could not produce the needed assets. The rapidly growing GIC business offered hope, with Harrison Givens promising limitless risk-free growth and Leo Walsh projecting that in 1985 GICs would provide $500 million in profits. There also was talk of merging with Mutual Life of New York (by then known as MONY), an ironic twist considering the ancient entanglements between the two companies. Although exploratory negotiations went far enough for Eklund to speculate about the merged company's name ("The Equitable Mutual" was his suggestion), the idea died.[34]

But the solution seemed to lie in other directions. Eklund was not opposed in principle to diversification. He was sure only that the efforts of the 1970's had been in the wrong direction and at too small a size to help The Equitable grow as he thought it should in the increasingly demanding and integrated financial environment of the 1980's. Henceforth, he decided, Equitable should measure itself relative not just to the life insurance industry or the old Equitable, but to the entire financial services business. In July 1981, he produced a plan, titled "Strategic Positioning" (but usually referred to as "20/20 Vision" because it looked forward and backwards twenty years), that proposed carrying on much as before but with diversification into other types of financial services. Here was another Eklund surprise: the insurance fundamentalist had become an entrepreneur. Before long, task forces and consultants were coming up with names of banks and brokerages as possible acquisition targets. And so Equitable began to make itself over again in response to a new set of upheavals going on around it — in this case, the worst inflation and most intense period of disintermediation in American history.

John B. Carter became CEO in a time of economic challenge and change.
He attempted to transform The Equitable.

CHAPTER XIX

TRANSFORMED IN THE 'EIGHTIES

I n 1982, Equitable's Chief Economist, Francis H. Schott, began an insightful paper on recent economic developments with a one-sentence summary of the extraordinary changes in America's economy since the nation's bicentennial six years earlier. "If the first 100 years of the country's history were a time of experimentation and growth and the second century a time of consolidation and development of traditions," he advised, "the third century has opened as if it were to be a time of transformation."[1]

That transformation was largely triggered by the worst peacetime inflation in American history, which some called The Great Inflation. The Vietnam War, the Great Society's programs of the 1960's, and the Arab oil boycotts of the 1970's, with their ten-fold increase in oil prices, spawned annual inflation rates of amazing heights. While inflation had rarely exceeded 3 percent between 1950 and 1966 and averaged about 8 percent over the next decade, from 1977 to 1981 it hovered at double digits. For a life insurance company during the Great Inflation, even more important than the price increases was the unusually volatile behavior of interest rates, which took large, unpredictable leaps to heights that seemed incredible. All this intensified the disintermediation trend that had been launched in the late 'sixties by stimulating people to "chase yield" with ever-increasing urgency.

Disintermediation also was energized by the inflation-stimulated, nationwide plunge of business and consumer confidence. The 'seventies was the first extended period since the Great Depression when most Americans experienced a decline in real income. In previous hard times, including the 1930's and 1890's, public distrust of the established order had been spurred by deep depressions; but now similar fears were stimulated by years of inflation in which the dollar lost value by 10 to 20 cents year after year, and people came to despair of ever again living in a stable economy. The writer Nicholas Lemann recalled, "The summer of 1979 was the only time I can remember when, at the level of ordinary life as opposed to public affairs, things seemed to be out of control."[2]

There was a cure, but it was as painful as the disease. To try to rein in inflation, the Federal Reserve Board in October 1979 sharply tightened the money supply. This brought even greater interest rate volatility in a surprising area, six-month Treasury bills, the safest and normally one of the most stable of all securities. Within six weeks of the Federal Reserve's action, the rate on Treasury bills increased from 10 percent to 11½ percent; and over the next two years, it varied from month to month by as much as 3 percent and reached as high as 16 percent. The entire country came to marvel at the yields of riskless six-month Treasury bills. Although the Fed's action eventually ended the Great Inflation, it did not stop the business upheavals: in 1980, corporate profits fell by 40 percent; in 1982, forty-two major American companies declared bankruptcy, the largest number of business failures in any year since the depression.

Equitable, fortunately, was already strong in two traditional hedges against inflation, real estate and common stocks. Its growing money-management business for third parties invested in these two areas, and one of its pioneering product lines, variable life insurance, was largely based on stock investments. Yet these advantages did not soften the blow of the wild interest rate fluctuations that came after the Federal Reserve instituted its tight money policy. Twelve days after the Fed's action, Robert Hendrickson, head of Equitable's Investment Affairs Department, reported cryptically and gloomily to his fellow officers: "Activity in corporate finance and real estate in condition of suspended animation.... [Equitable's] attitude: trying to maintain stability during turmoil — intense work on cash projections." That same day, Hendrickson described the company's new investment policy as one of extreme caution and selectivity: "It is expected that money markets will fluctuate widely," he explained.[3]

Disintermediation ran rampant. A telling indicator was the swing by Americans toward Treasury bills. In 1970, individuals held just under 14 percent of marketable Treasury debt; most of the remainder was in the hands of insurance companies, banks, and other intermediaries. But by 1980, individuals had a 21½ percent share. Many people financed these and other high-yielding investments by surrendering or borrowing against their insurance policies. Since the law prohibited an insurer from refusing most applications for policy loans and set their interest rates at about 5 percent, Equitable essentially had to make money-losing investments in its own customers. In 1981, the company's negative cash flow due to policy loans was $471 million; due to policy surrenders, $338 million. At the end of that year, Hendrickson referred to this drain when he warned Coy Eklund that his ambitions for expansion were being stunted by "inadequate financial nourishment."[4]

Dr. Francis H. Schott, Equitable's long-time Chief Economist.

Equitable was then preparing for another leadership transition. When Eklund reached the normal retirement age of sixty-five in 1980, and no likely successor was in place, the Board of Directors extended his term for two years while he considered a nominee. At first the candidates were two Executive Vice-Presidents in their fifties, James Attwood and Robert Hendrickson. Attwood's background was in group insurance, Hendrickson's in investments. (Asked later why the list did not include Chief Financial Officer Harry Garber, Eklund answered, "He was an actuary" — but so also was Attwood.) Eklund had Attwood and Hendrickson swap jobs in order to broaden their experience, although some board members sensed that he might also have been postponing his retirement. He asked for another year, but the directors told him to come up with a name soon. Eklund considered others and, in the end, proposed forty-seven year-old Executive Vice-President John B. Carter, a former agent and agency manager who was head of Insurance Operations. In September 1981, Eklund became Chairman of the Board (succeeding John Fey), remaining Chief Executive Officer, and Carter became the new President. Hendrickson took a position on Eklund's staff, and Attwood soon departed for the presidency of Mutual Life of New York (Leo Walsh succeeded him as Chief Investment Officer). After Eklund stepped down in 1983, former Secretary of the Army Robert Froehlke became Board Chairman.[5]

After more than four decades, Coy Eklund was no longer working for The Equitable. He had risen from a part-time agent selling $1,000 policies in a university's student union to positions in which he reorganized the agency force and, later, headed the entire company. Although he was most closely identified with the agency force, when he spoke of his seven years as CEO, Eklund was most pleased that he had focused the company on its profitability by divesting subsidiaries and cutting other costs. Surplus, which returned to $1 billion in 1978 after nine years at lower levels, increased almost three-fourths during his tenure as CEO, from $729 million in 1976 to $1.3 billion in 1982. Eklund would point out that this growth (without adjustments for inflation) was greater than the entire increase in surplus between 1939 and 1976.

An alumnus of Yale College and the Harvard Business School, John Carter had started out as an Equitable agent in New Haven and managed the agency in Saginaw, Michigan. In 1970, he was brought to the Home Office in the Agency Operations Department's Manpower Division, which assembled and analyzed data for recruiting agents. He spent a year in Virginia as field Vice-President for the company's eastern region, but when two influential agency officers, the brothers Jack and Gary Kinder, abruptly left Equitable for another insurance company, he was called back to the Home Office and promoted to a series of ever higher sales positions. In 1980, Carter assumed the $230,000-a-year job of Executive Vice-President in charge of Insurance Operations. A year later, he was President and heir apparent.

The appointment was greeted enthusiastically by the agency force and Home Office staff, for he was liked personally and respected for his Ivy League education, his openness to change, and his effective presence. After Carter's death in 1992, Robert Barth, who had managed a Philadelphia agency and later worked under him at the Home Office, recalled: "People were looking for a great leader, and John Carter had the ability to be a great leader. He had physical presence: he was big, bulky, and had a great voice. He also was a good human being." A generous, gregarious man with a deep religious faith and a family of eleven children, Carter could be counted on to take time from his busy schedule to comfort the troubled, visit the sick, and mourn the dead. John W. Riley expressed a widespread view in comparing Carter with his predecessor: "Coy was the type who would come into a crowded room and stand there and exert his magnetic personality without reaching out, while John Carter would reach out to everybody."[6]

Carter was receptive to many of the new ideas that were circulating during the economic upheavals. He read, and often quoted, the works of the futurists Alvin Toffler and John Naisbett as well as the management books and articles of the new generation of business writers who, stimulated by the challenges of the times and the rapid industrial advances in Japan, urged top-to-bottom corporate restructuring in order to liberate workers from bureaucracies. Carter told people that the company's future lay in decentralized decision-making, entrepreneurialism, and improved communications. After becoming CEO, he presented a personal computer to each member of Equitable's Management Committee of department heads and high officers, and instructed them to prepare themselves for the future by becoming computer literate. Yet for all his commitment to change, Carter revived images of the Equitable Family. He told agency managers: "Our challenge is to stick together, to work together, and, above all, to communicate. To communicate and communicate. We're not so big that we can't go one-on-one almost all the time."[7]

The Board of Directors also was urging the company to examine its organization and strategy. Since the Parkinson-related problems of the early 'fifties, the board had been quiet; business was steadily and predictably successful and management was trusted. "Staff-driven and not board-driven" was how Equitable of the 'seventies was characterized by Eleanor Sheldon. The board's institutional memory was hazy. For example, Raymond Wittcoff, who was elected to the board in 1980 and served on its executive committee for several years, knew nothing about the long, acrimonious, and significant battle between the agency and investment departments over Assured Home Ownership until he was told about it in 1994.[8]

The board's leader among outside directors in the 'seventies was Francis H. ("Hooks") Burr, a Boston lawyer who had been recruited to the Equitable board by Manly Fleischmann. Joining Burr were a number of demanding CEOs, board members, and legal advisors of fast-growing, technology-driven companies. They included Joseph Dionne, CEO of McGraw-Hill; Milton Mumford, former board chairman of Lever Brothers; Winthrop Knowlton, CEO of Harper & Row; William Agee of Bendix; Michael Blumenthal, formerly of Bendix and former secretary of the treasury; Drew Lewis, head of Union Pacific and former secretary of transportation; Raymond H. Wittcoff, of Transurban Corp., a St. Louis property developer; and Arthur Liman, a New York corporate lawyer who would be chief investiga-

tor on the Iran-Contra hearings. Their attitude was very different from that of the older board member who had complained when Eklund introduced the word *profit*. Liman captured the new mood correctly in saying, "I believe that even a mutual insurance company has to be profitable. Everything flows from that."[9]

As the new office of the Chief Financial Officer provided more data, and as the economic environment changed daily because of inflation and government deregulation in the Carter and Reagan administrations, the directors began asking more probing questions about the company and, especially, corporate planning and strategy. "Equitable had not given a thought to strategic planning — except for Henry B. Hyde at the very beginning," observed one board member, Lincoln Gordon, president of Johns Hopkins University. Eklund had made an effort at strategic thinking when he presented his "20/20 Vision" plan, but some directors did not think it had gone far enough; the future, as indicated by the plan, seemed to echo the recent past. Said Sheldon, president of the Social Science Research Council and a director of several big companies facing transition: "The board became individually — and, sometimes, in two or three or four members talking among themselves — more and more concerned about the future of the company."[10]

In 1983, the board created a committee of planning-focused directors and officers called the Corporate Development Committee, headed by Mumford and Dionne. The CDC established thirteen task forces to examine Equitable's business and prospects, from investments to new products to the idea of changing its status from a mutual to a publicly-owned company through the highly unusual step called demutualizing. The CDC retained a Washington-based consulting firm, Strategic Planning Associates, which had been introduced by Agee to advise on acquisitions, to develop a strategic program.

SPA's talented, energetic, and forceful staff swept through the Home Office, dug into files, interviewed officers and staff, and filed reports heavy with graphs showing the strengths and weaknesses of Equitable and the entire life insurance business going back to the first glimmer of change in the 1950's and 'sixties. "This was the first time I really understood what was going on in the company," said Sheldon. SPA developed a proposal for radical decentralization and cost-cutting in the Home Office, regional offices, and agencies that was projected to save as much as $322 million annually. On page 54 of its presentation, SPA summarized the new program in a multicolumn table, which, SPA head Walker Lewis told Carter, was "a direct attack on business practices and costs which prevent Equitable from having a strong bottom line." The Society, SPA repeatedly advised, must become more efficient. "We stayed there not to devise a corporate strategy but as cost-cutters and reorganizers," Lewis later said. "The key issue of life insurance is the tremendous cost of developing an agent. We analyzed the profitability of every account." With SPA's advice, Equitable cut back in several areas and eliminated others (although agency operations remained relatively untouched). Carter took to referring to the mammoth restructuring program by the code term *page 54*.[11]

In the 1970's, Eklund's More Profitable Growth program had introduced a modicum of decentralization by setting up departments as quasi-independent profit centers, each with its own incentive compensation plan. Carter took the concept much further to a radical decentralization scheme often referred to as downstreaming: shifting decision-making from a central authority to the entities most directly concerned. Besides the salutary effort to free people of restrictive management, downstreaming was also a cost-reduction measure intended to help pay for the company's

further growth and, therefore, its survival. The thinking was later explained by Leo Walsh, Carter's right-hand man first as Chief Investment Officer and then as Chief Operating Officer: "Downstreaming itself was a narrow subject. The goal was to cut overhead and central management expense. The idea was that if we didn't make the move we would die." What Hendrickson called "inadequate financial nourishment" had become the rule. While the dollar value of capital (the sum of surplus and the reserve against common stock investments) grew almost every year after the decline in the 'seventies, the fact was that capital growth did not keep pace with asset growth, even when capital was bolstered by surplus relief reinsurance, loans from other insurers in exchange for a share of Equitable's future premium revenues.[12]

To save money and stimulate productivity, Carter and Walsh aimed to eliminate the traditional centralized operation. By 1985, Equitable had fifty-one subsidiaries: nine operations in the insurance business, thirty in investments, and twelve in other fields. There even was a subsidiary to run the fleet of limousines so they could be leased out when they were not in use. Heads of subsidiaries were told to run their own operations much as they pleased so long as they made money. Each subsidiary had its own corporate structure; many had their own personnel programs, compensation schemes, and computer systems and were located where their CEOs thought best regardless of space available in buildings owned by Equitable. Departments and subsidiaries streamed out in all directions: some went to half a dozen buildings in Manhattan, pension operations were relocated in New Jersey, and George Peacock took real estate operations to Atlanta.

Some officers complained that downstreaming was not properly disciplined: many subsidiaries had computer systems incompatible with the one in the Home Office, several staffs had overlapping duties, some subsidiaries that seemed independent on paper actually were subsidized, and company-wide policy decisions over even small matters were made by groups of department heads hammering out their differences in long, acrimonious meetings under Carter's supervision. The idea that Equitable was a single company with a central focus was a thing of the past. When Equitable's Chief Administrative Officer, William McCaffrey, asked Carter why subsidiaries were allowed to lease offices in other buildings when there was empty space in the Home Office, Carter replied, "Bill, you just don't understand about decentralization." He promised that the confusion and conflicts would soon be dwarfed by the added revenues from new entrepreneurial energy.[13]

One recommendation by the consultants that Carter showed little interest in was importing officers from outside the Equitable family. Walker Lewis of Strategic Planning Associates advised Carter to "seed the place with outsiders who can provide role models for 'the new Equitable.'" While counseling against bringing in too many outsiders, which risked polarizing the company, Lewis contended that a transfusion was needed if the old, cautious mutual approach to business were to end: "Your *culture* has to be broken by fresh troops who *know* how a profit-oriented, market-driven, and customer-focused company feels," he told Carter's chief aide for restructuring, John Goddard. Although the concept was supported by several influential board members, Carter seemed blocked by loyalty from putting outsiders in key positions. One director, Joseph L. Dionne, believed this was because Carter himself was a product of the mutual system's traditional multichannel structure of specialists: "The real management problem at The Equitable was that it had silos of specialties. John worked in a silo and

had no thought of bringing people in from the outside." The few imports who were recruited to start new products and divisions had little support from Carter. In the end, said Lewis, "It was just a very hard culture to change."[14]

Meanwhile, the market was changing drastically. "You can draw the line at 1980 — that was the major break with the past," Equitable's Chief Investment Officer, Brian O'Neil said. "After the Great Inflation we no longer had a long-term product. It lost appeal in 1980 because people didn't want to buy a long-term bond any more." O'Neil's choice of words was apt: the Great Inflation was a break with history in which concerns about the long term had been overthrown by those about the short term. Like revolutions, major economic changes throw out old assumptions and undermine or even destroy institutions that do not quickly and accurately read and adjust to the new times.[15]

In its long history, The Equitable had correctly read changing circumstances on many occasions; the stories of tontines, group insurance, residential mortgages, variable insurance, pensions, and other products and services make that clear. In fact, the company sometimes threw itself into new projects so zealously that it had trouble hedging its risks and backing away as circumstances changed yet again. Yet for 120 years, with the exception of variable insurance, Equitable's main business had been to provide individuals and groups with long-term protection matched by long-term investments, most of them in seemingly safe, investment-grade bonds issued by the government or well-established corporations. But short-term thinking now dominated the economy, and in reply Equitable created families of investment-type life insurance and annuity products that addressed the contemporary demand for more investment yield.

Carter understood the drive to yield. In an interview in the first days of his presidency, he referred to Equitable's products as "funding vehicles." He later adopted a new finance-oriented corporate mission statement whose keystone was that Equitable's goal was to create and preserve personal wealth. Protection against life's crises was less emphasized. The new strategy was to make Equitable into a major shopping center for investment services, only some of which involved life insurance. For example, it introduced its own money market account and a line of mutual funds.[16]

An existing product that met the new demands was variable life insurance, which was finally fulfilling Harry Walker's expectations. After years of hard work to modify premiums and commissions in order to make policies competitive and appealing to agents, variable life found its market as Americans, many of whom had seen their fixed-income savings ravaged by inflation, left behind their distrust of common stocks. Variable life's premium income increased twelve-fold between 1980 and 1984 to $342 million. By 1987, it was more than $800 million. At the same time, variable annuities were growing into another successful product.

While Equitable was developing variable life insurance in the late 1970's and early 'eighties, a new product appeared in the industry: universal life insurance. Universal life was innovative in two major ways. First, there was no scheduled premium; policyholders could pay as much or as little as they chose, so long as the policy had enough money to cover the next month's charges. And second, unlike a traditional policy, a universal life contract clearly laid out the exact sales load, the mortality calculations, and — most important — the interest rate credited to the policy each year. This unprecedented amount of detail in an insurance policy invited consumers to engage in comparison shopping to find the best dividend yields. As it turned out, that yield often was provided by the youthful stockholder-owned life insurance companies specializing in universal life. Because these insurers were new, they did not have large investment portfolios of old, low-yielding assets. Their portfolios consisted largely (and in some cases entirely) of recently purchased, high-yield instruments, including commercial real estate and below investment-grade corporate bonds, sometimes called junk bonds. As a result, universal policies were extremely competitive, and these companies challenged the historic dominance of the mutuals.

Equitable took the industry lead in gaining New York State legislative and regulatory approval for the issuance of universal life. In 1983, the company introduced a new policy with some universal life features, though it required annual premiums. Called the Equitable Life Account, it sold very well except, at times, against pure universal life, with its flexible premiums. Equitable's alternative to universal life appeared in 1985: Incentive Life, a hybrid of universal and variable life. While offering flexibility in premium payment schedules and other features of universal life, Incentive Life gave policyholders the same control of the underlying investments that variable life offered, by allowing them to allocate premium payments to any of Equitable's many separate accounts. Incentive Life soon comprised over 60 percent of Equitable's new insurance sales, but it was an expensive effort. Administration of the complicated, custom-designed policies was unusually time-consuming, and sales costs were surprisingly high, since many Incentive Life policyholders made larger payments than anticipated in the first year, when agents' commissions were highest. In addition, many Incentive Life sales went to existing Equitable policyholders who surrendered their old policies in order to buy the attractive new ones. This transitory cannibaliza-

Incentive Life, a popular universal-variable product of the 1980's, heavily emphasized investment features over traditional protection.

tion process cost policyholders little or nothing and provided commissions to agents, but it was expensive to the company. Adjustments to the contracts eventually brought costs more in line with expectations.

Universal-variable and universal policies helped stimulate a rise in life insurance sales throughout the industry; insurance sales volume increased four-fold between 1980 and 1987. Despite the inflation, life insurance premiums kept shrinking ($1,000 of coverage cost $11.41 in 1975 and only $6.31 in 1985). Yet in the 'eighties, the proportion of national disposable income that went to premiums ended its twenty-year decline and remained stable at about 2½ percent through the end of the decade.[17]

Annuities also took new forms and became increasingly popular. In one, the client paid only one premium — somewhat like making a single deposit to open a savings account — and later received regular dividends on the tax-deferred

basis that applied to insurance products, so long as the funds were left in the policy. Single-premium deferred annuities were first offered by Equitable in 1978 and later became extremely popular after the 1986 overhaul of the federal tax code closed off many tax shelters without touching the tax advantages of either life insurance or annuities. They were keyed to prevailing interest rates and had complex investment features (Congress eventually shut off some tax advantages). In 1986, both in the industry and at Equitable, income from annuity considerations for the first time exceeded income from life insurance premiums.

These innovations helped trigger two developments in agency operations. One was the rise of extremely successful agents who specialized in certain types of products and customers and often worked independently of the Equitable agencies to which they were nominally assigned. Some of these agents exercised an influence within the company that previously had been limited to the managers of the largest agencies.

The other development was the appearance of large Equitable-owned agencies that came to be known as mega-agencies. The prototype was the Karr-Barth Agency in Philadelphia, Equitable's best-performing agency in sixteen of the seventeen years between 1978 and 1994.

When George W. Karr, Jr., founded the agency with no agents and three district managers in 1967, he was twenty-eight years old and the youngest agency manager in the company. Six years later, he and one of his district managers, Robert W. Barth, developed a plan for an innovative type of agency run by two co-managers. They were sure that by sharing the management burden and not tying themselves up in administration, they would be free to sell insurance on their own account, thereby keeping in touch with the market.

Until then, Equitable had long discouraged managers from making many sales calls, and there was only one other co-managed agency in the company. Karr and Barth took the idea to their Regional Vice-President, John Carter, who at first expressed reservations but eventually gave his approval. Karr and Barth developed an in-agency system of providing agents and clients with a range of services for the increasingly sophisticated financial marketplace. The staff soon included financial planners, lawyers, and other experts. The Karr-Barth Agency even had its own computer system for custom designing policy illustrations. In 1974, the agency earned $400,000 in first-year commissions; in 1984, it earned $3.7 million; and in 1990, almost $8 million. In 1978, when for the first time it was the company's top-selling agency, it had sixty-five agents; ten years later, it had 240. "The single most important factor in building an agency," Karr would say, was Equitable's new policy of encouraging agency managers to do their own personal production: "I have been able to help my associates sell insurance because I sell insurance and have to stay current and sharp."[18]

The Karr-Barth Agency's success influenced the creation of large, multiservice regional sales centers, called mega-agencies, with territories that sometimes stretched over state lines. Barth left the agency in 1984 for the Home Office to become head of The Equitable's sales organization; Carter later appointed him head of Insurance Operations.

Old barriers between financial institutions that had been raised by the federal government during the 1930's were being erased by deregulation and diversification during the 'seventies and 'eighties. Sears Roebuck, the clothing and home products retailer, acquired an insurance company and a securities brokerage. A provider of travel services, American Express, bought an investment bank. A manufacturer, American Can, was turning itself into a financial services company by acquiring, among other subsidiaries, twenty-two insurance companies (American Can soon completed its transformation by renaming itself Primerica). Commercial banks like J. P. Morgan & Co. and Bankers Trust, which had specialized in making loans, were lobbying to be allowed to underwrite securities; some bankers wanted to underwrite insurance, too. And a mutual life insurance company, Prudential, paid $385 million for a retail securities brokerage firm, the Bache Group.

Eklund to some extent and Carter more energetically wanted to make Equitable a leader in the broad area of financial services by expanding into the investment business. The company had long had indirect interest there as a source of funds and a money manager, but connections became closer. In 1977, Equitable loaned Kidder, Peabody & Co., a successful medium-size Wall Street investment banking and securities firm, $10 million (it was Kidder's first loan since the Great Depression); six years later, Equitable loaned Kidder another $20 million. (In the second loan, Equitable insisted on a provision for certain advantageous steps should Kidder, following the trend toward consolidation in the financial world, be purchased by another company. The agreement paid off for Equitable when General Electric bought Kidder in 1986.)

Carter's main goal was to acquire a Wall Street firm outright. The time was ripe; regulators as well as insurers were coming around to tear down the old walls. In 1982, the New York Executive Advisory Commission on Insurance Industry Regulatory Reform (known as the Heimann Commission, it included Davidson Sommers), recommended the end of the historic premise of the Armstrong laws that anything not specifically approved was illegal. This was an invitation to

The all-service Philadelphia agency co-managed by George Karr (right) and Robert Barth was the prototype mega-agency.

innovation and diversification on an unprecedented scale.

The question was what type of investment firm to acquire: one that could work with Equitable to distribute investment and insurance products (as Prudential was doing with Bache), or one that could complement the company's investment and money management operations. The company turned down opportunities to bid for retail brokerages because they competed for the same clientele as Equitable's agents. Later, in 1984, Carter held serious discussions with Kidder, Peabody about a possible acquisition, but Kidder's officers had doubts about the fit between their brokerage operations and Equitable's agency force, and the talks ended before a bid was tendered. The best fit thus seemed to be with a firm that did little retail brokerage, especially if it was strong in the fast-growing area of money management for pensions and other third-party accounts, in which Equitable

already had over $50 billion under management. In 1984, Equitable acquired a relatively small but well-established money manager, Calvin Bullock, for $16 million, and continued to search for larger acquisitions in the field.

One potential target was Donaldson, Lufkin & Jenrette (DLJ), a twenty-five year-old publicly held firm that specialized in money management, advisory, and brokerage services for institutions. It seemed a perfect fit. DLJ did not have retail brokerages to compete with agents, although its subsidiary, Pershing & Co., a stock clearing operation, offered direct access to hundreds of regional brokerage firms should Equitable wish to distribute policies and other products outside its agency force. Most appealing to Carter and Walsh, DLJ brought $20 billion of third-party assets (mostly pension funds) under management by its Alliance Capital Management and Wood, Struthers & Winthrop subsidiaries. Negotiations broke down for a while, then were renewed, and in 1985 Equitable acquired DLJ for $430 million (twice its book value) plus a $30 million cash payment to the firm's officers to ensure they would stay or, if they departed, to have them sign noncompete agreements. Alliance Capital became an independent subsidiary of Equitable, while Pershing remained in the DLJ fold and soon began executing securities trades for Equitable policyholders at discounted commissions.

Similar mergers had fallen into difficulties either because the acquisitions were a poor fit or because the new parent could not keep its hands off businesses very different from its own. While Equitable knew how a money management firm like Alliance Capital worked, it was not familiar with flexible, freewheeling, and very highly compensated enterprises like DLJ. But the firms were kept distinct and independent. They were housed in different buildings, had their own managements, and retained their own compensation and personnel policies. "We were treated as an investment by Equitable," said Alliance CEO Dave H. Williams. "It was hands off. We had little to do with each other." Joseph Dionne gave Carter full credit for the transaction and the continuing success of the relationship long after others between securities firms and their acquirers had ended in divestment: "John identified it and he produced it for an extremely good price. It was the only major acquisition of an investment firm that has worked."[19]

There was one nagging concern: Equitable's vast guaranteed interest contract (GIC) sector, the insurance industry's largest. Members of corporate retirement plans that were up for renewal were being urged by their companies, consulting actuaries, financial advisors, and others to transfer their money to the higher-yielding GICs offered by many of the aggressive new stockholder-owned life companies, including Executive Life and Charter Life, that offered lofty guarantees. This competition involved billions of dollars in retirement funds. Equitable's GIC-related assets totaled $10 billion in 1982 (up from $1 billion in 1975 and $4.3 billion in 1977) and were climbing rapidly. Some contracts coming up for renewal, and thereby subject to raids by competitors, reached into the hundreds of millions of dollars. With Equitable managing $10 billion in GIC assets, every percentage point of interest rate spread meant some $100 million in profits — assuming, of course, that the spread was positive.

Concerned about the potential loss of assets, Equitable introduced new, more liberal terms in order to compete. One allowed upward ratcheting of guaranteed rates indexed against Treasury bill rates. (The landmark rate was a 17½ percent guarantee for a contract for more than $100 million.) Another permitted new rates to apply retroactively. And a third applied the initial rate during an open period that lasted the term of the contract. Since contracts ran as

long as nine years, Equitable was locking itself into the rate for an extended period with no way to ratchet it downward should market rates decline. These new features were controversial inside Equitable's Pension Department, but they went into effect.

As competition intensified and interest rates continued high, the question was whether Equitable's investment yield could at least match the guarantees made to clients. The business was break even in 1982; the average guarantee and the average yield of its matching assets both were about 11 percent. But that year, the Federal Reserve, declaring victory in its war on inflation, allowed interest rates to drop. Guarantees to older clients had to remain at their old levels, and many clients took advantage of the contractual flexibility and poured new deposits at high interest rates into the open contracts, leaving Equitable with a negative spread.

The case history of a relatively small GIC is illustrative. In April 1976, one of Equitable's corporate clients made a $4.1 million deposit to open a 9.15 percent, seven-year GIC. Over the next four years, the company annually deposited between $600,000 and $1 million at that rate. Then came the interest rate spike, and in June 1980 the client invoked the ratchet clause and opened a new eight-year GIC at 12 percent; if the client chose, it would place all new contributions in this contract until 1988, when the contract would expire. When Treasury bill rates spiked to 16 percent in 1981, the client company withdrew $8 million from the Equitable GIC and moved it into Treasury bills. Then interest rates fell. When Treasury bill yields dropped to 9 percent in September 1982, Equitable's client deposited $10 million in the 12 percent GIC. It now had a 3 point positive interest rate spread, which meant that Equitable had a 3 point *negative* spread. Such a lose-lose sequence of events was known by the concerned pension people at The Equitable as the double whammy.

Equitable's investment income declined as rates dropped and holders of longer-term bonds and mortgages got out from under them through prepayment agreements. By the fall of 1983, some Equitable officers familiar with the GIC portfolio became convinced that the company faced a net negative interest rate spread. After a heated internal debate, the company set aside a special $300 million reserve against GICs that cut surplus that year by $106 million. The more than $100 million that GICs had contributed to the surplus over the previous years now began to look small. When the Board of Directors was asked to establish the huge reserve in the fall of 1983, it was the first time that many directors learned that the product had been experiencing serious troubles. Some were furious to discover that contracts had been held open for so many years, and that GIC liabilities and investment assets had become so mismatched. Hooks Burr recalled:

> *Every now and then I'd see a tremendous amount of money associated with GICs. Around 1983, we started to ask questions: "How did we get this way?" That was when we learned about ratcheting and open-ended deposits. From time to time we would get reports of the amounts of money involved that scared the pants off me. I would wake up in the middle of the night worrying about it.*[20]

Could the GIC problem be managed? One recommendation was to unload the GIC business at a cost, but since it was unclear what the liabilities were, the decision was made to set up large reserves, improve investment yields, and attempt to strengthen (but not greatly expand) the GIC business. New contracts were made less flexible by eliminating the ratchet clause, banning transfers to government bonds, and

shortening the open period for further deposits. But those restrictions could not be applied retroactively. Many of the contracts — valued at $11.6 billion in 1983 and eventually to grow to $15 billion in 1987 — had many years to run and carried guarantees higher than market interest rates.

To meet the high guarantees, Equitable established a new enhanced-return investment plan that consisted of stepping up the already large program of acquiring real estate and investing in high-yield bonds. The plan was controversial; many officers considered these instruments inherently risky either in their nature or in the degree to which funds were placed in them. In equity real estate, Equitable was the largest acquirer in the country from the late 1970's through the mid-'eighties. Among the developments in which the company participated, in this case as a 50-percent partner with Donald Trump, was one of the most glamorous buildings of the 'eighties, Trump Tower, which went up on the Equitable-owned Fifth Avenue site on which the company had long had a leaseback arrangement with Bonwit Teller. In 1984, Equitable set up a separate real estate subsidiary, Equitable Real Estate Investment Management. In one deal, it acquired nineteen shopping centers for $700 million for Prime Property Fund, its real estate operation for pension plans. During this period, real estate values rose rapidly thanks to a wave of property development sweeping through America and stimulated in part by foreign (especially Japanese) investors. At the peak of the market in the late 'eighties, Equitable profitably sold off many properties (including its share in Trump Tower), earning almost $1.5 billion in capital gains. For a while, handsome yields and capital gains from real estate held even with, and at times exceeded, GIC liabilities. Despite selling many properties, Equitable at the end of the decade still had over 30 percent of its assets invested in real estate.

As it enlarged its already extensive real estate portfolio, Equitable put almost 10 percent of its assets into some of the high-yield, below investment-grade, short-term corporate bonds that financed many of the takeovers, mergers, and leveraged buyouts of the 'eighties (some of these transactions also involved equity participation). Junk bonds had suffered very high default rates until the late 'seventies, when they appeared to be less risky. In 1984, Equitable invested $540 million to help start the Bass Investment Limited Partnership, a $660 million fund for purchasing junk bonds and financing leveraged buyouts. Its partners were the wealthy Bass family, in Texas, and Drexel Burnham Lambert, the investment firm that dominated the junk bond business. The fund, later renamed The Investment Limited Partnership and, finally, Airlie Group, had an excellent track record in its first five years. Investing largely in LBOs, it reported annual profits of about 20 percent. In 1987, Equitable allocated $500 million on a standby basis as part of $1 billion bridge loan fund that Donaldson, Lufkin & Jenrette assembled to provide temporary financing to companies going through leveraged buyouts or mergers before permanent financing could be arranged.

Equitable was not alone among insurance companies in buying junk bonds and real estate during the 1980's; high investment yields were in tremendous demand everywhere by institutions and by average people. Yet while some insurers were highly exposed in one or the other of the two enhanced-return investments, Equitable was unusual in taking very large stakes in both. So long as the junk bond and equity real estate markets held up, the company profited from their high yields, and the GIC problem seemed to be manageable.

While modern in appearance, Equitable Tower, with its enormous painting by Roy Lichtenstein, reprised Henry Hyde's theme of using architecture as both image-builder and investment.

CHAPTER XX

CAUGHT WITHOUT FUEL

W ith its transition from life insurance company to consumer investment supermarket launched, Equitable altered its image in the mid-1980's. Although the name given it by Henry Hyde remained the legal one, advertising copy identified the company as The Equitable Financial Companies. The corporate symbol of over a century — the Goddess of Protection, at once warlike and maternal — had already been modernized in a way that made her shield so flat that she became known informally in the Equitable family as "the pizza lady." Then the company stopped using the Goddess altogether.

Where the recent "There's Nobody Else Exactly Like You" advertising campaigns had concentrated on the varying needs of average middle-class people, the Society's new advertisements targeted a more upscale, ambitious market with hints and symbols of ease and wealth. One slogan was "Live the Good Life"; some ads in the mid-'eighties featured images of luxury yachts. The style of the company's annual reports also changed. During the Eklund years, they had looked and read like socially concerned consumer magazines, with articles by officers counseling readers about the economy and America's needs. But under Carter, they were less advisory and more glossily promotional of the style of personal wealth — less *Consumer Reports*, more *Town & Country*.

The most visible image of the new Equitable was the striking new Home Office building, which opened in 1986 at 787 Seventh Avenue, the other end of the block on which the twenty-five year-old former headquarters

stood. Twenty years earlier, Equitable's Home Office and investments in nearby real estate, including the Time & Life Building, had helped transform the Avenue of the Americas into one of New York's most striking business districts. The idea now was that a new Home Office, near another of Equitable's investments, the Sheraton Hotel, might do the same for Seventh Avenue. The new limestone and granite edifice was called Equitable Tower. Eighty percent of the old Home Office building was sold to Nippon Life, which renamed it the Paine Webber Building in honor of its main tenant, the securities brokerage. The entire block (including the new and old Home Office buildings and a galleria between them) was called Equitable Center and managed by Equitable. Equitable intended to occupy less than one-third of the office space in the new building, with the remainder leased at high rates to law firms, banks, and other companies. Following the principles of decentralization, many departments that had previously been under one roof were dispersed around the city and country as self-sufficient, freestanding divisions or subsidiaries.

Planning for the new building had begun under Coy Eklund and was propelled by the head of real estate, Benjamin Holloway, who took advantage of eye-catching, massive architecture and public art. Of course, there was nothing new about constructing grand new buildings to advertise Equitable's strength and relevance, or about earning income by leasing space. Henry Hyde had used this dual strategy with 120 Broadway when he "built for glory."

Benjamin Holloway (on left with a model of Equitable Tower) supervised construction of the new Home Office (right, in front of the old Equitable Building) near Times Square.

This time the symbol was not an allegorical statue group but three high arches — one set over the main entrance at street level, the other two, fifty stories up, over three-story windows facing west from the enormous, elegantly appointed boardroom and east from the Equitable dining room. "You have to go back to the Renaissance to find work on this scale," said the new building's architect, Edward Larrabee Barnes.[1]

Much of the public art in Equitable Center had a spirit of whimsy on classical and modernist themes, all on a grand scale. In the galleria, abstract murals looked down on oversized sculptures of an elephant and rabbit; and running along the upper walls of the bar of an adjoining restaurant, Palio, was a mural of a twelfth-century horse race. By far the largest and most arresting work was Roy Lichtenstein's *Mural with Blue Brush Stroke*, a 68-foot by 32-foot pop art painting that the artist painted in place — a cartoon full of references to art history, including the works of

Matisse, Léger, and more recent painters (including Lichtenstein himself), some of them partially wiped away by a gigantic hand to reveal office windows looking down on the atrium. The coolly intellectual, huge Lichtenstein, like Equitable Center itself, had a style of hip monumentalism whose message was no different from that of Hyde's first Home Office building at 120 Broadway, with its unusual height, exotic paneled elevators, and dramatic public art: each building announced that The Equitable was on the cutting edge, big, and powerful.

Around a corner from the Lichtenstein, near the elevator bank, hung a smaller, more energetic, and grittier work of art that, some thought, best represented Equitable's traditions. Thomas Hart Benton's realist mural, *America Today*, completed in 1931, is a ten-panel panorama of average Americans at work, at play, and — in one vivid scene of the Great Depression — in need. Brimming with vitality and human spirit, it was painted at the

New School for Social Research, in Greenwich Village; Benton's compensation was free use of brushes and paints. After fifty years, the New School sold it to a dealer, and New York Mayor Edward Koch asked Equitable to purchase it to prevent it from being broken up. Equitable paid $3.4 million for *America Today*, restored it, and hung it for all to see. Later, John Quincy Adams Ward's statue of Henry Hyde, who had so well understood the hopes and needs of people like those portrayed in Benton's painting, was placed nearby.

Equitable's art collection had been growing since the 1960's. At the suggestion of a board member, Nancy Hanks, former chairwoman of the National Endowment for the Arts, the Society collected systematically in the 'seventies and 'eighties, when it was advised by the Whitney Museum of American Art. The collection of 350 works, including the public art, was valued at over $7 million. Paintings, drawings, prints, and sculpture in Equitable's collection of American art were placed on display on the executive floors in the company's fifteen-story section of the Tower. Added later was a collection of portraits of early American business and political leaders, including many former directors of The Equitable, on loan from the New York Chamber of Commerce. Equitable also supported artists through a gallery for the Whitney Museum in the atrium and sponsorship of arts-related projects. Occupying donated space in Equitable Center was the Arts Resource Consortium, which comprised an arts library, a publisher of art books, and lawyers providing free legal assistance for artists. This corporate support for the arts was well received. A reviewer for the *New York Times* wrote that it was "a commitment to art on the part of a prominent American corporation that is as generous and innovative as any before."[2]

As when Hyde built his first Home Office, there was a mercantile purpose to the building and its large, lively use of the arts. Art, said Holloway, was "a way of attracting the kind of tenant we want, at the rental

Equitable bought Thomas Hart Benton's classic mural "America Today" at the request of New York City Mayor Edward Koch, seen here with John Carter and one of the panels.

prices we are asking." Carter said he hoped the center would have wide public appeal as "a valued urban oasis enjoyed by New Yorkers and visitors alike." The building seemed to meet both goals, judging by the number of rented offices and the crowds who paused in the cavernous atrium and concourse to view the art, make use of the adjoining shops and restaurants, or simply to relax.[3]

The sense of the new in the building seemed to reflect The Equitable's sometimes experimental developments in insurance marketing in the mid-'eighties. One effort at broadening the market was the placing of agents in kiosks and at sales desks in shopping malls and banks. During a trial run in 1984 in a mall in Indianapolis, an Equitable kiosk was staffed by three shifts of agents, two to a shift, eleven hours a day, working a computer that printed up personalized proposals for customers. Agents reported that people kept coming up to ask where the Equitable had been all these years. In another trial begun by Executive Vice-President and Chief Insurance Officer Ruth Block, in 1983 Equitable arranged with the First National Bank of Chicago to establish The Equitable Asset Management Account (TEAM), a cash management account, to be marketed by Equitable agents at fees lower than the usual commissions. Neither of those two experiments succeeded. After a disappointing test run in Colorado, the TEAM initiative was ended; and though sales and prospect-gathering at the kiosks seemed satisfactory, agents were not comfortable in them.

The ideas kept percolating. In 1984, Equitable established the Bank Marketing program in which Equitable agents set up shop in banks (sometimes near real estate agents and stockbrokers) to create a one-stop financial planning center where people could buy products that banks did not sell, among them life insurance and annuities. The pilot

program was in a bank in Des Moines; others were installed in banks in Alaska, New York, Pennsylvania, and Texas. By affiliating its agents with respected banks, Equitable hoped to make itself and its agents more visible to its target market of upscale people.

Those programs were intended to expand the job of an insurance agent. Another project, which took several forms, was to develop distribution of some insurance products outside the agency force. This notion had recently been rejected by Eklund, who was convinced it would undermine career agents, but it returned to the agenda in 1984 with John Carter's enthusiastic approval, so long as distribution of traditional life insurance remained exclusive to agents. The question was who should run this program and some other new ventures. Carter had opposed bringing in outsiders, but Block believed that the originality of the ideas required new blood. In the middle of 1984, she recruited a thirty-year veteran of Connecticut General Life, Peter Wilde, to start up and administer the alternative distribution project and a foreign venture.

Wilde nurtured relationships with the agency managers, most of whom were suspicious of distributing insurance products outside traditional paths, even as a complement to normal distribution. An early step was to drop the term *alternative distribution*, which he thought could be interpreted as a criticism of the agency force, and replace it with the less loaded *additional distribution*. One plan was to sell annuity and insurance products through banks and insurance brokerages under the brand name of Integrity. Another operation, called Tandem Financial, involved distributing annuities through the thousands of stockbrokers in the Merrill Lynch network. Equitable owned three-fourths of Tandem.

Besides creating additional distribution, Wilde developed an international operation. After a possible acquisition in Britain fell through, he succeeded in Japan, where life insurance was thriving in that country's savings-focused culture. Equitable enjoyed a long history of friendships in Japan, and the finance ministry was interested in having Equitable introduce variable life insurance. The process of gaining the necessary approvals moved slowly, but Equitable eventually founded a subsidiary with a $100 million infusion. While many Japanese insurance agents were part-timers, most of them women, Equitable of Japan's agency force consisted largely of male career agents.

Although these ambitious new programs brought in substantial premium income — additional distribution produced about $2 billion in new premiums annually — and were forecast to have strong futures, they were not long lived, for two reasons. Carter's initial support of additional distribution faded under pressure from the agency force, but the chief reason for the end of the period of marketing experimentation in the mid-1980's was that Equitable was running short of capital. Starting up and running the new products until they became profitable was expensive, and surplus strain from obligations concerning the large volume of new sales made great demands on Equitable's liquidity. Wilde looked back: "I like to tell people it's like the tank corps out in front of the infantry as they advance. The tanks run out of gas and stop. The drivers call back and somebody says, 'I knew we forgot something.'" Remembered Robert W. Barth, then head of Insurance Operations, "The bombs had started falling by the middle of 1987, and that was when we started to contract. The single most important reason for the end of Integrity was the shortage of capital."[4]

Consultants and some officers had predicted there would be plenty of money to carry the new programs through their expensive start-ups until they became profitable, but

now those assurances seemed overly sanguine. The jumpy economy took part of the blame; the stock market crash in October 1987 substantially sliced DLJ's and Alliance Capital's profits and left Equitable's profits almost 60 percent lower than in 1986. The new Home Office building went over budget. So did sales costs for the popular new universal-variable Incentive Life policies. And downstreaming, rather than controlling costs as intended, increased them by freeing subsidiaries to expand unrestrained. "John Carter will not turn the faucet off organizational growth," Wilde told colleagues at a conference in 1986. "It's not his style. I've asked John, 'How will we continue to grow?' He said, 'We can't stop. I can't tell anybody in the organization not to grow after I've primed the pump.'" As Wilde told his associates, "The problem is, the faster you grow, the more you lose." Wilde soon left for Citibank to develop an international insurance business.[5]

Some problems were recognized and dealt with. One was Equitable's old bailiwick of group life and health insurance, which were performing erratically. Group insurance had become extremely volatile, alternately losing and making money. Equitable's largest group contract was still in Pittsburgh, but instead of covering 60,000 industrial workers at U.S. Steel, it was for the 27,000 employees of the University of Pittsburgh. In 1986, at Carter's instigation and with the intention of spinning off the company's group business, Equitable merged its large group life and health operation with the Hospital Corporation of America, an owner of for-profit HMOs and hospitals. The new entity was called Equicor. Despite encouraging projections about synergistic fit, Equicor was an awkward operation, with its management divided geographically between New York and Nashville, and administratively between Equitable's and HCA's different operations.

Leo Walsh took charge and soon closed the New York offices, but Equicor continued to require large subsidies.

All these projects and ideas were costing some money at least some of the time, but the overwhelming problem was the guaranteed interest contract. The bailout plan had not succeeded. "GIC worries drove everything," remembered Walker Lewis of Strategic Planning Associates. In 1986, Equitable's GIC business totaled $15.6 billion in obligations whose average guarantee was 12 percent, while Equitable's average investment yield was only 10 percent (including substantial one-time capital gains from sales of real estate). In other words, the company was losing 2 percent on one-fourth its assets. An internal task force recommended in 1987 that the GIC business be capped and cut back by almost $1 billion a year from its current $15 billion level. More reserves were set aside and, in order to boost yields, more investments were made in junk bonds and real estate. Among insurance companies, Equitable became the second largest investor in real estate. By 1989, 39 percent of the company's assets were in real estate or junk bonds, well above the life insurance industry's average of 27 percent. With those two markets at their highest in the late 'eighties, Equitable's investment performance was among the best in the insurance industry. Yet investment yields still could not match the high rates the company was contractually obligated to pay on the huge block of GIC obligations.[6]

Although the task force optimistically projected that GICs would be in the black by the early 'nineties, there were serious bouts of second-guessing the GIC actuarial model, the business decisions taken to make the contracts more flexible in order to be competitive, and the drive to build assets that lay behind the introduction and expansion of the business. Some critics suggested that the 'seventies'

environment of interest rate volatility was inherently inhospitable to a product designed to work according to the law of averages. Many fingers were pointed at Leo Walsh, who ran the business side of GICs; some also were aimed at the work of the deceased Harrison Givens, who had drawn up the actuarial model and introduced some of the flexibility that eventually caused trouble. Only a few years earlier, in the late 1970's, GICs had been widely hailed within Equitable as a triumph at meeting the goal of building assets. Harry Garber, who had quietly criticized GICs as early as 1976, summarized their rise and decline:

> This business just became sensationally popular. We were the first, and we were the most aggressive. And that became the danger: it was too successful. At one stage 40 percent of our new business was in GICs. Nobody looked at the dark side. Later, Coy Eklund decided to pass Metropolitan Life in size, and so GICs became important to him. Leo Walsh was the father of all this, so he kept piling all the chips on the table. Then there was the unanticipated inflation. Also, we assumed that the individual employee was the decision-maker — but the employer was the decision-maker. The law of averages collapsed on you.

The result, Garber ruefully admitted in 1993, was mixed: "The GIC concept was both a tremendous success and a tremendous failure."[7]

Still, in 1986 Equitable seemed strong in many fundamentals. It was the third largest insurer in assets, was responsible for 5 percent of all life insurance in force in America and was the second largest manager of pension and other tax-exempt funds. While capital was not growing dramatically, there was every anticipation that the restructuring of the company and changes in the economic environment

The Equitable's Board of Directors in 1988: (left to right) Don Johnston, Joseph L. Dionne, John T. Hartley, Jewel S. Lafontant, Raymond H. Wittcoff, Robert M. Hendrickson, James R. Jones, William T. Esrey, Leo M. Walsh, Peter S. Heller, Winthrop Knowlton, Eleanor B. Sheldon, George J. Sella, Jr., John B. Carter, Harry D. Garber, Richard H. Jenrette, Richard S. Ross, Marion Stephenson. (Not present) Norman C. Francis, James J. Howard III, Arthur L. Liman.

would lead to an increase of profits and sur-plus. A new indicator of success entered the picture. As banks and savings and loans every-where in the country became strained or failed during the 'eighties, state and federal regulators as well as private credit-rating agen-cies began to ask tough questions of all types of financial institutions. Until 1984, the insur-ance industry had been rated by only one

Equitable, 1959–1989 (in billions)

| YEAR | NET INCOME | | ASSETS | CAPITAL |
	PREMIUM	INVESTMENT		
1959	1.1	0.4	9.7	0.6
1964	1.3	0.5	11.7	0.8
1969	1.8	0.7	14.0	1.0
1974	3.0	1.0	17.6	0.6
1979	5.8	2.1	30.8	1.1
1984	7.9	3.6	46.0	1.4
1989	7.4	4.3	61.7	2.1

rating agency, A. M. Best, but as an increasing number of insurers faced troubling erosions of their capital base, Standard & Poor's, Moody's, and other agencies started to rate the insurance industry after studying financial statements and investment portfolios and rigorously interviewing officers. When The Equitable's ratings were released, they were surprisingly low, indicating to officers and outsiders alike that the company was weaker than most people had believed. These credit-rating reports, which were closely read in the financial community, influenced prospective policyholders in their choice of an insurer, and markdowns in ratings were publicized by agents for competing insurers.

If the rating agencies' concerns were troubling, so were worries about John Carter's management. He could be either arbitrary or indecisive. In 1984, after complaints by agency managers that universal-variable policies were being processed too slowly by the regional service centers, Carter called for the resignation of some of the staff without consulting with the top officer involved, Ruth Block. Block, in protest, threatened to resign, and though Carter publicly backed down, Block took early retirement in 1986, after thirty-five years at Equitable. Carter also allowed his schedule to be so tied up in conferences that Walker Lewis warned he was caught in "meeting entrapment," and executives complained they were spending more time on process than on actual management. Some directors were disappointed that Carter appeared to view his job as that of ambassador for Equitable, and though he was very well regarded in the insurance industry, that job had been assigned by the board to Chairman of the Board Robert Froehlke. Day-to-day management was left to Walsh, who became Chief Operating Officer and Senior Executive Vice-President in 1986. Directors noticed that when Carter did not have an answer for their questions, he usually turned to him. While Walsh supplied the information, board members expected more from Carter. Still, the directors, many of whom were themselves CEOs struggling with times of unprecedented challenge, sympathized with Carter's position: he had inherited many trying problems, including GICs, and he faced a difficult economy. And his decisive handling of the acquisition of Donaldson, Lufkin & Jenrette and of the spinoff of group and health insurance showed that he was capable.[8]

Early in 1988, Froehlke retired and Carter suggested that he be elected Chairman of the Board and that Walsh succeed him as President. This did not please the directors. They wanted to see Carter take command, not give it up, and they also were unhappy with reports of unusually tense relations and high resignation rates among officers. The outside directors on the board's Organization and Compensation Committee met in April and agreed it was time to inform Carter of

their dissatisfaction. According to directors who were present, they wanted only to advise Carter generally that they expected changes, not instruct him to take any specific action. But after Joseph Dionne, the committee's chairman, conveyed their concern, Carter quickly dismissed Walsh. Richard H. Jenrette, who had come to The Equitable with his firm, Donaldson, Lufkin & Jenrette, in 1985, and who had been Chief Investment Officer since 1986 (when Walsh became Chief Operating Officer), was elected Chairman of the Board and given all responsibility for investments; Carter, as President and CEO, oversaw insurance operations.

Walsh himself believed that Carter had been the messenger of the board's decision to fire him. In any case, Carter's chief of staff specified language for the press release that, for such announcements, was unusually blunt in indicating that he had been dismissed. This press release appears to have suggested to business editors that something was amiss at The Equitable. Within a few months, there appeared in the business press a series of critical probes of the company. The first, in the September 1988 *Forbes*, was titled "The Mess at Equitable Life." While it mentioned difficulties at other companies, the article concentrated on Equitable and characterized Walsh's departure as a boardroom coup. The piece stimulated questions and doubts about the company's situation and future among two important audiences, the company's agents and prospects for Equitable policies. The *Forbes* analysis was followed over the next two years by faultfinding articles in the *Wall Street Journal*, *Business Week*, and other magazines.

Carter did take charge. Concerns over the cost of decentralization stimulated him to revise his mission. He no longer aimed at making Equitable a high-growth financial supermarket but planned to return the company to something akin to its traditional role as a provider of protection and savings. He pleased the critical directors by taking more control over daily operations, cutting back on his personal staff, and instituting an inside expense review and a series of cost-cutting transactions. Tandem and Integrity were sold to Merrill Lynch and an Australian company, National Mutual, respectively. The leasing company, one of the few survivors of the diversification movement of the 'seventies, was also sold. Alliance Capital Management was taken public in a limited partnership in which a majority interest was owned by Equitable and minority interests were held by Alliance employees and the public. Carter ordered a study of Equitable of Japan but decided not to pursue a sale. And after internal studies of Equicor concluded that a further investment of as much as $1 billion would be needed for it to grow into a major player in health insurance, Carter in 1990 sold Equitable's interest in the subsidiary to CIGNA at a $100 million capital gain. Equitable, which had pioneered group insurance eight decades earlier, was now out of it completely.

The financial environment changed once again. The year 1988 was superb for investments until commercial real estate began to slide, and then in the middle of 1989, the junk bond market crashed after insider-trading and other criminal charges were brought against Michael Milken of Drexel Burnham Lambert, the investment firm that dominated the market in below investment-grade bonds. The consequences of these two collapses were grim for anybody who was heavily exposed in either real estate or junk bonds. But they were especially hard for The Equitable: outside of only a couple of other life insurers, the company had the largest concentration in the industry of investments of both types. Rather than sell the real estate at depressed prices, Equitable set aside $415 million from the general account as a loan to the GIC segment. Equitable's capital position kept dropping well below peer companies.

Standard & Poor's cut the company's rating to A+, four notches below the top rating of AAA.

Despite these unhappy reports, Carter's mood and that of many of his subordinates remained buoyant in 1989, so much so that he sliced a $100 million cost-cutting plan in half. "There were not a lot of people to talk to about bad news," Harry Garber reminisced. "The company was living off of optimistic forecasts." Jerry de St. Paer, then a financial officer and later Chief Financial Officer, compared this time of energetic cheerfulness with the phony war in the early months of World War I, when whole nations convinced themselves that the problem could be solved by patriotic fervor and a few quick cavalry attacks, only to be trapped in trenches, confronted by tanks and machine guns.[9]

As sanguine as Carter seemed, he explored major initiatives in three directions: demutualization, a merger, and spin-offs of Equitable's investment arms. The idea of taking the company public had been reviewed several years earlier by a subcommittee of the Corporate Development Committee. Harry Garber, who had chaired the demutualization study, was a leader of the industry committee that drafted the New York demutualization law. For a while in 1986 and 1987, in meetings with agents and staff members, Carter and Walsh spoke of going public as a lively option. But that spark of interest died. Not only did demutualization seem too complicated and expensive, but Carter was optimistic that such an overhaul would not be needed.

The merger project was a possible marriage with Metropolitan Life. It was afoot during the winter of 1988–89. At Jenrette's suggestion, Carter seriously explored a consolidation that would have created the world's largest life insurance company, ahead even of Prudential. It seemed a good match. Met Life, the old industrial insurer, had a predominately middle-class policyholder base; Equitable's was upscale. Together they would

Joseph L. Dionne.

manage assets total-
ing more than $200
billion. A committee
of Equitable officers,
led by Garber, met
several times with a
Met Life group in
an apartment in
the Stuyvesant Town
complex that Met
Life owned. Equitable directors who were
informed showed interest, but except for some
officers who believed that the merger would
solve the company's financial problems, management was not happy with the idea. Before it
was formally presented to the board, Met Life,
the larger partner, indicated that the top jobs
in the new operation would go to its officers,
and Carter ended the discussions.

The third idea, which Carter discussed
with increasing frequency, was selling part or
even all of DLJ and Alliance Capital, which by
then were regarded by the Board of Directors
as Equitable's crown jewels. Brief negotiations
with a potential buyer of DLJ had ended in
1987 when its officers showed no enthusiasm
and the price seemed low. When Carter again
broached the idea of selling DLJ and Alliance
Capital two years later, they were providing
over half of Equitable's earnings. Alliance was
rapidly becoming one of the largest money
managers in the country, and a respected survey of the investment business gave DLJ top
rankings in three investment specialties and
ranked it fourth out of 500 American firms in
institutional sales and trading. All this indicated to Equitable's Board of Directors that
the two subsidiaries were more valuable to
Equitable than whatever price they would
bring on the current depressed market.

The proposal to sell the crown jewels, the
persistent GIC losses, the drop in credit
ratings, the collapse of the high-yield invest-

ment program, and Carter's seeming indeci-
siveness in the face of evidence of serious
difficulties — all together stimulated the
directors to act boldly. While the directors had
been careful not to go around Carter and talk
to his subordinates, Joseph Dionne took
Garber aside at a Christmas party and interro-
gated him about the Society's problems.
Garber spoke frankly about the very thin ice
under the company's skates. Dionne then
spoke to other directors and gradually built
support for a major move.

On May 17, 1990, he and other outside directors on the Organization and
Compensation Committee, Eleanor Sheldon,
Winthrop Knowlton, Raymond Wittcoff, and
Arthur Liman, met in Liman's office in the
Paine Webber Building. Sheldon recalled,
"There was an increasing sense that things
were coming apart, that we did not have a handle on the company. We knew the company
was in very poor shape." The group decided
to ask Carter to resign. It was a startling step
for a major U.S. business at that time. A few
years later, the boards of IBM, General
Motors, and several other large corporations
would relieve CEOs of their jobs. But until
then, for a board of directors of a major company — and a mutual insurance company at
that — to even talk seriously about discharg-
ing a CEO was an extremely rare event.[10]

To replace Carter, the board chose Jenrette,
whom many directors knew not only within
Equitable but from his other activities as a leading figure in the investment and securities
businesses. He was deeply experienced in
capital formation, he was respected in the international financial community, and as a relative
newcomer to The Equitable and not locked
into what Dionne called a career "silo," he
could apply necessary detachment to the solution of problems. Liman agreed: "In Dick we're
bringing in someone who was not breast-fed at
the Equitable" (a quote that, when repeated,

Dan W. Lufkin, Richard H. Jenrette, and William H. Donaldson in the first year of their new securities firm.

upset several long-time members of the company's family). Later that day, at a scheduled board meeting, Carter and Jenrette (who had been forewarned) were asked to leave the room. The committee presented its observations and proposal to the board, which approved. The directors' sense of urgency was enhanced by their awareness that Jenrette had recently been approached by the nominating committee of the New York Stock Exchange regarding the exchange's chairmanship, but had made no decision. (The position went to his former partner William H. Donaldson.)[11]

Early the next morning, Dionne broke the news to Carter, who took it with remarkable calm. "It was a very civilized breakfast," Dionne recalled. "He obviously was a man of great faith who accepted the hand that was dealt him. He certainly turned out to be the man I thought he'd be, if not the manager." An Equitable officer who had heard the news, Bob Jones, ran into Carter on the street that afternoon and proffered his condolences. Carter's response was to reach out: "Bob, don't be sorry. Let's talk about *you*." And he went on to discuss Equitable's future.[12]

Richard H. Jenrette was born on April 5, 1929, in Raleigh, North Carolina, the son of an insurance agent. Showing aptitudes for both journalism and management, as a teenager he covered sports for a Raleigh newspaper and organized local baseball teams; and at the University of North Carolina he was president of his fraternity and edited the campus daily newspaper, while also doing well enough in the classroom to be elected to Phi Beta Kappa. After two years selling insurance for New England Mutual, he served a tour in the army, then went back to insurance sales. He soon realized it was not his life's calling ("I wanted to control things; I wanted to run things," he later said emphatically), and, returning to school, earned an MBA at Harvard Business School. He went to work for Brown Brothers, Harriman, a private bank in New York involved with the family of Edward H. Harriman, who had played an important role in The Equitable's history at the turn of the century.[13]

As he was learning the banking and investment business, Jenrette was approached by two friends from business school who also were working on Wall Street, William H. Donaldson and Dan W. Lufkin. They asked him to join them in founding a new firm that would provide specialized research in emerging growth companies for the rapidly increasing population of institutional investors. Most institutions, including Equitable, depended for at least some of their investment research on statistical departments in securities firms, and these departments subscribed to the conventional wisdom of concentrating investments in the common stocks of well-known blue-chip companies, like General Motors, General Electric, and U.S. Steel. These stocks had performed exceptionally well during the 1950's (giving trusteed pension plans an advantage over Equitable's pension business), but the three men believed that they had become overpriced. Their new firm would specialize in providing research about companies like Haloid Xerox, which had a new type of copying technology. The trick was to seize the opportunity before the big, old-line securities firms realized it was there. "If a new company could have very low overhead, it could get under the radar of the larger firms," Lufkin later explained. Donaldson, Lufkin & Jenrette (DLJ) opened its doors in 1959 with six employees — three staff members and the three founders, who paid themselves salaries of $7,500 in the first year (a $1,000 raise for Jenrette), shared profits, and made no policies without unanimous agreement. "Our philosophy was one of partnership and complementary areas of expertise and experience," Donaldson recalled.[14]

DLJ became an extremely successful securities firm specializing in institutional research (an early client was The Equitable). The founders earned a reputation for contrarianism by exploiting niches in the securities markets and, in 1970, successfully challenging the Wall Street establishment and making DLJ the first New York Stock Exchange member firm to be publicly owned. After Donaldson and Lufkin departed for other activities, Jenrette took over DLJ just as it encountered the demanding period of the mid-'seventies, when the government deregulated previously fixed commissions on securities sales at the same time as the economy was in a shambles. "I felt like old Mother Hubbard whose cupboard was so bare," he looked back. "There we were with rising interest rates, rampant inflation, and unfixed commission rates. It seemed like the end of the world." Jenrette regards life as a continuum between difficult challenges, or what he calls "defining moments," and this was one of them: "When the market would collapse and everyone would think it was the end of the world, I'd get optimistic. I'm basically a contrarian. I'm somewhat that way in the corporate world. I think I do my best work under adversity." DLJ survived its trials to build successful operations in new fields, including money management in its Alliance Capital Management subsidiary. Years later, Jenrette would say that leading DLJ through that rough period was the best training he had for the challenge he faced at The Equitable.[15]

Jenrette in the 1990's at Millford, his plantation near Columbia, South Carolina.

Jenrette was president of the Securities Industry Association in 1984 when he met John Carter at a U.S. Senate hearing on deregulation of the financial services industry. The two men agreed that the walls between specialties would be broken down inevitably; before long, DLJ was acquired by Equitable, to which Jenrette went as Vice-Chairman of the Board. His friends expected him to soon retire to go into academia or indulge his hobby of restoring antique houses, but he surprised them by becoming busy at Equitable. He effectively protected entrepreneurial DLJ and Alliance Capital against bureaucratic restrictions, advised in the investment area, visited agencies and agents' meetings, learned about the company's long history (he especially admired Henry Baldwin Hyde, another contrarian), and completed his CLU certification, which he had started in the 'fifties. While he believed in the principle of decentralization, he thought Equitable had gone too far and had too many overlapping entities. Soon after taking full control of investment operations on Leo Walsh's departure in 1988, Jenrette merged Equitable's own two investment management companies into one, Equitable Capital Management, and ended the duplication among many jobs in the corporate holding company and the life insurance company.

Although he got along well with John Carter, Jenrette seemed out of place in the Home Office, with its constant infighting for position. "He was terrible at office politics — he would even admit when someone on his staff made a mistake!" said Brian O'Neil, who later became Chief Investment Officer. "What he had going for him was that he was such a big person outside Equitable. This impressed directors but upset other officers." Jenrette also found Carter's regimen of seemingly endless meetings stifling: "Sorry I've been so locked up in meetings lately — help!" he wrote a colleague in desperation.[16]

Jenrette's own management style was more personal and informal. It differed markedly from the dramatically charismatic approach of many of his predecessors. "Farsighted and balanced, not carried away with the moment, and an information sponge," was how he was characterized by Dave H. Williams, the head of Alliance Capital Management. Jenrette preferred meeting with subordinates in small ad hoc groups or one-on-one, and in moments of crisis would go to the center of the action — a trading floor during a stock market collapse or a corporate relations department struggling to control a

false rumor — to provide assistance and encouragement. After a disagreement, he was known to telephone apologies to people to whom he felt he had been unduly sharp; he was widely referred to as "the last gentleman on Wall Street." This combination of qualities, and the success that it helped bring, attracted a loyal following. "He has the ability to get very good people to work very hard for him," said John Chalsty, DLJ's Chief Executive Officer. "There is an extraordinary and perhaps unique loyalty to DLJ that characterizes the firm. Dick's legacy has a lot to do with that."[17]

In his public appearances, Jenrette's speeches often appeared to be works in progress. Pacing behind the microphone, absentmindedly fiddling with his eyeglasses, he tossed out rushes of financial data in his soft Carolina accent. He often argued his main point by repeating one or two financial figures, especially the ratio of the company's capital to its liabilities, which he considered the single most reliable indicator of health. Sometimes he made a point through wry humor. Appearing before Equitable's agency managers for the first time as chief executive, in July 1990, he was introduced by former Equitable President Coy Eklund, who in his remarks appeared to absolve recent Equitable CEOs of responsibility for the guaranteed interest contract. Rising to the podium, Jenrette observed that since it appeared that none of his immediate predecessors had approved the GIC, he could only surmise that it had been invented by Henry Hyde. The punch line brought down the house and made the telling point that the time had come for The Equitable to face up to its past.

The question about Jenrette in the spring of 1990 was whether — already wealthy and, at sixty-one, probably within a few years of retirement — he was motivated to assert the necessary urgency and dedicate the enormous energy needed to revive The Equitable. But he spoke of the situation not just as another business challenge but in terms of personal commitment: this, he said, was a mission to restore Henry Baldwin Hyde's creation to greatness. Like Hyde, he was happiest and functioned at his best with his back against the wall, in a fight for survival. In the tense moments before Equitable made its public stock offering in 1992, he wrote his staff:

Perhaps as an incurable romantic, on principle I am unwilling to agree that once a nation, a company, an individual, or even a fine old house fall on hard times, they cannot be resurrected.... Yes, Virginia, I believe in turnarounds. And The Equitable is going to be another example that there is inherent virtue in great names that can be repolished and made to shine again.[18]

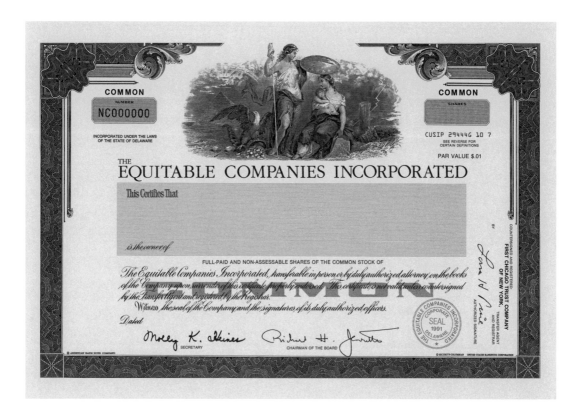

The new stock certificate used the same Protection Group image
that Henry Hyde had placed on The Equitable's original shares in 1859.

CHAPTER XXI

TAKING EQUITABLE PUBLIC

"At the time Dick became CEO, the threat to the company was *severe*," Equitable Chief Financial Officer Jerry de St. Paer recalled. The danger of a fifteen-year drain on capital finally had become obvious to all, as had the requirement, after several years of experimentation, for decisive direction. People demanded firm corporate purpose. "It really has to do with who's running the show," Robert Barth, Equitable's head of Insurance Operations, told a journalist soon after Jenrette took over. "I think a sense of urgency is instituted at the top."[1]

Jenrette's decisive first steps were aimed at reestablishing public and business confidence in the company by bolstering the bottom line and imposing strong central direction. He announced he would cut $100 million in annualized expenses in the first 100 days (he had originally aimed at $200 million until his staff protested). Some of the savings came by reducing the employee population, eventually by one-fourth to 4,800, and by trimming luxuries that had accumulated during the fat years, including a fleet of limousines and weekly distributions of fresh flowers on executive floors. Other cost reductions came by adding new financial controls and merging operations.

As Jenrette cut away, he sent calming signals to the anxious agents to minimize defections and policy surrenders by their clients. The Home Office told the agents that Equitable would understand if they sold other companies' policies in order to close a sale. Although new sales dropped, most agents

maintained their affiliation with Equitable. To further assure the agents and to indicate to the insurance industry and regulators that he was as attentive to their concerns as he was to financial issues, Jenrette determined that he should have at his right hand, in charge of Equitable's insurance operations, a senior, well-known authority with a background outside the company. Donald L. Bryant, Sr., retired in Florida, recommended Joseph J. Melone, president of Prudential. Impressed by Melone and his reputation in the insurance industry, Jenrette offered him Equitable's number two position as President and Chief Operating Officer. Melone arrived at The Equitable in November 1990. A longtime high officer at Prudential, Melone also had a distinguished background in business and insurance education. He held a Ph.D. from the University of Pennsylvania, was a former professor at the Wharton School of Finance, and had written books on pensions and insurance. "His insurance experience perfectly complemented my Wall Street background," Jenrette happily looked back.[2]

Melone's appointment strongly boosted the spirits of the company as a whole and, most important, of the agents, who were taking a beating from competitors. His knowledge of insurance and unflappable personality were respected nationally and internationally (for years he was responsible for the operations of Sony-Prudential Insurance Co. of Japan). In giving up the second most important job at the world's largest insurance company, he implicitly endorsed Equitable's health and future.

Joseph J. Melone joined Equitable in the fall of 1990 and took chief responsibility for the agency force.

As head of agency operations, Equitable appointed Mel Gregory, a favorite with the field force who had been with The Equitable as agent, manager, and officer for more than three decades. He and Melone promptly took to the road to visit agencies and provide quiet encouragement. Back in New York, they and their staffs worked backbreaking schedules to answer agents' questions and offer assurance that The Equitable would survive.

Jenrette noticed the difference immediately. Where he had been receiving as many as sixty telephone calls a day from agents alarmed by reports of Equitable's situation, the calls largely stopped when Melone came on board. Jenrette was freed to concentrate on corporate strategy — most particularly on his ambitious and extraordinarily complicated two-pronged plan to raise large amounts of capital and take Equitable public through demutualization.

With cost-cutting well under way, the focus changed to raising capital in order to replenish the depleted surplus. The business environment was not good late in 1990: a gradually deepening recession in the United States was coupled with worldwide caution in capital markets after Iraq's invasion of Kuwait. What should be done? Selling part or all of Alliance or DLJ would provide little short-term help since, in a time of worldwide financial retrenchment, they would have fetched low prices — assuming that Jenrette and Equitable's Board of Directors even wanted to divest what many people called Equitable's crown jewels. The only solution seemed to lie in going public, that is, in demutualizing. Not long after he was elected CEO, Jenrette sat down with a pencil to outline his thoughts. In handwriting cramped by the tension of the moment, he started, "Equitable needs to raise new capital — $500 million at *minimum*." Over the next three pages he went point by point through the pros and cons. In July 1990, at a lunch of senior officers, he summarized his conclusions in a five-point plan. Equitable should cut costs at an annualized rate of $162 million and redesign products to make them more profitable. It should develop new ways to provide incentives for employees and rebuild the company's image both internally and externally. And the company had to end the capital squeeze that had affected so many decisions and stimulated the downgrading of its credit ratings. To do all this meant going public and raising half a billion dollars in a public offering to preserve the crown jewels and produce a better and stronger company.[3]

In his initial cryptic jottings, Jenrette had written, "Time to get ready for rainy day is *when* sun is shining." But the sun was no longer shining over Equitable. The slide in commercial real estate became a collapse, and many previously solid deals crumbled. For example, almost ten years earlier Equitable had loaned more than

$100 million to the developers of 1.5 million square feet of space in three new office buildings in New Orleans at 13 percent interest. The owners went under, Equitable foreclosed, and now the space could be rented out only at low rates. Problems also reached buildings in which Equitable had an equity stake. In October 1990, Equitable and its partners put into bankruptcy a large office building at 1515 Broadway, in Times Square. Intended to forestall what were deemed to be worse problems in a rapidly declining real estate market, the bankruptcy ended up on the front page of the *New York Times* and stimulated a suit by Manufacturers Hanover Trust, the lender to Equitable and its partners. (The suit was later settled.)[4]

While its investment problems were widely publicized, Equitable was not alone in having them. As a national recession deepened during the last half of 1990, and the country slowed down in anticipation of a war in the Persian Gulf region, other well-established mutuals, including Mutual Benefit and Mutual of New York, took writedowns of hundreds of millions of dollars for bad real estate loans and below-investment grade bonds. Where there had been no failures of life companies in 1981, there were twenty-seven in 1989. One of the most successful life companies of the 'eighties was Executive Life, which had invested mostly in junk bonds and had produced one of the industry's highest investment yields. But after the crash of the junk bond market, Executive Life would be seized by the California Insurance Department in the spring of 1991.

At Equitable, there had been hopes that GIC losses would be less than $100 million in 1990, but as investment returns plummeted they turned out to total $415 million, after writedowns for poor performing assets. Insurance operations continued to lose money, $300 million in 1990 alone. Something had to be done — and quickly. Jenrette decided that the only solution was to raise a huge amount of money by taking the company public.

It was a bold decision for any company even in good circumstances, but given Equitable's precarious financial situation and the intricacy and unfamiliarity of the demutualization process, the most serious concern was whether the task could even be carried off. Said Equitable director Hooks Burr, "Some thought demutualization would be a good idea, but I thought, 'This is so complicated we're just whistling Dixie.'" Only 125 mutual property and life companies had gone public since 1850, just fifteen of them since 1970. All had been small companies, and even then, judging from recent experience, the process of meeting the demands of regulators, policyholders, and financial markets had been onerous at best. The largest previous demutualization had taken more than three years, when Union Mutual Life, a Maine company, was converted into a publicly owned disability insurer, Unum Corp., in 1986. The New York Insurance Department was certain to be cautious in its application of the state's 1988 demutualization law. Among the difficult questions involved was the rights of voting policyholders in the old mutual to compensation, in the form of stock in the new company or a cash payment, in exchange for their control. Recently, an attempted demutualization of an insurance company in another state had been halted when regulators required that the company compensate policyholders more than it wished.[5]

Equitable's sense of urgency was extreme: significant progress had to be made by June 1991. That deadline had been set by the credit rating agencies when they indicated that if there were no improvement in the company's condition or serious prospects by then, they would further lower the company's ratings. Lower ratings could very likely set off a wave of policy surrenders.

To move the process along, Jenrette set up a committee of top officers and appointed as its coordinator Jerry de St. Paer, who had a background in international finance and a flair for making deals. He had worked on the initial public offering of Alliance's stock, the sale of the leasing and group insurance operations, and the study of a possible sale of Equitable of Japan. In June 1990, Jenrette strolled into his office, told him about his plans to take Equitable public, and asked him to help organize it. There would have to be two steps, he said. First, because demutualization would be time-consuming, they would need to raise money up front through a private placement of debt that later would be convertible into equity in the demutualized company. Then, once demutualization was approved, there would be an initial public offering of additional stock. De St. Paer confidently predicted that the first step would be completed in a year, the second in another year, but most of the insurance industry was convinced that Equitable would not become a public company for four or even five years — if at all, since the task was so daunting. In the end, de St. Paer's predictions were off by less than three weeks.

As project coordinator under Jenrette and Melone, de St. Paer worked closely with other officers, including Harry Garber, who, having drafted the New York demutualization law, was intimately familiar with the legal requirements; General Counsel Stephen Friedman, who oversaw the intricate legal problems; Chief Financial Officer Thomas Kirwan, a former CFO at CBS who was widely respected in and outside the company; and Chief Administrative Officer William McCaffrey, who in his more than thirty years at Equitable had become famous for his ability to meet deadlines and oversee complex projects. The early planning group of a dozen officers rapidly grew to more than 100 actuaries, accountants, public relations experts, financial people, lawyers, investment bankers, and other specialists whom de St. Paer assembled for weekly and, later, daily meetings.

The fall of 1990 was spent developing a draft prospectus and a plan for the two-step procedure. Equitable was advised by investment bankers at Donaldson, Lufkin & Jenrette, Goldman, Sachs & Co., and J. P. Morgan & Co. Jenrette, as a student of history, was delighted by the symmetry of Morgan's involvement: eighty years earlier, Pierpont Morgan and his bank had owned a majority interest in The Equitable and had played a key role in making it a mutual.

But before the demutualization plan was implemented, it was almost upset by a wild rumor of Equitable's imminent doom. On November 27, 1990, a small investment newsletter in London published an article suggesting that an unnamed American life insurance company had missed a bond payment, was almost insolvent, and soon would declare bankruptcy. The story was seen by a reporter for Reuters, who prepared to send it out over an international newswire. In fact, there was an insurance company in such straits (or almost — insurers can become insolvent, but they cannot file for bankruptcy protection). That company turned out to be a small Massachusetts-based insurer, yet the Reuters reporter believed it was Equitable.

Just why this false assumption was made, and why other reporters as well as bankers readily believed it, will never be known for certain. Very likely, there was a cumulative effect of the recent news of the bankruptcy of the Times Square building in which Equitable had an interest and memories of Equitable's executive shakeup, downgraded credit ratings, and well-known GIC woes. Whatever the reasons, on the morning of November 27, the Reuters reporter called Equitable's Home Office for a comment and spoke with Nancy Amiel, in the Corporate Relations Department. She denied the allegation so fervently that she found herself shouting. But the story went out over the

Jerry de St. Paer (left) was project coordinator for the intricate demutualization effort. Among the other key members of the group were Chief Financial Officer Thomas Kirwan (center) and Chief Administrative Officer William McCaffrey.

Reuters wire and around the world through newswires, information services, and financial institutions. Amiel and her colleagues were swamped by dozens of calls, from as far away as Japan, demanding more information.

Jenrette was out of the country, and Melone, who had come over from Prudential only two weeks earlier, was in a meeting. Equitable got some support from other institutions. An officer of Rothschild & Co., an investment bank, telephoned to volunteer both a public denial of the rumor and an endorsement of Equitable's security. And the Deputy Superintendent of the New York State Insurance Department, Kevin Foley, told the Dow Jones Newswire that the department had no reason to believe the rumor. The report went out that afternoon, too late to stop two institutional investors from cashing in $100 million of Equitable's commercial paper, which represented one-third of the company's short-term unsecured debt. When a large bank called Melone for a comment, he realized what Amiel already knew: the rumor was taking on a dangerous life of its own. "That was when we got into crisis mode," he later said. After Melone's wife was stopped in a shopping mall by a woman who told her that her family's retirement rested in Equitable's hands, he telephoned the

woman with reassurance. As Equitable struggled all afternoon and evening to snuff out the rumor, the threat of a collapse of public trust in Equitable — and perhaps even a run on its assets — loomed large. When the bankruptcy rumor reached one of Equitable's retirement plan clients, DeFrancisci Machine Corp., a Queens manufacturer of pasta machines, the workers walked off the job until they were told their plan was safe. "The employees were ready to rip my face off," the office manager told *Business Week*. "Fortunately, Equitable people convinced everybody it was nonsense."[6]

While there never was concern during this crisis about Equitable's ability to pay claims, Melone later said, there was a deep worry that a sudden collapse of public trust would frighten policyholders into fearing for the future of their benefits and making a panicky run on the company's treasury. Jenrette agreed: "I thought that if it had gotten out of control, it could have been a national crisis because of Equitable's size and importance. It was a scary period." He telephoned secretary of the treasury Nicholas Brady and Federal Reserve chairman Alan Greenspan, two old friends, as well as the president of the New York Federal Reserve, Gerald Corrigan, to assure them that the story was untrue and warn them of the consequences of a run on Equitable. In case a run did start, Equitable established a $2 billion fund of liquid assets to be available at two branches of the Chase Manhattan Bank to allow policyholders to cash in their policies. There was no run, Jenrette and Melone were sure, because the agency force advised their customers that there was no reason to worry. Said Melone, "Thank God for the agents. The result is they hung in."[7]

News reports of the bankruptcy rumor said nothing about the company's plan to demutualize, which had been kept under wraps. On December 11, 1990, Jenrette announced the plan with the words, "This is a step that opens the future for us." That day, Standard & Poor's cut Equitable's credit rating again, from A+ to A and put the company on a credit watch, meaning that further rating reductions were possible. The agencies gave the company half a year to demonstrate progress. "The company recognizes its need to seek significant external capital," the agency commented. But qualified as this appraisal was, it seemed almost like a vote of confidence compared with what was being written about Equitable.[8]

Asked if he had regrets about his two-year effort to demutualize Equitable and take it public, Jenrette replied that the only one concerned the unfortunate but unavoidable timing. "Obviously I would rather have done it at another time," he said. "But we didn't have the luxury of waiting. So we had to damn the torpedoes and go full speed ahead." The company's problems were deepened by a lengthy recession as well as by intensely critical articles in the business press that, Jenrette and his colleagues believed, unfairly focused on short-term, cyclical problems (such as real estate, which until recently had been very profitable) or on other problems that the company was on the way to solving (for example, guaranteed interest contracts).[9]

What the press was ignoring, he thought, were Equitable's historic resilience and vitality in a number of areas. Its 8,300 agents included the largest groups in the industry of Chartered Life Underwriters, Chartered Financial Consultants, and licensees of the National Association of Securities Dealers. The average size of new policies, at $200,000, was four times the industry average. Equitable was one of the largest money managers in the world, with over $100 billion in third-party assets under management. The stock of one of the money management arms, Alliance Capital was tripling in value, while Donaldson, Lufkin & Jenrette was one of the more successful Wall Street firms (DLJ's bridge loan fund, in which Equitable had provided a pool of stand-by funds, steadily earned more than 20 percent and was called by one financial writer "the envy of every firm on Wall Street"). Equitable Real Estate Investment Management was the country's largest manager of real estate assets for pension plans and other tax-exempt organizations; its subsidiary, COMPASS Management and Leasing, founded in 1990, was becoming one of the nation's largest property managers.[10]

But these strengths were generally skirted by the critics. "There was a time when the first name of the company seemed to be *troubled*," remembered Jerry de St. Paer. "We were always referred to as 'troubled' Equitable." All this bad news had one benefit: it helped convince the New York State Insurance Department that the company's situation was sufficiently serious that demutualization was necessary and had to be accomplished quickly ("The press made our case for us!" Jenrette said). Yet the steady barrage of critical reports discouraged Equitable's people, especially the agency force. The articles themselves tested the agents' and customers' loyalty and confidence; so did the reprints of those articles that were circulated by agents of other insurance companies. The frustration was bitter. When George Karr, the head of the prototype mega-agency in Philadelphia, was presented with an award by an industry agency managers organization in March 1991, he devoted almost half his acceptance speech to attacking "company bashing," which, he told the other managers in the room, was as dangerous to the life insurance industry as the threatened loss of federal tax advantages:

> As many of your companies have followed Equitable into the group business, the health insurance business, the variable life business, etc., your company may follow us into the bad press business. I hope for you and your agents that you'll miss this one. But should you not, I would hope that no one is waiting to recruit your career agents and falsely scare your policyholders into moving their business.[11]

To cheer his colleagues, Jenrette often quoted slogans that had helped him during tough times at DLJ. "Turn a problem into an opportunity" was one. Another was an encouragement to ignore the nagging commentators: "Perception lags reality." A third, which he offered when roadblocks appeared, was a picturesque quote from Albert Camus: "The dogs bark but the caravan moves on."[12]

Jenrette, after a long career of working in and around publicly owned enterprises, believed that the discipline of bottom-line accountability to stockholders would be good for Equitable. Yet he admired some aspects of the culture of a mutual company: "I don't want to convert it — I think Wall Street is too frantic, too hyper," he told a reporter soon after he became Chief Executive Officer. Then he added, "But it may be too much the other way here." His faith in demutualization initially was

not widely shared at The Equitable, which throughout its history had promoted itself as a mutual in either function or legal status. According to an old, widely held conviction among mutual insurers' agents, employees, and policyholders, mutuals were more successful, effective, and socially responsible than stock companies because they did not focus on short-term profitability. Raymond Wittcoff, a board member, had shared this conviction, yet he was won over in part by contemporary events in another part of the world:

> What changed my thinking on this was two things. First, financial exigencies; we had to raise new capital. And the other — which may sound far afield — was the revelation that some of the world's worst environmental degradation was caused by nonprofit companies in Eastern Europe. The culture of a company depends on the people running it, whether they have integrity and a high sense of social responsibility. People of this caliber may be found in both mutuals and stock companies.[13]

Doubts about demutualization were especially strong in the agency force, which for decades had been citing mutual status as a selling point against stock-owned insurers. Jenrette recalled: "One of the traumatic moments was when we revealed the demutualization plan to the agents, who had been weaned on the mutual concept." To bolster his argument, he presented stacks of financial data demonstrating that mutuals were no longer as successful as they had been. While income and assets had grown, capital simply had not kept up. In 1970, mutual companies had controlled two-thirds of the life insurance industry's assets and half its capital; but by 1989, they held less than half the industry's assets and only one-third its capital. Mutuals had also lagged behind other financial institutions: the level of capital in securities firms had been one-third that of mutual insurers until 1984; but only five years later, the securities industry was far better capitalized — $38 billion as against $25 billion. Jenrette said, "To me, these figures were the handwriting on the wall for mutuals."[14]

Citing these data, Jenrette, Melone, Harry Garber, agency head Mel Gregory, and other officers told the agents and agency managers that the company's survival depended on quickly raising large amounts of capital, and that the best way to do that was to demutualize. They assured agents that stock ownership, handled responsibly, would produce a healthier Equitable as well as a windfall of shares in the new company for the more than 2 million voting policyholders. The Old Guard and the National Agents' Forum eventually accepted the idea. "Joe was so important in providing credibility, calming agents, and keeping spirits up. He deserves much of the credit," Jenrette said of Melone. At Gregory's suggestion, Equitable recognized agents and managers who remained especially loyal during this time of troubles by naming them to a new honor organization, The Founders Circle. The names of the more than 500 honorees were placed on a plaque located near the Equitable boardroom under a tribute that begins, "When we needed you, you were there."[15]

The effort to bolster morale called on the resources of the company's traditions and history. Jenrette ordered that the company's oldest symbols, the Protection Group and the Goddess of Protection, be brought back and used in the company's literature and advertising. The Protection Group was placed on the stock certificates that were issued during the demutualization — a fitting decision since the Group had made its first appearance on the shares that Henry Hyde issued when founding The Equitable in 1859. In November 1991, The Equitable Life Assurance Society, which

recently had been just one of several subsidiaries, once again became the company's main operating entity through a reorganization that created a new holding company, The Equitable Companies Incorporated. Under Equitable Life were placed the four other operating companies: Equitable Variable Life; Alliance Capital Management; Donaldson, Lufkin & Jenrette; and Equitable Real Estate Investment Management.

Jenrette's original plan for the demutualization was to assemble a small syndicate of strategic investors to make a $500 million subordinated loan that, after demutualization, would be converted into shares totaling no more than 25 percent of the company. Important prospects included U.S. institutions, such as the General Motors pension plan and European and Japanese investors, some of them reinsurers that had made surplus relief loans to Equitable. Among the companies that expressed interest was American International Group, the American insurance giant known for acquiring troubled companies, which suggested a possible $1 billion bid for 100 percent of Equitable. The idea never reached the stage of a formal proposal; in providing nothing for the policyholders, it almost certainly would have been blocked by the New York State Insurance Department.

The company that did become the major investor was introduced in January 1991 by one of Jenrette's business school classmates. Michel François-Ponçet was the chairman of Banque Paribas, a French bank whose American offices were located in the Equitable Tower. When François-Ponçet called on Jenrette, he heard him speak of Equitable's need for an investor. He suggested Claude Bébéar, the head of a rapidly growing French insurer, Groupe AXA, in which Paribas had a minority interest and on whose board François-Ponçet served. In the previous sixteen years, Bébéar had transformed

Melone at The Founders Circle plaque with agency managers Don Hobley (Troy, Michigan) and Derry Bishop (Woodland Hills, California).

AXA from a small regional company to the second largest insurer in France and eighth largest in Europe, with $42 billion in assets and $8 billion in capital. After Jenrette expressed interest, François-Ponçet flew to Paris to speak to Bébéar, who he knew was looking for an American acquisition.

Groupe AXA was descended from some of France's oldest insurance companies, including a fire insurer founded in 1817 in Normandy that came to be called Groupe Ancienne Mutuelle. In 1958, Bébéar, a graduate of one of France's elite schools, the Ecole Polytechnique, went to work for the company as an actuary. He quickly rose through the ranks, founded the company's Canadian life insurance subsidiary, and in 1974 was made head of the parent company, by then called Mutuelles Unies. Based in Rouen, it was the twenty-fifth largest insurer in France.

A charismatic and ambitious man with a grand vision of life — he hunted big game and motivated his people by taking them on rigorous group trips to the Sahara and China — Bébéar began a dizzying round of mergers that turned Mutuelles Unies into a major European property and casualty company. Explaining his business strategy, he said, "I buy, consolidate, and go off again. I am not a gambler; my risks are calculated." He diversi-

Claude Bébéar, the head of the French insurer Groupe AXA.

fied into other businesses, including a fur company, a publisher, and a cement factory, then sold them off at a profit. In the mid-'eighties, Bébéar moved the headquarters to Paris and began looking for large acquisitions abroad. He had already undertaken some foreign transactions but came to see that they were too small: "The best way to defend against global companies taking over your business is to become a global company yourself and spread your risks abroad. When you try to go global, you have to be big in the countries in which you are doing business." When he changed the company's name in 1985, he chose AXA, which had no intrinsic meaning, largely because it could be read and pronounced in any language. "Our strategy," he said, "is to be one of the biggest players in the world."[16]

An obvious target was the huge U.S. market. In 1990, AXA tried to acquire a California-based property and casualty insurer, Farmers Group, as a part of a large hostile takeover bid by Sir James Goldsmith, the British financier. After the takeover collapsed, AXA was approached by several U.S. insurance companies seeking financing, but Bébéar turned them down. Then, in January 1991, Michel François-Ponçet paid him a call to tell him about his conversation with Jenrette:

Michel came to me and said, "Equitable wants $500 million and is willing to give 25 percent of the company for it. You should take a look at it." I wanted a larger stake, but Michel urged me to go with him to see Dick anyway. I was pessimistic when I went to New York; I thought it would be just a courtesy visit. During lunch, I decided it was possible to do something, but not for 25 percent. I told Dick, "I must be a major shareholder." I offered $1 billion for 40 percent of the company. I told Dick, "You think you need $500 million, but if you get $1 billion, it will provide the psychological shock that is needed to revive the confidence of the agency force so business will come back."

The two men got along extremely well. After conversations with his Board of Directors and staff, Jenrette told Bébéar that he was prepared to talk further.[17]

Although the two companies had no history of relationships, there turned out to be several overlaps from the era of The Equitable's foreign empire. An AXA subsidiary, the British life insurer Equity & Law, had helped Henry Baldwin Hyde gain a license to sell insurance in Britain in the 1870's. One of AXA's French companies occupied offices in Rouen that had once been used by an Equitable agency. AXA later acquired Equitable's former Paris headquarters, which James Hyde had worked so hard to have built early in the century. An Australian insurance company in which AXA later acquired a majority stake, National Mutual, not only had purchased Equitable's Integrity line of products but had owned Equitable's former buildings in Melbourne and Sydney — the same buildings that, at their construction a century earlier, had excited respect for "the shrewd businessmen who manage the affairs of The Equitable Life Assurance Society."

At their initial meeting in January 1991, Jenrette and Bébéar forged a close relationship. AXA offered $1 billion for 40 percent of Equitable.

In order to gather data for negotiating a formal contract, dozens of AXA representatives came to the Home Office to pore over Equitable's books. "The news about Equitable was very negative, but the newspapers didn't know the company," Bébéar recalled. "After studying the company for five months, we knew it very, very well, and it was clear it was not in such bad shape. It was a good company that had been poorly managed, but we were sure it would recover very quickly with Dick and Joe Melone." Negotiations went on through the spring of 1991. After the 1990 financial figures showed further decline in Equitable's surplus, Jenrette and Melone fully concurred that AXA's potential stake should be raised to $1 billion.[18]

The agreement was subject to the approval of the New York State Insurance Department, which, guided by the new demutualization law, was expected to be characteristically conservative. Not only would the transaction give a substantial, if not dominating, stake in Equitable to a foreign company, but it and the subsequent demutualization would concern the interests of the mutual company's policyholders. Equitable's demutualization had to pass two crucial, challenging requirements imposed by the law.

One of these requirements was the so-called "closed block" of assets. Worried that a hostile raider might buy a majority interest in a demutualized company and then misuse the assets guaranteeing life insurance policies, the state legislature and regulators had insisted that insurance guarantees be protected inside a subsidiary-like entity akin to a trust fund in its invulnerability to invasion. De St. Paer likened the closed block to "an invisible force field inside which the hard-core mutual liabilities and assets are stuck." Calculating the size and type of assets to go into the block was a complicated task requiring detailed estimates of mortality rates and investment yields for years into the future. In the end, Equitable's closed block contained more than $7 billion of assets, none of which could be used in another way by an outside investor.[19]

The other key requirement was a "market test." It concerned the rights of voting policyholders to shares in the new stock company in exchange for giving up their interest in the old mutual company. The issue was how many shares should be issued or, put another way, what the price of the shares should be. Besides fairness, this question concerned the strategy of the demutualization, since the larger the proportion of shares distributed to policyholders, the smaller would be available for investors. Equitable had hoped to raise capital through a private placement at a fixed percentage that would give the new outside investors no more than 40 percent in return for their $1 billion investment. But the State Insurance Department disagreed with that approach. The price, it said, must not be fixed by Equitable and its investment bankers; rather, it must be set by an initial public offering of the stock and an adjustment for trading in the aftermarket for sixty days following the IPO. The department believed that this test of the public market would hold off any perception and subsequent legal action to the effect that policyholders had been shortchanged. The department was cautious on other issues, as well. For instance, it prohibited officers and directors from buying Equitable stock for two years after the demutualization, even through stock option plans.

These concerns were understandable considering the unprecedented size of the transaction and the department's historic fears about violations of public trust. Still, the regulators' circumspection was frustrating for Jenrette and his colleagues, who were eager to bring a quick solution to the continuing nagging questions about The Equitable's solvency — which had made the demutualization plan necessary in the first place. The closed block complicated matters by removing valuable assets from the table during negotiations with bidders, and the market test required an initial public offering that would be cumbersome, expensive, and, possibly, difficult to sell. (The demutualization and capital raising eventually cost more than $70 million, all of which, including fees to the insurance department's advisors, was paid by Equitable.)

The market test also imposed a large degree of ambiguity on the transaction: nobody would know until after the offering what the stock was worth and, therefore, how many shares AXA and other investors got for their money. All that was known for sure was that, according to the agreement between Equitable and AXA, AXA would end up with a stake of at least 40 percent and no larger than 49 percent; if the initial share price warranted a stake of 50 percent or more, the excess would be placed in convertible preferred stock not to be exchanged for common shares until 1994, should AXA choose to do so. "Like playing Russian roulette with $1 billion" was how Jenrette wryly described his and AXA's situation under these provisions. Despite the indeterminacy of future ownership, Equitable had no choice but to take the gamble; as Jenrette would say, "the caravan had to move on." Otherwise, the deal with AXA would be canceled with a penalty, leaving the company in worse shape than ever. In June 1991, as the two sides went into their final intense talks, A. M. Best reduced the company's credit rating, and Moody's announced it was putting Equitable under review for a downgrade.[20]

The Equitable-AXA agreement was approved by the New York State Insurance Department and signed by both parties on July

Flanked by Equitable General Counsel Stephen Friedman (left) and Debevoise & Plimpton attorney Martin F. Evans, Jenrette testifies at the state hearing on the demutualization.

18, 1991. Under it, AXA provided $750 million in secured notes and $250 as a subordinated loan to strengthen Equitable's surplus. The loan increased Equitable's capital by 42 percent and raised the important capital-to-liabilities ratio from 4 percent to 6 percent. Board members and officers would be exchanged, and there would be cooperation in developing and marketing products. At the press conference for what Equitable and AXA called "a global partnership," while Bébéar said that AXA's stake was controlling, he made it clear that Jenrette was still in charge of Equitable. And Jenrette spoke of "this challenge of turning around the Equitable and bringing it back to greatness."[21]

AXA's $1 billion check arrived just in time. "A day later and there might have been a run on Equitable," Jenrette said. That was because a day later Mutual Benefit Life, a large, respected old-line company that also had invested heavily in commercial real estate, was taken over by New Jersey insurance regulators. The largest insurance company seizure in history, it could have started a run on Equitable had the company not been strengthened by the timely announcement of AXA's $1 billion investment. Even with the boost in confidence of the AXA financing, Equitable's policyholders were withdrawing money at near-record levels; during the first nine months of 1991, loans and surrenders totaled $1.88 billion, half again as large as in the same period in 1990. The percentage of investments categorized as "troubled" continued to grow, despite substantial markdowns for deflated real estate values. These withdrawals and losses further drained the company's liquidity, already strained by the remaining GIC obligations.[22]

Yet there were indications that Equitable was putting some of its problems behind it.

New York Stock Exchange Chairman William H. Donaldson, Jenrette, and Bébéar celebrating on the floor of the exchange as Equitable's stock was listed for the first time.

While the company reported a pretax loss of $898 million for 1991, about two-thirds of it resulted from additional loss reserves in the GIC business, which was officially discontinued in that year; GIC obligations would decline as old contracts expired, until termination in 1995. As a result of the new capital that was raised, surplus was down only $16.7 million in 1991, much less than the previous year's $203.5 million. Subsidiaries continued to be shed; the company began negotiations to sell Equitable of Japan.

Equitable and its advisors got to work writing the prospectus for the public offering and demutualization to submit to the voting policyholders, who had to approve the plan with at least a two-thirds vote before any further steps were taken. The 180-page prospectus was extraordinarily candid about Equitable's situation. Arguing that they were protecting Equitable against possible lawsuits, the lawyers

for the company, Debevoise & Plimpton, and for the underwriters, Davis Polk & Wardwell, insisted that the disclosure section of the prospectus contain not only all the bad news but several worst-case scenarios. Even more dour than many of the disparaging reports running in business magazines, the prospectus became a source for a number of frightening articles. The document's frankness was praised by analysts: "This is a level of disclosure that could force everybody to go to a higher level," one analyst told a reporter. Another considered

Guaranteed Interest Contract Business, 1980-1995
(in billions)

EQUITABLE LIABILITIES

1980	8.3	1989	10.6
1983	11.6	1992	4.7
1986	14.3	1995	0.0

it proof that Equitable had mended its ways: "These documents make it clear that this is a company that is going through pains to clean up its act." While Jenrette understood the lawyers' concerns — in annual reports, he drafted wary cautions under such titles as "What Could Go Wrong?" — he called the document "one of the scariest prospectuses I've ever seen" and complained, "I had to go out and sell the damned thing." In the end, the deal was done with unusually little litigation, which was quickly resolved. In 1994, Equitable was cited by the Association for Investment Management and Research as the insurance company with the best record for honest public reporting.[23]

The task of selling the public offering was made no easier by the inhospitality of the economic climate. The country was still foundering in recession in the summer of 1992. Real estate, in which Equitable had almost one-third its assets, was in terrible shape; one of North America's largest developers, Olympia & York, went into foreclosure, and Equitable in late 1991 and early 1992 wrote down the value of its real estate assets by $1.3 billion. Then in May, *Barron's* ran a brutally critical piece about Equitable's real estate investments. Now there were fears about the success of the initial public offering, on which the final stage of the demutualization depended. According to the agreement with AXA, Equitable had to raise a minimum of $300 million or the deal was off. With a maximum of 50 million shares offered, that meant a price of $6 a share, which, though well under what Equitable had hoped for, was deemed by some skeptics to be too high for the weak marketplace.

First came the effort to win policyholders' approval. Over eight days beginning Saturday, March 15, 1992, William McCaffrey and his staff at Equitable sent out the thick prospectus for the demutualization plan with other information and a ballot. The packages, each totaling 336 pages and weighing 1 pound, went

to the almost 2.2 million voting policyholders — people who held participating life, health, and annuity policies and contracts (holders of variable policies, which are nonparticipating, were ineligible). The Great Mailing, as it was called, broke volume records for the U.S. Postal Service in three categories: personalized packages, self-designed envelopes, and Priority Mail distribution. To deal with policyholders' queries, a special twenty-four-hour information hot line with its own toll-free telephone number was set up. There were automated responses for simple questions, but 125 operators, most of them with backgrounds in insurance or finance and many fluent in several languages, were ready to handle complicated matters, most of which concerned worries that the demutualization would affect policy benefits. The hot line took almost 100,000 calls in the first four weeks (the peak was almost 11,000 on March 23).

In late April 1992, in another step in the long process that Jenrette likened to running a gauntlet, Equitable officers testified in a public hearing of the Insurance Department. The only serious criticism of the plan came from the administrator of the 50,000-member United States Steel & Carnegie Pension Fund, a large holder of Equitable policies. While praising the demutualization strategy, he complained about the formula for distributing shares to policyholders, which allotted at least three shares per participating policy, the number to be based on the policy's size, type, and age. When one policyholder asked if demutualization was a guarantee that Equitable would stop making mistakes, Jenrette responded frankly: "I can't guarantee that we won't make mistakes in the future, but we do have a new management team."[24]

It came to a head in May. Of the almost 900,000 policyholders who voted on the plan, an overwhelming majority of 92.3 percent approved it. Then New York State Insurance

The Equitable's flag flies from the New York Stock Exchange. This event was highlighted on the cover of The Equitable's 1992 annual report.

Superintendent Salvatore Curiale sanctioned the plan. On May 26, Equitable filed the registration statement with the Securities and Exchange Commission with an estimated price between $11 and $14 a share. The underwriters were top-tier: Goldman Sachs, DLJ, J. P. Morgan Securities, Salomon Brothers, and Banque Paribas (the bank of the invaluable go-between, Michel François-Ponçet).

Next, the transaction had to be sold to prospective investors. For several weeks in June, Jenrette and Melone traveled around the country and abroad on a twenty-eight stop road show to make Equitable's case to pension funds, investment firms, mutual fund managers, and other institutional investors. With them, besides the investment bankers, was a team of Equitable financial people. Jerry de St. Paer (now Chief Financial Officer after Tom Kirwan died of a heart attack in May) explained the unfamiliar demutualization plan and the IPO. Chief Investment Officer Brian O'Neil, in presentations and in response to questions, minutely laid out the quality of the company's assets down to and including the occupancy rates of Equitable-owned buildings. And Senior Vice-President Gregory G. Wilcox described the company's plans for its future as a public company. Many of the people who came to hear the presentation knew Jenrette well from his years at DLJ, and held him, Equitable's investment subsidiaries, and the investment bankers serving as Equitable's underwriters in high regard. A boost came from the insurance industry in Japan. Melone, de St. Paer, and Coy Eklund had many friends there; and Yul Rhee, a longtime Equitable officer who had accompanied three generations of the company's CEOs on visits to the Far East, and

Aritoshi Soejima, a friend of Eklund's, were extremely helpful. Ten Japanese insurers announced in July that they would invest $61.5 million, and some Korean insurers also took an important stake.

The job of finding buyers was not easy. There were many hard questions about real estate and about the market test to determine how many shares AXA would receive. One investment banker had complained, "I can't tell you I think this is a good idea because I won't know what the terms are until the damn thing is done. How can I make a recommendation? No one's ever seen anything like this." While Jenrette had not believed Equitable would get the $14 price, he was surprised by the negativity the offering encountered and especially by the pessimism about real estate. On July 15, Equitable, on the advice of its underwriters, dropped the price to $9 a share.[25]

The next day, Equitable became a stock company once again when its shares were listed as EQ on the New York Stock Exchange. All 50 million shares were sold to raise $450 million in additional equity capital. On July 22, AXA's $1 billion in loans were converted to equity comprising 49 percent of Equitable, with an additional 7 percent in convertible preferred stock to give it a potential stake of 56 percent. The policyholders' portion of almost 16 percent of outstanding stock was smaller than had been expected; but it provided policyholders with a stake in a recovering company at no cost to themselves. By the end of 1992, Equitable's shares were trading for almost $15; by September 1994, when they were at $31, equity held by policyholders was worth $800 million, and Equitable was a much stronger, better capitalized company than it had been in years.

Equitable Comes Roaring Back

Insurer Remodels And Branches Out

By MICHAEL QUINT

When Richard H. Jenrette was named chairman of the Equitable Life Assurance Society in 1990, the company resembled one of the run-down mansions he is fond of restoring. The company had a glorious past, but had been neglected and mismanaged to the point of ruin.

But in the last four years, Equitable has been renovated. And with a rebuilt foundation — the capital base needed to grow and assure policyholders that their claims would be paid — Equitable's insurance business is standing on its own and expanding rapidly.

Rumors of insolvency, which were widespread early this decade, have been replaced by glowing reports from securities analysts, as the stock price of the Equitable Companies, the parent, has more than doubled since it issued shares in mid-1992. The stock market as a whole, measured by the Standard & Poor's index of 500 stocks, rose only 13 percent in the same period.

But unlike old houses, where restoration is aimed at recreating a historical ideal, the new Equitable is not trying merely to fix its problems and return to its past.

'A Huge Savings Problem'

Instead, Equitable is pushing a new line of offerings — variable life insurance and variable annuities, whose returns to customers vary with the stock and bond markets. The offerings are tailored to well-off members of the aging baby boom generation.

Seventy-five percent of Equitable's new insurance polices are variable, and the company has 25 percent of that market, with a third of the agents — 8,000 — of the industry leader, Prudential Insurance, with 40 percent.

"We have a huge savings problem emerging in America," Mr. Jenrette said. "As more people realize that the Government just can't pay the retirement benefits they are expecting, there will be a growing concern about how to prepare for their old age."

To meet that concern, which he expects will loom ever larger in the public psyche for the next 15 to 20 years, Mr. Jenrette and a cadre of insurance executives imported from other companies flipped Equitable's line away from traditional insurance and toward variable offerings.

The variable insurance policies and annuities have the advantage of offering returns that over long periods of time should be significantly higher than the returns offered by insurance companies on traditional life and an-

Continued on Page D7

William E. Sauro/The New York Times, 1990

Equitable Life has undergone a broad renovation since Richard H. Jenrette was named chairman in 1990. Mr. Jenrette has led the turnaround from the company's board room in Manhattan.

Back on Track

After several years of steep losses, Equitable has bounced back, spurred by steady sales in its insurance and mutual funds divisions.

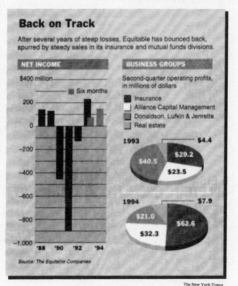

NET INCOME

$400 million

■ Six months

200

0

-200

-400

-600

-800

-1,000

'88   '90   '92   '94

Source: The Equitable Companies

BUSINESS GROUPS

Second-quarter operating profits, in millions of dollars

■ Insurance
□ Alliance Capital Management
■ Donaldson, Lufkin & Jenrette
■ Real estate

1993

$4.4
$29.2
$23.5
$40.5

1994

$7.9
$62.6
$32.3
$21.0

The New York Times

The hard criticisms of 1990–92 were left behind as Equitable, with almost triple its old capital, recovered to profitability. This story ran in September 1994.

CHAPTER XXII

REDEMPTION

Demutualization and the financial disciplines implemented before and after it succeeded by three standards: they raised a vast sum of capital, they generated growing profits, and they stimulated new confidence in Equitable by outside observers.

The recovery story can be told in words and in numbers. Starting with the number of most acute concern, Equitable's capital grew from $1 billion to $3.4 billion between 1991 and 1994. (Those figures are according to generally accepted accounting principles. Under insurance statutory accounting, capital grew from $1.7 billion to $3.1 billion.) The main sources of the increase were AXA's $1 billion investment, the $450 million raised by the initial public offering from other investors, and $779 million subsequently raised in April 1993 through an issue of 1.6 million shares of convertible preferred stock (half this amount was subscribed by AXA, whose stake in the company thereby increased to 60 percent).

Between 1991 and 1994, Equitable Life, the company's main operating entity, more than doubled its ratio of statutory capital to liabilities from 4.9 percent to 11 percent, the highest among peer life insurers ("That would have pleased Henry Hyde," Jenrette observed, referring to the founder's passion for building surplus). Standard & Poor's lifted its creditwatch warning after demutualization. Subsequently, at a time when the industry generally experienced a decline in credit quality, Equitable was one of the few insurers to earn rating upgrades. In October 1995, it was returned to an AA rating.[1]

The company returned to the black, reporting $343 million in pretax profits in 1993, $482 million in 1994, and $253 million in the first six months of 1995 (when total revenues increased by 23 percent). Investment operations continued to improve in the volatile 1990's; the portfolio's net investment yield rose from 6.2 percent in 1991 to over 7.5 percent in 1993 and 1994, despite lower interest rates in the capital markets. Total assets under management by Equitable and its subsidiaries, including Equitable's own assets and assets of pension funds and other third parties, increased by half from $126 billion in 1990 to $190 billion in July 1995.

Alliance Capital Management, into which Equitable merged its asset management operation in 1993, was the nation's largest publicly traded asset manager and fourth largest provider of tax-exempt assets. Its demand for office space in its midtown Manhattan building grew so much that when Alliance signed a new lease in 1994, its name went up on the building. Donaldson, Lufkin & Jenrette's name would also be placed on *its* building after DLJ's planned move to midtown in early 1996. One of the top four securities firms in equity underwriting volume, DLJ in August 1995 managed the largest common stock offering ever by a single manager, a $933 million offering of 31 million common shares by WorldCom that took only four days to complete after the filing with the Securities and Exchange Commission. That October, part of DLJ was sold in an initial public offering and to employees, leaving Equitable

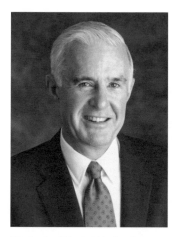  

The heads of Equitable's three investment subsidiaries: (left to right) John S. Chalsty of Donaldson, Lufkin & Jenrette; George R. Puskar of Equitable Real Estate Investment Management; and Dave H. Williams of Alliance Capital Management.

with an 80 percent stake in the securities firm, whose value was now about $1.7 billion.

In real estate, thanks to a recovery in the market and an energetic program of property sales to bring Equitable's portfolio more in line with the industry's, the company's problem loans fell from almost $400 million in 1993 to under $100 million in 1994. One controversial investment, the office building in Times Square at 1515 Broadway that had declared bankruptcy, was largely rented out in 1994 (its major tenant was Viacom, the cable television company) and had a potential capital gain. Equitable's real estate business had changed dramatically. In 1984, two-thirds of the activity in Equitable Real Estate Investment Management's $2.3 billion portfolio had

involved Equitable's own assets in the general account, while a third had involved the assets of client pension plans and other third parties. In 1988, Equitable became the nation's largest manager of tax-exempt real estate assets and did not lose the lead. By 1994, the mix of the portfolio (by then valued at $13 billion) was reversed, with the company's activity as an equity investor much smaller than its work for third-party clients. Equity real estate had constituted a third of assets during the 1980's; it made up only 10 percent in 1995. (One of the properties sold that year was Gateway Center, the historic Pittsburgh development.)

Meanwhile, public confidence in Equitable improved by the important indicators: stock price, insurance sales, and coverage by the media. After opening at $9 in July 1992, Equitable's stock rose to highs of $31.50 in 1993 and $30 in 1994; in September 1995 it was just under $27. Insurance premiums in 1994 totaled $5.4 billion, up 12 percent, the steepest growth among major life insurance companies. First-year premiums and considerations increased at more than double that rate, by 25 percent.

Of all the indicators of revival, the one that Jenrette found most satisfying, after three years

Equitable, 1990–1994 (in billions)

YEAR	CONSOLIDATED STATUTORY CAPITAL	CAPITAL-TO-LIABILITIES RATIO (%)	TOTAL ASSETS UNDER MANAGEMENT
1990	1.7	4.6	126
1991	1.7	4.9	145
1992	2.3	7.5	151
1993	3.1	10.6	173
1994	3.1	11.0	174

of enduring the media's negativity, was the wave of complimentary articles about The Equitable. After 1992, gloomy media reports about life insurers concerned other companies subjected to investigations of alleged misconduct by some of their agents or securities salesmen. Stories about The Equitable in newspapers and magazines ran under such headlines as "Equitable Comes Roaring Back" (in the *New York Times*) and "Redemption" (in *Financial World*). These articles often quoted positive reports of securities analysts. Typical were comments by Margaret Alexandre, of Salomon Brothers, who, after profits were announced in 1993, described "the renaissance of The Equitable" and exclaimed, "What a difference a year makes." Equitable, she wrote, had made "all the right moves."[2]

Equitable continued to restructure operations in many areas, including the agency force. To run insurance sales and operations, early in 1993 Joe Melone, as President and Chief Operating Officer of Equitable Life, hired James M. Benson to be Senior Executive Vice-President. Benson was a former officer and agent at Pacific Mutual Life and officer at Management Compensation Group, a consultant on corporate insurance. For several years, he had commuted between his home in California and the group's office in New York. "What particularly well suited Jim for this leadership position," Melone said, "were his technical and financial strengths in addition to his considerable sales ability." Jenrette described Benson as "one of life's real winners — a quick study who exudes tremendous vitality and energy, and is extremely disciplined and well organized."[3]

The combination of Benson and Melone was historic for Equitable: not since the very early years of its 134-year history had its insurance operations been led by two people who had not been raised in the company. The two

James M. Benson making a presentation during the long agency road show in 1993.

men also made an interesting match in their outlooks, which mingled the modern with the traditional. Melone would speak of the growing importance of strategic analysis in the life insurance business: "Macro demographic forces, including the aging of the population, and their impact on personal savings needs and longer-term financial planning, will drive the insurance business for decades to come." In the meantime, Benson, in the tradition of Pick Embry and Coy Eklund, would talk emotionally of the needs of the individual agent in the trenches out in the field: "It's a real free enterprise, no-holds-barred business, a business that's easy to get into and tough to stay in," he said of the agent's lot. "You have to have credibility to sell a product whose delivery lies in the future. It's all trust and credibility. If you have the gumption to make the calls, the company will support you with its distribution infrastructure, training, and computer support."[4]

To introduce themselves and the restored Equitable to agents and their clients, in 1993 Benson, Melone, and Jenrette made a nationwide tour of agencies, two or three cities a week for twenty-five weeks. Benson attended every session during this exhausting schedule, while Jenrette and Melone alternated. The main

Continuing the old tradition of the Home Office spurring on the agency force, Joe Melone talks with two agents during the Albany, New York, presentation on the road show.

event at each stopover was a half-day seminar where agents and managers were told the story of Equitable's financial turnaround and learned about new tools being developed for agents, such as a sophisticated computerized work station. To bolster agents' spirits, the officers also dispensed large rations of encouragement of the sort that the Home Office had been providing since Henry Hyde made a Pullman car his home away from home. "Part of it was pure reassurance," Melone said of the tour. "Salespeople generally need a lot of personal contact; selling is still a lonely assignment." Sales improved 24 percent during the six months of the road show.[5]

To improve agent retention rates, Melone and Benson began restructuring and consolidating the agency force, imposing new, tighter recruiting standards and targeting lawyers, accountants, and other professionals as prospec-

tive agents and district managers. The force became more compact, with 7,800 agents in 1994. The company also revisited the old territory of insurance sales outside the agency force. When tried in the 'eighties, alternative distribution had produced large volume before it was ended by the capital shortage. To implement a new program of what was now called complementary distribution, Melone brought back Jerome Golden, who had helped draw up the first variable life contracts. This market was expected to expand as deregulation led to ever increasing consolidation of financial services. Equitable developed a new line of annuities to be sold by banks, securities firms, Equitable agents, and others.

Since Equitable had sold or was selling off its group, health, and disability insurance arms, agents concentrated on the company's historic two core products, individual life insurance and individual annuities. Industry-wide as a percentage of all insurance sales, the market share of variable life insurance more than tripled between 1990 and 1994, from 6 percent to 20 percent. Equitable was the second largest company in the variable life business, with about one-fourth of the market. The demand for annuities and mutual funds also increased dramatically as the large, aging baby boomer generation looked for ways to save for old age and retirement. In 1994, Equitable had $1.7 billion in new variable individual annuity considerations, and sold almost $1 billion worth of mutual funds.

As Jenrette, who turned sixty-five in 1994, began to look toward his retirement, he and the Board of Directors assigned Melone and Benson increasing responsibility. In 1994, Melone, already CEO of Equitable Life, was elected Chairman of the Board, and Benson became President and Chief Operating Officer. Jenrette remained chairman and CEO of the entire enterprise, The Equitable Companies.

In returning to financial fitness, The Equitable had again demonstrated the resilience that Jenrette, in the tense times before demutualization, had described as "inherent virtue in great names that can be repolished and made to shine again." Vision and determination had helped the company through several trials over its long history. In the period of economic stringency of the 1990's,

Jenrette restored Equitable by refocusing it on business fundamentals and by taking the bold step of making it the first major American life insurer to transform itself from an undercapitalized mutual into a strong, public company. Four decades earlier, James Oates had shaken the company out of its doldrums by steering it into new ventures in separate accounts and variable products, as well as into a leadership role in social reconstruction. Sixty years before Oates, in the shadow of the debilitating fight and takeover attempts for The Equitable, Paul Morton had regained public trust by setting Equitable on the road to mutualizing, and by making it the pioneer in group insurance.

Equitable in the 1990's seems in striking ways to have come full circle back to its youth under its redoubtable founder, whose mainspring mottos, "call it *pressure*" and "*jam it through*," might have been those of a few of his successors. Henry Hyde built his Society into one of the world's great financial institutions using a global marketing strategy and a product, the tontine, that, like today's variable annuity, addressed the nagging problem of paying for old age when the economy is a "restless, booming anarchy." Whether the vigorous steps that Hyde and his successors took will be needed again cannot, of course, be predicted. History neither repeats itself precisely, nor can it be rewritten. Yet history, properly understood, often lays out pathways of understanding to guide us safely around hazards and on into the future.

SOURCES

⁓

INTERVIEWS

Walter Adlard
Nancy M. Amiel
Betty Anderson
Gerald A. Anderson
Robert Barth
Claude Bébéar
James M. Benson
Ruth S. Block
Michael A. Boyd
Paul Brown
Donald L. Bryant, Sr.
William Buhl
Francis H. Burr
John S. Chalsty
William T. Clifford
Darwin N. Davis

Gordon G. Dinsmore
Joseph L. Dionne
William H. Donaldson
Coy G. Eklund
Harry D. Garber
Jerome S. Golden
Albert H. Gordon
Lincoln Gordon
Alan D. Grant
Nancy H. Green
Mel H. Gregory
James Gurley
Eleanor Hamill
John H. Jacobus
Richard H. Jenrette
Robert S. Jones, Jr.

William Kiernan
Walker Lewis
Lester L. Lovier
Dan W. Lufkin
William T. McCaffrey
Jane C. Mahoney
Joseph J. Melone
Samuel V. Merrick
Edward Monahan
James E. Obi
John O'Hara
Brian S. O'Neil
Howard A. Osman
Yvonne Pinnow
Newton Press
John W. Riley

Frank Russell, Jr.
Jerry M. de St. Paer
Francis H. Schott
Harris T. Schrank
Thomas W. Shade
Davidson Sommers
Marion Stephenson
Leo M. Walsh
Peggy Ward
Robert Wenzlaff
Peter A. Wilde
Dave Williams
Raymond H. Wittcoff
Clarence M. Wright

ORAL HISTORIES

*In the Equitable
Archives:*

Eugene D. Badgley,
1979

Joseph L. Beesley,
1979

Ruth S. Block,
1992

Donald L. Bryant Sr.,
1979

Neil M. DeVries,
1979

Coy G. Eklund,
1975 and 1985

A. M. Embry,
1955

Don Finn,
1979

Richard C. Hageman,
1979

Benjamin D. Holloway,
1990

Calvin D. Kanter,
1992

Frank E. Kuhn,
1979

Leroy E. Long,
1979

Robert W. McCabe,
1979

Edward Nichols,
1979

John P. Pierce,
1979

John W. Riley,
1991

Edward A. Robie,
1992

Francis H. Schott,
1991

Eleanor B. Sheldon,
1993

Eloise Showalter,
1988

J. Henry Smith,
1985

Davidson Sommers,
1985

Jule E. Stocker,
1988

Other:

Robert I. Peters,
in Betty Anderson
collection, Kovacic
Agency, Pittsburgh,
Pa., undated.

ARCHIVES AND MANUSCRIPT COLLECTIONS

There are two large and, for the historian, indispensable collections of documents relating to The Equitable's history. One is the Equitable Archives. Located in the company's Home Office in New York City, the archives contain a vast amount of internal correspondence, news clippings, advertisements, photographs, and other materials concerning most aspects of the company's long history.

The other collection is the Equitable Life Assurance Society Collection in the Baker Library at the Harvard University Graduate School of Business Administration, in Boston, Massachusetts. It contains internal correspondence from the period 1859-1905 removed by James Hazen Hyde, the founder's son and intended heir, when he left the company under a cloud in 1905.

SELECTED BIBLIOGRAPHY

Albion, Robert Greenhalgh. *The Rise of New York Port, 1815-1860*. New York: Scribner's, 1939.

Alexander, James W. *Forty Years' Familiar Letters of James W. Alexander D.D.* Ed. John Hall. 2 vols. New York: Scribner, 1870.

Alexander, William. *The Equitable in the Early Days: Personal Reminiscences of William Alexander*, 1919, typescript in Equitable Archives.

—. *My Half-Century in Life Insurance*. New York: Harper, 1935.

Allen, Everett T., Jr., Joseph J. Melone, Jerry S. Rosenbloom, and Jack L. Vanderhei. *Pension Planning*. 7th ed. Homewood, Ill.: Irwin, 1992.

Armstrong Committee Hearings. *Joint Committee of the Senate and Assembly of New York to Investigate and Examine into the Business and Affairs of Life Insurance Companies Doing Business in the State of New York: Testimony*, Lyon Edition, 7 vols. New York: n.p., 1906.

Bishop, George A. *The Response of Life Insurance Companies to Changes in Monetary Policy.* New York: Life Insurance Association of America, 1971.

Bogart, Michele H. *Public Sculpture and the Civic Ideal in New York City, 1890-1930*. Chicago: University of Chicago Press, 1989.

Bruchey, Stuart. *Enterprise: The Dynamic Economy of a Free People*. Cambridge: Harvard University Press, 1990.

Bruno, Laurens F. *Memories: My Equitable Odyssey*. N.p.: n.p., 1990.

Buley, R. Carlyle. *The American Life Convention, 1906-1952: A Study in the History of Life Insurance*. 2 vols. New York: Appleton-Century-Crofts, 1953.

—. *The Equitable Life Assurance Society of the United States, 1859-1964*. 2 vols. New York: The Equitable Life Assurance Society of the United States, 1967.

Carosso, Vincent P. *Investment Banking in America: A History*. Cambridge: Harvard University Press, 1970.

—. *The Morgans: Private International Bankers, 1854-1913*. Harvard Studies in Business History. Cambridge: Harvard University Press, 1987.

Chapin, Charles. *Charles Chapin's Story, Written in Sing Sing Prison*. New York: Putnam's, 1920.

Chernow, Ron. *The House of Morgan*. New York: Atlantic Monthly Press, 1990.

Clarke, Sally H. *Regulation and the Revolution in United States Farm Productivity*. New York: Cambridge University Press, 1994.

Cleveland, Harold van B. and Thomas F. Huertas. *Citibank: 1812-1970*. Cambridge: Harvard University Press, 1985.

Clough, Shepard B. *A Century of American Life Insurance: A History of the Mutual Life Insurance Company of New York, 1843-1943*. New York: Columbia University Press, 1946.

Conklin, George T. Jr. "Institutional Size — Life Insurance," *Law and Contemporary Problems*, 17 (Winter 1952), 219-38.

Cooper, Robert W. *An Historical Analysis of the Tontine Principle*. Homewood, Ill.: S. S. Huebner Foundation for Insurance Education/Richard D. Irwin, 1972.

Coss, Jonathan. "Baseball at The Equitable," unpublished, 1994. Equitable Archives.

Creamer, Robert W. *Babe: The Legend Comes to Life.* New York: Simon & Schuster/Fireside, 1992. (Originally published 1974.)

Dear Old Greene County. Catskill, N.Y.: n.p., 1915.

Dictionary of American Biography.

Experience of Thirty-Four Life Companies Upon Ninety-Eight Special Classes of Risks. New York: Actuarial Society of America, 1903.

Fabritius, M. Manfred and William Rogers. *Saving the Savings and Loans: The U. S. Thrift Industry and the Texas Experience, 1950-1988.* New York: Praeger, 1989.

Fackler, David Parks. "An Account of the Various Dividend Systems Adapted by American Life Insurance Companies up to This Time...," Actuarial Society of America *Papers,* 1 (1889), 3-9.

Frick Committee Report. *Report to the Directors of the Equitable Life Assurance Society of the United States at its Meeting of May 31, 1905, of the Committee appointed April 6, 1905, to "Investigate and Report upon the Present Management of the Society."* Equitable Archives.

Garraty, John A. *Right-Hand Man: The Life of George W. Perkins.* New York: Harper, 1960.

Goldsmith, Raymond W. *Financial Intermediaries in the American Economy Since 1900.* Princeton, N. J.: National Bureau of Economic Research/Princeton University Press, 1958.

Goodheart, Lawrence B. *Abolitionist, Actuary, Atheist: Elizur Wright and the Reform Impulse.* Kent, Ohio: Kent State University Press, 1990.

Graham, William J. "Reminiscences of William J. Graham," unpublished, 1960. Equitable Archives.

Grant, James. *Money on the Mind: Borrowing and Lending in America from the Civil War to Michael Milken.* New York: Farrar, Straus & Giroux, 1992.

Hendrick, Burton J. *The Story of Life Insurance.* New York: McClure, Phillips & Co., 1906.

Henry Baldwin Hyde: A Biographical Sketch. New York: The Equitable Life Assurance Society, 1901.

Herrick, Clay. *Trust Companies: Their Organization, Growth, and Management.* New York: Bankers Publishing, 1909.

Hirsch, Mark D. *William C. Whitney: Modern Warwick.* New York: Dodd, Mead, 1948.

Historical Statistics of the United States: Colonial Times to 1957. Washington, D.C.: U.S. Bureau of the Census, 1960.

"History of the National Bank of Commerce in New York, 1839-1919," unpublished, 1929. Equitable Archives.

Hone, Philip. *The Diary of Philip Hone.* Ed. Allan Nevins. 2 vols. New York: Dodd, Mead, 1927.

Horowitz, Daniel. *The Morality of Spending: Attitudes Toward the Consumer Society in America, 1875-1940.* Baltimore: Johns Hopkins University Press, 1985.

Howells, William Dean. *A Hazard of New Fortunes.* New York: New American Library/Meridian Classic, 1983. (Originally published 1890.)

Hughes, Charles Evans. *The Autobiographical Notes of Charles Evans Hughes.* Ed. David J. Danelski and Joseph S. Tulchin. Cambridge: Harvard University Press, 1973.

Ibbotson Associates, *Stocks, Bonds, Bills, and Inflation: 1993 Yearbook.* Chicago: Ibbotson, 1993.

Ilse, Louise Wolters. *Group Insurance and Employee Retirement Plans.* New York: Prentice-Hall, 1953.

Institutional Investor, editors of (ed.). *The Way it Was: An Oral History of Finance, 1967-1987.* New York: Morrow, 1988.

Jennings, Robert M., Donald M. Swanson, and Andrew P. Trout. "Alexander Hamilton's Tontine Proposal," *William and Mary Quarterly,* 3rd Series 45 (January 1988), 107-15.

Jessup, Philip C. *Elihu Root.* 2 vols. New York: Dodd, Mead, 1938.

Jones, Lawrence D. *Investment Policies of Life Insurance Companies.* Boston: Harvard University Graduate School of Business Administration, 1968.

Keller, Morton. "The Judicial System and the Law of Life Insurance, 1888-1910," *Business History Review,* 35 (1961), 317-35.

—. *The Life Insurance Enterprise, 1885-1910: A Study in the Limits of Corporate Power.* Boston: Belknap/Harvard University Press, 1963.

Kennan, George. *E. H. Harriman: A Biography.* 2 vols. Boston: Houghton Mifflin, 1922.

Klein, Maury. *Union Pacific: The Rebirth, 1894-1969.* New York: Doubleday, 1989.

Kwolek-Folland, Angel. *Engendering Business: Men and Women in the Corporate Office, 1870-1930*. Baltimore: Johns Hopkins University Press, 1994.

Lemann, Nicholas. "How the 'Seventies Changed America," *American Heritage*, July-August 1991, 39ff.

Levesque, Paul A. "The Equitable in Canada, 1916-1984," unpublished, 1984. Equitable Archives.

Logan, Andy. "Building for Glory," *The New Yorker*, October 21, 1961, 139ff.

Lord, Walter. *The Good Years: From 1900 to the First World War*. New York: Harper, 1960.

Martin, George. *Causes and Conflicts: The Centennial History of the Association of the Bar of the City of New York, 1870-1970*. New York: Houghton Mifflin, 1970.

May, Earl Chapin and Will Oursler. *The Prudential: A Story of Human Security*. Garden City, N.Y.: Doubleday, 1950.

McNalty, J. Bard, ed. *The Correspondence of Thomas Cole and Daniel Wadsworth*. Hartford, Conn.: Connecticut Historical Society, 1983.

Milligan, John W. "The Entrepreneur and the Equitable," *Institutional Investor*, September 1990, 80-85.

Mott, Frank Luther. *A History of American Magazines*. 5 vols. New York and Cambridge: Appleton and Harvard University Press, 1930-1968.

Myers, Margaret G. *The New York Money Market*. 3 vols. New York: Columbia University Press, 1931-32.

Nevins, Allan. *Grover Cleveland: A Study in Courage*. New York: Dodd, Mead, 1948.

Noble, Louis Legrand. *The Life and Works of Thomas Cole*. Ed. Elliott S. Vesell. Cambridge: Belknap Press, 1964.

Nocera, Joseph. *A Piece of the Action: How the Middle Class Joined the Money Class*. New York: Simon & Schuster, 1994.

Norris, George A. *A History of the National Association of Life Underwriters*. Washington, D.C.: National Association of Life Underwriters, 1989.

Norris, James D. *Advertising and the Transformation of American Society, 1865-1920*. Contributions in Economics and Economic History. New York: Greenwood Press, 1990.

North, Douglass C. "Capital Accumulation in Life Insurance between the Civil War and the Investigation of 1905." In William Miller, ed., *Men in Business: Essays on the Historical Role of the Entrepreneur*. Expanded edition. New York: Harper Torchbooks, 1962, 238-253.

—. "Life Insurance and Investment Banking at the Time of the Armstrong Investigation of 1905-06," *The Journal of Economic History*, 14 (1954), 209-228.

Oates, James F. Jr. *Business and Social Change: Life Insurance Looks to the Future*. New York: McGraw-Hill, 1968.

—. *The Contradictions of Leadership: A Selection of Speeches*. New York: Appleton-Century-Crofts, 1970.

The Old Guard. New York: The Equitable, 1955.

Pinckney, James D. *Reminiscences of Catskill: Local Sketches*. Catskill, N.Y,: n.p., 1868.

Powers, Richard Gid. *G-Men: Hoover's FBI in Popular Culture*. Carbondale, Ill.: Southern Illinois University Press, 1983.

Pritchett, B. Michael. *Financing Growth: A Financial History of American Life Insurance Through 1900*. Homewood, Ill.: S. S. Huebner Foundation for Insurance Education/Richard D. Irwin, 1985.

Pusey, Merlo J. *Charles Evans Hughes*. 2 vols. New York: Macmillan, 1952.

Ransom, Roger L. and Richard Sutch, "Tontine Insurance and the Armstrong Investigation: A Case of Stifled Innovation, 1868-1905," *Journal of Economic History* 47 (June 1987), 379-90.

Reddell, Arthur H. "The Equitable at the Turn of the Century," unpublished, 1957. Equitable Archives.

—. *Publicity Methods for Life Underwriters*. New York: F. S. Crofts, 1927.

Report of the Executive Advisory Commission on Insurance Industry Regulatory Reform. New York: n.p., 1982.

Riley, John W. Jr., ed. *The Corporation and its Publics: Essays on the Corporate Image*. New York: Wiley, 1963.

—. "Social Research and Life Insurance," *American Behavioral Scientist*, 6 (May 1963).

Roosevelt, Theodore. *The Letters of Theodore Roosevelt*. Ed. Elting E. Morison. 8 vols. Cambridge: Harvard University Press, 1951-54.

Ryan, Thomas F. "Why I Bought The Equitable," *North American Review*, 198 (August 1913), 161-77.

Schiff, Jacob H. *Our Journey to Japan*. New York: New York Co-Operative Society, 1906.

Schott, Francis H. "A Time of Change for Financial Institutions," paper submitted to the New York Executive Advisory Commission on Insurance Industry Regulatory Reform, 1982. Author collection.

Securities and Exchange Commission, *Variable Life Insurance and the Petition for the Issuance and Amendment of Exemptive Rules*, 1973.

Seligman, Joel. *The Transformation of Wall Street: A History of the Securities and Exchange Commission and Modern Corporate Finance*. Boston: Houghton Mifflin, 1982.

Sellers, Charles. *The Market Revolution: Jacksonian America, 1815-1846*. New York: Oxford University Press, 1991.

Seymour, Harold. *Baseball: The People's Game*. New York: Oxford University Press, 1990.

Sharp, Louis I. *John Quincy Adams Ward: Dean of American Sculpture*. Newark, Del.: University of Delaware Press, 1985.

Smith, James G. *The Development of Trust Companies in the United States*. New York: Holt, 1927.

Smith, James Henry. *Great Ideas for Living*. Ed. Wendell M. Smith. N.p.: Polestar, 1994.

Snow, Richard F. "American Characters: James Hazen Hyde," *American Heritage*, August-September 1981, 96-97.

Stalson, J. Owen. *Marketing Life Insurance: Its History in America*. Homewood, Ill.: Richard D. Irwin-McCahan Foundation, 1969. (Originally published 1942.)

Stone, Mildred F. *The Teacher Who Changed an Industry*. Homewood, Ill.: Irwin, 1960.

Sullivan, Mark. *Our Times: The United States, 1900-1925*. Vol. 3. New York: Scribner's, 1930.

Swaine, Robert T. *The Cravath Firm and Its Predecessors, 1819-1947*. 2 vols. New York: n.p., 1946.

de Tocqueville, Alexis. *Democracy in America*. Trans. George Lawrence. Garden City, N.Y.: Doubleday-Anchor, 1969.

Toker, Franklin. *Pittsburgh: An Urban Portrait*. University Park, Pa.: Pennsylvania State University Press, 1986.

Van Zandt, Roland. *The Catskill Mountain House*. New Brunswick, N.J.: Rutgers University Press, 1966.

Walker, Guy Morrison. *Trust Companies: A Study of the Nature of Their Business and the Source of Their Great Earning Power*. Boston: n.p., 1903.

Wall, Joseph Frazier. *Andrew Carnegie*. New York: Oxford University Press, 1970.

Walter, James E. *The Investment Process: As Characterized by Leading Life Insurance Companies*. Boston: Division of Research, Harvard University Graduate School of Business Administration, 1962.

Weed, Thurlow. *The Autobiography of Thurlow Weed*. Ed. Harriet A. Weed. Boston: Houghton Mifflin, 1883.

Wilkens, Mira. *The Emergence of Multinational Enterprise: American Business Abroad from the Colonial Era to 1914*. Cambridge: Harvard University Press, 1970.

—. *The Maturing of Multinational Enterprise: American Business Abroad from 1914 to 1970*. Cambridge: Harvard University Press, 1974.

Williamson, Harold F. and Orange A. Smalley. *Northwestern Mutual Life: A Century of Trusteeship*. Evanston, Ill.: Northwestern University Press, 1957.

Woods, Lawrence C., Jr. *Half a Century: A History of the Edward A. Woods Company*. Pittsburgh: Woods, 1930.

Wyllie, Irvin G. *The Self-Made Man in America: The Myth of Rags to Riches*. New Brunswick, N.J.: Rutgers University Press, 1954.

Zelizer, Viviana A. Rotman. *Morals and Markets: The Development of Life Insurance in the United States*. New York: Columbia University Press, 1979.

PHOTO CREDITS

All photographs and illustrations are property of the Equitable Archives or are in the public domain unless otherwise indicated below.

PAGE

5	*Catskill, New York Public Library.*
6-7	*Johnston, Northwestern Mutual; Homans, Society of Actuaries; Winston, Mutual of New York (MONY); Wright, New England Life.*
8-9	*New York City, Museum of the City of New York; Fifth Avenue Presbyterian, New-York Historical Society (NYHS); Alexander, Princeton Theological Seminary.*
12	*Lord, NYHS.*
21	*Robinson, MONY.*
73	*Perkins, New York Life.*
82-83	*Schiff, World Wide Photos (WWP); Depew, WWP; Coach race, NYHS.*
90-91	*Morgan, WWP; Roosevelt, WWP; Harriman, WWP.*
95	*Ryan, WWP.*
101	*Ryan, Brown Brothers.*
108	*Cleveland, WWP.*
110-111	*Armstrong, Brown Brothers; C. E. Hughes, WWP.*
121	*DuPont, Bettman.*
144-145	*Airplane, TWA; H. Hughes, WWP; McCarthy, WWP.*
146-147	*Cartoon,* Finance *magazine; Groundbreaking, Carnegie Library, Pittsburgh.*
159	*Huebner, The American College.*
175	*Freeman, WWP.*
178	*McLaughlin, New York Times (NYT) Pictures.*
186	*Hyde, WWP.*
193	*Fleischmann, Mrs. Alison F. Kimberly.*
223	*Merton, Columbia University.*
229	*Christmas party, Mrs. Peggy C. Ward.*
236	*Beavers, LeRoy A. Beavers, Jr.*
301	*Jenrette, Michael Mundy.*
320	*NYSE, Cheryl Rossum.*
322	*Roaring Back,* The New York Times, *Sept. 8, 1994. William E. Sauro, NYT Pictures.*
325-326	*Benson and Melone, Carl Howard, Black Star.*

COLOR PHOTOGRAPHY

CHARLES UHT	*Henry B. Hyde frontispiece, stained glass window, and all chief executive officer portraits except John B. Carter.*
DAVID HAYS	*Portraits: John B. Carter and Grover Cleveland.* *Equitable buildings: 120 Broadway lithograph and 393 Seventh Avenue.* *Advertisements: calling cards poster, French poster of international offices, New York City Currier & Ives print, Equitable lifeboat, 1870 policy,* Truth in a Nutshell *pamphlet, "Strongest in the World" calendar, and 1900 presidential flyer.*
JEFF WATTS	*Richard H. Jenrette portrait.*
DOROTHY VEIDMAN	*Benton murals.*
GRANT PETERSON	*Goddess and mother head sculptures.*

ENDNOTES

Note: Endnotes are arranged by paragraph and cite the initial words of the quote. Full citations of published sources may be found in the bibliography.

CHAPTER I

1. "Call it *pressure*": William Alexander memorandum in Alexander 1884-85 file, Equitable Archives (henceforth EqAr). "*Jam it through*": R. Carlyle Buley, *The Equitable Life Assurance Society of the United States, 1859-1964*, 185 (henceforth *The Equitable*). Emphasis in originals.

2. "The most daring": Morton Keller, *The Life Insurance Enterprise, 1885-1910: A Study in the Limits of Corporate Power*, 57. "The greatest organizer": J. Owen Stalson, *Marketing Life Insurance: Its History in America*, 360. "Reckless": Bray Hammond in William Greider, *Secrets of the Temple: How the Federal Reserve Runs the Country*, 259.

3. "The wild magnificence": J. Bard McNalty (ed.), *The Correspondence of Thomas Cole and Daniel Wadsworth*, 1.

4. "Streets and lots": James D. Pinckney, *Reminiscences of Catskill: Local Sketches*, 79. "It is a thrifty": in Roland Van Zandt, *The Catskill Mountain House*, 44.

5. "He was a tall": *Henry Baldwin Hyde: A Biographical Sketch*, 13.

6. "The departure": Burton J. Hendrick, *The Story of Life Insurance*, 95.

7. "A genuine": Buley, *The Equitable*, 48. "I come to": *Henry Baldwin Hyde: A Biographical Sketch*, 16. "Without doubt": Buley, *The Equitable*, 156.

8. "He entered": *Henry Baldwin Hyde: A Biographical Sketch*, 14. "Mr. Hyde": Buley, *The Equitable*, 51.

9. "Mr. Hyde had": William Alexander, *The Equitable in the Early Days*, 5.

10. "A man of": Hendrick, *The Story of Life Insurance*, 82.

11. "Gentlemen": *Henry Baldwin Hyde: A Biographical Sketch*, 157. "Organized upon": Buley, *The Equitable*, 9.

12. "The Lord Almighty": George Martin, *Causes and Conflicts: The Centennial History of the Association of the Bar of the City of New York, 1870-1970*, 24 ftn. "Mr. Hyde always": William Alexander, *The Equitable in the Early Days*, 12.

13. "A half-way": Hyde to Valentine P. Snyder, December 2, 1897. Equitable Life Assurance Society Collection in the Baker Library at the Harvard University Graduate School of Business Administration (henceforth Hyde papers, HBS).

CHAPTER II

1. "Choose any American": Alexis de Tocqueville, *Democracy in America*, 404. "Hyde's genius": J. Owen Stalson, *Marketing Life Insurance: Its History in America*, 600-601. Quotes from southern tour letters: Buley, *The Equitable*, 114-115. Emphasis in originals.

2. "The attitude of," "Mr. Hyde": William Alexander, *The Equitable in the Early Days*, 17, 14.

3. "I have often": Alexander, *The Equitable in the Early Days*, 34.

4. "While nothing": Daniel J. Boorstin, *The Americans: The Democratic Experience*, 175. "Actuaries tend": Harry D. Garber interview with author, 1994.

5. "The hands of": Buley, *The Equitable*, 31.

6. "Like gnats": Stalson, *Marketing Life Insurance*, 43. "I remember": Weed, *The Autobiography of Thurlow Weed*, 433.

7. "Poor New York": Hone, *The Diary of Philip Hone*, vol. 1, 461.

8. "Gambling made": Viviana A. Rotman Zelizer, *Morals and Markets: The Development of Life Insurance in the United States*, 68. "Mathematically determined": Lawrence B. Goodheart, *Abolitionist, Actuary, Atheist: Elizur Wright and the Reform Impulse*, 145. "Like St. Paul": Buley, *The Equitable*, 155.

9. Lambert quotes: *Henry Baldwin Hyde: A Biographical Sketch*, 174. "I knew when": Buley, *The Equitable*, 68.

10. "I want hustling": Buley, *The Equitable*, 538, ftn. "Make use of": Zelizer, *Morals and Markets*, 128.

11. "Great is": Keller, The Life Insurance Enterprise, 29. "Your work": Hyde to James W. Alexander, December 29, 1887. Hyde papers, HBS.

12. "His nervous": Hendrick, *The Story of Life Insurance*, 115. "It takes away": Buley, *The Equitable*, 156.

13. "Henry B. Hyde": Buley, *The Equitable*, 347.

14. "To insure": William Alexander, *The Equitable in the Early Days*, 18.

15. "Life assurance," "this one thing": *Henry Baldwin Hyde: A Biographical Sketch*, 78, 154.

Chapter III

1. Henry Hazen Hyde quotes, "the Success of": Buley, *The Equitable*, 78, 81.

2. "The one striking": Hendrick, *The Story of Life Insurance*, 100-1.

3. "They need to": Harry D. Garber interview with author, 1993.

4. "Many persons": Buley, *The Equitable*, 93.

5. "The assurants": Roger L. Ransom and Richard Sutch, "Tontine Insurance and the Armstrong Investigation: A Case of Stifled Innovation, 1868-1905," *Journal of Economic History* 47 (June 1987), 379. "He realized": Richard H. Jenrette interview with author, 1993.

6. "Life insurance," "It is": Keller, *The Life Insurance Enterprise*, 57. "Its principle is": Greene, *Tontine: What it is; How it Works*, ca. 1881. Historical Collection, EqAr.

7. Data: Ransom and Sutch, "Tontine Insurance and the Armstrong Investigation," 387.

8. "It was": William Alexander, *The Equitable in the Early Days*, 31.

9. "The bane of": Stalson, *Marketing Life Insurance*, 534.

10. "Time expended": Buley, *The Equitable*, 265.

11. Codes: Code Book. Historical Collection, EqAr.

12. "Bold, persistent": Stalson, *Marketing Life Insurance*, 448.

13. "I am watching": Hyde to James A. Taber, November 20, 1883. Hyde papers, HBS.

14. "Artists, diplomats": memorandum on interview with H. I. Schoofs, 1951. Russian Agency file, EqAr.

Chapter IV

1. "Big, caring": Foote, Cone & Belding to Equitable, March 23, 1960. Advertising Department file, EqAr.

2. "Purely religious": Charles Sellers, *The Market Revolution: Jacksonian America, 1815-1846*, 371.

3. Prime quotes: Buley, *The Equitable*, 62. Emphasis in original.

4. Beecher quotes: *Truth in a Nutshell*. Historical Collection, EqAr.

5. "Any searching": Zelizer, *Morals and Markets*, 7.

6. "If a," "will blot": Arthur H. Reddall, *Publicity Methods for Life Underwriters*, 271, 269.

7. "The pastor": *Equitable News*, December 1902.

8. "Thy shield," "the most dignified": Lewis I. Sharp, *John Quincy Adams Ward: Dean of American Sculpture*, 184, 185.

9. "The company": Morton Keller, *The Life Insurance Enterprise*, 98. See Morton Keller, "The Judicial System and the Law of Life Insurance, 1888-1910," *Business History Review*, 35 (1961), 317-335.

10. "Men and firms": B. Michael Pritchett, *Financing Growth: A Financial History of American Life Insurance Through 1900*, 12. "I can't transact": Hendrick, *The Story of Life Insurance*, 154.

11. "Building buildings": Andy Logan, "Building for Glory," *The New Yorker*, October 21, 1961, 144. "I would very": Hyde to various correspondents, July 5, 1895. Hyde papers, HBS.

12. "Hyde's folly": Hendrick, *The Story of Life Insurance*, 123. "Marble quarry": William Alexander, *The Equitable in the Early Days*, 33. "As if it," "an indescribable," "the hub": Logan, "Building for Glory": 146, 154, 154.

13. "The marble halls," "on the outside": William Dean Howells, *A Hazard of New Fortunes*, 12, 13.

14. "The shrewd": Buley, *The Equitable*, 474.

15. "If we do not": Hyde to George T. Wilson, August 16, 1896. Hyde papers, HBS.

16. "With him": Buley, *The Equitable*, 188.

17. "I have": Buley, *The Equitable*, 534.

CHAPTER V

1. "After fussing": Arthur H. Reddall, "The Equitable at the Turn of the Century." EqAr.

2. Office details: S.G.M. Day, Herbert Rudd, and H.B. Whitman in *The Equitable Spirit*, October 26, 1933.

3. "There is no": Harold Seymour, *Baseball: The People's Game*, 215.

4. "Hooray!": Jonathan Coss, "Baseball at The Equitable," 1994. EqAr.

5. "I have a": Tarbell to William Alexander, November 9, 1897. Tarbell letter book, EqAr.

6. "Thus the whole": Buley, *The Equitable*, 85.

7. "Men brought up": Hyde to George T. Wilson, July 10, 1896. Hyde papers, HBS.

8. "I can get": Buley, *The Equitable*, 381. "Here lies": Hendrick, *The Story of Life Insurance*, 110. "A massive": Zelizer, *Morals and Markets: The Development of Life Insurance in the United States*, 129.

9. "It may be": in William Alexander 1884-85 file, EqAr. Emphasis in original. "I agree": undated circular. Historical Collection, EqAr.

10. "The interests": James W. Alexander memorandum, October 1, 1886. Historical Collection, EqAr. "Every agent": Woods, *et al.* to agency force, August 25, 1894. Historical Collection, EqAr.

11. "There never has": Alexander to agency force, September 1, 1893. Historical Collection, EqAr.

12. "The important": Hyde to Tarbell, June 17, 1896. Hyde papers. HBS.

13. "I was": *The Equitable Spirit*, October 26, 1933.

14. Wilson quotes: *The Equitable Spirit*, October 26, 1933.

15. "I have found": William Alexander to George Woods, July 15, 1886. Woods Agency file, EqAr. "A drive": Lawrence C. Woods, Jr., *Half a Century: A History of the Edward A. Woods Company*, 13.

16. "Probably originated": Stalson, *Marketing Life Insurance*, 582.

17. Notebook quotes: Edward A. Woods notebook, Woods Agency file, EqAr.

18. "There was a very": Robert I. Peters oral history, undated. Audiotape in Betty Anderson collection, Kovacic Agency, Pittsburgh, Pa.

19. "To hold your": Edward A. Woods to William M. Duff, January 30, 1911. Woods Agency file, EqAr.

20. "You have to": Hyde to Tarbell, July 9, 1896. Hyde papers, HBS.

21. "When he was": Frank L. Jones to Alexander McNeill, September 15, 1936. Retired directors file, EqAr.

22. "Of inexhaustible": *The Equitable News*, January 1902. "Hammer and": Buley, *The Equitable*, 588. "We must have": Tarbell undated memorandum (1904?). Hyde papers, HBS. "After signing": *The Equitable Spirit*, October 26, 1933. "You should go": Tarbell to Powell, October 1905. Tarbell file, EqAr.

23. Hyde quotes: Hyde to Tarbell, January 25, 1897. Hyde papers, HBS. "I think we": Tarbell to Hyde, undated (1896). Tarbell letter book, EqAr.

CHAPTER VI

1. "Some day": R. Carlyle Buley, *The American Life Convention, 1906-1952: A Study in the History of Life Insurance*, vol. 1, 199.

2. "A serious": Buley, *The Equitable*, 379. "Every time": Hyde to Marcellus Hartley, July 29, 1896. Hyde papers, HBS.

3. Data, "of late": James G. Smith, *The Development of Trust Companies in the United States*, 335.

4. "For many years": Van Cise to William A. Day, March 22, 1907. Eklund file, EqAr.

5. "The general cry": Alexander to James H. Hyde, March 25, 1904. Hyde papers, HBS. "A struggling": Tarbell to Alexander, December 19, 1901. Tarbell letter book, EqAr.

6. "We have": Keller, *The Life Insurance Enterprise*, 141.

7. "I do not": Van Cise to Hyde, May 27, 1897. Hyde papers, HBS. "The time has": Buley, *The Equitable*, 485.

8. "A small matter": Keller, *The Life Insurance Enterprise*, 109.

9. "The worst": Hamilton to Wilson, February 3, 1913. Foreign agencies file, EqAr.

10. "Please Alexander": John A. Garraty, *Right-Hand Man: The Life of George W. Perkins*, 70.

11. "I have": Hyde to John Quincy Adams Ward, February 10, 1896. Hyde papers, HBS.

12. "Don't deal with": Hyde to George T. Wilson, August 3, 1896. "It is really": Hyde to Wilson, August 14, 1896. "It is worth": Hyde to Tarbell, January 25, 1899. Hyde papers, HBS.

13. Data: Buley, *The Equitable*, 555 ftn.; *Historical Statistics of the United States*, passim; and Pritchett, *Financing Growth*, 6, 19.

14. Hyde quotes: Hyde to Alexander, December 29, 1897. Hyde papers, HBS.

15. "A man of": Buley, *The Equitable*, 541. "The handsomest": Charles Chapin, *Charles Chapin's Story, Written in Sing Sing Prison*, 238. "Wise guidance": *Henry Baldwin Hyde: A Biographical Sketch*, 155. "The institution": James W. Alexander, "Some Prejudices about Life Insurance," *Atlantic Monthly*, July 1900.

16. "Here is the": Alexander notations on actuary's memorandum, August 27, 1900. Hyde papers, HBS. "Take out": Alexander to James H. Hyde, March 28, 1903. Hyde papers, HBS.

17. "The old idea": Stuart Bruchey, *Enterprise: The Dynamic Economy of a Free People*, 343. "Become the": Buley, *The Equitable*, 577.

18. "This great": Hendrick, *The Story of Life Insurance*, 15.

19. "For months": transcript, Complainant's Testimony, *U. S.* v. *Northern Securities Company*, Third Circuit Court, vol. 1, 335.

20. "Life insurance": Bruchey, *Enterprise*, 318. "When I was": transcript, Armstrong Committee Hearings, 1906, vol. 1, 599-600.

21. "The trust": Thomas W. Lawson in Keller, *The Life Insurance Enterprise*, 146.

22. "It is something": Alexander to Hyde, May 7, 1897. Hyde papers, HBS.

23. Data: Equitable 1906 annual report. EqAr.

24. "I got too": Buley, *The Equitable*, 699.

25. "I had always": Keller, *The Life Insurance Enterprise*, 42.

26. "Jauntily downtown": Mark Sullivan, *Our Times: The United States, 1900-1925*, vol. 2, 33. "I have": Garraty, *Right-Hand Man*, 162. "Altogether": Buley, *The Equitable*, 686.

27. "Getting thick": Alexander to Hyde, March 28, 1903. Hyde papers, HBS.

28. "The many transactions": Price Waterhouse and Haskens & Sells Supplementary Report to Equitable, January 30, 1906, 198. EqAr.

29. Alexander quotes: Buley, *The Equitable*, 582.

30. "Let us hoist": Morton Keller, *The Life Insurance Enterprise*, 254. "The opinion prevailed": Tarbell to Alexander, February 1, 1900. Tarbell letter book, EqAr.

31. "The Western," "anyhow we": Buley, *The Equitable*, 596.

CHAPTER VII

1. Alexander quotes: James W. Alexander, "Do Governments and Lawmakers Regard Life Assurance from the Right Point of View?", paper for the International Congress of Arts and Sciences, St. Louis, September 1904. Transcript in James W. Alexander file, EqAr.

2. "The very great": Alexander to James Hyde, March 25, 1904. Hyde papers, HBS. "They are": Buley, *The Equitable*, 579.

3. "Bold manipulator": Keller, *The Life Insurance Enterprise*, 137.

4. "A quite really": Arthur H. Reddall, "The Equitable at the Turn of the Century." EqAr. "The worst," "no one worked": Maury Klein, *Union Pacific: The Rebirth, 1894-1969*, 35, 53.

5. "Independent men": Buley, *The Equitable*, 410.

6. "Yes this": Tarbell to R. J. Mix, January 16, 1905. Tarbell letter book, EqAr.

7. "I *very much*," "matters of": Tarbell and Alexander to several directors, January 31 and February 2, 1905. Tarbell letter book. EqAr. Emphasis in original. "The future": Frick Committee Report. EqAr.

8. "Large responsibility": R. Carlyle Buley, *American Life Convention*, vol. 1, 200 ftn. "The Strenuous Life": Richard F. Snow, "American Characters: James Hazen Hyde," *American Heritage*, August-September 1981, 96. Mr. Dooley quote: Finley Peter Dunne, "Mr. Dooley on the Life Insurance Investigation" *Collier's*, November 4, 1905, 12.

9. "A personal," "his youth": Frick Committee Report.

10. "Serious and," "rush rush," "the enemies": Frick Committee Report.

11. "Open aggressive": Frick Committee Report.

12. "Tremendous evil": Frick Committee Report.

13. "While polite": Hyde notes on February 12, 1905, meeting. Hyde papers, HBS.

14. "We are in": Hyde memorandum of record, undated. Hyde papers, HBS. Emphasis in original. "Now more," "God damn": Philip C. Jessup, *Elihu Root*, vol. 1, 440.

15. "*Equitable Fight*," "Hyde's chief": *New York American*, April 5, 1905.

16. "Such a damnable": Robert T. Swaine, *The Cravath Firm and Its Predecessors*, vol. 1, 753.

17. "Sane and": Joseph Frazier Wall, *Andrew Carnegie*, 936. "A very difficult": Jessup, *Elihu Root*, vol. 1, 438.

18. "Great panic": Gulliver to Hyde, March 8, 1905. Hyde papers, HBS.

19. Board of Managers quotes: minutes, meeting of April 3, 1905. Old Guard minute book, EqAr.

20. "The heart and," "insurance workers," "this brother," "I drink": Alexander and Hyde speeches, general agents' meeting April 1905. Transcripts in Hyde papers, HBS. "You may," "gentlemen": Buley, *The Equitable*, 638.

21. "The Society," "Alexander and": minutes of ad hoc board meeting, May 8, 1905. Hyde papers, HBS.

22. Report quotes: Frick Committee Report.

23. "If Ryan," "American Louvre": Mark D. Hirsch, *William C. Whitney: Modern Warwick*, 466. "There was hardly": Jessup, *Elihu Root*, vol. 1, 437.

24. "The most": Hirsch, *William C. Whitney*, 466. "No more serious": Thomas Fortune Ryan, "Why I Bought The Equitable," *North American Review*, August 1913, 161.

25. "I will use," "we are likely": Buley, *The Equitable*, 658.

CHAPTER VIII

1. "God watched": William J. Graham, undated letter enclosed in the copy of Graham, "Reminiscences of William J. Graham," 366. EqAr.

2. "You have": Theodore Roosevelt, *The Letters of Theodore Roosevelt*, vol. 4, 1,214.

3. "Paul Morton," "so live": Edwin Lefèvre, "Paul Morton — Human Dynamo," *Cosmopolitan Magazine*, October 1905. "The situation," "it is a big": Buley, *The Equitable*, 658-59, 665.

4. "I can," "if he": Buley, *The Equitable*, 757, 758.

5. "Powerful cable": Buley, *The Equitable*, 717. "Our old": Buley, *American Life Convention*, vol. 1, 203. "I feel": Allan Nevins, *Grover Cleveland: A Study in Courage*, 760.

6. "Six months," "honest conservative": Buley, *The Equitable*, 668.

7. "My dear": Charles Evans Hughes, *The Autobiographical Notes of Charles Evans Hughes*, 121.

8. "His was an," "as unemotionally": Swaine, *The Cravath Firm and Its Predecessors*, vol. 1, 757, 758. "The dreadful," "we had": Keller, *The Life Insurance Enterprise*, 250, 140.

9. "Were not incorporated": Armstrong Committee Hearings, vol. 7, 294-5.

10. "Some of the," "rather drastic": Swaine, *The Cravath Firm and Its Predecessors*, vol. 1, 760, 761. "While they are": Tarbell to Morton, February 26, 1906. Tarbell letter book, EqAr. "Of course": *The Reminiscences of Bertrand J. Hendrick* (1949), in the Oral History Collection of Columbia University.

11. "Armstrong Report": Shelby Cullom Davis, "Common Stock Investments by Life Insurance Companies." *Analysts Journal*, July 1945.

12. Loading data: Van Cise to William A. Day, March 22, 1907. Copy in Coy Eklund files, EqAr.

13. "Was maintained": Minutes of General Agents Association Executive Committee meeting, January 15, 1909. Old Guard minute book, EqAr.

14. "Organizing and": Tarbell to George E. Griffin, February 11, 1907. Tarbell letter book, EqAr.

15. "The Equitable": Morton, fiftieth anniversary banquet speech, July 28, 1909. EqAr.

16. "The department": *New York Insurance Department Report on The Equitable*, 1909. "The history of": Alexander to William Day, February 26, 1912. Secretary's file, EqAr.

17. "I thought it best": Vincent Carosso, *The Morgans: Private International Bankers, 1854-1913*, 637.

18. "We must never": Executive Order no. 425, February 20, 1919. Day file, EqAr. Emphasis in original. "Supply the": Day, "The Significance of the Increasing Volume of Life Insurance," speech, 1919. Transcript in Day file, EqAr.

19. "The more or less": General Agency Association minutes, January 9, 1913. Old Guard minute book, EqAr.

20. "Dodo Birds": Buley, *The Equitable*, 920. "The backbone": *The Old Guard*, 4.

21. Data, "a veritable": Andy Logan, "Building for Glory," 160.

22. "I like conceiving": Buley, *The Equitable*, 818 ftn.

CHAPTER IX

1. "The present": General Agency Association minutes, March 6, 1907. Old Guard minute book, EqAr.

2. "An essential": Daniel Horowitz, *The Morality of Spending: Attitudes Toward the Consumer Society in America, 1875-1940*, 53. Data: Horowitz, *Morality of Spending*: 53, 124-25, 178; Raymond W. Goldsmith, *Financial Intermediaries in the American Economy Since 1900*, 319.

3. "If this thing": Buley, *The Equitable*, 773.

4. "There is a much": Morton speech at fiftieth anniversary dinner, July 28, 1909. Transcript in Morton file, EqAr.

5. "Group Insurance": Day, "Group insurance: Its Aims and its Field," address 1913. Transcript in Day file, EqAr.

6. "A lot of," "group insurance": Buley, *The Equitable*, 784, 791.

7. "A menace": Louise Wolters Ilse, *Group Insurance and Employee Retirement Plans*, 48. "Your pay check": R. Carlyle Buley, *The American Life Convention*, 421 ftn.

8. Mortality statistics and quotes: *Experience of Thirty-Four Life Companies Upon Ninety-Eight Special Classes of Risks, passim*. EqAr.

9. "It was": J. Henry Smith oral history, 1985. EqAr. Emphasis in original.

10. "An unexplained": Eugenius Outerbridge, "Group Insurance as an Influence in Promoting Stability in Labor Groups," speech to the Association of Life Insurance Presidents, December 6, 1918. Transcript in group insurance file, EqAr.

11. "Justified in": Buley, *The Equitable*, 800. "The practical": Klein, *Union Pacific*, 349.

12. "Not looking": Graham, "Reminiscences of William J. Graham," 210. Typescript in EqAr. "Our greatest," Frank H. Davis speech, "Life Insurance in 1950", meeting of the Association of Life Insurance Presidents, December 11, 1924. Transcript in Davis file, EqAr.

13. "Social insurance": Buley, *The Equitable*, 908.

14. "To help inspire," "take advantage": Graham, "Reminiscences," 336.

Chapter X

1. "Moral fiber," "what we need": Buley, *The Equitable*, 942, 940.

2. "You won't do": *New York World-Telegram & Sun*, October 20, 1951.

3. "Snappy work": Buley, *The Equitable*, 869.

4. "He is not only": Day to Abraham Brittin, October 5, 1927. Day file, EqAr.

5. "Persistence": Buley, *The Equitable*, 1012 ftn. "His hobby": *Eastern Underwriter*, July 24, 1933.

6. "I am ready": *Insurance Observer*, November 1930. "Was almost": Recommendations on Agency Management, undated (1936?) memorandum. Woods Agency file, EqAr.

7. "I often": Buley, *The Equitable*, 976.

8. "I said profits": *National Underwriter*, life insurance edition, July 9, 1948.

9. "The compulsion": Mendel memorandum, January 22, 1964. Mendel file, EqAr.

10. "Break its": Shelby Cullom Davis, "Common Stock Investments by Life Insurance Companies," *The Analysts Journal*, July 1945. Copy of draft in Ferguson file, EqAr.

11. Data and "a concentrated": Lawrence D. Jones, *Investment Policies of Life Insurance Companies*, 264. "The great": Grant Keehn, speech to agency managers, Boca Raton, Fla., January 29, 1960. Transcript in Keehn file, EqAr.

12. "In any amount," "there is nothing": Sally H. Clarke, *Regulation and the Revolution in United States Farm Productivity*, 223, 225.

13. "In metropolitan": Laurens F. Bruno, *Memories: My Equitable Odyssey*, 77.

14. "I can say": Pierson to Robert E. Dineen, April 21, 1947. R. Carlyle Buley notes, EqAr.

15. "Should have credit": James F. Oates, Jr., *Business and Social Change*, 51.

16. "Our dear": Joseph Frazier Wall, *Andrew Carnegie*, 817. "An unmanageable": Roy Stryker and Mel Seidenberg, *A Pittsburgh Album, 1758-1958*, 84. "In the mid-twentieth": Theodore Hazlett, Jr., in Robert C. Alberts. *The Shaping of the Point: Pittsburgh's Renaissance Park*, 7.

17. "There is a": Pittsburgh *Press*, September 29, 1957.

18. "Leaps of faith": Pittsburgh *Post-Gazette*, June 24, 1960.

19. "Again the": *Pittsburgh Press*, June 24, 1960.

20. "Get Mr. Oates": Mark Higgins, draft of article, 1959. Group insurance file. EqAr. "The Equitable and": Robert S. Jones, Jr., interview with author, 1994.

Chapter XI

1. "T. I. Parkinson": Donald L. Bryant, Sr., oral history, 1979. EqAr.

2. "A manpower": Leroy E. Long oral history, 1979. EqAr.

3. "How a young": *Equitable News*, November 1901. "There is no": Woods notebook, Woods Agency file, EqAr.

4. "We meet": *Equitable News*, March 1903.

5. Davis quotes: Merle Crowell, "The World Makes Way for a Man Who Knows Where He's Going," *American Magazine*, June 1923. "To hell with": C. G. James to R. Carlyle Buley, May 31, 1963. Davis file, EqAr.

6. "Forget policy," "Billy Sunday": Buley, *The Equitable*, 925, 921.

7. Embry quotes: A. M. Embry oral history, 1955. EqAr.

8. "Lots of people": Embry oral history.

9. "Embry did": Robert Wenzlaff interview with author, 1994. "Back in those": Embry oral history.

10. "There were all": Bryant oral history.

11. Formula: Bryant oral history.

12. "It was just": Wenzlaff interview.

13. "He made the district": Wenzlaff interview.

14. "Everything I": James Gurley interview with author, 1994.

15. "The basis," "if you": George A. Norris, *A History of the National Association of Life Underwriters*, 30.

16. "Joint selling": Robert I. Peters oral history, undated. Audiotape in Betty Anderson collection, Kovacic Agency, Pittsburgh, Pa.

17. "Sieve," "if you can": Woods in Report to Committee on Scientific Salesmanship, National Association of Life Underwriters, September 29, 1919. Woods Agency file, EqAr.

18. "My friends": Mildred F. Stone, *The Teacher Who Changed an Industry*, 162-63.

19. "Buy yourself": Robert S. Jones, Jr., interview with author, 1994. "One of the": Bruno, *Memories: My Equitable Odyssey*, 1.

20. "Became acquainted": Richard C. Hageman oral history, 1979. EqAr.

21. "It's got," "after two": Coy G. Eklund oral history, 1975. EqAr.

22. "Clarence Metzger": Eklund oral history, 1975.

23. Data: Angel Kwolek-Folland, *Engendering Business: Men and Women in the Corporate Office, 1870-1930*, 30, Table 3.

24 "An absolute": *Equitable News*, March 1903.

25. "It shows": *Equitable News*, March 1903.

26. "Life insurance": Woods to Parkinson, January 19, 1939. Woods Agency file, EqAr.

27. "Two and A Half," "who had seen": letters and promotional materials. Metzger file, EqAr.

28. "Serving on the": Francis H. Burr interview with author, 1994.

29. "Yes, I guess": Robert W. Creamer, *Babe: The Legend Comes to Life*, 274.

30. "I just can't": Graham, "Reminiscences of William J. Graham," 345.

31. "To your," "in nearly": Richard Gid Powers, *G-Men: Hoover's FBI in Popular Culture*, 222.

32. "The Equitable": *Best's Insurance News*, life edition, December 1947.

CHAPTER XII

1. "The future": Parkinson undated (1927?) speech. Parkinson file, EqAr.

2. "A crooked": Buley, *The Equitable*, 993. "When the life": *Weekly Underwriter*, July 30, 1949. "They tell me": Harry T. Wright to Parkinson, April 10, 1945. Advertising file, EqAr.

3. "A wow": *National Underwriter*, life edition, September 3, 1948.

4. "A storm": *National Underwriter*, life edition, December 12, 1950. "Timid and": *National Underwriter*, life edition, December 24, 1948. "If Mr.": *Insurance Field*, November 26, 1948.

5. "It was": *Insurance Advocate*, March 3, 1950.

6. "Privately gobbled": *Spectator*, August 1949.

7. "It is enough": program for dinner, October 16, 1952. Parkinson file, EqAr.

8. "Equitable was just": Richard H. Jenrette interview with author, 1993. "Paternalistic in": Edward A. Robie oral history, 1992. EqAr.

9. "Very articulate": Coy G. Eklund oral history, 1975. EqAr. "Kingmanship," "people who did": J. Henry Smith oral history, 1985. EqAr.

10. "Seldom sitting": Equitable Board of Directors tribute to McLaughlin, 1963. McLaughlin file, EqAr.

11. "The most inarticulate": testimony before Senate Judiciary Committee, May 27 1944. Transcript in antitrust file, EqAr. Sommers anecdote: Davidson Sommers oral history, 1985. EqAr. "Technical legal": Insurance Department audit of Equitable, 1950. EqAr.

12. "Father and": in McLaughlin to Parkinson, August 9, 1951. McLaughlin correspondence file, EqAr.

13. "Tightly laced," "the hand": Buley, *The Equitable*, 1208 ftn., 1211.

14. "Untrustworthy": Mertens, Report of Special Counsel to Insurance Department, March 31, 1953. Secretary's file, EqAr.

15. "Will be": *Spectator*, September 1953.

16. "I don't look": *New York Herald Tribune*, October 30, 1953. "Not a well": *Wall Street Journal*, November 2, 1953.

17. "At no time": Parkinson letter to Equitable Board of Directors, November 4, 1953. Parkinson file, EqAr.

18. "I cannot temporize": Bohlinger statement to Equitable Board of Directors, November 4, 1953. Secretary's file, EqAr.

19. "A very warm": Robie oral history.

20. "This he regarded": Horace H. Wilson to Clarence Axman, April 17, 1953. Murphy file, EqAr. Emphasis in original.

21. "We'll have": *Wall Street Journal*, November 6, 1953. "There is": *New York Journal-American*, November 6, 1953.

22. "He protected": Edward Monahan interview with author, 1994.

23. "We used to joke": Robert Wenzlaff interview with author, 1994. "The bane of": Coy G. Eklund oral history, 1985. EqAr.

24. "A savior sent": Smith introduction of Davidson Sommers at Equitable banquet, Grand Bahamas, March 7, 1973. Sommers file, EqAr.

CHAPTER XIII

1. "Instead of being": J. Henry Smith oral history, 1985. EqAr.

2. "I would say": Davidson Sommers oral history, 1985, EqAr.

3. "A man of": Smith oral history. "Know all": speech at dinner, May 1976. Transcript in Oates file, EqAr.

4. "It would be": *Equinews*, January 1958, 20. "That sort of" Smith oral history. "Bill McCaffrey sir," "Billy," "after that": William T. McCaffrey interview with author, 1993.

5. "I believe": Oates speech to Equitable Veterans Legion, May 1, 1957. Transcript in Ray Murphy file, EqAr. "The Dignity of Selling": in Oates, *Contradictions of Leadership*. "Must have in": *National Leaders Magazine*, March-April, 1967, 29. "A set of," "unrelated to": *A Code to Work By*. Black Advisory Panel file, EqAr.

6. "He had the": Lincoln Gordon interview with author, 1993. "I'm constituted": in Oates undated interview. Oates biographical file, EqAr. "Springboard," "create a mood": Eklund journal, July 5. 1960. Eklund collection, EqAr. "He turned": Coy G. Eklund oral history, 1985. EqAr.

7. "Forbidding gauntlet": "Report on Innovation," 1959. Harvard Report file, EqAr.

8. "Equitable is," "people at": "Report on Innovation." Emphasis in original.

9. "Their effectiveness": "Summary of Conclusions of Officers' Committee Regarding Harvard Report Recommendations," November 16, 1959. Harvard Report file, EqAr.

10. "He was the kind": Smith oral history.

11. "He certainly": Smith oral history. "He had almost": John W. Riley oral history, 1991. EqAr.

12. Mission statement quotes: *The Fundamental Purpose, Business Objectives, and Implicit Goals of The Equitable Life Assurance Society of the United States*, 1960. Eli Ferguson file, EqAr.

13. "I believe": Oates speech to Board of Directors, October 9, 1963. Ferguson file, EqAr.

14. "There was a": Sommers interview with author, 1994. "You were": Sommers to Oates, February 20, 1973. Oates file, EqAr.

CHAPTER XIV

1. "Here was," "he outlined": Keehn speech to Old Guard, May 1964. Transcript in Keehn file, EqAr.

2. "I do not": Sommers to J. Henry Smith, September 19, 1973. Sommers personal collection.

3. "He could": Jule E. Stocker oral history, 1988. EqAr.

4. "I don't think": Davidson Sommers oral history, 1985. EqAr. Keehn quotes: Keehn, notes for speeches at dinners, New York, January-February 1959, sponsored by Investment Banking Group and Blyth & Co. Index cards in Keehn file, EqAr.

5. Data: Keehn to Oates, May 13, 1959. Keehn file, EqAr.

6. "We have maintained": Hines memorandum, October 27, 1958. Hines File, EqAr.

7. "Fixed income": Sommers oral history.

8. "You don't have": Sommers interview with author, 1994.

9. "A trust": Stocker oral history.

10. "Ball park," "I would": Sommers oral history.

11. "Actuaries like": Sommers interview.

12. "In effect": Sommers oral history.

13. "In recent years": Keehn to Oates, May 13, 1959. Keehn file, EqAr.

14. "An important: Keehn to Oates, May 13, 1959.

15. "Perhaps I am": *The Investments of the Equitable: A Talk to the Field Forces of The Equitable*, pamphlet, September 1928. EqAr. Mendel letter and Keehn comments: Mendel to Keehn, January 14, 1959. Keehn file, EqAr.

16. "This rate," "I certainly": Keehn's reconstruction of speech to managers meeting, Boca Raton, Florida, January 29, 1959, with handwritten Oates comment. Keehn file, EqAr.

17. "One of our": Keehn to Oates, May 13, 1959. Keehn file, EqAr.

18. "A bitter": John W. Riley interview with author, 1994. "He would not": Robert Wenzlaff interview with author, 1994. "This was really": Joseph L. Beesley oral history, 1979. EqAr.

19. "God damn": Ralph Hardison to Grant Keehn, July 7, 1971. Keehn file, EqAr.

20. "A workshop talk," "this is a": Keehn speech, managers meeting, Boca Raton, Fla., January 29, 1960. Transcript and note cards in Keehn file, EqAr.

21. "The Equitable": Leroy E. Long oral history, 1979. EqAr. "It has come": Calvin D. Kanter oral history, 1992. EqAr. "I never thought": Sommers oral history.

22. "It is clear": Eklund to Oates, October 30, 1967. Copy in Keehn file, EqAr.

23. "To do so": Oates to General Policy Committee, March 26, 1964. Keehn file, EqAr. "I may have": Associated Press article, February 21, 1964. Clipping in Oates file, EqAr.

CHAPTER XV

1. "The view was": Harry D. Garber interview with author, 1993. "Kind of": Leroy E. Long oral history, 1979. EqAr.

2. "Dual career": *Equitable Items*, October 29, 1951.

3. "Getting men": Joseph L. Beesley oral history, 1979. EqAr.

4. "If you ever": Robert Wenzlaff interview with author, 1994.

5. Kanter quotes: Calvin D. Kanter oral history, 1992. EqAr.

6. "Being an insurance": Mark Higgins, draft of article, 1959. Group insurance file. EqAr.

7. "Many and many": Eugene D. Badgley oral history, 1979. EqAr.

8. "A somewhat": Coy G. Eklund oral history, 1985. EqAr.

9. "It was a sleepy": Garber interview.

10. "At that time": Donald L. Bryant oral history, 1979. EqAr. "It irritated": Richard C. Hageman oral history, 1979. EqAr.

11. "The Old Guard's power": Wenzlaff interview. "A very close": James B. Gurley interview with author, 1994.

12. "Company": *Life Insurance Reveille*, August 1947. "She is": Welch to Pierson, August 26, 1947. Pierson File, EqAr.

13. "However well": Laurens F. Bruno, *Memories: My Equitable Odyssey*, 24.

14. "Our heart was": Newton Press interview with author, 1994. "After all": *Association Quarterly*, September 1964, 10.

15. "The Home Office": Press interview. "This insurrection": Bruno, *Memories: My Equitable Journey*, 35.

16. "John Kennedy": Kanter oral history.

17. "Way out there": Coy G. Eklund oral history, 1975. EqAr.

18. "Have you ever": Eklund oral history, 1975.

19. Eklund quotes: Eklund oral history, 1975.

20. "To the man": Eklund inscription on program, May 19, 1976. Oates file, EqAr.

21. "It is the": Eklund oral history, 1985.

22. "Believing always": Eklund speech to managers, Boca Raton, Florida, January 29, 1959. Transcript in Keehn file, EqAr. "This is a": Eklund, "Looking at Manpower," March 8, 1962, Ohio State University Insurance Conference, Columbus, Ohio. Transcript in Henry Lloyd file, EqAr. "*Élan* and *éclat*": Wenzlaff interview. "The presence of": Eklund speech to Baltimore Chapter of CLU, October 8, 1968. Henry Lloyd file, EqAr. "I'm saying this": Robert W. McCabe oral history, 1979. EqAr.

23. "Some threw," "a kind of": John W. Riley interview with author, 1994. "You've been seduced": John W. Riley oral history, 1991. EqAr.

24. "Two-span bridge": Eklund journal, 1959-60. Eklund file, EqAr. "It was a": Riley interview. "To assist": Merton to Eklund, May 23 1960. Merton file, EqAr.

25. John W. Riley Jr., ed., *The Corporation and Its Publics: Essays on the Corporate Image*, and "Social Research and Life Insurance," *American Behavioral Scientist* 6 (May 1963). "People had never": Riley interview.

26. "It was a": Riley oral history.

27. "Sales manpower": Eklund, "Looking at Manpower."

28. "People do not": Eklund speech to Equitable Board of Directors, July 19, 1962. Transcript in Henry Lloyd file, EqAr.

29. "He wasn't": Gurley interview.

CHAPTER XVI

1. "The premium": Don Finn oral history, 1979. EqAr. "In the old": Howard A. Osman interview with author, 1993.

2. "If we fell": *Business Week*, January 15, 1966.

3. "Everybody used," "it was," "you wanted": Peggy Ward interview with author, 1994.

4. "It is ironic": Oates, *Business and Social Change: Life Insurance Looks to the Future*, 88-89.

5. "We haven't thought": Harry D. Garber interview with author, 1993.

6. "An older": Neil M. DeVries oral history, 1979. EqAr.

7. "They weren't": J. Henry Smith oral history, 1985. EqAr.

8. "Most managements": Edward A. Robie oral history, 1992. EqAr.

9. "One of the": Ruth S. Block oral history, 1992. EqAr.

10. "This activity": Block oral history.

11. "To effectively sell": *The Fundamental Purpose, Business Objectives, and Implicit Goals of The Equitable Life Assurance Society of the United States*, 1960. EqAr. "These are that": Oates, *Business and Social Change*, 3.

12. "I think it": Robie oral history.

13. "One could": Smith oral history. "Where and how": John W. Riley oral history, 1991. EqAr.

14. "Let's get": Joseph L. Beesley oral history, 1979. EqAr.

15. "Somewhere someone": Oates, *The Contradictions of Leadership*, 153-54.

16. "This was not": Block oral history.

17. "To cater only": *Time*, May 15, 1978, 77.

18. "While it is": Andrew R. Baer to David Monfried, October 25, 1972. Copy in Donald L. Bryant, Sr., file, EqAr.

19. "People from": Riley oral history.

20. "Tender as": Foote, Cone & Belding to Equitable, March 23, 1960. Advertising Department file, EqAr.

21. "Bob asked us": Harris Schrank interview with author, 1994.

CHAPTER XVII

1. Data: George T. Conklin, Jr., "Institutional Size — Life Insurance" *Law and Contemporary Problems* 17 (Winter 1952), 222-24. American Council of Life Insurance, *Fact Book*, 1994, 72.

2. Data: Joseph J. Melone, "A Growth Franchise," speech to Merrill Lynch Insurance Investor Conference, February 1995. Copy of outline in author collection,

3. Data: Lawrence D. Jones, *Investment Policies of Life Insurance Companies*, 8.

4. "An unmistakable": Schott, "The 1975 Outlook for the Life Insurance Industry — a Broad View," July 15, 1968. Alan R. Thomander file, EqAr.

5. "The market": Davidson Sommers oral history, 1985. EqAr. "That was the": Mel H. Gregory, interview with author, 1993.

6. "Coy has": John W. Riley interview with author, 1994.

7. "I guess": J. Henry Smith, *Great Ideas for Living*, 54.

8. "The trouble": Smith, *Great Ideas for Living*, 132. "Coy Eklund had": Benjamin D. Holloway oral history, 1990. EqAr. "Without meaning": Smith to Donald L Bryant, February 8, 1973. Bryant file, EqAr.

9. "I must tell": editors of *Institutional Investor, The Way it Was: An Oral History of Finance, 1967-1987*, 212.

10. "Chase yield": Joseph Nocera, *A Piece of the Action: How the Middle Class Joined the Money Class*, 220.

11. "We no longer": Francis H. Schott oral history, 1985. EqAr.

12. "A financial": Oates, *The Contradictions of Leadership*, 148.

13. "Variable life was": Harry D. Garber interview with author, 1993.

14. "It was," "Coy leave": Coy G. Eklund oral history, 1985. EqAr.

15. "I had seen": Donald L. Bryant, Sr., interview with author, 1994. "I think it": *Wall Street Journal*, July 9, 1971.

16. "A four-hour": Bryant interview.

17. "Chipping away": Jerome Golden interview with author, 1994. "Once there was": *New York Times*, September 16, 1976.

18. "Given a new": Raymond H. Wittcoff retirement speech to Equitable Board of Directors, December 15, 1993. Transcript in author collection.

19. "Probably the most": *Business Week*, November 7, 1977, 114.

20. "In the past": Raymond H. Wittcoff interview with author, 1994.

21. "The word ancillary": Bryant interview.

22. "My idea was": Bryant interview.

23. "This kept": Bryant interview.

24. "Employers were": Joseph J. Melone to auther, September 5, 1995.

25. "(1) Growth assets": Minutes of group annuity task force, no date [1969?]. Walsh file, EqAr.

CHAPTER XVIII

1. "Namer of things": Coy G. Eklund oral history, 1985. "Equicake": Benjamin D. Holloway oral history, 1990. EqAr.

2. "Coy had a": Robert W. Barth interview with author, 1994. "Coy was brilliant": Nancy H. Green interview with author, 1992.

3. "A means of": Eklund oral history, 1985. Eklund quotes: Coy Eklund, *Reminders for MC's*, Equitable pamphlet, 1981. Eklund collection, EqAr. "He served under": Robert Wenzlaff interview with author, 1994.

4. "EVLICO management": EVLICO President's Report, February 11, 1977. EVLICO board minutes file, EqAr.

5. "There is no": Joseph Nocera, *A Piece of the Action: How the Middle Class Joined the Money Class*, 120.

6. "Variable life": Alan Grant interview with author, 1994. "Agents tend": Lester Lovier interview with author, 1994. "I can remember": Grant interview.

7. "It was like": Harry D. Garber interview with author, 1993.

8. "Quite satisfactory": Givens memorandum, October 19, 1966. Givens file, EqAr.

9. "The confidence": Garber interview, 1994. "The principal": Givens draft, April 24, 1968. Givens file, EqAr.

10. "Harrison Givens": Leo M. Walsh interview with author, 1994.

11. "Aggressive sales": Smith report to Board of Directors, 1973. Hendrickson file, EqAr.

12. "We have assumed": Separate Account 9 Business Plan, appendix, 1976. Eklund file, EqAr.

13. "The guarantee": Walsh interview. "Life insurance companies": Givens speech to New York Society of Securities Analysts, December 16, 1977. Transcript in Givens correspondence and office file, EqAr.

14. "The GIC is": Walsh interview.

15. "Harrison was": Gordon G. Dinsmore interview with author, 1994.

16. "A development of": Givens to Charles B. Strome, June 28, 1974. Givens file, EqAr.

17. "This new": Walsh to Vice-Presidents in charge of group field sales regions, June 6, 1974. Walsh file, EqAr.

18. "GICs were big": John H. Jacobus interview with author, 1994.

19. "We must become": Eklund to Garber, February 25, 1976. Gubar file, EqAr. "In the end": Garber to Eklund, March 12, 1976. Gubar file.

20. "Debate went on": Walsh interview.

21. "Hand-wringing": Givens to Walsh, October 1974. Walsh file, EqAr. "There would be": Givens to Schott, May 29, 1975. Givens file, EqAr.

22. "We were convinced": Walsh interview.

23. "Our only requirement": *Time*, July 11, 1977.

24. "You will note": Garber undated note on Van Cise to Day, March 22, 1907. Eklund file, EqAr.

25. "Common stocks": Eklund memorandum to senior officers, August 23, 1978. Eklund corporate relations file, EqAr.

26. "Corporate finance": Eklund oral history, 1985.

27. ."No more": *Wall Street Journal*, December 11, 1979.

28. "The Equitable": John O'Hara interview with author, 1994. "It would never": Edward Monahan interview with author, 1994.

29. Action memo 352: Eklund to Broms, December 25, 1979. Eklund file, EqAr.

30. "There's no such": Eklund oral history, 1985.

31. "They decided": Jerome S. Golden interview with author, 1994.

32. "Henry was": Eklund oral history, 1985.

33. "From bigger": Grant interview. "A challenging": Hendrickson to Eklund, August 7, 1981. Hendrickson file, EqAr. Emphasis in original.

34. "The Equitable Mutual": Eklund oral history, 1985.

CHAPTER XIX

1. "If the first": Francis H. Schott, "A Time of Change for Financial Institutions," paper submitted to the New York Executive Advisory Commission on Insurance Industry Regulatory Reform, 1982. Copy in author collection.

2. "The summer of": Nicholas Lemann, "How the 'Seventies Changed America," *American Heritage*, July-August 1991, 46.

3. "Activity in": Robert Hendrickson memorandum, October 18, 1979. Hendrickson file, EqAr. "It is expected": Hendrickson to Carleton D. Burtt, Benjamin D. Holloway, and James E. Hayes. October 18, 1979. Hendrickson file, EqAr.

4. "Inadequate financial": Hendrickson to Eklund, December 12, 1981. Hendrickson file, EqAr.

5. "He was an": Coy G. Eklund interview with author, 1994.

6. "People were looking": Robert W. Barth interview with author, 1994. "Coy was the": John W. Riley interview with author, 1994.

7. "Our challenge": Carter speech to Equitable National Agency Leaders Conference, San Francisco, March 25, 1983. Transcript in Carter file, EqAr.

8. "Staff-driven": Eleanor B. Sheldon oral history, 1994. EqAr.

9. "I believe that": John W. Milligan, "The Entrepreneur and the Equitable," *Institutional Investor*, September 1990, 82.

10. "Equitable had": Lincoln Gordon, Equitable Board of Directors retirement speech, September 18, 1985. Gordon collection. "The board became": Sheldon oral history.

11. "This was the": Sheldon oral history. "A direct attack": Lewis to Carter, April 16, 1984. Carter file, EqAr. "We stayed there": Walker Lewis interview with author, 1994.

12. "Downstreaming itself": Leo M. Walsh interview with author, 1994.

13. "Bill you": William T. McCaffrey interview with author, 1993.

14. "Seed the place": Lewis to John Goddard, March 14, 1984. Goddard SPA file, EqAr. "Your culture": Lewis to Goddard, October 8, 1984. Carter file, EqAr. Emphasis in original. "The real management": Joseph L. Dionne interview with author, 1994. "It was just": Lewis interview.

15. "You can draw": Brian S. O'Neil interview with author, 1994.

16. "Funding vehicles": *Wall Street Journal*, September 18, 1981.

17. Data: Joseph J. Melone, "A Growth Franchise," speech to Merrill Lynch Insurance Investor Conference, February 1995. Copy of outline in author collection.

18. "The single most": George W. Karr, Jr., acceptance speech for Agency Management Hall of Fame, General Agents and Managers Association, 1991. Copy of transcript in author collection.

19. "We were treated": Dave H. Williams interview with author, 1994. "John identified it": Dionne interview.

20. "Every now": Francis H. Burr interview with author, 1994.

CHAPTER XX

1. "You have to go back": *Art & Auction*, October 1985, 153.

2. "A commitment": *New York Times*, February 23, 1986.

3. "A way of": *Art & Auction*, October 1985, 152. "A valued": *Real Estate Weekly*, December 9, 1985.

4. "I like to": Peter A. Wilde interview with author, 1994. "The bombs had": Robert W. Barth interview with author, 1994.

5. "John Carter": Equitable Financial Services strategic planning meeting, April 23, 1986. Audiotape in EqAr.

6. "GIC worries": Walker Lewis interview with author, 1994.

7. "This business": Harry D. Garber interview with author, 1993.

8. "Meeting entrapment": Lewis to Carter, April 16, 1984. Carter file, EqAr.

9. "There were not": Garber interview.

10. "There was an": Eleanor B. Sheldon oral history, 1993. EqAr.

11. "In Dick we're": John W. Milligan, "The Entrepreneur and the Equitable," *Institutional Investor*, September 1990, 82.

12. "It was a": Joseph L. Dionne interview with author, 1994. "Bob don't": Robert S. Jones, Jr., interview with author, 1994.

13. "I wanted": Richard H. Jenrette interview with author, 1993.

14. "If a new": Dan W. Lufkin interview with author, 1994. "Our philosophy": William H. Donaldson interview with author, 1994.

15. "I felt like": Jenrette interview. "When the market": "The Equitable's Race for Assets," *Chief Executive*, March 1995, 46.

16. "He was": Brian S. O'Neil interview with author, 1994. "Sorry I've": Jenrette comments on Robert Hendrickson memorandum to Jenrette, October 29, 1986. Hendrickson file, EqAr.

17. "Farsighted": Dave H. Williams interview with author, 1994. "He has the": John S. Chalsty interview with author, 1995.

18. "Perhaps as an": Richard H. Jenrette to Eric Miller, June 2, 1992. Scott Spencer file, EqAr.

CHAPTER XXI

1. "At the time": Jerry M. de St. Paer interview with author, 1995. "It really has": John W. Milligan, "The Entrepreneur and the Equitable," *Institutional Investor*, September 1990, 85.

2. "His insurance": Richard H. Jenrette to author, March 1995.

3. "Equitable needs": Jenrette undated memorandum, 1990. Copy in author collection.

4. "Time to get": Jenrette memorandum.

5. "Some thought": Francis H. Burr interview with author, 1994.

6. "That was when": Joseph J. Melone interview with author, 1993. "The employees": *Business Week*, December 24, 1990.

7. "I thought that": *Washington Post*, September 6, 1992. "Thank God": Melone interview.

8. "This is a": *Wall Street Journal*, December 12, 1990. "The company": *Los Angeles Times*, December 12, 1990.

9. "Obviously I would": "The Equitable's Race for Assets," *Chief Executive*, March 1995, 46.

10. "The envy": *New York Times*, July 21, 1995, D4.

11. "There was a": de St. Paer interview. "The press": Jenrette to author, March 10, 1995. "Company bashing," "as many of": George W. Karr, Jr., acceptance speech for Agency Management Hall of Fame, General Agents and Managers Association, 1991. Transcript in author collection.

12. Aphorisms: Richard H. Jenrette interview with author, 1994.

13. "I don't want": Milligan, "The Entrepreneur and the Equitable," 85. "What changed": Raymond H. Wittcoff interview with author, 1994.

14. "One of the": Jenrette to author, March 10, 1995. Data: in Terrance L. Little collection. "To me": Jenrette to author, August 20, 1995.

15. "Joe was so": Jenrette to author, March 10, 1995.

16. "I buy": *Le Nouvel Observateur*, September 8-15, 1994 (translation). "The best way": Claude Bébéar interview with author, 1995. "Our strategy": *New York Times*, June 4, 1991.

17. "Michel came to me": Bébéar interview.

18. "The news": Bébéar interview.

19. "An invisible": de St. Paer interview.

20. "Like playing": Robert Stowe England, "Redemption," *Financial World*, September 1, 1994, 29.

21. "A global": *Financial Times*, July 19, 1991. "This challenge": *New York Times*, July 19, 1991.

22. "A day later": England, "Redemption," 29.

23. "This is," "these documents": *New York Times*, April 7, 1992. "One of the": "The Equitable's Race for Assets," 46.

24. "I can't guarantee": *Financial Times*, April 24, 1992.

25. "I can't tell": Nancy Hass, "Who Will Buy?", *Financial World*, November 12, 1991, 23.

CHAPTER XXII

1. "That would have": Jenrette to author, September 10, 1995. Data in this chapter: Equitable annual reports, 1991–94, and various public statements and internal reports in Terrance Little and author collections.

2. "Equitable Comes": *New York Times*, September 8, 1994. "Redemption": Robert Stowe England, "Redemption," *Financial World*, September 1, 1994. "The renaissance," "what a difference": Salomon Brothers equity research report on The Equitable, February 6, 1993. "All the right moves": quoted in Equitable annual report, 1993.

3. "What particularly": Melone to author, September 8, 1995. "Jim Benson": Jenrette to author, September 11, 1995.

4. "Macro demographic": Joseph J. Melone interview with author, 1993. "It's a real": James M. Benson interview with author, 1993.

5. "Part of it": Charles Butler, "Man on a Mission," *Sales & Marketing Management*, March 1994, 63.

INDEX

❧